Edinburgh for Under Fives

The Family Friendly Guide

Edition 12

Compiled by local Parents and Carers
including members of the
National Childbirth Trust

Published by Edinburgh for Under Fives

1st edition   1987, reprinted 1987
2nd edition   1989
3rd edition   1991
4th edition   1993
5th edition   1995
6th edition   1997
7th edition   2000
8th edition   2002
9th edition   2004
10th edition   2006
11th edition   2008
12th edition   2010

Edinburgh for Under Fives Committee 2009-2010
Amy Reilly (convenor)
Sophie Kelsall (treasurer)
Helen Maguire
Kathy McGlew
Diahann Whitefield
Alison Macdonald-Ewen
Jo Drew
Rachel F Freeman
Mary Ross
Melissa Corkhill

Editor: Jude Thomas
Efuf Logo: Ann Ross Paterson
Map: Brendan Reilly

Published by: Edinburgh For Under Fives
© Edinburgh for Under Fives 2010
ISBN 978-0-9555161-1-5

INTRODUCTION

Welcome to Edinburgh For Under Fives. We hope that this NCT guide will help you find moments of happiness and fun with your young family.

Edition 12 has had a makeover with a fresh layout and colour scheme. It is bursting at the bindings with new and updated information highlighting what Edinburgh and its surroundings have to offer for babies, toddlers, pre-schoolers, the very young at heart, parents and carers.

There are new case studies written for anyone on a budget or those with twins, and plenty of tips from Ed if you're stuck for ideas. The popular "Places to Eat" and "Places to Go" sections have new symbols to enable you to find amenities in a venue via a quick skim.

The breadth of material covered could not have occurred without the hard work of a team of over 30 volunteer researchers and the steering committee consisting also of volunteers and a tireless Editor. The committee extends a huge "Thank You" and raises a rattle to the editor Jude Thomas, to all the researchers for sharing their insight and experience of Edinburgh for Under Fives and also to all advertisers, booksellers and our supporters and readers. The proceeds of the book are used to finance the printing of forthcoming editions and also to support the work of the Edinburgh NCT. We strive for increased awareness of this valuable resource and hope that it also makes life just a little bit more exciting for anyone wishing to indulge in Edinburgh with their young family.

Jo
Kathy
amy
Melissa
Helen

May
Diahann
Alison.
Sophie.
Rachel.

Edinburgh For Under Fives committee
July 2010

CONTENTS

CONTENTS

We'd love to hear from you.

- Let us know what you think of the book.
- Tell us how we can improve it.
- Suggest places that should be included in the next edition.
- Or offer to help research the next edition.

www.efuf.co.uk

v

NOTES

Out & About

INTRODUCTION

The aim of this section is to give you as much information as is currently available at the time of writing to enable you to be prepared as you get out and about in Edinburgh. The current options for travel in and around Edinburgh are by air, bus, cycling, car, walking, taxi, train and soon to be trams. We try to offer you relevant information for travelling by those methods here, including pertinent knowledge for travelling with under 5s, e.g. with pushchairs. Useful general contacts are detailed below.

Traveline Scotland
0871 200 22 33 (24 hour hotline)
www.travelinescotland.com
For information about public transport, such as timetables, details of available concessions, bus times to your mobile or details of transport for people with disabilities. The site can help with journey planning on public transport in Scotland and to major centres in other parts of the UK. It can also direct you to other sites e.g. transport direct, and help you plan a journey in Wales, Northern Ireland or England.

The Traveline Scotland website features a useful journey planner.

Traffic Scotland
0800 028 1414
(24 hr Freephone Customer Care Line)
www.trafficscotland.org

NB: If calling from a mobile, phone 800 028 1414. This service provides up-to-date information on all motorways and trunk road networks in Scotland. This includes information on road accidents, traffic congestion, park & ride facilities, major events and even weather warnings.

Visit our website for updates:
www.efuf.co.uk

Edinburgh Council
www.edinburgh.gov.uk/transport
This is a useful site for finding out about general options for public transport in Edinburgh, walking and cycling options and e.g. roadworks affecting bus routes. It's also a useful site for current information about trams.

Tourist Information Centre
3 Princes Street
EH2 2QP
0845 22 55 121
www.edinburgh.org
The centre offers free literature, a booking system, various discounts and transport information. There is also a centre based at the airport.

Visit Scotland
Ocean Point One
94 Ocean Drive
EH6 6JH
www.visitscotland.com
This service provides booking and information for the whole of Scotland, including a useful travel section.

BY AIR

Edinburgh Airport
EH12 9DN
0844 481 8989
Live flight information 0870 040 0007
www.edinburghairport.com
The airport is located 8 miles west of Edinburgh, and is easily accessible by car, just off the A8 dual carriageway to the west of the city and close to the M8 and M9 motorways. The website provides live flight information, how to get to and from the airport, flight destinations from Edinburgh, how to book flights, plus information on parking, hotels nearby and airport security.

Pick-up and drop-off

For picking up passengers, signs will lead you to the Pick Up Zone which is located on the ground floor of the multi-storey car park. For dropping off, follow the signs to the Set Down Zone, close to the terminal building, next to the multi-storey car park.

PARKING

Short Stay

There is a new Fast Track service in operation, which offers 150 dedicated spaces located a one minute walk from the terminal building, these are currently charged at £21 per day and are bookable in advance.
Pick Up/2 Hours Max Short Stay Parking has its own dedicated car park, and prices are up to £6 for 2 hours.
General Short Stay Parking is available for a few hours or for short trips, and prices currently range from £1.50 for 15 minutes to £18 for 18–24 hours. Short Stay parking can be booked in advance for convenience.

Blue Badge holders can park on the ground floor of the short stay car park in designated spaces for 15 minutes free of charge. This is validated at the ticket desk on the ground floor of the car park.

Long Stay Edinburgh

Located within the airport boundary, linked to the terminal by a courtesy coach service, which runs every 10 minutes and is a 5 minute journey.

NCP Scotpark Edinburgh

Located outwith the airport boundary, the complimentary coach runs approximately every 7 – 10 minutes and takes 5 minutes.

Both of these are monitored 24 hours, and can be pre-booked for a slightly cheaper price rather than just turning up on the day, cost approximately £7 per day.

BUS LINKS

Buses pick-up and drop-off outside the terminal building, just by the main entrance. Lothian Buses operate the 3 main services into Edinburgh. Details about other longer distance buses can be found on the airport website. Journey times may be affected by trams/tram works.

Airlink 100 - 0131 555 6363
www.flybybus.com

This runs to and from Waverley Bridge to the airport. The journey time is approx 25 mins with buses leaving Waverley Bridge every 10 mins during the day. Most Airlink buses are of the low floor, easy access type. Fares: adult £3.50 single, £6 open return; child £2/£3; under 5s free.

Night Bus N22 - 0131 555 6363
www.nightbuses.com

This runs from the airport to the city centre (via South Gyle) and onto Ocean Terminal, Leith 7 nights a week. It runs every 30 minutes and takes 28 minutes from the airport to Waverley. Fare is a flat fee of £3.

Service 35 - 0131 555 6363
www.lothianbuses.com

This also runs from the airport to the city centre and onto Ocean Terminal. Drop-offs include the RBS Headquarters, Scottish Parliament and Holyrood House. This service runs every 15 minutes at peak times, and takes about an hour from the airport to Holyrood. Fare is £1.20 per adult, and a day ticket currently costs £3.

Service 64 - 01506 432251
www.horsburghcoaches.com

E & M Horsburgh run this hourly service from the airport to the Western General Hospital, stopping throughout North Edinburgh including Pilton, Muirhouse, Davidson's Mains, and Cramond. The journey time to the hospital takes about 1 hour.

TAXIS

Onward Travel
0131 272 8222
www.onwardtravel.com
There are three taxi ranks available outside the east end of the terminal, near to UK Arrivals. There are private airport taxis, black cabs and advance-booked taxis available. Journey time into the city centre is approximately 25 minutes, and all arrangements are managed by Onward Travel.

CYCLE
In front of the International Arrivals entrance, there is a bicycle parking rack and shelter available.

THE AIRPORT TERMINAL

Security
The rules around security are constantly being updated, so best to check the airport website section on Security Control before you fly for rules regarding liquids, medicines, baby milk and foods etc.

Baby Changing
There are 4 changing rooms available within the terminal building. They are located before security in UK arrivals near Costa Coffee and on the first floor near Borders. After security they are available near Gate 11. For arriving passengers, it is located in the international baggage reclaim hall.

Play Areas
There are some interactive play screens dotted about the airport, and a play area near Gate 3 (after security) with some toys and puzzles.

Under 5s Essentials
Boots in the airport has a supply of nappies, formula and wipes, and most eating facilities in the airport offer a children's menu.

Airport & Tourist Information
The desk can be found in the International Arrivals area. The staff will help you with details on airport facilities, places of interest, accommodation and car hire.

Car Hire
There is a new car rental building, outside the terminal which can be reached by following the signs from the domestic arrivals part of the terminal building.

Flying with under 5s
Always let the airline know in advance that you are travelling with a baby or toddler and check out the facilities available on board and at your destination airport when booking, along with any relevant airline policies e.g. baggage. If you have a lively toddler, it may be worth finding out if you can use a car seat on board. You may have to pay for the seat, depending on the airline and how busy the aircraft is. Other options include booking a separate seat for your child, though this is usually charged at adult price, or some airlines allow you to select your seats when booking your tickets, so you can select a block of seats together. Car seats and pushchairs can also travel in the hold – but check your baggage allowance. Take tried and tested snacks and toys for in-flight entertainment. During take-off or landing, swallowing food or drinks, or bottle-feeding, will help prevent earache arising from changes in cabin pressure. Nappy changing facilities vary with each aircraft.

Flying while Pregnant
It's always best to check with individual airlines as to their policy, as well as checking your insurance policy, but general advice is that the safest time to fly is after week 14 and before week 28. Most airlines will require a medical certificate after 28 weeks in order to allow you to travel.

BY BUS

Two companies – Lothian Buses and First Bus – provide the majority of services in and around Edinburgh, although other operators provide localised transport.
Lothian Buses' livery has gold and red squares on maroon and white, and all buses are low floor and easy access. First Bus operates fewer routes in the city centre, but has more buses which service the outlying zones of the city. First's livery is white, indigo and red for the majority of the fleet.

Bus fares

Under 5s travel free on the understanding that they will surrender their seat for a fare-paying passenger. A maximum of two under 5s may accompany one adult, and a standard child fare must be paid for further children.

Fares are a flat rate for both adults and children, as well as for concessionary travel: currently, adults pay £1.20 for a single journey. The child's half-fare in Edinburgh is 70p. People who have concession passes for Edinburgh, East Lothian and Midlothian can travel free apart from on night buses and tour buses.

There are also bargain day tickets available (currently around £3) which means you can hop on and off their buses as you require. As well as the day tickets, there's a raft of saver options available, so if you use buses frequently, it might be worth taking the time and working out what's your best option: weekly, monthly and even yearly passes are available. There is also a RidaCard ticket available, paid by direct debit.

Pushchairs on buses

There has recently been a great deal of controversy in the media about travelling by bus with a pram or pushchair, but hopefully this seems close to being resolved. If there is already a pushchair on the bus you are boarding, you may need to be prepared to fold your pushchair if possible or wait until the next bus. Spaces may also need to be vacated for wheelchair users. Lothian Buses are currently trialling a new dedicated unfolded buggy space on the 22 service, which will exist in addition to the dedicated space for wheelchair users, which if successful may be rolled out to other services. There may be some issues with using the bus if you have certain types of side-by-side double pushchairs due to lack of space on the bus itself, it's probably best to check with the bus company first before travelling, or chat to other parents.

Bus times

Real time bus information for in and around Edinburgh can be obtained from
www.mybustracker.co.uk
This can also be accessed via a wap-enabled phone.

Lothian Buses
Annandale Street
EH7 4AZ
0131 554 4494
Email: mail@lothianbuses.com
www.lothianbuses.com

Bus Times & Information 0131 555 6363

Lothian Buses Travelshops – for enquiries, tickets and timetables.

Hanover Street
Opening times: 8.15-18.00;
closed Sun and Bank Holidays

Shandwick Place
Opening times: 8.15-18.00;
closed Sun and Bank Holidays

Waverley Bridge
Opening times: 8.15-18.00; Sun 9.30-17.15

Contact head office/customer services for more information about access on Lothian Buses. Lothian Buses are moving towards making 100% of their bus fleet accessible.

Lothian Buses Lost Property
Annandale Street
0131 558 8858
Email:lostproperty@lothianbuses.co.uk
Opening times: 10.00 – 13.30 Mon – Fri (excluding Bank Holidays).

First Bus
Carmuirs House
300 Stirling Road
Larbert
FK5 3NJ
01324 602 200
08708 72 72 71 (customer services)
www.firstgroup.com/ukbus/scotland/sescot

The following 2 companies are taking over some routes in Edinburgh. Lothian tickets are not valid on these services.

E&M Horsburgh
01506 432251
www.horsburghcoaches.com

Edinburgh Coachlines
0131 554 5413
www.edinburghcoachlines.com

FURTHER AFIELD
Long distance buses operate out of St Andrews Square. There are services to many parts of Scotland, and other parts of Britain. This is a relatively new bus terminal, which is much sleeker – and much less draughty – than its predecessor. One thing to watch out for is the automatic doors which screen the waiting area from the bus ranks. There is a lift down from street level on St Andrews Square. The following companies provide coach travel from Edinburgh to various destinations. If you're not sure which company goes where, try Traveline for information (see beginning of chapter for details).

Scottish Citylink Coaches
Buchanan Bus Station
Killermont Street
Glasgow
G2 3NP
08705 50 50 50
www.citylink.co.uk
NB: One under 5 not occupying a seat, and accompanied by an adult fare-paying passenger, will be carried free of charge. Any additional under 5s, accompanied by the same adult, and all children aged 5 to 15 years inclusive, can get discounts of up to 30% off normal fares.

Stagecoach Scotland
10 Dunkeld Road
Perth
PH1 5TW
0871 200 2233 (24 hours)
www.stagecoachbus.com
Website gives information on individual bus stations across Scotland, along with timetables, fares, and online booking.

Megabus
08705 505050
www.megabus.com
Stagecoach also provides the Megabus.com inter-city service. You can book tickets online.
NB: Under 3s go free, but they are not guaranteed a seat – unless a specific seat has been purchased for them and the reference number provided.

National Express
PO Box 9854
Birmingham
B16 8XN
08717 818181
www.nationalexpress.com/coach
On National Express buses, under 5s travel free, but on coaches this is only applicable to under 3s.

BY BICYCLE

Given the numbers of hills in and around Edinburgh, cycling may not be the first thing you think of doing with your baby or toddler, but with a wealth of off-road routes in and around the city, maybe you will be inspired! Your child will certainly be thrilled by feeling the breeze and watching people and objects speed by.

Bicycle Safety

Before taking off, a few guidelines. Firstly, get your bike checked over at a specialist shop and keep it well maintained, especially the brakes and the wheels, as they will be under greater strain than normal. Next, buy the best child seat you can afford. Finally, wear a helmet and ensure that your baby, toddler or child wears a helmet at all times both on road and off road.

Whether you cycle alone or with your child, dress brightly and make use of fluorescent strips to maximise visibility and if it may get dark while you are out, remember to have working front and back lights. The use of a flashing red rear light in addition to the legally required steady red light is recommended. Beware of the effect other road users' actions may have on you, such as car doors opening unexpectedly, and of the effect your actions may have on other road users, such as overtaking a stationary queue of traffic at a junction. Never jump the red lights at pedestrian crossings.

Compared with cycling alone, you will find that the bike feels heavier with a child on or attached to your bike. That's what those low gears are for. If using the more common rear-mounted child seat, it is advisable to carry any necessary luggage in front panniers to balance the weight front and back. You may find that wider handlebars give better control over the steering, but if you are using a mountain bike, change the knobbly tyres for smooth ones to reduce resistance on off-road paths and tarmac surfaces.

Although some keen cyclists have been known to tow babies as young as a few weeks old in child trailers, it is advisable not to take them cycling until the baby can support its head and sit up unassisted, usually around 6 months. Babies and toddlers can be taken cycling in a child trailer towed behind the bike or in a rear-mounted child seat, which clips into a bicycle's rear rack. There are pros and cons to both and what is most suitable for you will depend on the type of cycling you intend to do and your budget.

Once the trailer or child seat has been outgrown (3-4 yrs depending on size), the choice is a trailer cycle, which attaches to your bike or a tandem bicycle. Again there are pros and cons to both. For fully comprehensive information you could try a book such as 'Bicycling with Children' by Trudy E. Bell.

Bicycles on Trains

Cycles travel free of charge on Scotrail trains, though reservations may be required. It's best to make your enquiry when you are booking your ticket.

Cycling in Pregnancy

If you are reasonably fit and used to cycling, there is probably no reason not to keep cycling during pregnancy, but do follow your doctor's advice. www.nhs.uk does advise that you shouldn't cycle after 26 weeks due to the risk of falls. Consider lower gears and inverting dropped handlebars to enable a more upright sitting position for greater comfort. Be aware that your balance may change as your bump grows.

Useful general cycling contacts listed as follows:

CTC
Cotterell House
Parklands
Railton Rd
Guildford
GU2 9JX
0870 736 8450
Email: cycling@ctc.org.uk
www.ctc.org.uk
The CTC is Britain's largest national cycling organisation. It campaigns for all cyclists regardless of age, ability or type of bike. Members receive a range of services, and there is a local group, the CTC Lothians District Association.

Local contact:
Bill Coppoch (Secretary)
Email: secretary@ctclothians.org.uk
www.ctclothians.org.uk

Spokes
St Martin's Church
232 Dalry Rd
EH11 2JG
0131 313 2114 (answering machine)
www.spokes.org.uk
A Lothian cycle group which campaigns for better conditions for cyclists, Spokes is an entirely voluntary organisation. It produces Cycle Maps of Edinburgh and surrounding areas, including off-road routes.

Sustrans Scotland
Glenorchy House
20 Union Street
Edinburgh
EH1 3LR
0131 539 8122
Email: scotland@sustrans.org.uk
www.sustrans.co.uk
A charity working on sustainable transport projects, the flagship project being the National Cycle Network. Sustrans maps and guides are available from bike shops, bookshops or direct. Sustrans also offers advice on Safe Routes to School projects.

Cycling Scotland
24 Blythswood Square
Glasgow
G2 4BG
0141 229 5350
Email: info@cyclingscotland.org
www.cyclingscotland.org
This organisation aims to establish cycling as an acceptable, attractive and practical lifestyle choice.

BY CAR

Edinburgh is a fairly accessible city by car, if you have a good A-Z and can avoid travelling during rush hour. However, at time of writing, tramworks seem to be the biggest problems for road users in Edinburgh, which can slow your journey down along the tram routes, including for example Princes Street and South Gyle.

Car parking
The main headache in Edinburgh is not driving (despite the tramworks), but parking. If you choose to visit one of the outlying shopping complexes, this problem is negated by the provision of ample and free parking at centres such as the Gyle, Fort Kinnaird, Ocean Terminal, Straiton, Hermiston Gait etc. However, sometimes parking in or near the city centre cannot be avoided. In the last few years parking restrictions have become tighter and charges have become steeper.

There are now various parking zones around the city. The Central zones 1–4 run from Haymarket to the West of the city centre to Calton Road to the East; and from Heriot Row to the North to Melville Drive to the South. In the Central zones, restrictions generally apply Mon-Sat 08.30–18.30 and are generally charged at £2/hour. Central zones 5–8 generally apply Mon–Fri 08.30–17.30 and include areas such as Dean Village and Bruntsfield. There are also peripheral and controlled parking zones which charge at least 70p/hour.

There is also now a facility called mpark which you can register for using your mobile phone and a credit/debit card. This is particularly handy if you don't have any change for the meter.

Parking Operations

0131 469 5400
E-mail: parking@edinburgh.gov.uk
www.edinburgh.gov.uk

There are also several different parking facilities available throughout Edinburgh:

Park Easy

Information about on- and off-street parking in and around the city, leaflets are available in shops and NCP car parks or available to download from the above council website, or www.ncp.co.uk

Greenside Row Car Park

The largest car park available in Edinburgh is Greenside Row at the top of Leith Walk. This has an elevated walkway through to St. James Centre and is pushchair friendly.

Park Green Scheme

This scheme aims to make savings on resident's parking permits for those owners of cars with more fuel efficient vehicles paying less. Details on council website as above.

Park & Ride

There are 6 Park & Ride facilities available in Edinburgh. These are generally free and secure and are currently based at the following sites: Ingliston, Hermiston, Straiton, Sheriffhall, Newcraighall and Ferrytoll Fife.

 Your child may be entitled to parking concessions under the blue badge scheme. You can get a blue badge if you receive the higher rate of the mobility component of Disability Living Allowance or if you have a permanent and substantial disability which means you are unable to walk or have considerable difficulty in walking. Although children under the age of three years are not entitled to receive the mobility component of Disability Living Allowance, children aged two years may still qualify to receive a blue parking badge if they have considerable difficulty walking caused by a permanent or substantial disability. Your child may have to be assessed to check that they qualify. For further information contact Travel Concessions:
0131 469 3891 / 3540 / 3840

Motability

www.motability.co.uk
Many parents with children who are entitled to the higher rate mobility component of DLA choose to surrender this part of their award and pay a non returnable deposit (for some cars this deposit is nil) in return for the hire of a new vehicle of their choosing. Insurance and repair costs are met over the three year rental period. There are a wide variety of cars to choose from, with MPVs being a popular choice among families with younger children. The cost of the deposit varies depending on the car chosen. For more information on the schemes available, how to apply and current prices visit the website.

If you need a disabled parking bay outside your home, contact Clarence:
0800 232323

Car Safety

For up to date information on travelling safely and within the law with under 5s, please see
www.childcarseats.org.uk

CITY CAR CLUB

An alternative to owning a car in Edinburgh is to join the City Car Club. You pay for the time you use a car for, plus a mileage charge.

You can join and book your car either on-line or by phone. Once you have registered, you can even book your next car in-car. Individual membership is currently £50 per annum. For a hatchback, charges range from £5 for an hour to £104 for 72 hours. You get 50 miles free fuel included in the first 24 hours, and 24p/mile afterwards. Insurance is included within the membership fee, with a £500 excess. Cars are accessed by membership card and PIN. Keys are located inside the vehicle and cars are located through the city. The Club does not provide car seats for children, so you would need to provide your own.

Visit our website for updates:
www.efuf.co.uk

City Car Club
24 hour enquiries 0845 330 1234
www.citycarclub.co.uk
Edinburgh-specific 0845 258 2985
E-mail: Edinburgh@citycarclub.co.uk

WALKING

Built on seven hills, Edinburgh is pretty steep in places with a lot of steps! It's not always the easiest city to negotiate with pushchairs or with young children in tow. However, it is a great city to explore on foot with under 5s, especially the city centre which is fairly compact.

The council published a walking strategy in 2006 as part of their priorities to promote more sustainable modes of travel. Useful resources for walking and road safety listed below.

www.walkit.com
A useful site when planning a walking route in Edinburgh, however they do not currently include information on accessible or pushchair friendly routes.

www.schooltravelwise.org.uk
A relatively new scheme set up for Nurseries and Schools, who, once signed up, can tap into information on travel and journey planning.

Scottish Road Safety Campaign
Heriot-Watt Research Park (North)
Riccarton
Currie
EH14 4AP
0131 472 9200
Email: enquiries@roadsafetyscotland.org.uk
www.srsc.org.uk

Children's Traffic Club
www.trafficclub.co.uk
A road safety programme specifically aimed at 3 – 4 year olds, teaching them how to keep safe when out and about. This is free to join for children in Scotland, and your child will receive an invitation to join from the Health Authority.

Edinburgh is a city of hills and cobbles, both of which contribute to Edinburgh's appeal as a historic city. Cobbles don't bide particularly well with the pushing of wheelchairs, nor the wearing of high heels (particularly hazardous if these two activities are combined!) and hills can be a work-out at the best of times – not least when pushing a pushchair or wheelchair up them!

If you can't manage the hills, then there are plenty of areas that have good access and pathways. The Meadows area has good views of Arthur's seat, extensive and well kept grasslands and good parking if you have a blue badge. Inverleith Park and the Botanics have good parking and toilet facilities (the Botanics has disabled toilet facilities) and the choice of completely flat walkways or some gentle hills. Lots of squirrel and duck feeding opportunities and good ice-cream on site. Inverleith Park offers a safe environment for a child learning to use a cycle, with wide flat walkways. Although bikes are not permitted in the Botanics, the rule may be overlooked if your child uses a special needs trike with a pull bar. For a seaside walk, Portobello Promenade is flat, wide, has good parking facilities close by, and the toilet on the prom near Straiton Place Park has good wheelchair access.

For information on walking around the Pentland Hills area have a look at:
www.edinburgh.gov.uk/phrp/
disabledaccess/disabledaccess.html

For information on disabled access to walks in other areas throughout Scotland have a look at the Walking Scotland website:
www.walking.visitscotland.com
(and click on disabled access)

BY TAXI

There are 2 types of taxi in Edinburgh, black taxis and some private hire cars. Black taxis are able to be flagged down and take up to 5 passengers plus a wheelchair, and most vehicles are accessible. Private hire cars must be booked in advance and can take up to 8 passengers. All taxis should display licences and have ID badges shown, and they should all be registered with the council and have standard rates operating under a meter system.

Travelling with under 5s by taxi can be tricky but you should be able to fit your car seat in the taxi should you wish, or secure your pushchair in the case of black taxis, e.g. with wheelchair straps.

♿ Your child may be entitled to a taxi card (from age 2). Card holders are entitled to travel with selected taxi companies for a reduced fare. Contact travel concessions for further information: **0131 469 3891 / 3540 / 3840**

Handicabs
www.handicabs.org.uk
0131 447 9949
Handicabs offer a door-to-door transport service for people unable to use ordinary public transport. Two services are provided – Dial-a-Ride and Dial-A-Bus. The Dial-A-Ride service may be useful if your child uses a wheelchair as all buses are adapted to carry wheelchair users. This service offers door-to-door transport seven days a week. The fare is reasonable, particularly for longer journeys. May be used for holidays or for getting to the airport. Bookings need to be made in advance.

BY TRAM

This section is most likely to be out of date due to frequent change, and it's hard to imagine at present the impact of trams on Edinburgh, but current information is as follows.

All trams are due to go from the airport to Newhaven by 2012, with approximately 6 trams running per hour. There are further links planned but not yet in progress. Pushchairs will be welcome on trams, and there will be 2 dedicated wheelchair spaces on board. There won't be any steps to/from trams so they should be fully accessible. Trams will be charged at the same price as Lothian buses.

For further, more up to date information, see
Edinburgh tram
www.edinburghtrams.com
0800 328 3934
E-mail: info@edinburghtrams.com
or visit the council website
www.edinburgh.gov.uk

BY TRAIN

National Rail Enquiry Service
www.nationalrail.co.uk
08457 48 49 50 (24 hours)
For all train times and fare enquiries. It operates on a call-rotation system.
If you are planning a journey, you could also check out Traveline (as listed at the start of this chapter).

There are currently 4 main passenger service operators in and around Edinburgh:

First Scotland
(within Scotland)
www.scotrail.co.uk
08457 550033

Virgin Trains
(West Coast to London)
www.virgintrains.co.uk
08457 222333

East Coast
(East Coast to London/Inverness/Aberdeen)
www.eastcoast.co.uk
0871 200 49 50

Arriva Cross Country
(England via East Coast)
www.crosscountrytrains.co.uk
0844 811 01 24

For train times and tickets, www.thetrainline.com is also a useful resource.

Train Stations

Although there are around 11 stations in the Edinburgh area, there is limited use for trains within Edinburgh due to the current lack of suburban services. The following gives relevant information on the 4 main stations for carers of under 5s.

Station	Postcode	Accessibility	Toilets	Parking
Edinburgh Waverley	EH1 1BB	North and south entrances step free. Lifts to all platforms.	Nappy changing available.	Limited, buses stop near station.
Edinburgh Haymarket	EH12 5EY	No step-free access to platforms 2, 3 or 4.	Nappy changing available.	Reduced due to current engineering works.
Edinburgh Park	EH11 4DF	Step-free access to all parts of station.	No	At shopping complex.
South Gyle	EH12 9EU	Step-free access to all parts of station.	No	Yes

For more detailed information see
www.nationalrail.co.uk
Check with individual train companies with regards to accessibility on the actual trains themselves.

National Rail produces a rail map for people with reduced mobility, which can be helpful when planning your journey.
Of the train stations in and around Edinburgh, those where wheelchair access to all platforms without having to use any steps is possible and where staff are available to assist are: Edinburgh Waverley, Inverkeithing, Kirkcaldy, Falkirk High, Stirling, Glasgow and Perth.
Those stations where there is wheelchair access to all of the platforms but staff may not be available to assist are: Brunstane, Newcraighall, Musselburgh, Wallyford, Longniddry, Drem, North Berwick, Dunbar, Aberdour, Dunfermline, Cardenden, Bridge of Allan, Drumgelloch and Shotts.

Those stations where there are steps to some or all of the platforms are:
Edinburgh Haymarket, Prestonpans, Carstairs, Dunblane, Markinch, Ladybank, Springfield, Cupar and Gleneagles. At Edinburgh Haymarket only platform 1 is wheelchair accessible, platforms 2, 3 and 4 are not wheelchair accessible and there are a large number of steps to the platforms.

These details were correct at time of writing but may have changed since. Call Scotrail for information on accessibility at particular stations:
08456 015929

Train fares

As a general rule, under 5s travel free, on the understanding that they will give their seats up to fare paying passengers. An adult can be accompanied by up to two free under 5s. A variety of special fares are available for families, including saver, cheap day returns and family railcard. Always ask to check the cheapest way to travel before buying your ticket. There is usually an abundance of leaflets with special deals available.

TOILET STOPS

There are 29 public toilets in Edinburgh for which the council's Environmental and Consumer Services are responsible.

For any comments or for more information on them, contact:
City of Edinburgh Council
Environmental and Consumer Services
0131 529 3030

env.con.svs@edinburgh.gov.uk
Please note that the Council reserves the right to alter opening times,etc. There are other automated loos (eg. St Andrew's Sq and Portobello Prom) but you'll need to spend much more than a penny to operate them!

Toilets in Edinburgh

We have listed the toilets by their opening times. Key:
D = facilities for people with disabilities. These toilets are part of the national key scheme.
N = facilities for changing nappies, usually a pull down shelf and separate bin.

8.00-20.00
Castlehill (8.00-18.00 in winter)
Castle Terrace Car Park (D,N)
Haymarket (D,N)
Ross Band Stand (D) (summer only)
St James (N)

8.00-22.00
Hunter Square (D,N)
Mound (D) - gents only. Ladies are within Weston Link (N)

10.00-18.00
Bruntsfield
Canaan Lane (N)
Canonmills (N)
Colinton
Cramond (N)
Currie
Hamilton Place
Hope Park
Joppa (N)
Juniper Green
Middle Meadow Walk
Nicolson Street
St John's Road
Taylor Gardens (N)

10.00-20.00
Ardmillan (N)
Bath Street
Hawes Pier (18.00 in winter)

 Any information missing or incorrect? Tell Ed. Contact Ed via our website www.efuf.co.uk or send an email - info@efuf.co.uk

Location Location

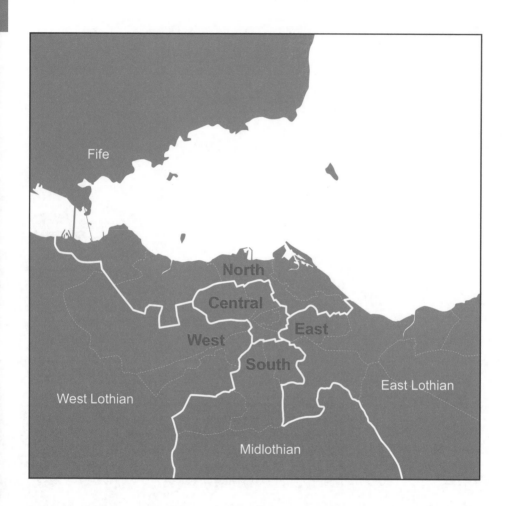

Fife

North

Central

East

West

South

West Lothian

East Lothian

Midlothian

Map

With sat-navs and internet searches making it easier to locate addresses we have endeavoured to include postcodes wherever possible throughout the book.

To help you plan days out and find your way about we have listed entries in geographical groupings. The map above and the table on the opposite page show how we have organised the information included in this edition.

Area	Places	Postcodes
Central	Old Town, New Town, Stockbridge, Canonmills, Broughton, West End, Tollcross	EH1, EH2, EH3
North	Dean Village, Comely Bank, Clermiston, Barnton, Cramond, Blackhall, Ravelston, Craigleith, Crewe Toll, Drylaw, Pilton, Muirhouse, Granton, Trinity, Newhaven, Leith, Restalrig, Craigentinny, Meadowbank, South Queensferry	EH4, EH5, EH6, EH7, EH30, Fife and beyond
East	Newington, Prestonfield, Canongate, Holyrood, Northfield, Mountcastle, Piershill, Portobello, Joppa, Duddingston, Liberton, Cameron Toll, Craigmillar, Niddrie, Gilmerton, Ferniehill, Moredun, Mortonhall, Musselburgh, Wallyford, Whitecraig, Gullane, Prestonpans, Cockenzie, Port Seton, Tranent	EH8, EH15, EH16, EH17, EH21, EH31, EH32, EH33, East Lothian and beyond
South	Marchmont, Grange, Blackford, Bruntsfield, Morningside, Fairmilehead, Merchiston, Lasswade, River Esk, Polton, Bonnyrigg, Straiton, Loanhead, Dalkeith, Danderhall, Mayfield, Newtongrange, Gorebridge, Rosewell, Roslin, Penicuik	EH9, EH10, EH18, EH19, EH20, EH22, EH23, EH24, EH25, EH26, Midlothian and beyond
West	Haymarket, Gorgie, Stenhouse, Saughton, Sighthill, Murrayfield, Corstorphine, Gyle, Ratho, Oxgangs, Colinton, Slateford, Chesser, Craiglockhart, Longstone, Wester Hailes, Juniper Green, Currie, Balerno, Kirknewton, Newbridge, Kirkliston	EH11, EH12, EH13, EH14, EH27, EH28, EH29, West Lothian and beyond

Accessible Edinburgh

Additional information on accessibility is available throughout this book. Look out for more details wherever you see this symbol.

We cannot possibly cover everything in this book, but it is hoped that the information provided will help families have fun days out, as well as find the support they need.

Ed Loves.....

Our city is home to lots of green businesses and ethical ventures. Show some heart:

Ethical coffees - Always Sunday, Cafe Newton and Gallery cafe

Fair trade retail - Flux and the One World Shop

Give great gifts - Green Gift Company and Ollie & Forbes

Go Green - www.changeworks.org.uk for practical advice on being greener

Go Real - The Real Nappy Project

Locally sourced ingredients - Henderson's and the Edinburgh Farmers' Market

Organic beauty products - Neal's Yard Remedies

Reuse - Get some great bargins at NCT Nearly New Sales

Support local training initiatives - The Engine Shed and Out of the Blue

Think transport - Join the City Car Club or go for a cycle (Edinburgh Bicycle Co-op)

Places To Go

DAYS OUT

There are dozens of different types of venue where you can enjoy a really great day out with under 5s – in Edinburgh and throughout Scotland. We have concentrated on those places that most children should enjoy and which could be visited comfortably by parents with young babies. We have tried to ensure that our entries will appeal to different age groups and interests, thereby providing something for everyone.

While children are welcome at all these venues, parents should be considerate to other visitors. Every child is different, and so please be aware that not every venue might be ideal: the content of some may offer little interest or stimulation to a toddler, but could catch the attention of a four year old, or are great for visiting with a baby; others, due to the physical structure of the buildings (dark rooms and corridors, narrow turnpike stairs, etc) may concern rather than excite your particular child.

No matter what your preference is – indoor or outdoor, active or more reflective – there are some considerations which concern every parent: will my child be able to access most or all of the venue; are there suitable toilets and nappy changing areas; and if we want to eat, is the venue geared up to catering for children? We've tried to answer these points too!

As ever, the same rules always apply: when out and about with young children, try to account for every eventuality. With your first child, you might find yourself a little overwhelmed with the amount of planning needed, but rest assured, if you go with the old adage, 'if something can go wrong, it will', you'll get most bases covered. So, lightweight waterproofs are always worthwhile; put anything spillable or burstable in a sealable pocket or in a plastic bag; and always take a change of clothes. In the nice weather always remember the sunscreen and a sunhat - a child's skin must always be protected.

In this section we have listed the different types of venue by geographical areas under the following main headings:

- All creatures great & small - animal parks, aquaria, farms and zoos

- Art attack - art galleries, cinemas, crafts and theatres

- Grand designs - castles, country houses and palaces

- The great outdoors - beaches, gardens, parks and playgrounds

- Planes, trains & automobiles - boats, buses, railways and waterways

- Rainy days - libraries, leisure centres, museums and soft plays

- Festivals & events - plenty to entertain all year round

Key to symbols

We've introduced some symbols to provide a quick overview of the facilities available:

P	Car Park	**NTS**	National Trust for Scotland
♿	Accessible	**M**	Membership/Season Tickets
£	Entrance Fee	🍴	Refreshments (see Places to Eat)
F	Free	**S**	Shop
HS	Historic Scotland	🎁	Children's Parties

Many of the historic places to visit are managed by Historic Scotland (HS), Tel: 668 8600 or the National Trust for Scotland (NTS), Tel: 243 9300. Contact them for further information on membership and discounts. Please note that the National Trust for Scotland does not permit pushchairs or backpacks into some of its stately homes for safety reasons regarding your children and their property – babies in a front sling are permitted.

ALL CREATURES GREAT & SMALL

There are numerous farms, animal parks and aquaria in Scotland and we've listed many of them here. All offer something different, be it rare or non-native breeds, adventure playgrounds, train rides or playparks.

NORTH

Craigie's Farm
West Craigie Farm
South Queensferry
Edinburgh
EH30 9TR
0131 319 1048
john@craigies.co.uk
www.craigies.co.uk

Come for a walk and enjoy the wonderful views of the Forth while following the nature detective trail. Make beautiful engravings using the brass-rubbing stations. Pick-your-own fruit (there's a huge range on offer throughout the summer and early autumn). Don't forget to go and collect a few eggs (so fresh they are still warm!) from the chicken coop and swing by to say hello to the rare breed pigs before you leave. A great outing for children and adults alike!

    F   S

Deep Sea World
Battery Quarry
North Queensferry
KY11 1JR
Tel: 01383 411880
info@deepseaworld.co.uk
www.deepseaworld.com

Located just off Junction 1 off the M90 - well sign posted. Free coach and car parking. Journey time is approx 20 mins from Edinburgh.

This award-winning aquarium offers a spectacular fishes'-eye view of the marine environment. It's divided into various areas, including 'Krakatoa', with deadly species from around the Indo-Pacific; Amazonia which has the ever popular pirhanas; and the Underwater Safari. This is fascinating, as you stand on a moving walkway to observe the fish which swim all around the tunnel you're in. Toddlers will be fascinated by the sharks – especially at feeding time.

On entry check the feeding times and touch pool demonstrations. Free face painting, animal handling sessions and family talks and activity sessions.

    £   M   S

Fife Animal Park
Auchtermuchty
01337 831830

On the B937 half a mile south of A91 Milnathort to St Andrews road.

Exhibition, information area, as well as 2 play areas, trampolines and an outdoor trail. All facilities fully accessible for pushchairs and wheelchairs, and play areas fully enclosed. Small animal handling room.

Restaurant with high chairs and children's menu.

     £   S

Muddy Boots

Balmalcolm
Fife
KY15 7TJ
01337 831222
muddyboots@live.co.uk

Muddy Boots is a working farm which provides a great family day out. The facilities are all very new and modern. The café cooks with the farms own produce as well as other local produce and is very bright and comfortable, with additional sofas around a wood burning stove. There is a farm shop selling local and farm produce. At the back of the farm shop there is a ceramic workshop where children and adults can design their own pottery.

The outside features an area with farm animals including hens, sheep, and rabbits and children are encouraged to pet the animals. There is a large play area for children with grass sledging, buggy rides, a large sandpit and bouncing pillow.

There is a large indoor play area with plenty of toys which would specifically suit the under 5s. The toilets are modern and very child friendly.

The Scottish Deer Centre

Cupar
KY15
01337 810391

Located on A91, 4 miles before Cupar. Stagecoach bus Edinburgh to Cupar passes the Deer Centre. There's a deer farm walk to meet the deer, nature trail, picnic area, aerial walkway, etc. There are also falconry displays three times a day, and trailer rides in summer. Covered all-weather adventure barn. Superb outdoor adventure playground. Restaurant, coffee shop and shops.

£

St Andrews Aquarium

The Scores
01334 474786
www.standrewsaquarium.co.uk

Take M90 to J8, then A91 East. Stagecoach operates services from Edinburgh. Train from Edinburgh to Leuchars and then local bus service into St Andrews town centre.

Special feature exhibitions include tropical fish and touch pools – get up close and personal with piranhas. The centre also rehabilitates seals for release into the wild, with talks. Access to the actual aquarium area from the pay desk is down a set of stairs, but if you have a pushchair or wheelchair access to the lower level of the aquarium is via an external ramp.

Café with children's menu and bar open to all – check opening times.

Gift shop with marine merchandise.

 £

Vane Farm RSPB Nature Reserve

By Loch Leven
Near Kinross
01577 862355
vanefarm@rspb.org.uk
www.rspb.org.uk

This RSPB Nature Reserve has two nature trails. The Woodland trail (1.6 km) is a pretty but steep walk through a birch wood to a viewpoint at the top of Vane Hill. The Wetlands trail is a flat walk alongside Loch Leven and features three hides from which you can observe - even identify! - the birds using the colourful displays within the hide. Both trails require appropriate footwear and binoculars (which can be hired from the shop). Children can borrow one of the 'explorer packs' containing binoculars plus a variety of spotting, collecting and drawing activities. The café observation area has five telescopes and camera views to observe activity on the loch, and informative displays.

 £ M

Active Kid Toys and Adventure Park
Burnside
Stanley
PH1 4QB
01738 827286
sales@activekid.co.uk
www.activekidadventurepark.co.uk
An excellent day out for the family, lots to keep all ages occupied, guaranteed to have tired children by the end of the day. The murals around the site by a local artist give the park a more individual feel. The outdoor facilities include a large fort; pedal go-carts; 3-lane astra slide; trampolines; football targets; crazy golf and a tipee which can be booked for parties. There are tables and marquees for picnics. There are even a few farm animals too! Large range of TP toys to try out and buy. The indoor facility consists of a large pre-school play area; a lovely café; a well-stocked shop and a party room.

 £ M S

Auchingarrich Wildlife Centre
Comrie
Perthshire
PH6 2JE
01764 679469 / 670486
info@auchingarrich.co.uk
www.auchingarrich.co.uk
Take the M9 past Stirling to A9. From A9, take A822 towards Crieff, then 2nd turn off on to B827, then follow signs to Wildlife Centre.
Set in the heart of Perthshire with a range of birds and animals (highland cows, ponies, sheep, pigs, rabbits and guinea pigs; cockerels); prairie dogs popping out of holes; and there is a hatchery where you can hold newborn chicks and maybe see them hatch! Has an outdoor play area with a sandpit, mini tractors, a play barn with picnic tables, swings, climbing frame, etc., and a soft play barn with a separate area for under 5s and under 2s. Picnic tables can be found in a field with space hoppers, golf and space to run around. The new owners have plans to develop the café and play areas.

  £   S

Highland Wildlife Park
Kincraig
Kingussie
Invernessshire
PH21 1NL
01540 651270
www.highlandwildlifepark.org
If you're up North, take a trip to the Highland Wildlife Park. You can view animals there that you won't see anywhere else in Scotland, such as Przewalski horses, wolves, European elk and bison. There are also smaller animals, such as beavers, otters, polecats and owls, and internationally endangered animals of mountains and tundra. The Snow Monkeys by the cafe are particularly entertaining. You'll also be able to see Mercedes the Polar Bear who moved here from Edinburgh Zoo.

  £ M S

Brechin Castle Centre
Brechin
Angus
DD9 6SG
01356 626813
enquiries@brechincastlecentre.co.uk
www.brechincastlecentre.co.uk
Located off the A90, mid-way between Dundee and Aberdeen.
Large complex including a model farm and play park. The farm has a range of animals, including horses, sheep, goats, rabbit, guinea pigs etc. There are also displays of vintage farm equipment (lots of big wheels and old tractors!).
The Dragon's Lair playpark has imaginative equipment. There is also a miniature railway which runs, weather permitting, in the summer, plus a large ornamental lake.
Garden centre and a shop area, which sells a range of children's books, as well as some clothing, foods, and kitchenware.

 £ M S

EAST

Scottish Seabird Centre
The Harbour
North Berwick
EH39 4SS
01620 890202
www.seabird.org
Located by the harbour in North Berwick. Car parking in streets around or in town carparks.
Award-winning visitor attraction perched on the sea. A great family day out. Children's workshops during holidays and at weekends, and boat trips out to the Bass Rock. Centre has a wildlife cinema, events and exhibitions. Interactive live cameras allow visitors to watch gannets, puffins and other nesting seabirds on the Bass Rock and Fidra, and grey seals on the Isle of May. Cute seal pups live on camera are a great attraction! Seals and dolphins can sometimes be seen from the observation deck. In the main area downstairs there is a small children's soft play area suitable for toddlers.

 £ M S

Ed's Top Trips.....

There are so many great places it's hard to choose (everyone will have their own favourites). Here are a some suggestions from Ed:

Almond Valley

Dominion baby screenings

East Links

Edinburgh Zoo

Gorgie Farm

National Museum, Chambers Street

Royal Botanic Gardens

Soft Play (Tumbles at Craiglockhart Sports Centre and Scrambles at EICA)

Vogrie Country Park

Yellowcraig Beach

What would you recommend?
Tell Ed
email ed@efuf.co.uk

East Links Family Park

Dunbar
East Lothian
EH42 1XF
01368 863607
07775 7136646
grant@eastlinks.co.uk
www.eastlinks.co.uk

Loads to do at this 20 acre farm park - you can easily spend the whole day playing and exploring. The site is fully pushchair accessible (some gravel areas may be more difficult), with pushchair "parking" available where necessary. A range of outdoor activities (trampolines, a giant "jelly belly", pedal tractors, go-karts, toboggan run, giant maze, milk can skittles, kids rabbit warren, pirate ship play area, horseshoe pitching) and indoor activities (haybarn, climbing wall, bouncy castle, soft play) that will keep the whole family entertained. A new two level indoor "ball blast arena" and activity fortress add to the fun. If you want a rest after all the activities hop on board the 1 km narrow gauge railway for a trip around the park. You'll get a good view of many of the animals – particularly the sheep and lamas who like running by the train! You can also see chickens, turkeys, pigs, goats, donkeys, deer and rhea which you are welcome to feed with the animal food located throughout the park. Smaller animals such as rabbits, guinea pigs and chicks are also to be found.

The park is open year-round, and at Christmas-time, there are special activities and displays such as Santa's sleigh train, and a Nativity scene featuring animals from the park.

Outdoor picnic tables, as well as a spacious covered picnic area are available if you bring a packed lunch. You are also welcome to visit "Tea in the Park", the on-site tea room serving a variety of hot and cold dishes. The park is happy to host birthday parties – please contact them for details.

NOTE: Show this copy of Edinburgh for Under Fives when paying in to receive a free animal feed token!

   M

 Ample parking. Toilet for the disabled provided. Ask about a carer's discount – carers get in to the park for the price of a child. All of the park is accessible by wheelchair, including the small animal barn and the animal feeding activities. The narrow gauge railway has ramp access to a carriage that can accommodate a wheelchair so access shouldn't be a problem. All in all – top effort!

SOUTH

Butterfly & Insect World

at Dobbies Garden World
Lasswade
Midlothian
0131 663 4932
info@edinburgh-butterfly-world.co.uk
www.edinburgh-butterfly-world.co.uk

Located on A7, nr Dalkeith.

One of Europe's largest butterfly farms. Popular attraction with a minimum of 500 free-flying butterflies on display, although the numbers can escalate to 1200 at times. The butterflies live amidst a landscape of tropical plants, little waterfalls and pools, which contain fish and terrapins.

Individual displays of other creatures – tarantulas, 'glow-in-the-dark' scorpions, snakes, lizards, beetles, stick insects etc - some of which you get a chance to touch. The "Nocturnal Zone" is dark (of course!) which some children may find scary. Entrance is though the shop, where there's a good selection of books and gifts. Fully accessible for wheelchairs and pushchairs.

There's a restaurant in the garden centre, serving meals, snacks, etc. There are a couple of play & picnic areas – one adjacent to the restaurant, and one situated between Butterfly and Insect World and Dobbies Garden World.

  £   S

Jedforest Deer and Farm Park
Jedburgh
01835 840364
www.jedforestdeerpark.co.uk
Follow A68 south, 5 miles from Jedburgh, signposted on main road, turn off right and travel a mile to the first farm you come to.

Quite a long way from Edinburgh but well worth the journey. Farm includes deer such as 'white' red deer, red deer and muntjacs, plus many rare varieties of most farm animals, such as Soay sheep, Belted Galloway cattle and Tamworth pigs. The pigs have a lovely wooded area to potter in. There is a 'clapping' area where children can touch and sometimes help to bottle feed animals. Walks in wooded area and round the whole farm and pond following colour-coded signs lasting ½ -1½ hrs.

Large and small adventure playgrounds, including go-karts which older children love. There is also an indoor barn with ride-on tractors and straw bales. Ranger Activities available according to season: mini-beast hunts, tree safari, pond dipping, crafts.

Falconry Scotland is also based in the park, and even if there is no display you can still see the birds at rest.

Barbecues for hire, picnic area, café with high chair and separate play area, and farm animal themed shop.

 £   S

WEST

Gorgie City Farm
51 Gorgie Road
Edinburgh
EH11 2LA
0131 337 4202
info@gorgiecityfarm.org.uk
www.gorgiecityfarm.org.uk

A great place for children to experience farm animals. There are lots of lambs and piglets born at the farm during the year. There are two entrances from Gorgie Road, the first (coming from town) is for cars and the second for pedestrians. It is just before Tynecastle High School.

The pet lodge houses small birds, gerbils, guinea pigs and a snake amongst others. There is a sensory herb garden which is also home to the ducks, a wildlife garden which has the owl and a small pond where there are lots of frogs to spot in the summer. The main farm has goats, sheep, a pony, a cow, pigs, lots of chickens and turkeys and rabbits. There are chickens wandering freely round the farm which the children seem to enjoy and a big red static tractor which is a firm favourite with everyone. There is also an area where children can see vegetables being grown.

There is a café selling coffee, tea, sandwiches and basic meals. The cafe is trying to promote healthy eating and uses produce from their own gardens and has homemade soup every day. There are also tables and chairs outside for when the weather is fine.

The education centre can be hired for parties and also by people who want to use it as a venue for classes.

 £ S

Parking is limited but convenient for the farm if you can get a space. There's disabled access to all facilities, although the terrain is slightly rough in parts and the play park area has a bark ground covering. There are toilet facilities for the disabled. If you consider having a birthday party here for your child, they will be happy to change from the usual party room to one that is more accessible.

Edinburgh Zoo
134 Corstorphine Road
Edinburgh
EH12 6TS
0131 334 9171
info@rzss.org.uk
www.edinburghzoo.org.uk

Set in 82 acres of splendid parkland 10 mins from the city centre. Home to over 1000 animals and one of Europe's leading zoos.

With an inspiring array of daily events and much to see and do you will be kept busy. Upon entry you will be given a map and an events list (with times for penguin parade, animal antics, keeper talks, feeding times), there is usually a notice board as you enter with any new arrivals/babies.

The wonderful Rainbow landings is a walk through lorikeet aviary. There is room outside to leave pushchairs and before you enter it is worth buying a pot of nectar. The birds are surprisingly gentle so even the youngest toddler can feed them. Don't miss the impressive Budongo Trail, a huge chimpanzee experience where you can watch the chimpanzees indoors and out.

The famous penguin parade takes place daily at 14.15 - get there early to get a good space. Enjoy the underwater viewing where the penguins come right up to the glass to have a good look at you.

It is impossible to mention everything but some of our favourites are feeding times with the otters and red pandas, the lions, the monkey house, the UK's only koalas, and a trip on the hilltop safari.

 If you can cope with hills, the zoo can be a great day out. All enclosures and animal houses are accessible and a courtesy vehicle, with wheelchair access, runs about every 15 minutes and goes up to the top of the zoo where the wild cats and zebras live (not together!). The courtesy vehicle is very popular so you may have to wait in long queues during peak times. At present, there is no priority given for those who can't manage the walk, which can be a little frustrating. Parking is nearby and there are blue badge parking bays, which may not always be available during peak times. Parking is free for members.

Carers get in free and it's worth knowing that if you buy an annual membership for your child, their card should state 'plus carer' on it; this can be an affordable option if you plan to visit fairly regularly. There are several cafes, all of which are accessible, although the café on the lower floor of the member's house has a 'no pushchairs' rule. This can be quite strictly enforced and may cause difficulties if your child has a 'buggy' style wheelchair that passes for a pushchair – be prepared to explain this to staff if you visit this cafe. Overall, an enjoyable day if the weather's nice and it's not too busy. A visit during the day in school term-time might be best.

Whitmuir
Whitmuir Farm
Lamancha
West Linton
EH46 7BB
01968 661908
heather@whitmuirorganics.co.uk
www.whitmuirorganics.co.uk

Organic farm shop only 20 mins drive from Hillend, Edinburgh, on A701, 4 miles south of Leadburn Inn junction. Well-stocked shop including fresh locally reared beef, pork, mutton and lamb from own butchery, and home-grown seasonal soft fruit and vegetables. Delivery run to Edinburgh every Thursday for farm supporters (pay by regular standing order). The cafe and gallery are definitely worth a visit. Customers to the shop receive a warm welcome and are invited to explore the farm. On a recent visit I made, while my shopping was packed for me, the farmer took me and my 3 sons to see the turkeys and 12-day old piglets delightfully running about in the woods with their mum. A fantastic learning experience for kids to really see where their food comes from and beats a large supermarket any day!

Almond Valley Heritage Centre

Millfield
Livingston
EH54
01506 414957
info@almondvalley.co.uk
www.almondvalley.co.uk

Award winning museum, farm, and discovery centre, where the whole family can spend the day together exploring and having fun. A good range of indoor and outdoor activities. A new soft play area is attached to Morag's Milk Bar offering parents/carers the opportunity to sit and have a cup of tea while watching their children have fun. "Bones and Stones" is another recent addition, where children can take part in a simulated archaeological dig by sifting through the sand looking for buried artefacts. A new mine-themed outdoor play area has plenty to climb on, and a chute to slide down. Longstanding attractions, such as the tractor course, in-ground trampolines, museum, working mill, under 5s soft play, and adventure zone, are still favourites and well worth visiting. Also offers trailer, tractor and narrow-gauge railway rides (seasonal). There are a range of animals and during our visits, we have spotted giant bunnies, lambs, goats, cows, horses, and donkeys to name a few. There are usually daily talks and encounters with the animals scheduled.

Look out for special events throughout the year, such as "Easter Eggcitement", "Spooky Happenings" at Hallowe'en and "Santa at Almond Valley" at Christmas-time.

Bring a packed lunch and eat it at one of several picnic benches around the site, or, in the covered picnic barn. A range of hot and cold dishes and snacks are available in Morag's Milk Bar. At the end of your visit, there is a well-stocked gift shop offering a range of pocket-money and good quality farm-related toys/books/games.

  £ M S

 The majority of the centre is accessible to wheelchair users. Due to the nature of the land, with its hills and bumps, access may be a little tricky, but everything that can be done to make the centre accessible has been. While the terrain near the animal enclosures may be rough, it should be accessible to pushchairs and wheelchairs, and ramps have been provided to assist access. On the narrow gauge railway trip there is no ramp access to the carriage and a child may need to transfer from their wheelchair to the carriage seats, staff are more than willing to assist with the storing of chairs and equipment. Ask for help if you need it – it's part of the staff ethos to assist parents where they can. There are accessible toilet facilities and blue badge parking bays – parking shouldn't be a problem.

Five Sisters Zoo
Gavieside
West Calder
EH55 8PT
01506 872924
enquiries@fivesisterszoo.co.uk
www.fivesisterszoo.co.uk
Located just outside Polbeth in West Lothian. This is a great animal park, just the right size for under 5s to walk around, pushchair-friendly, lots of small and active animals. You can feed the lemurs or take part in a touch and feel session with some smaller animals. Lots of special events during the year, see website for details.

Blairdrummond Safari Park & Adventure Park
Blairdrummond
by Stirling
FK9 4UR
01786 841456
Follow M9 to junction 10 and take A84 for about 3 miles.
Exciting day out with lots to do. Drive through safari to see wild animals – lions, tigers, bisons, rhinos, ostriches etc. Drive takes about ½hr. Also giraffes, elephants and zebras can be viewed on foot, and there are elevated walkways for viewing bears and lions. Domestic animals – pigs, goats, llamas – are in a field where you can walk and touch them, with areas where they can 'escape' if they need a rest. Facilities for washing hands afterwards are provided. Lemurs can be seen pottering around and there is also a lemur enclosure that you can walk through. The sea lion show and bird of prey show are both very entertaining. Also a boat ride to see the chimpanzees on an island.
Large adventure playground is suitable for toddlers and older children. Includes 'pirate ship' for climbing and sand area with buckets and spades, which is lovely for younger under 5s. Amusement park (extra charge) and restaurant with a good range of food too. Tables available for your own picnics and DIY barbecue area.

ART ATTACK

ART GALLERIES

Children of any age can be fascinated by paintings and sculpture and Edinburgh offers a wide variety of opportunities to expose the young enquiring mind to art. Holding young children up to see properly and giving constant reminders not to touch can be tiring but well worth the effort. Sometimes a gallery may just be a different place to go with a baby and meet friends.
There are also some great examples of art in the environment throughout Edinburgh – the best central location is probably Princes St Gardens – and here you can look and touch!

Galleries are generally free, but you will have to pay for certain exhibitions.

CENTRAL

The City Art Centre
2 Market Street
Edinburgh
EH1 1DE
0131 529 3993

Hosts a collection of Scottish art and temporary exhibitions, often with a very broad appeal. Some exhibitions are aimed at children with workshops for under 5s. Access to all floors by lift and escalator. Toilets for the disabled on the ground floor have nappy change facilities. Pleasant café adjacent to the centre.

doggerfisher
11 Gayfield Square
Edinburgh
EH1 3NT
0131 558 7110
mail@doggerfisher.com
www.doggerfisher.com

A bright white contemporary art gallery in a converted tyre garage which showcases the work of international contemporary artists. Exhibitions run periodically and the gallery is open for private viewings for collectors of contemporary art. Easily accessible with pushchairs, equipped with nappy-change area and toilet facilities. Always a cheery welcome.

Fruitmarket Gallery
45 Market Street
Edinburgh
EH1 1DF
0131 225 2383
info@fruitmarket.co.uk
www.fruitmarket.co.uk

Contemporary art gallery showcasing the work of international artists and emerging talent. Pram and wheelchair accessible, with lift to upper floor. Ground floor café (highchairs), contemporary culture bookshop and toilet for disabled visitors. No nappy-change station.

   S

National Gallery
The Mound
Edinburgh
EH2 2EL
0131 624 6200
0131 332 2266 (recorded information)
enquiries@nationalgalleries.org
www.nationalgalleries.org

Events worth taking your 3+ child to are education events on Sundays such as Art Cart. The permanent exhibitions may have some beautiful art, but due to how the pieces are hung – it is not child friendly for perusal. It is a super place to go if your baby is asleep and you want time to soak up some culture.

Weston Link (garden level)
Part of the National Gallery Complex
The Mound

This is the best place to start and end your visit to either the National Gallery or the Royal Academy because of the coat check, toilet facilities, gift shop and restaurant. The large windows allow for a super view East towards the Balmoral, Princes Street Gardens, North Bridge and beyond. The It Gallery offes interactive screens for educational purposes, but this is more for children pushing 5 and up. The temporary exhibits on the walls in the Gallery are more easily viewed for small people than the galleries upstairs.

   S

Scottish National Portrait Gallery
1 Queen Street
Edinburgh
EH2 1JD
0131 624 6200
0131 332 2266 (recorded information)
enquiries@nationalgalleries.org
www.nationalgalleries.org

Closed until late 2011.

PLACES TO GO - ART ATTACK

NORTH

The Dean Gallery
73 Belford Road
EH4 3DS
0131 624 6200
0131 332 2266 (recorded information)
enquiries@nationalgalleries.org
www.nationalgalleries.org

If you park in the car park, the rear of the building is facing you. Here you will find the access for disabled visitors and you can also use this for access with prams. The lift provides access to all levels of the building. The imposing grade A listed building has been transformed by architects, with great features for the under 5s such as a see through floor and porthole type windows to fire the imagination. Good pushchair access. The gallery has a lovely setting, with an expanse of grass lawn to the front. Here you'll find several installations – ideal for youngsters to explore on a warm day. The Dean Gallery is dedicated to 20th century art – including Dada and Surrealist collections. Highpoints are Paolozzi's Vulcan (the 2 room-high iron man) and the reconstruction of the artist's London studio, which is stuffed with a wonderful collection of items. Shop sells a range of gifts, cards, books etc. Lift to brightly tiled toilets in basement where nappies can be changed.

    S

Scottish National Gallery of Modern Art
Belford Road
EH4 3DS
0131 624 6200
0131 332 2266 (recorded information)
enquiries@nationalgalleries.org
www.nationalgalleries.org

Can be accessed from the Water of Leith, lovely walk from Stockbridge through Dean village. Gallery car park is free. Ramped entrance and pushchair access to all floors via the lift.

Scotland's finest collection of 20th century paintings, sculpture and graphic art. Includes works by Picasso, Matisse, Moore, Hockney, Davie, Campbell and Wiszniewski. The front garden has been landscaped with an award-winning design by Charles Jencks, with steep, curved banks and ponds. This is fun for children to walk on but due caution is necessary as the banks are very steep in places: you can get Edinburgh's most artistic grass stains on your rear! Walled sculpture garden at the back.

    S

WEST

Jupiter Artland
Bonnington House Steadings
Wilkieston
EH27 8BB
01506 889900
www.jupiterartland.org

Artworks set in a stunning outdoor location. Allow at least an hour and a half to walk round the site. Paths are not suitable for pushchairs, younger children best carried in a sling, and wellies are a good idea if it's been raining. Seasonal opening hours as this is part art gallery and part private home. Visit website for opening hours, to book and for news of events.

 £ **S**

Visit our website for updates:
www.efuf.co.uk

THEATRES & ART CENTRES

Theatres are becoming more child friendly and there are often shows for under 5s, particularly during the Children's Theatre Festival as well as the Fringe. However, be aware that theatres may not be suitable for pushchairs. If a show is advertised as being for children, it's still best to check beforehand on age restrictions and the content and duration of the show. Refreshments may not always be suitable for children.

Prices vary by venue and depending upon the performance. Contact venues or visit their websites for more details.

Various theatre brochures and festival publications give information on facilities such as parking, toilets and access. For up-to-date information about theatre performances for children and families in Scotland try:

Young Audiences Scotland
c/o Catherine Wheels Theatre Co
Brunton Theatre
Ladywell Way
Musselburgh
EH21 6AF
0131 653 5255
info@youngaudiencesscotland.com
www.youngaudiencesscotland.com

♿ City centre theatre venues have good access for the disabled (this may not be the case in the Festival when everything but your granny's living room turns into a venue). When booking tickets ask about a carer's discount as some venues will give carers a concessionary rate, and consider whether or not you wish to book the seats allocated for wheelchair users. Sometimes these seats can be in a good location, with plenty of room around them for ease of access, although this is not always the case. If you book these seats your child will be expected to stay in their chair (or can sit on your knee) and a seat will be provided for a carer next to the wheelchair space. If you don't need this facility, it should be possible to book end of row seats, which may make things easier for you. If your child has a 'buggy' style wheelchair, you may be asked to leave it outside and may need to explain to staff that it is a wheelchair.

CENTRAL

Assembly Rooms
54 George Street
Edinburgh
EH2 2LR
0131 220 4348
enquiries@assemblyroomsedinburgh.co.uk
Hired as a venue for family events during the Edinburgh International Science Festival (Mar/Apr), and the Children's Festival (May). The venue is also used by various clients for craft fairs, ceilidhs, private parties etc, and is one of the main venues during the Festival Fringe.

There is a lift to the 1st floor and there are nappy changing facilities in the main foyer. Quiet area available on request for breastfeeding.

Playhouse Theatre
18-22 Greenside Place
0870 606 3434
www.edinburgh-playhouse.co.uk
A wide variety of shows including opera, musicals, ballet and rock concerts. Occasional children's shows. Toilets on ground floor. Some restricted views.

Scottish Storytelling Centre
43-45 High Street
Edinburgh
EH1 1SR
0131 556 9579
reception@scottishstorytellingcentre.com
www.scottishstorytellingcentre.co.uk
The Centre includes the historic John Knox House and the Netherbow Theatre. Offers a programme of regular storytelling for under 5s: Tiny Tales (6mths -3yrs) and Story Space (2-5yrs). Events happen monthly, but best to check dates and times on the website (also worth joining the mailing list). During the Edinburgh Fringe, they offer a wide range of children's theatre, storytelling and puppetry; some are suitable for children 3+ yrs. Finally, look out for the Puppet Animation Festival in the spring!

Traverse Theatre
10 Cambridge Street
Edinburgh
EH1 2ED
0131 228 1404
boxoffice@traverse.co.uk
www.traverse.co.uk
Occasional children's shows including the Children's International Theatre Festival (May). Generous discounts to most performances. The Traverse Bar Café is licensed for children until 20.00. Children's portions available all day. Lift to eating area and toilet with nappy changing facilities.

George Square Theatre
George Square
Edinburgh
0131 651 1930
A venue which is used during university holidays for shows, including children's shows. However, this is a university lecture theatre and consequently there are no specific facilities for young children or babies.

King's Theatre
2 Leven Street
Edinburgh
EH3 9LQ
0131 529 6000
Traditional theatre. Occasional children's shows, some specifically aimed at under 5s. Some shows with special low price tickets. Book early for a good seat. Ice cream and refreshments available. Toilet with nappy changing facilities on ground floor.

Royal Lyceum Theatre
30 Grindlay Street
Edinburgh
0131 248 4848
www.lyceum.org.uk
Family show at Christmas. Has also been used as a venue for the Scottish International Children's Festival in May. Lifts to all levels. Toilets for the disabled on the ground floor. Nappy changing facilities. Traditional-style theatre – very ornate and plush inside, once you are past the modern glass façade.

NORTH

Theatre Workshop
34 Hamilton Place
Stockbridge
0131 226 5425
www.theatre-workshop.com
Many shows geared for school children and occasionally under 5s. Also exhibitions, classes and workshops. Concession rates apply to children's tickets. Nappy changing facilities.

North Edinburgh Arts Centre
15A Pennywell Court
Edinburgh
EH4 4TZ
0131 315 2151
admin@northedinburgharts.co.uk
www.northedinburgharts.co.uk
Purpose-built arts centre offering a variety of performances and other arts activities for children, including some for the very young. Full programme of theatre and dance performances, plus Saturday workshops for families in a range of art forms. The Centre offers summer schools and other holiday arts activities, also suitable for under 5s.
Fully accessible centre with nappy changing facilities, garden with play structure and a family friendly café.

Out Of The Blue Drill Hall
36 Dalmeny Street
Edinburgh
EH6 8RG
0131 555 7100
www.outoftheblue.org.uk
A great space that is home to a community of artists. The Drill Hall is a venue for various Edinburgh festivals throughout the year and regularly hosts exhibitions. Also home to classes, a cafe and quarterly markets. Spaces are available to hire and the venue is very child-friendly. Visit the website for more information and news of events.

EAST

Festival Theatre
13/29 Nicolson Street
Edinburgh
EH8 9FT
0131 529 6000
www.eft.co.uk
Occasional children's shows for 3+ yrs. Café on the ground floor is licensed for children until 20.00. Toilet with nappy-changing facilities on 1st floor (lift access). Although the façade is very modern, the actual theatre is traditional and some seats have a slightly restricted view.

Craigmillar Arts Centre
58 Newcraighall Road
Edinburgh
EH15 3HS
0131 669 8432
craigmillarcommunityarts@gmail.com
www.craigmillarcommunityarts.org.uk
Very friendly and spacious old church just opposite the Fort Kinnaird Shopping Centre. Full of free art materials, best suited for the artistic parents among us with babies who would happily sleep in the pram while you express yourselves, or parents with pre-school aged children who would like to participate themselves. Adults should watch out as the space is fairly crammed with potentially risky objects. The centre also has scheduled events, such as Karaoke, Music Workshop, Photography Workshop etc. Please check the arts centre's website for further details.

Brunton Theatre
Ladywell Way
Musselburgh
EH21 6AA
0131 665 2240
boxoffice@bruntontheatre.co.uk
www.bruntontheatre.co.uk
Brunton Theatre is situated in Brunton Hall on the main street that runs through Musselburgh's west end. Big free car park to the back of theatre. Wonderful bistro within the building.
Theatre has a very varied programme, with shows (many shows suitable for the whole family), dance performances, concerts, films and children's events (shows, pantomimes, films). Many children's events have matinee showings.
The auditorium is of a good size, with all seats having a good view of the stage. There is a licensed bar within the foyer and a kiosk open during performances. Pushchairs are parked in foyer. A lift takes you to the east entrance of auditorium with a wheelchair gallery. Stairs lead to the west entrance. Many workshops also take place in the theatre.

Anything out of date?
Let us know -
info@efuf.co.uk

SOUTH

Church Hill Theatre
33a Morningside Road
Edinburgh
EH10 4RR
0131 447 7597
This venue is owned by Edinburgh Council and rented to theatre groups. Some shows are of interest to under fives. They publish a brochure with details of what shows are on. The cafe area is large, but does get very busy when there is a children's show on. Staff are always friendly and keep the facility very clean.

WEST

St Bride's Centre
10 Orwell Terrace
Edinburgh
EH11 2DY
0131 346 1405
Children's theatre and film shows, usually in school holidays. Also hosts arts and crafts class, parent and tots gorup, and after-school club. Café with large enclosed play area and reading corner. Nappy changing facilities. St Brides programmes detailing children's events and classes is distributed through local schools and libraries.

Don't forget to have a look at the Ceramic Experience advert on the back cover of this book!

Macrobert Arts Centre
University of Stirling
Stirling
FK9 4LA
01786 466666
www.macrobert.org
Located on University of Stirling campus. Follow M9 to the Dunblane roundabout then follow signs to Bridge of Allan. Travel through Bridge of Allan and the university is on left as you exit the village. Fabulous arts centre designed with children in mind. Lots to interest under 5s. Varied programme for the whole family including children's theatre productions and current films. Panto at Christmas. Art, dance and theatre workshops for a variety of age groups and a handy crèche facility. Spacious foyer area with small tables for little ones, colouring activities and toys.
Fully accessible, with parking pushchairs near to main entrance. Private area for feeding in baby care room.

CERAMIC CENTRES

NORTH

Ceramic Experience
Ocean Drive
Ocean Terminal
EH6 6JB
0131 554 4455
anna@theceramicexperience.com
www.theceramicexperience.com
All ages are catered for with free soft play for young children, a cafe area to chill out in, and then there are the tressel tables where you can get stuck into ceramic painting, glass making and body casts. 80% of the customers are mothers and babies and the studio specialises in childrens bitrthday parties, helping to take the pressure off you. The staff are friendly and walcoming so even if you just want to see what goes on, pop in for a coffee and a chat or some inspiration!

Potter About
267 High Street
Burntisland
KY3 9AQ
01592 873680
info@potterabout.co.uk
www.potterabout.co.uk
Decorate your own plates, bowls, ornaments and other gifts. Café serving snacks/home baking and a play corner. Available for party hire.

Ceramic Experience
17b Elgin Street Industrial Estate
Dunfermline
KY12 7SN
01383 840640
www.theceramicexperience.com
Facilities include café, soft play, ball pool.

Ceramic Experience
Bennybeg
Muthill Road
Crieff
PH7 4HN
01764 655788
www.theceramicexperience.com
Facilities include Soft Play, café, ball pool.

SOUTH

Ceramic Experience
28 Marchmont Crescent
Edinburgh
EH9 1HG
0131 662 6666
marchmont@theceramicexperience.com
www.theceramicexperience.com
A family friendly studio where you can paint and decorate items such as coasters, mugs and plates. Clay imprints of babies' hands and feet are also possible. Café, ball-pool and soft play area onsite. Nappy changing facilities and highchairs are available, and there is plenty of space for pushchairs. A great venue for a birthday party.

Doodles
29 Marchmont Crescent
Edinburgh
EH9 1HQ
0131 229 1399
painting@doodlesscotland.co.uk
www.doodlesscotland.co.uk
Very friendly staff - obviously experienced at working with children – will provide help in creating a fun ceramic workshop experience for all the family. Baby hand and foot prints make great presents, and older children can paint their own designs on items ranging from egg cups to large plates. Group rates available for parties and birthday party packages are available. Plenty of room for pushchairs.

CINEMAS

There's a good range of cinemas in Edinburgh, from the independently owned Dominion where the manager greets you in the foyer, or the more 'arty' Cameo and Filmhouse, to the sprawling megaplexes, which seem to be showing every film released in the past six months: take your pick. You never quite know how your child will take to their first cinema outing. Remember that the sound volume can be overwhelming, as can the dark. However, there are the chairs, big and plush to little ones, the décor, such as the planetoid carpet of Vue at Ocean Terminal and the lure of ice cream! Some cinemas have children's film clubs – check out your local one for details.

 It's worth knowing that most cinemas in Edinburgh admit a carer free of charge. Some may have an Cinema Exhibitors Association card (http://www.ceacard.co.uk/) that you need to apply for to enable you to gain free entry. When choosing seats consider whether or not you would like to book the seats reserved for wheelchair users. Some cinemas will operate a 'no pushchairs' rule but should be accommodating to children in wheelchairs (although storing wheelchairs in the aisle may be a no-no for health and safety reasons). All new build cinemas are wheelchair accessible, with the older cinemas accessible to varying degrees. The Cameo has two of its three screens fully accessible to wheelchair users (screens 1 and 2) and the bar area is accessible by the side entrance (there is also an accessible toilet). The Filmhouse is fully accessible and has good toilet facilities. The Dominion (a listed building) has steps into every screen so is not accessible.

CENTRAL

Vue
Omni Centre
Greenside Place
Edinburgh
EH1 3AA
08712 240 240
www.myvue.com
Parking behind complex, in side streets or NCP St James. Twelve-screen cinema complex, centrally located. Accessible by escalator and lift. Toilets with nappy changing facilities. Good views down on to the traffic (and the fantastic giraffes!) from the huge glass-fronted façade. Snacks on sale above ticket sales, so you can get to the screens without passing by, if you take the stairs.

 £

Cameo Cinema
38 Home Street
Edinburgh
08707 551231
www.picturehouses.co.uk
Car parking is poor, try parking at Chalmers St and walking down to Tollcross, or park at Castle Ter/Semple St and walk up. Friends cardholder scheme available offering discounted tickets at all times. Babies and children of all ages admitted at parents' discretion and subject to normal film certification. Ice cream, popcorn and a wide range of confectionery on sale in the foyer. Children allowed in the bar up until 20.00. There is a permanent nappy changing station located in the cinema.

The Big Scream
Offers screenings exclusively for parents/carers of young children on Thursdays at 10.30. Entry is only valid for a carer, plus one other adult (must be must be accompanied by a baby under 12mths). A pre-screening complementary tea or coffee is included in the ticket price. Pushchair parking, bottle warming and nappy changing facilities are all provided. To be updated specifically on Big Scream events please email: cameo.marketing@picturehouses.co.uk.

 £

 Don't forget to let businesses know you saw them in the EFUF book!

Filmhouse
88 Lothian Road
Edinburgh
EH3 9BZ
0131 228 2688
www.filmhousecinema.com
Three screen cinema with a more varied programme than the larger chain cinemas, showing independent, art house and world cinema.

For Crying Out Loud
The Filmhouse's scheme for carers/parents with young children. Screenings are on Mondays at 10.30. Up to two carers, who must be accompanied by a child under 12mths.

Odeon Cinema
118 Lothian Road
Edinburgh
EH3 8BG
0871 22 44 007
Parking – not plentiful: a choice of on-street, 'pay and display' or the car park behind the cinema in Semple Street.
Four-screen cinema showing mainstream films. Easy pushchair access and lifts. Nappy changing facilities. Comfy chairs in retail area and on concourse to screens.

Odeon Newbies
Odeon offer newbies baby parent and baby screenings.

NORTH

Vue
Ocean Terminal
Ocean Drive
Victoria Dock
Leith
EH6 6JJ
08712 240240
www.myvue.com
One of the most liberating experiences as a new mum is making it out to the cinema with your baby for the first time. Mother and baby screenings available during term times are a mecca for the maternity leave bunch and the enjoyment needn't stop there. Kids AM shows childrens films every Saturday and Sunday at discounted rates while accompanying adults go free! There are also family discount tickets and cheap day Tuesdays. Use a baby carrier instead of a buggy to avoid health and safety issues with pushchairs at mother and baby screenings.

SOUTH

Dominion Cinema
18 Newbattle Terrace
Edinburgh
EH10 4RT
0131 447 4771
directors@dominion-cinema.co.uk
www.dominioncinemas.net
One of the last remaining family-run cinemas in Edinburgh, and long may it continue. A cosy gem of a place that has just had a substantial refurbishment to create a 22-seat private cinema which can be booked for parties. Allow plenty of time to park near the cinema, especially if it's a popular film and/ or during the school holidays. Parking is metered from 8am – 6pm Mon-Fri and 8am – 1.30pm Sat.

UGC Fountainpark

Fountainpark
130/3 Dundee Street
Edinburgh
EH11 1AF
0871 200 2000
0870 902 0417 (24 hr information)
Access car park via Western Approach Rd, or via Dundee St. Yearly passes available.

Large cinema complex located in a purpose built leisure park in a central location. Underground car park; fee refunded on exit with voucher supplied by cinema or other outlets. Cinema offers booster seats for children. Parties hosted in a special 'party' room. Phone for further information and booking.

   £

Westside Plaza

120 Westerhailes Road
Edinburgh
EH14 2SW
0870 5050007
Eight-cinema complex. Next to Wester Hailes station. Easy parking and access is all on one level. Ice-cream, popcorn etc. Nappy-changing facilities. Family tickets available. Under 18mths free if sitting on parent's knee.

   £

GRAND DESIGNS

Despite changes in legislation regarding access to buildings, you should remember that in the case of historic buildings, some areas of castles, palaces and even houses and museums may be hard to access, due to the age of the building and the nature of the architecture. Slings/papooses are recommended for very young children. You may find that backpacks are forbidden in many historic buildings. Rememer, if you're a member of Historic Scotland or The National Trust for Scotland, you gain free entry to many monuments, and if you have National Trust or English Heritage membership you may also get free entry.

Many historic sites now carry Green Tourism awards, which are awarded for the introduction of energy saving measures, which can be anything from using low-energy lightbulbs or movement–sensitive lighting, recycling, using local produce, or promoting wildlife areas or sustainable transport.

We've a wealth of castles and palaces on our doorstep: there are castles straight out of fairy tales to those stark, eerie hulks that are straight out of nightmares, and all points in between.

While a visit to a country house may not be high on the list of things to do with young children, please bear in mind that many stately homes now have facilities to attract families, including decent tearooms and nappy changing facilities. The interior of the houses may hold no interest for an under 5, but the estates are usually a different matter, and many now have nature trails and play areas.

CENTRAL

Edinburgh Castle
Castle Rock
Edinburgh
EH1 2NG
0131 225 9846
www.historic-scotland.gov.uk
Nearest parking on Castle Ter and Johnstone Ter. If you choose a clear day to visit, you can enjoy stunning views over Edinburgh and across to Fife from the Esplanade. Within the castle walls are various historic attractions such as St Margaret's Chapel, the Honours of Scotland, the Stone of Destiny, the famous cannon Mons Meg and the prison vaults (might be too dark and scary for the very young). There's also the One O'clock Gun and a related exhibition.

Guided tours and CD-ROM audio tours available. There isn't an awful lot to take younger children's interest and there are some steep cobbled paths that are not ideal for toddlers or pushchairs. Over 3s might enjoy a short visit – or they might be happy with a walk round the esplanade!

 £ HS S

 Top marks for accessibility! You may not believe it, given that the castle was not built with access in mind, but a trip to the castle can be fun, educational and easy! If you have a blue badge you can park on the esplanade. A courtesy vehicle will then transport you and your child through a 'secret tunnel' that cuts through the rock and up the steep cobbled hill to the top area of the castle. The wheelchair accessible courtesy vehicle can transport you up and down again although, if you can brave the cobbles, you may wish to walk back down. Truly VIP treatment! Almost all of the exhibitions, including the crown jewels and the prisoner of war exhibit/dungeons, have alternate wheelchair access (although note that the accessible entrance to the dungeons may be closed in high winds and that there are a small number of steps within the dungeons). The staff are fantastically helpful, do ask if you need assistance. There are toilets for the disabled at various levels. Carers and under 5s get in free so, if it's just the two of you, it may not cost you anything! A visit comes highly recommended.

John Knox House
43-45 High Street
Edinburgh
EH1 1SR
0131 556 9579
reception@scottishstorytellingcentre.com
www.scottishstorytellingcentre.co.uk
In the same building as The Storytelling Centre, this atmospheric 16th century house has massive metre-thick walls, a stone spiral staircase, and views over the bustle of the High Street. Look out for a false keyhole and sliding panel designed to confuse thieves, and a cloak and hat to dress up in. It is not suitable for pushchairs, but might be interesting for pre-school children.

St Giles Cathedral
High Street
Edinburgh
EH1 1RE
0131 225 9442
www.stgilescathedral.org.uk
A magnificent building steeped in history. As well as being a living church with an active congregation, it is host to some 400,000 visitors every year. Inside there a is great deal of space to explore and for a toddler this is quite exciting. There is no particular focus for children, but mine enjoyed the stained glass, and running through the chairs. Children are welcome and the space is big enough for you not to worry about disturbing someone in prayer. Be aware that some parts are roped off and may be a challenge for the more adventurous child. The Thistle Chapel is worth a visit - it's full of detail and we enjoyed spotting the beautifully carved animals, look out for the angels playing bagpipes.

Volunteer guides are on duty each day to answer questions and conduct guided tours on request. There are information desks situated at the main West entrance and at the Thistle Chapel. Permits for photography, including camcorders, are available from the Information Desk.

 S

Gladstones Land
477b Lawnmarket on Royal Mile
08444 932100
Gladstone's Land was the home of a prosperous merchant in the 17th century. It is authentically decorated and furnished to evoke Edinburgh's Old Town some 300 years ago. Remarkable painted ceilings, reconstructed shop booth and bar parlour and a fine collection of 17th century Dutch paintings. There is a shop.

£ NTS   **S**

Greyfriars Tolbooth and Highland Kirk
Greyfriars Place
Top of Candlemaker Row
0131 226 5429
www.greyfriarskirk.com
Home to the Church of Scotland congregation of Greyfriars Tolbooth and Highland. The kirk takes its name from the pre-Reformation Franciscan friary that stood nearby. It was the first church built in Edinburgh after the Reformation and opened in 1620. The church is primarily a place of worship, prayer and music.
Information, souvenirs and an audio-visual programme is available in the kirk visitor centre. Greyfriars also offers visits for groups of nursery age children.

S

Greyfriars Bobby
A statue dedicated to Greyfriars Bobby is situated opposite the kirk gates, at the junction of Candlemaker Row and George IV bridge. The story of the faithful dog is always popular and to prove it's true, both Bobby and his master are buried in the churchyard.

The Georgian House
7 Charlotte Square
Edinburgh
EH2 4DR
0844 493 2117
www.nts.org.uk
The Georgian House is an exquisite 18th century town house in Edinburgh's New Town, designed by master architect Robert Adam The house is beautifully furnished, with collections of period china, furniture, art, and silver gracing three floors of elegant rooms, decorated as they would have been when the house opened in 1796.
Visitors to the house can view a video presentation which explores the history of New Town and the living conditions of those who inhabited Georgian House. Visitors also have a chance to see what life was like "below stairs", with access to the restored kitchen, as well as the wine cellars and china closet.
The best bit is the insight into Georgian Life. Visitors with very active toddlers might find they have to restrain their little ones from touching antiques etc. The Georgian House runs a variety of children's events through the year with the Easter Egg Hunt being a particular favourite. There is an activity room on the top floor which is always open and where children can paint, draw and try on costumes. They are also working on devising some activities for the under 5s to supplement the quizzes and activity sheets for the over 5s. The staff are exceptionally friendly and helpful.

£ NTS

 In most cases under 5s go free!

NORTH

Lauriston Castle
2a Cramond Road South
Davidsons Mains
Edinburgh
EH4 5GD
0131 336 2060
lauristoncastle@edinburgh.gov.uk
www.edinburgh.gov.uk/lauriston
Under 5s are discouraged from the house and tours, however, welcome to explore the gardens and grounds. Set in 30 acres of parkland and formal gardens with fabulous views overlooking the Firth of Forth, the house itself is a fine example of Edwardian Edinburgh. The grounds offer a series of pushchair friendly gardens to stroll. On the whole well maintained but take care in the Japanese Garden which has fallen into disrepair. Wellies are a must on a wet day.

Toilets are basic, but has a bench that can be used for nappy changing. Group picnics can be arranged through the warden. A diary of activities can be found on the website.

Hopetoun House
South Queensferry
EH30 9SL
0131 331 2451
www.hopetounhouse.com
Described as 'Scotland's finest stately home' and approaching it via the sweeping drive certainly creates quite an impact. There is a magnificent art collection throughout the impressive rooms – and pleasant guides who will explain interesting features such as serving bells to under 5s.

The gardens are extensive with lots to explore for more adventurous children. Watch out for ha-has though (ditches to keep animals in fields – there's one to the left of the main drive), and the large pond to the rear of the house. Also a picnic area, nature trails and deer. In the old stable block there is a flora and fauna exhibition for older children.

Various events throughout the year.

 £

Abbot House Heritage Centre
Maygate
Dunfermline
01383 733266
www.abbothouse.co.uk
The oldest house in Dunfermline: 'The People's Tardis'. Permanent displays of Dunfermline/ Scottish life from the Picts to the 1960s and of famous people, such as Andrew Carnegie. Also hosts exhibitions and craft fairs. Upper floors unsuitable for pushchairs. However, the café with highchairs and the shop on the ground floor are accessible. Café has a 'sitooterie' with a view of the Abbey. Under 5s can play in the gardens and in the adjoining Abbey grounds, but beware of attractive hazards such as the fountain.

  S

Aberdour Castle
01383 860519
www.historic-scotland.gov.uk
Aberdour lies about 5 miles E of the Forth Bridges on the A921. The castle is next to Aberdour railway station, and near a bus stop

Built in the 13th Century, this partially ruinous step-gabled castle is brilliant for children – especially those interested in knights and castles. The winding stairs are fascinating for older toddlers and children, but are obviously no use for a pushchair! The interior is furnished and accessible.

Tearoom open during summer and weekends in winter. The shop has reasonably priced themed toys for children's role play (knights' helmets etc).

Make a day of it with a trip to one of the beautiful Aberdour beaches too.

    HS   S

Falkland Palace

Falkland
Cupar
Fife
KY15 7BU
0844 4932186
www.nts.org.uk

A palace straight out of a fairy tale, built by Stewart monarchs as a country residence/-hunting lodge. Pleasant gardens, with viewing access to the oldest 'royal tennis' court in Britain – built in 1539 and still in use. Partly roofed, with some fully furnished rooms from all eras of the palace's use, the palace itself is of minimal interest to under 5s – best to give it a miss unless you are interested in the historic aspects (and have a baby in a papoose or sling). Having said that, there are 'I-Spy and Garden Activity sheets for their younger visitors, and a young persons guide to palace on sale at reception. Palace often hosts weekends with guides in historic costume (check with property for details for these dates, plus other special events).

 £ NTS S

Lochleven Castle

On an island in Lochleven
KY13 8UF
01577 862670
07778 040483
www.historic-scotland.gov.uk

Situated off the M90 at Kinross. Follow signs from Kinross. A great day out. This castle is situated on a tiny island and is only accessible by a small motor boat (warm jackets recommended) which takes about 10 minutes to cross the loch. The castle is steeped in history: Mary Queen of Scots was imprisoned and forced to abdicate here before managing to escape. After exploring the castle and island, follow the footpath opposite the ticket office round the loch for 50m to a great play park. Loch Leven is a National Nature Reserve and an important site for waterfowl. The ticket office shares premises with a cafe (independently owned) and small visitor centre. You could also visit the nearby Vane Farm Nature Reserve while you are here.

 £ HS S

Castle Campbell

At the head of Dollar Glen
FK14 7PP
01259 742408
www.historic-scotland.gov.uk

Located 10 miles east of Stirling on the A91. Imposing 15th century castle and seat of the Clan Campbell set amidst beautiful countryside. A climb to the top of the tower brings lovely views of the Ochil Hills and Dollar – don't forget to count the steps to answer the question on the Children's Quiz Sheet. There is an interactive model of the castle with buttons to press and sound effects and pretty terraced gardens with picnic tables and benches. Best suited for pre-schoolers rather than younger under 5s. There is only one toilet cubicle for the castle which has a queue at busy times and no nappy changing.

 £ HS S

Hill of Tarvit

01334 653127
www.nts.org.uk

On A916 nr Cupar. Well-signposted from A91 and A92.

The house, which is just over 100 years old, has large collection of furniture, paintings and porcelain with lots for the family to see. There's also an awful lot of 'below-stairs' preservation, which makes for some interesting viewing. Back pack carriers not allowed. Free activity sheets for children available at reception. Children should be supervised in house. Large gardens with lots of space for children to run around plus a steep walk up the hill to the monument. Picnic tables in garden. House also offers various family activites. Toilets and nappy changing facilities. Dogs welcomed on woodland walks (not at the front of the house). Keep all dogs on leads.

 £ NTS S

Scone Palace
Perth
PH2 6BD
01738 552300
www.scone-palace.co.uk
In the past, the kings of Scotland were crowned on Moot Hill in the grounds of this impressive looking palace. Young children will enjoy the extensive grounds to run around in, but there is also an adventure playground suitable for under (and over) 5s and a butterfly garden. However, the high point of our visit was the Murray Star Maze and the fountain to be found in the middle of it. Peacocks roam the grounds (and can be fed with peanuts purchased from the shop), and there are donkeys, a Highland pony and Highland Cattle. The palace interior has little to interest under 5s (apart from two stuffed bears), although older children may enjoy the 'I spy' trail for primary school age children.

   £   S

Where would you suggest?
Tell us -
ed@efuf.co.uk

EAST

Palace of Holyroodhouse and Holyrood Abbey
Foot of Royal Mile
Canongate
Edinburgh
0131 524 1120
The Palace is closed when The Queen or Her Commissioner is in residence. Joint admission tickets for Palace and Queen's Gallery available.
This is The Queen's official residence in Scotland and all state and historic apartments are open to the public. Audio tour equipment is provided, including a special 'family' edition. You can also visit the ruins of Holyrood Abbey, dating back to the 11th Century. There is a limited amount of interest for under 5s. Pushchair access is limited to the ground floor.

Queen's Gallery
Situated in the Mews area of the Palace. Contains exhibitions from the Royal Collection. Toilets are available in the Royal Mews where changing and feeding facilities for babies are available. There is also a café and gift shop with helpful staff.

£   HS   S

Craigmillar Castle
Craigmillar Castle Road
Edinburgh
EH16 4SY
0131 661 4445
www.historic-scotland.gov.uk
A great place to visit particularly on a sunny day. Take a picnic and enjoy exploring this very well preserved medieval castle – one of the best in Scotland. Many rooms to explore – the great hall, the 'Mary Queen of Scots' room, kitchen and basement prison. Fantastic views of Edinburgh from the battlements. The Castle is surrounded by a large garden including the remains of a large ornamental fishpond in the shape of the letter 'P' for Preston, the castle's owners. Recommended for children who are walking, as there are steep turnpike stairs without handrails, different levels and long drops from low windows and balconies.

   £   HS   S

Arniston House
Gorebridge
01875 830 515
www.arniston-house.co.uk
Located approx 40 mins from central Edinburgh, from A7 turn right on to B6372, signposted as Penicuik and Temple, turn right after about a mile.
Large private house, which has lovely, well maintained grounds for walks. Access for pushchairs. Toilets. No nappy-changing facility. Toilet with disabled access.
Arniston House is lovely, but while the guided tour may be of interest to parents, there's little to interest under 5s. The tour involves a fair amount of stairs – not suitable for a pushchair, but fine if you have a baby in a papoose. Most of the tour is accessible by visitors in wheelchairs, there are some steps, but there is a ramp, and also a stairclimber to access the hall from the porch.

 £

Crichton Castle
Near Pathhead
EH37 5QH
01875 320017
www.historic-scotland.gov.uk
Situated 2.5 miles south-south-west of Pathhead, off the A68. Built for the Crichtons in the late 14th Century and later occupied by the Bothwells, the castle stands alone amidst Midlothian countryside and has an unusual diamond-faceted courtyard facade added in the 16th Century. This is a small castle which is great fun for older under 5s to explore. Bear in mind that there are no toilet facilities at the castle, so if you're not also visiting Vogrie Country Park (5 mins drive away), the nearest public loos are at Fordel Services on Lauder Road, between Pathhead and Dalkeith.

 £ HS

Preston Mill
East Linton
EH40 3DS
08444 93 21 00
In East Linton 23m east of Edinburgh off A1, 7m south of North Berwick.
A water-driven meal mill has existed here for four centuries, and these attractive stone buildings date from the 18th century. Watch the still intact mechanism at work, and learn about milling in the exhibition. Picturesque millpond and doocot. There is a shop and a picnic area.

£ NTS S

Dirleton Castle and Gardens
01620 850330
www.historic-scotland.gov.uk
In Dirleton, 3m W of North Berwick. Take A1 then A198 towards North Berwick. Next to the car park there is a small play park, with bucket swings, roundabout, slide etc and picnic table.
Fantastic castle built in the 12th century, great for exploring by young and old alike, but do take extra care with little ones. Famous gardens include an Arts and Crafts herbaceous border – the longest one in the world according to the Guinness Book of Records. Make a day of it by visiting Yellowcraig Beach too.

 £ HS S

SOUTH

Floors Castle
Near Kelso
Roxburghshire
TD5 7SF
01573 223 333
A beautiful castle, built in 1721, and set in stunning grounds. It is the largest inhabited castle in Scotland. State rooms with priceless works of art open to public. Woodland and river walks. Children's quiz in castle. Well-maintained adventure playground.

 £ S

Hermitage Castle
01387 376222
www.historic-scotland.gov.uk
5½ miles NE of Newcastleton, take the B6399, and watch out for the signs.
A looming, eerie fortress set deep in the Borders and scene of many dark deeds – it is said that one of its first owners was boiled alive in his own cauldron! Open in the summer only, and even then bring wellies! From the outside, it's just about everything you'd want from a castle. Inside there's a covered well, a view down into the prison pit and good views out into the bleak countryside. It can be viewed externally in the 'closed' season. The terrain around is uneven and banked, so perhaps best viewed with active children rather than toddlers or babies – the same goes for the interior. There's a ruined chapel and graveyard if you turn left once you have crossed the access bridge rather than right towards the castle. There's a giant's grave outwith the chapel's walls; he was called the Cout o' Kielder and owned magic chainmail – ideal story-fodder for children! When at the Hermitage or the chapel, watch out for the river. Picnic area and toilets.

 £ HS

Paxton House
Berwick upon Tweed
TD15 1SZ
01289 386291
info@paxtonhouse.com
www.paxtonhouse.com
54 miles from Edinburgh. Signposted 3 miles from the A1 Berwick upon Tweed bypass on B6461.
This beautiful house is in the 18th century Palladian style, with interiors by Robert Adam. It houses the largest collection of Chippendale furniture in Scotland. Guided tour only – with 'Teddy Bear' trail for children. Lift to 1st floor only. Not suitable for toddlers or pushchairs – and it could be a little too rarified for more active youngsters.
However, there's plenty outside to whet (and exhaust) the most active appetites. There are 80 acres of woodland, parkland and gardens. Nature detective trails for children and 1 mile of riverside walks – accessible by pushchair if dry. Ponies and Highland cattle can usually be seen in the estate fields. Wildlife includes rare red squirrels, which you might be able to see from the red squirrel hide. There's also an adventure playground, which has various structures, and a croquet lawn. Various annual activities and events – phone for details. Winner of various awards.

 £ S

Jedburgh Abbey
01835 863925
www.historic-scotland.gov.uk
Take the A68 from Edinburgh. Jedburgh is an historic town, set in the heart of the Borders.
Impressive building, founded in 1138. Visitor centre which houses many priceless artefacts found during excavations at the site. Cloister and herb garden. There is also an interactive area. Car park. Toilets. Shop. Reasonable access with pushchair. Picnic area.

 £ HS S

Visit our website for updates:
www.efuf.co.uk

Melrose Abbey
01896 822562

The town of Melrose can be a lovely spot to break off a longer journey, or for a day trip. The town nestles below the Eildon Hills – fairy hills or the resting place of King Arthur and his Knights, if you believe the tales. Take the A7 or A68 from Edinburgh.

The majestic ruins of the abbey offer plenty of intricate carving to admire. You can see them along an adjoining path, rather than going in, if you prefer, as there is little really to interest under 5s, although Robert the Bruce's heart is allegedly buried in the Abbey grounds – a plaque marks the spot.

Smailholm Tower
01573 460365
www.historic-scotland.gov.uk
Near Smailholm village, 6m W of Kelso on the B6937, then turn on to the B6404
Smailholm Tower sits high on a rocky outcrop with a safety rail for safer viewing of the outlying land. It is a typical example of the 'bastles' that once stood all around the country. Inside there is an exhibition of tapestries and costume dolls. Open all summer and at the weekends in the winter. If you visit Kelso, it might be worth the detour just for the look. No toilets.

 £ HS

Traquair House
Innerleithen
01896 830323
enquiries@traquair.co.uk
www.traquair.co.uk
Oldest continually-inhabited house in Scotland, set in picturesque grounds. It looks very different to many of the other stately homes of Scotland, as it isn't Georgian. Look out for the gates that were locked in 1745 and are not to be opened until a Stewart returns to the throne. No pushchairs permitted inside - there are many stairs to negotiate, including the secret priest's stairs. Excellent maze and pleasant children's play area.
Traquair hosts family events throughout the year.

 £   S

Threave Castle
07711 223 101
www.historic-scotland.gov.uk
3m W of Castle Douglas on the A75. This is one straight out of days of old when knights were bold. The castle itself stands on an island in the River Dee. To access it, you ring a bell and a steward will come to ferry you over: boat jetty is ½ mile walk from car park. There are toilets (inc disabled) in the car park, but none on the island. There is a picnic area on the island. The last boat leaves the island at 18.00. Not suitable for prams due to the boat ride.

 £ HS

WEST

Corstorphine Dove Cot
Dovecot Road
Corstorphine
EH12 7LE
www.historic-scotland.gov.uk
Maintained by Historic Scotland, this is a large circular 'beehive' shaped dovecot. It's possible to walk round the outside, but there are some steps. An interesting educational visit to tie in with doing other activities in the area.

F HS

House of the Binns
Near Linlithgow
West Lothian
EH49 79A
0844 4932127
houseofthebinns@nts.org.uk
www.nts.org.uk
Located on the A904. There is a woodland walk suitable for children who are good walkers and can manage steps. Not suitable for pushchairs. Walk takes approx 15mins and offers fantastic views. Picnic tables provided near the car park. Admission to the house includes a tour, but this is less suitable for under 5s. Great place for a picnic and a walk. Remember to look out for the peacocks!

 £ NTS

Linlithgow Palace
01506 842896
In Linlithgow. It is best to park your car and walk up to the palace.

Built as a pleasure palace by various Stuart monarchs and acknowledged as one of the most beautiful palaces in Europe. Now roofless and partially ruined. Full of nooks, crannies and turnpike staircases which make it unsuitable for pushchairs. Probably best visited with tiny babies in a papoose or with older children; there's certainly a lot to fire the imagination of little princes and princesses. Information boards provided in key rooms in various languages. There's a huge fireplace in the Great Hall – stand inside and look up!

Look out for a skittles slab, courtyard fountain, the Presence Chamber with its unique floor patterning and the charmingly named 'vomitorium'. There are toilets with disabled access, a picnic area, plus a shop. There is not a café, but there are plenty in Linlithgow.

 £ HS S

Callendar House
Callendar Park
Falkirk
FK1 1YR
01324 503770
www.falkirk.gov.uk (arts and culture link)
Take the M9, J5, turn left along the Laurieston Bypass. At the end, turn left, then right. Pass the grassy banking of the Antonine Wall and the park entrance is on your left, signposted, at a roundabout. Callendar House is well worth a visit as all sorts of Royal intrigues and battles took place in Falkirk. The house is set in extensive grounds with play park and woodland trails. Inside are four 'interpretative areas' with costumed guides: the 1828 kitchen, the General Store, the Clockmaker's Workshop and the Printer's Workshop. You get to eat things in the kitchen and the general store. There are also temporary exhibitions of art and history, as well as permanent displays .

Shop selling handmade preserves and sweets and traditionally-made replicas of products from the famous Carron Ironworks.

  £ S

Stirling Castle
Stirling
FK8 1EJ
01786 450 000
www.historic-scotland.gov.uk
One of Scotland's most impressive castles and superb for energetic toddlers and adults, even on rainy days. Audio-visual exhibits in the kitchens and palace, interactive displays, gargoyles on the walls and secluded corners where there are probably ghosties! Take care if you decide to walk around castle walls. Cannons for pretend play, grassy gardens and stunning views, shop and restaurant. The restored Great Hall is swagged with heavy drapes, has a stunning beamed roof, but for young children, its main attraction is as a running space. The military museum holds little to interest young children and is up some narrow stairs. If possible, take a good look at the map you get with your ticket before setting out from the ticket office so you can be clear about the best route to take with under 5s because the space is large and the signposts are informative but not descriptive.

Castle has various toilets facilities, but there's a good one hidden away within the Great Hall, complete with a nappy change unit.

  £ HS S

The Pineapple
NTS maintained gardens, building leased to the Landmark Trust. 7m E of Stirling, off A905, then off B9124, 1m W of Airth.

If you are going home from Stirling by the 'low road' (the A905) through Fallin, Throsk etc, look out for the signs to the Pineapple before you get to Airth. Follow the narrow road to a small car park. Through the gateway in the wall, you'll enter what was a large orchard and set in the midst is The Pineapple – a 45ft (14m) high building built in the shape of, you've guessed it, a pineapple. Built in 1761, it is now holiday properties, so you can't get inside, but it makes a quirky quick stop-off point.

 F NTS

THE GREAT OUTDOORS

BEACHES

Swimming in the Sea

Paddling and swimming in the sea can be great fun but remember sea water can be extremely cold even on sunny days so be ready to wrap up warm afterwards. Edinburgh's beaches from Cramond to Musselburgh are generally reasonably clean, but standards can change from season to season and after heavy rain, so always check before going into the water, and always obey the notices posted – just because it looks clean doesn't mean it's safe. The Scottish Environment Protection Agency (SEPA) monitors and reports on water quality of other recreational waters as well as those which are EC recognised (see www.sepa.org.uk for latest results). Some of the beaches in urban areas can be affected by sewage debris and have higher bacterial concentrations during and immediately after heavy rain, caused by storm sewer overflows and run off from streets. All the EC recognised beaches in Edinburgh, Lothians and Fife meet EC water quality standards. Other beaches away from towns are generally safe to play on but simply do not have official EC recognition because they are too sparsely used.

NORTH

Cramond Beach and Esplanade

A broad paved promenade runs for 2 miles from Cramond through Silverknowes to Granton Point West Shore Rd. An attractive area for walking with the pram, roller-skating or for learning to ride a bike. Plenty of seats and shelters. Superb views across to Fife on clear days. Suitable for picnics on the Grassy Banks at Silverknowes where there is parking along Marine Drive – but look out for dog mess. You can also walk up to Lauriston Castle from Silverknowes.

Tide charts are available for reference in summer. Ice cream vans, pipe bands and entertainment over some summer weekends. The beach itself is sandy at Cramond and stony elsewhere. It can be oily and there are often pollution warnings about collecting shellfish. The beach is gently sloped but the tide can come in fast and maroon you on a sandbank – be prepared to paddle!

Fife is wonderful for the bucket-and-spade brigade. Great sandy beaches include:

Aberdour

There are two lovely beaches – the Silver Sands (café, toilets and a car park) and the Black Sands (limited parking, no amenities), a winner of the Seaside award from Tidy Britain Group.

Kinghorn (Pettycur Bay)

Safe, sandy, award-winning bay with two ice-cream shops /cafés on the front. Fife Council Environmental Health Department gave it a good/ excellent rating for its water quality.

St Andrews
East and West Sands Beaches

Two lovely large sandy beaches. Clean – and the water status is checked regularly. West Sands continues to hold a Blue Flag award.

Tentsmuir (near Leuchars)
2 miles from the B945. Follow signs to Tentsmuir Forest and Beach.
A huge sandy beach and forest with extensive walks and cycleways. There is a car park, picnic and barbecue area with toilets, a play area, and an information board. The car park kiosk sells a small selection of snacks.

Elie Harbour Beach
Large, sandy, blue-flag beach with a café at the harbour, and also a pub (The Ship Inn), which has a beer garden, BBQs every Sunday May-Aug and overlooks the beach where the local team play cricket on Sundays. Elie Watersports (Tel: 01333 330962) at the harbour hire out pedaloes, inflatable rides, canoes, dinghies, windsurfers, etc.

EAST

Portobello beach and promenade
Rain or shine, Edinburgh's seaside has something to offer: Sandcastles and ice creams in the summer and puddles and bracing walks in the winter. Stretching from Seafield Rd (near the Edinburgh Dog and Cat home) to Esplanade Ter in Joppa (just near the solar-powered public toilets!), the promenade is a wide paved space ideal for pushchairs, bikes, scooters and for exploring on foot (no traffic to worry about). There are a couple of play parks along its length and the pool at one end and the bowling club at the other make ideal places for snacks and toilet stops. The Seafield end is the more commercial area with amusement arcades and fast food bars, while the promenade and beach nearer Joppa are much quieter. The beach is very clean (early morning visitors can enjoy watching the tractors skim the sand) but is used by a lot of dog walkers so best to watch out! There's plenty of free parking along Portobello's streets and on the Musselburgh Rd and a public car park in Bridge St.

East Lothian has many good beaches along its shores and all of them are worth exploring. Our particular favourites, and those especially good for pre-school children, are listed here:

Aberlady
Drive through Aberlady on the A198 towards North Berwick. There is a car park on the left, and a wooden bridge provides access to the RSPB reserve. From here it is quite a long walk through the reserve, but well worth the adventure as the beach is beautiful and usually quite empty. Not very suitable for pushchairs, best to take a backpack or sling.

Gullane
Easy-to-find beach 40 mins from Edinburgh. From A1, take A198 towards North Berwick. In the village follow sign to the left into a paying car park (Easter-Sep). Pleasant beach with grassy area and dunes behind. Play area with toilets nearby.

North Berwick
Take the A198 from the A1. The town has a one way system, but the beaches and car parks are all signed. There are beaches to the east and west of the harbour and Seabird Centre. The beach to the east is long and sandy, with plenty of rock-pools and easy parking along the adjacent road. There is a paddling pool which refills naturally when the tide comes in, and when the tide is out makes a good swimming and boat sailing environment for youngsters (and their carers!). Award-winning toilets nearby.

Seacliff Beach
East of North Berwick on A198. Private beach. You'll need correct money for unmanned barrier. Beautiful bay, rock pools, tiny harbour, island and lovely view of Bass Rock. Car park. Toilets.

Tyninghame

Take the A199 out of Haddington and turn on A198 towards North Berwick. After passing Tyninghame village there is an unmarked turn off to the right, through an avenue of trees, leading to a small car park. From there a track leads down to the beach, and also off through the trees for various woodland walks. Not ideal for pushchairs, so take sling or backpack. The beach has lots of rock pools and can be quite exposed. No toilets. There is a café with gift shop and toilet in nearby Tyninghame village.

Yellowcraig Beach

Drive through Dirleton and turn left just before you leave the village. Paying car park (Easter-Sep). Beautiful beach and nature trail through the woods. Difficult with a pushchair, take a sling or backpack. There is a climbing frame play park next to the car park, themed on a pirate ship, with a separate area for toddlers and chipped bark on the ground.

GREENSPACE

This section covers all the wonderful greenspaces in and around Edinburgh. It covers country parks where you can get your walking boots on, formal gardens where the beautiful array of plants can be admired, and the plentiful supply of playgrounds and parks with play equipment.

Edinburgh is blessed with over 4500 acres of green space – where children and adults can relax or let off steam, without having to travel miles out into the country.

We've included some suggestions for country places within the City of Edinburgh or at least very close by. The walks in this section range from carefully tended public gardens to wild open hillsides. We have tried to give some indication of the terrain in terms of accessibility for pushchairs and small bikes; of course, children can also be carried in a packpack or sling. Remember that conditions can vary on non-surfaced paths, dependent on the season or the weather: what can be a pleasant stroll on a dry summer afternoon, can be a mire on a November morning! A map of the city's cycle paths, published by 'Spokes', the cyclists' organisation, is useful for walks where pushchair accessibility is needed.

If it's play equipment that you're after there is plenty to choose from - too many for us to include them all. Each playground should have a notice displaying the name of the playground and a contact number to report any damage. Many of the newer playgrounds have equipment made from tough plastic designed to be hard wearing and to withstand vandalism – although sadly this can mean that the vandals become more inventive. Nearly all playgrounds have benches and litter bins.

Remember, if your local playpark is vandalised contact the Council (Tel: 332 2368 for the Park Ranger Service). That way you know that they are aware of the damage and repair may be more quickly effected.

NB. While lack of nearby toilets is still a problem at many playgrounds, the Recreation Department has no say in the allocation of public toilets.

♿ Design of playgrounds in the Edinburgh area now takes into consideration the needs of wheelchair users and of children with a wide variety of special needs. There are, however, still many parks in the Edinburgh area that were designed before access for all was considered. It's rather a case of trial and error: there may be some parks that are particularly good for your child and others that offer them little in the way of play opportunities. If you feel your local park is unsuitable for your child's needs it may be worth contacting your local council (you can also do this to report glass or other dangerous litter in the park). If you are looking for more information on which parks are currently accessible or on plans to improve accessibility in Edinburgh, then it may be worth contacting the Parks Division of Edinburgh Council on 0131 529 7898.

CENTRAL

Calton Hill

Great spot for strolling with a pushchair. Fabulous views over the city. Good open space to run around and a brass cannon to climb on.

Home to "Edinburgh's shame" a monument based on the Parthenon that was started in 1822 but never completed. This provides climbing opportunities for older children. Also home to the Observatory and Nelson's Monument, but neither are particularly suitable for young children.

Pedestrian entrance off Regent Rd unsuitable for pushchairs due to steps. Gate next to Parliament House provides step-free route. Pushchair access also possible from quieter Royal Ter, but this is somewhat steeper.

Princes Street Gardens
Princes Street

The City's most famous park runs alongside Princes St under the lee of the castle. The park is a useful rest point for weary parents, mid-shopping, as there are plenty of seats and trees for shade on a sunny day. It also provides an open space for toddlers to let off steam after the confines of the pushchair in the nearby shops. The playground is in the West Garden, see below.

There are lawns, trees, flowerbeds and many statues and sculptures to interest parents and children. Look out for a tree with a hole through it (near the gardener's lodge in the West Gardens). The park's patrol officers will be pleased to point this out, or help you out with any other questions or problems. The gardens are locked at sunset or 22.00 (23.00 during the Festival). Please note that dogs must be kept on a lead.

The presence of the railway line in the gardens is a bonus, especially the bridge behind the Ross Bandstand from which children can safely and easily see the trains coming and going and drivers usually oblige with a wave and a toot!

The gardens are a good place for a picnic: some stores on Princes St sell sandwiches, yoghurt, fruit, etc, and there are many sandwich shops on Frederick St, Hanover St and Rose St. Ice cream kiosks are dotted around the park.

East Gardens

The park is divided in two by the Mound. The East Gardens may be accessed from the Mound, Waverley Bridge and Princes St. Access to the lower level of the gardens is via steps at the Mound end and via a steep sloping path at the Waverley end. The Scott Monument, a Victorian, high-gothic memorial to the author Sir Walter Scott, and a convenient landmark, can be climbed for an admission fee. The spiral stairs are very steep and narrow near the top and would probably not be enjoyed by small children or mothers-to-be!

Next to the Scott Monument is a kiosk selling sweets, ices, hot and cold drinks to take away. There are plenty of birds and squirrels to feed and some of the kiosks sell nuts and bird food. The station platforms and trains can be viewed from the path at the side of the National Gallery.

The East Gardens are the venue for Edinburgh's Winter Wonderland with an ice rink, children's fairground rides and food kiosks.

West Gardens

Accessed from the Mound, Princes St, Johnstone Ter and King's Stables Rd. The famous Floral Clock, next to the steps down to the park at the junction of Princes St and the Mound, is a source of delight for both children and adults alike. The clock is composed of up to 35,000 small plants and functions all year round except when being replanted. A cuckoo emerges briefly from a wooden house every quarter hour. It was the original idea of an Edinburgh clockmaker in 1903 and there are now copies all over the world. There are several rain shelters at the Mound end of the gardens, close to the foot of the Floral Clock steps.

Be ready to listen out for the Castle's 1 o'clock gun – it is loud and might give you a fright if you're not prepared for it. There is some vehicle traffic in the gardens, especially when the Ross Bandstand is being used, but many under 5s will enjoy admiring forklift trucks and the gardener's tractors.

The Ross Bandstand is situated in the middle of the West Gardens. This is used for various events throughout the year and during the Edinburgh Festival Fringe there are usually daily events and entertainment. Also during the summer festivals a carousel and a bungee dome usually operate near the Ross Fountain.

Over the railway, the South side of the gardens is less formal, with a steep grassy slope leading up to the castle. The slope is covered with daffodils in the spring. There is a gate into the castle esplanade via a steep zigzag path with steps, but the gate can be locked at times (especially during the Edinburgh Military Tattoo). There is a level entrance to the Gardens from King's Stables Rd opposite the multi-storey car park and a sloped entrance from Johnstone Ter round the side of the castle. These paths join up and cross a railway footbridge (no view of trains) into the gardens near the playground. A path also leads from the bridge, alongside the railway to another bridge (excellent view of trains) at the Ross Bandstand and then further on along a path leading up over the railway alongside the Mound and back to the Floral Clock. Toilets are near the playground.

Princes Street Gardens Playground

The nearest entrance is from Princes St; the second gate from the West end is best, as the first gate has a long flight of steps. Also level access from King's Stable Rd or through St Cuthbert's Churchyard.

This playground is large and has a great variety of equipment, though sadly no swings. Loosely based on a castle theme, the multiplay has ramps, tunnels, slides and walkways suitable for toddlers and a climbing wall, upper level and covered slide for older children. There are many other activities around it, including a hammock popular with parents!

Although the playground is unfenced, dogs in the gardens are supposed to be kept on leads.

Toilets are near the playground with nappy changing facilities. The key can be obtained from the attendant on duty. Note there is no ramp up to Princes St from these toilets. Toilets at the Ross Bandstand are open in the summer (no nappy changing facilities).

George V Park
Eyre Place

A good variety of things for children under 5, such as a climbing frame with slide and fireman's pole. There are baby swings and grown up swings! The ground is covered in wood chippings rather than concrete which is good for falls but my kids were wearing sandals and stopped every 5mins to remove bits from their shoes.

It is a friendly play park cordoned off from the main park, so there are no dogs etc within the play park area. The surrounding area is grass and provides plenty of space to run around if the park is busy or the kids want a different scene, but beware of dog mess.

The Yard
70 Eyre Place
EH3 5EJ
0131 557 899

Aims to provide creative and adventurous play opportunities for children and young people with additional support needs. While many of the clubs are geared towards older children, the family days (Saturdays and Thursday evenings) may provide a stimulating play environment for younger children and their siblings. Equipment includes: a wide range of adapted bikes, a large bedswing and ballcone, an enormous sandpit and a soft play area. There is also a sensory garden, a music trail, a stream, musical instruments, an art room and a calming sensory room. The yard is staffed by professional play-workers and volunteers, who will assist your child in play. The environment may be daunting for younger, less mobile children at times when there are lots of older children and young people playing. Phone prior to your first visit so that someone can meet you on arrival. Parking can be problematic due to the central location but there should be yellow line parking available nearby if you have a blue badge. There is no charge for families, although donations are welcome. Toilets and facilities are accessible. The Yard hosts a variety of community events including a bonfire night and community summer festival.

Royal Botanic Garden Edinburgh

20a Inverleith Row
EH3 5LR
0131 552 7171
www.rbge.org.uk

This is a favourite of many generations of Edinburgh families and a definite 'must' on the Edinburgh under 5s trail! The 'Botanics' is a fabulous place to visit at any time of year; come rain or shine, in winter or summer, it's always truly wonderful! You can pop in for a short relaxing stroll, or attend one of the many events for young children organised throughout the year. The aquarium exhibits (free) and the glasshouses offer plenty of excitement for the curious mind (and welcome shelter when the weather turns…).

Two main entrances for members of the public: the East Gate on Inverleith Row and the West Gate on Arboretum Avenue through the stunning new John Hope Gateway.

The Glasshouse Experience

Entrance to The Glasshouse Experience is through the grandest of the old buildings, the Tropical Palm House built in 1834. Leaflets for adults and children are available. Pushchairs can be left at the cash desk if you wish, as some paths between plants are quite narrow. Some ponds have no railings so hold on to active youngsters. There are old and new glasshouses, at various temperatures and humidities. Look out for dinosaur footprints, life-size animal sculptures and the banana plants. As you come outside again after the cactus house don't miss the rest of the Glasshouse Experience round the corner past the Exhibition Hall.

Visit our website for updates:
www.efuf.co.uk

NORTH

Cammo Estate

Cammo Road

A fantastic introduction to countryside walking and nature, the cammo estate comprises of 85 acres of woodlands, meadows, marshes, a ruined estate house, stables and folly (which under 5s think looks like a mini castle.) If you are travelling by bus you can take any bus that goes down Queensferry Rd, get off at the Barnton junction, turn left into Cammo Rd and follow the path to the estate. There is no entrance fee, no shops, no cafes, no ice cream vans - take a picnic and enjoy the countryside. There are many routes suitable for beginners, some for the more advanced, and some suitable for pushchairs and wheelchairs. Under 5s will love playing hide and seek behind the giant trees, watching nature change with the seasons, especially frogspawn in the giant pond at springtime, and exploring the ruins. There is a visitor centre at the main entrance, open Tues and Sun 2-4 and Thur 10-4. Here you will find lots of information on the estate, leaflet on walks (useful if you visit regularly)and toilets.

Cammo and the River Almond

The paths along the River Almond can be joined from Cammo. These routes are not really suitable for pushchairs, as they are narrow, uneven and overgrown.

Start the walk on Cammo Rd. A signpost leads you through a gate on the right and down a rough wide path to the river. Here the riverbank is very steep. The path continues to follow the river upstream towards the airport. There are stepping stones about halfway along or turn up the path to the left near the bridge and you will eventually rejoin Cammo Rd again. Along this path you pass Craighall Temple, a locked tower, or turn right over Grotto Bridge. The river is very narrow here and looks spectacular after rain, as the water thunders underneath. Just over the bridge is a cattle grid, which has been known to capture clambering youngsters! The path follows the river downstream and can be rough with some steep steps down to the water. It ends near the Cramond Brig Hotel.

Cramond Walled Garden
Cramond Glebe Road
(behind Cramond Kirk)
EH4

Play structure in the shape of a ship. Suitable for under 5s.The end of the slides are quite high off the ground so it is advised that an adult stands at the bottom ready to catch.The ship structure is fully enclosed with a gate so no little ones can run off and the floor is covered in wood chips. Adjacent is a large grassy area great for little ones to run off steam. Also provides challenging climbing frames and basketball hoop, handy if you have under 5s and older children, as there is something to keep everyone happy. It is abit off the beaten track so tends to be quite quiet and is away from any traffic. If you are travelling on foot there is a pathway from Whitehouse Rd, entrance by the bus stop nearest the doctors surgery which is a much quicker route.

Walks from Cramond

The village is situated at the mouth of the River Almond. There are swans and seagulls to feed and lots of small boats to look at. Walks radiate in all directions from the yachting centre. There is a large car park on Cramond Glebe Rd, below Cramond Kirk and above the Cramond Inn. A ramp leads down to the esplanade. Below the Inn are public toilets. There are also two cafes serving teas and ice creams.

Cramond was home to an established Roman settlement. There is a partially excavated site in the upper car park, beside the 17th Century Cramond Kirk.

North – To Cramond Island

There is a causeway across the tidal mudflats out to Cramond Island, which is negotiable at low tide. Tide charts are pinned up at the start of the causeway monthly but often get torn down. Check the tide times with Forth Ports or the Ranger Service before setting out. Take a picnic to your own small uninhabited island. Good views of the Forth Bridges but keep an eye on the time for returning before the tide comes in again.

South – The River Almond

About 1½ miles, the walkway starts on the esplanade, near the yachting centre, and follows the river upstream on a wooded path. The path is wide and on the level, and is suitable for pushchairs and bikes, but can be muddy. The river is tidal up to Cockle Mill Cottages, where the path opens out into a grassy area, watch out for dog fouling. There is also a small car park, access from Whitehouse Rd via School Brae. The path continues up to Fair-a-Far Mill where there is a waterfall and a fish ladder. The mill is now a ruin and children can enjoy running through the arches and up a few steps. The river is railed at this point but toddlers can get underneath quite easily. People throw pennies into the top of the fall and children collect them later! The path continues up to the Cramond Brig Hotel and Haugh Park, but there is a steep flight of steps and pushchairs would have to be carried.

East – the Esplanade

A broad paved footpath runs for 2 miles from Cramond through Silverknowes to Granton Point, West Shore Rd. An attractive area for promenading with the pram, roller-skating or for learning to ride a bike. Plenty of seats and shelters. Superb views across to Fife on clear days. Suitable for picnics on the Grassy Banks at Silverknowes where there is parking along Marine Drive – but look out for dog mess. You can also walk up to Lauriston Castle from Silverknowes.

Tide charts are available for reference in summer. Ice cream vans, pipe bands and entertainment over some summer weekends. The beach itself is sandy at Cramond and stony elsewhere. It can be oily and there are often pollution warnings about collecting shellfish. The beach is gently sloped but the tide can come in fast and maroon you on a sandbank – be prepared to paddle!

West - across the River Almond

There is no bridge across the Almond at Cramond, and unfortunately the passenger ferry which used to operate is no longer there. At present there are no plans to reinstate it. The land on the west bank of the river belongs to the Dalmeny Estate.

Haugh Park
Brae Park Road
Barton
EH4

This is a lovely, quiet, safe playground, situated in a beautiful location alongside a field with Shetland ponies. There is a variety of equipment, including a dish swing and multiplay. It is completely enclosed with 2 self-closing gates, though these are easy for toddlers to open. There is a small, grassed area and one picnic table and there are also several benches situated around the playground. It is for a wide age range, so toddlers need to be supervised. Access is either via Brae Park Rd (off Whitehouse Rd) or the River Almond walkway.

Davidson's Mains Park
East Barnton Avenue
Playground within large grassy park.

Clermiston Park
Clermiston Gardens
Playground with two bucket swings, separated from the rest of the playground by a metal fence, four other swings, a multiplay with rope climbs and slides, roundabout, seesaw, and two springy animals, all set on rubber matting. Benches and litter bins. The surrounding park is grassy with lots of young trees. There is a hard surface area next to the playground with basketball nets.

Ravelston Park and Playground
Craigcrook Road
Blackhall
An enclosed playground surrounded by a grassy park lined with trees and spring bulbs. There are paths up through Ravelston Woods, for those interested in a small nature expedition. The playground has two bucket swings, two swings, a roundabout, a seesaw, two 4-seater buckabouts and a large multiplay. The multiplay has a high slide, a medium slide, climbing wall, hanging rope tube, steps, and dangling rope seat. At ground level there is a car dashboard with steering wheel and gear lever and also a colourful spinning 'picture-maker' game.

The equipment is set on a rubberised surface with interesting coloured pictures, there is a hopscotch game marked on the tarmac. This decent-sized playground is ideal for toddlers and older children, and is popular with families. Easy parking on Craigcrook Rd. There are two benches within the playground and three more just outside. There is a fenced tarmac area (old tennis court) next to the playground useful for football, bat and ball etc. The tarmac path around the edge of the park is good for bikes. The park is popular with dogwalkers but fouling does not appear to be a problem.

Inverleith Park and Playing Fields
Inverleith
Various entrances from Arboretum Pl, Inverleith Pl, East Fettes Av, and Portgower Pl. A large tree lined park with paved footpaths, playing fields (cricket pitch in Summer, rugby and football pitches), large duck/swan pond (where on a Sunday you can watch the remote control boats), a rose garden with sundial, free tennis courts, five-a-side court, boules area and playground. The park often hosts festivals and events throughout the year, including Treefest, Taste of Edinburgh and in the Summer holidays has various organised activities for school age children.

The playground is located near the south end of Arboretum Pl and is fenced off from the rest of the park with two gates, one at each side (only problem is that these are quite easy for toddlers to open and are often left open by other children/adults). Dogs are not permitted inside the playground boundary. It has seating and litterbins and generally is clean and tidy. The centrepiece is a large ship in three sections, the wheelhouse, mast and bow which incorporates a slide, rope ladders, rigging and crow's next. There is also a smaller multiplay with slide, steps, climbing wall and gangway, two bucket swings, four swings, seesaw, sit-in wobbly whale and a higher climbing structure for older childen. All equipment is located on a rubberised surface.

Muirhouse Linear Park and Playground
Near Muirhouse Drive
Playground with adjacent grass area, basketball court and skateboard park.

Pennywell Gardens
At east end of Pennywell Gardens
Playground only.

Pennywell Road
Pennywell Grove/Pennywell Gardens
Playground only.

Granton Crescent Park
Granton Crescent
Edinburgh
EH5 1NY
Small playpark on grassy slope with views to the Firth of Forth (just visible behind the towerblocks!). Bucket swings, seesaw, slide and climbing frame and two benches for parents. Good for under 5s but wouldn't keep older children entertained. Surrounding grassland provides opportunity for ball games.

Granton Mains
Granton Mill Crescent
Off West Granton Road
Playground with two multiplays, plus other stand alone equipment: adjacent basketball court.

St Mark's Park
Warriston Road
Playground with two multiplay units, plus a roundabout. Grassy area within and round the playpark.

Victoria Park and Playgrounds
Between Newhaven Rd/Craighall Rd
Trinity/Newhaven
A lovely 18-acre park with two excellent playgrounds. The first is near Newhaven Rd and is suitable for toddlers. This enclosed area includes; a multiplay unit with a slide, two bucket swings, a small hemispherical climbing frame, a 4-seat buckabout, and a roundabout – all set on rubberised surfaces. The second is near to Craighall Rd. This is more suitable for 3+ yrs although younger kids will enjoy some of it if closely supervised. The playground is made up of modern tough plastic equipment. It has interlinked climbing frames, bridges, walkways and slides, one with a roller surface, and a whole variety of climbing, swinging and bouncing equipment. This is all fenced off and set in wood chips. Picnic tables and benches nearby.

The park also has a floodlit, all-weather, five-a-side football pitch and a basketball court. There are several cycle paths running through the park. Busy at lunchtimes with pupils from nearby Trinity Academy.

Pilrig Park
Bonnington Road/Pilrig Street
A good range of play equipment, suitable for babies/toddlers and older children. There are toddler swings and standard swings, so it is a good park if you have children in different age ranges. There are also opportunities for sliding, bouncing and climbing. All the equipment is well-spaced and there is good space for running about and benches for a well earned rest. Easy area to get to and reasonably clean and litter-free.

Sandport Playpark
A stop off park, not worth a visit on its own, but adequate to pass 15 mins on your way somewhere. There are no cradle swings, just two big swings, a wooden climbing area made of drilled poles, with a bridge and slide, but most under 5s will need help climbing up, and the only thing aimed at younger children is a rocking seat. The park has a wood chip base, and unfortunately tends to have litter. There are no benches for carers.

Anything out of date?
Let us know -
info@efuf.co.uk

Leith Links and Playground

48 acres of grass, trees and spring bulbs complete with hillocks, which are the remains of 16th century gun emplacements. There are benches and paths, which are lit in the evenings, suitable for pushchairs. The fenced playgrounds are to the North West of the park.

The toddler area has a Noah's Ark themed multiplay complete with slide and rope ladder, four bucket swings, a sit-on animal roundabout and two horse buckabouts, all set on rubberised surfaces. There's a picnic table and other seating, a litterbin and also a fenced grass area to the side of the playground for running around and picnics, this has an interesting carved wooden bench.

The junior area set on bark chips has a large multiplay climbing frame with chain scramble netting, slide, steps, ladders and monkey hoops. There is also a tyre commando slide and a tyre swing. Some of this is suitable for under 5s under close supervision. Again, seating is provided.

There's a third area which has an 'Eiffel Tower' climbing net and a basic balancing frame. This area is set in sand. The equipment is only really suitable for older children but all ages can enjoy the sand. These playgrounds are extremely popular and are usually in pretty good condition.

Keddie Gardens Playground
Largo Place
Off Ferry Rd

Playground with toddler multiplay and other equipment, includes helter-skelter slide. Adjacent grass area close to steps down to Water of Leith walkway.

Dalmeny Street Park

Entrances on Dalmeny St, Iona St, Sloan St and Dickson St. Playground and adjacent grass area.

Hopetoun Street Development
McDonald Rd

Playground only (small).

Beaverbank Playground
Broughton Rd
EH7

Lovely modern park with soft matting under all equipment and benches, plus a small grassy area with pergola. Low and high slides both off climbing frame with rope bridge and climbing net, toddler swings and a large bowl swing, a rope roundabout and bouncy see saw. Metered parking on Broughton Road.

Lochend Park and Playground
Lochend Road

Fenced playground set within the 23-acre park. Playground equipment includes a multiplay unit which is suitable for both toddlers and juniors. Park has fenced-off pond.

Montgomery St Playground
Montgomery Street
EH7

Centrally located on Montgomery St, this large park is not the most modern but has a great variety for all ages; smaller climbing frames, slide and swings for toddlers, and also more advanced and exciting things for older children including a tractor climbing frame with slide and another with a bridge tunnel, swings, and a high helter skelter slide too. Railings separate the playpark from the road and a large concrete basketball/football area, and there is also an adjoining grass park with benches.

Handy for Leith Walk and London Rd (and Pearce and Renroc cafes which are both excellent for children), there is metered parking all around the edges of the park. Both entrances are suitable for pram and wheelchair access, one at ground level and one ramped.

Redbraes Park
Broughton Road
EH7

Fenced off modern playpark set in large grassed park on Broughton Rd towards Pilrig St, which has free and open parking. Toddler and regular swings, climbing frame with chute, good for all ages, soft matting surrounds all equipment.

Dalmeny House and Estate
0131 331 1888
www.dalmeny.co.uk
Take the A90 and then B924. There is a bus service from St Andrew Sq to Chapel Gate, 1 mile from the house.

While we'd not recommend Dalmeny House as a place to visit with young children, the estate itself is pleasant to walk around – fields, shore and woodland with cows, sheep, pheasants and a statue of a racehorse. There is a sheltered woodland walk through the rhododendrons and azaleas of the garden valley. No dogs allowed. Picnics only by prior arrangement. No fires.

The house can also be reached by the 4½ mile Shore Walk from Long Craig Gate in South Queensferry, east towards Cramond (you can no longer go all the way to Cramond this way). The path is open all year round to pedestrians only. It is negotiable with a pushchair or manageable with small children in backpacks, and passes through several designated Sites of Special Scientific Interest – including nesting and feeding grounds for several rare species of birds, as well as giving wonderful views of the Forth. There are lovely beaches in the estate, particularly the ones near Barnbougle Castle and also just past Dalmeny House, known to locals as the 'shell-beds'.

Lochore Meadows Country Park
Crosshill
Lochgelly
KY5 8BA
01592 583343
Travel north on M90. At J2A, take Kirkcaldy, A92 turn off. Follow Lochgelly exit from this road, then the B920 to Crosshill. Park is signposted on the left. Car parking available.

Park offers a multitude of activities including a playground, woodland trail, orienteering routes, picnic and BBQ areas, cafe, bird watching, canoeing, hillwalking, sailing, horse riding and golf/putting. There is a wheelchair accessible bird watching hide at the west end of the loch. Building all on one level. Maps showing waymarked walking routes are available to buy at the Park Centre.

Pittencrieff Park
Dunfermline
KY12 8QH
01383 722935
Lovely park close to Dunfermline Abbey, with wooded glen, wide open areas and play park. Animal houses, glasshouses, and pavilion selling coffee, ice cream etc. Free entry to park. Pittencrieff House Museum in the centre of the Park is worth a visit, free entry.

Craigtoun Country Park
By St Andrews
Fife
KY16 8NX
01334 473666
Located 3 miles SW of St Andrews off B939. Admission charges apply but all facilities are free after payment of entry fee, phone to check details. Plenty to do for all the family including: miniature railway, trampolines, bouncy castle, boating, putting, crazy golf, adventure play park, toddler play area, aviary, formal gardens and glasshouses. Countryside Centre and lots of parkland to roam. Calendar of events throughout the year.

Toilets at various points in the park. Nappy changing facilities in toilets for the disabled.

EAST

Holyrood Park

Car parks at Dunsapie Loch, near the entrances at Duddingston Loch, Holyrood Palace and Meadowbank Ter.

A rugged park, including Arthur's Seat (823ft), Salisbury Crags, and three small lochs. A surfaced road, Queen's Dr, runs around the park for approximately 5k. Apart from a small stretch of surfaced path from the Holyrood Palace entrance up Haggis Knowe towards St Anthony's chapel (about 200yds), all the other routes are rocky or on grass. The climb to Arthur's Seat is a steep one for youngsters (shortest route from Dunsapie Loch) but there is an excellent view at the top with a trig point and cairn indicating surrounding sites of interest. Lower down there are good views from Dunsapie Hill (523ft). It is possible to walk round St Margaret's Loch with a pushchair to see the ducks, geese and swans. In the south east of the park is Duddingston Loch, a bird sanctuary.

Leaving Queen's Dr, below Salisbury Crags and to the south-east of Pollock Halls is a cycle track and footpath, suitable for pushchairs, known as the Innocent Railway.

Northfield Broadway

Next to Northfield Community Centre
Toddler playground.

Figgate Park

Portobello

Entrances on Duddingston Rd, Hamilton Dr and Mountcastle Cres. A large park set around Figgate Burn, which has recently been drained and landscaped. A wooden boardwalk runs along one end of the pond, dotted with seating areas and viewing points - good place to observe and feed the local wildlife, although the gaps between the fencing are just wide enough for an agile toddler to wiggle through! At the northeast end of the park is a large enclosed play area. It has two parts, bucket swings, a climbing frame and slide for younger children and a junior multiplay with more challenging versions of the same for older children. The play area has soft tarmac and bark chippings to cushion falls.

Joppa Quarry Park

Portobello

Entrance on South Morton St or over the bridge from Morton St. An enclosed play park sited in a large grassed area ideal for ball games, or just running around. The play park has a large multiplay with a slide, scramble net and climbing rope. This is a little challenging for the under 2s and requires close supervision. More easily tackled are the bucket swings, springy rides and sensory boards. For older children there is a whirling 'hang-on' roundabout, swings, climbing wall and a standard more sedate roundabout. The whole area is on rubberised matting. A safe space to play and explore with the added attraction of trains to spot nearby!

Rosefield Park

Portobello

Entrances on Rosefield Pl and West Brighton Cres. Rosefield Park itself is a grassy area near to Figgate Burn. The real attraction is the playpark to the left as you enter from Rosefield Pl. A small enclosed space, it has two sets of swings – bucket seats for the younger visitors – a roundabout and a climbing frame with two slides. The smaller slide is accessed by a ladder rather than steps so younger children may need a boost. This is a pleasant park and its close proximity to the library makes it ideal for a quick swing before doors open at 10am.

Straiton Place

Portobello

Entrance from promenade or Straiton Pl. A boat-themed play park set in a fenced grassy area just off the beach. Particularly good for the younger under 5s, it has an easy-to-tackle slide with sturdy steps (and only two possible exits at the top of the steps, so easily covered by one person supervising), a small table and chairs, a climbing net and a couple of springy animals on rubberised matting. Good as a stop-off point rather than a destination. It has a handy superloo right next to it which can accommodate a double pushchair.

Tower Bank
Portobello

Entrance between Bath St and Beach Lane, off the promenade. Just off the beach and near to the primary school, so can get busy in the afternoons. This has the usual complement of play equipment – swings, springy animals and a multi-play climbing area with slides. The multiplay is challenging for the under 2s – this is probably a park aimed more at slightly older children.

Glenvarloch Crescent
Glenvarloch Crescent
Liberton

Bright enclosed playground set in the centre of a grassed area, with quiet estate roads on four sides. Two multiplays and also stand-alone equipment.

Craigmillar
Niddrie House Square
Multiplay plus other equipment.

Prestonfield Park
EH16

This is a nice local park. The play area is fenced off from the majority of the park. It was upgraded in 2009. There is one large piece of equipment incorporating multi level play for all age groups. This includes a walkway, helter skelter, fireman's pole and small slide. Additional equipment includes two traditional swings, roundabout, see-saw, multi person swing and springy animal. Benches and picnic table are a welcome addition for parents. Access to the park can be from Prestonfield Av or Prestonfield Rd.

Gracemount Leisure Centre
Captain's Rd, entrance of Gracemount Dr, to rear of car park. Playground only. Small but ideal for toddlers. Two bucket seats, two spring bouncers, a roundabout and two slides.

Inch Park
Access from Glenallen Drive

A play area set in large green parkland. The park is best accessed through Glenallan Dr, though the main park can also be entered at Cameron Toll shopping centre car park.

The playground is divided into three separate sections – a main fort playground, a basketball court and a high wire. The fort is the main focus and centre of the play area, which also includes bucket swings, tyre swing, slides and walkways. This section would be best used for pre-school upwards as some of the equipment might be too challenging for younger children. This area is fenced off from the park to increase safety and reduce dog access.

Magdalene Community Centre Playpark
Magdalene Estate
Off Milton Road
Edinburgh

The small playpark is situated in between the primary school and the community centre. The park has three pieces of play apparatus which each stand on a soft surface for landing on. The park would suit children from walking age. There are three chutes to use. Lots for climbing on but there are no swings in the park. Surrounding the playpark is a fence with two gates, therefore the park can be made secure.

The playpark is open even when the school and community centre are closed. Access is gained through the school gates.

Seven Acre Park
Stanedykehead
Liberton

This park is a hidden jewel where town meets country, if you can manage to avoid all the pot holes on the long private road leading to it which is only partly tarmaced. There are brightly coloured bucket swings, a roundabout, bouncer, and a large climbing frame with two slides, rope ladders and bridges within a fenced area. This is surrounded by a grass area with a football pitch and then onto farmland. There are stunning views across the whole city and beyond to Fife on a clear day. But definitely to be avoided on a windy day!

Musselburgh Links Playground
Musselburgh

Fisherrow Links off New St. Follow signs for Links and Bowling Green. Themed around pirates, this play park is imaginatively designed and is packed with interesting and unusual play equipment. There's an outdoor gym for older children, a crow's nest slide complete with skull and crossbones hiding a seating area, large sandpit with diggers, huge swinging hammock, plus smaller swings for the younger children. There's also a multiplay unit with slide, climbing wall and balancing beam, a few springy animals and a balancing beam on its own (for walking the plank?). Challenging for my 17mth old but it didn't stop him giving everything a go. Brilliant for slightly older under 5s. We'll be going back.

John Muir Country Park
01620 827279

Take A1 east towards Dunbar, turn left at roundabout signposted Dunbar onto A199, turn right along A1087 for 1 mile, and turn left into Linkfield car park and then turn right by East Links Family Park. Or for Shore Rd, continue further ½ mile into West Barns.

Large country park with a lovely beach, clifftop trail, and woodland walks. Not always suitable for a pushchair – take a sling or backpack. Picnic sites at Linkfield car park and Shore Rd car park. Adventure playground on grass with bark chips at Linkfield car park. Barbecues for hire at Linkfield. Toilets with disabled units served by radar key at both car parks. There are interpretation boards at various points throughout the park.

Lauderdale Park
Bayswell Road
Dunbar

Excellent park for all ages and abilities. The Garden Path Cafe within the park serves a fine range of light meals and snacks. Combined with a visit to the swimming pool this is definitely a great day out.

A lot of thought has gone into the design of the park and it may be enjoyed by older/able bodied children as well as less mobile children. Facilities that may be enjoyed by children with limited mobility include a very large diaphragm-shaped swing, water and sand features and a roundabout with a seat with back and sides on it. There's plenty for everyone and nearby picnic seats have spaces for wheelchairs and some seats with back and sides. Walkway access to the park is good and the nearby public toilet facilities are fantastic – disabled toilet key is held by attendant.

SOUTH

Bruntsfield Links

Parking on various nearby streets; some are metered, some are single yellow lines, some are not. Acres of space to run in the middle of town. During the summer, the area is popular with all sorts of people, from dog walkers to frisbee throwers and football players: most of the walkways have cycle ways on them, so try to stay on the pedestrian side of the line.

Meadows Playpark

Probably the best play park in Edinburgh. It appeals to kids of all ages (and some adults I am sure), so it is ideal if you have older children too. There are swings for babies, older children and also for those with disabilities. The sandpit area is always a huge a favourite and there are climbing frames suitable for most ages. There is a also a zip slide for the brave! There are plenty of benches and also tables for snacking and snatching a rest if you can.

It does get pretty busy on a nice day and can also be a bit of a challenge if you have children of different ages all running of in different directions. There are also plenty of nice cafés near by in Marchmont which do great take out coffee.

Where would you suggest?
Tell us -
ed@efuf.co.uk

Morningside Park

Morningside Park is a lovely, well-used play-park, which has been repainted and spruced up generally with new plants and a picnic table thanks to the recently formed "Friends" group. Four toddler swings, four traditional swings, toddler multi-play, climbing frame/slide, helter-skelter and sit-in roundabout. There are also grassy areas, hopscotch, a tennis court and a large hard-surfaced area for football, bike riding etc. The park can get very busy, especially in late afternoon, when it is sometimes used by the local after-school club.

The Braids

Grassy slopes and hills, good for kites, walking and sledging. Access and parking at the entrance to the Braid Hills Public Golf Course on Braid Hill Approach and along Braid Hill Dr. There are usually horses to be seen in fields nearby at Liberton Tower Farm.

Hermitage of Braid and Blackford Hill

69 Braid Road
Edinburgh
EH10 6JF
0131 447 7145
countrysiderangers@edinburgh.gov.uk
www.snh.org.uk

A great open parkland in the city where you can spend a good few hours and the views from the top of the hill are well worth the climb. Most routes are suitable for a pushchair, but some include steps and streams and are less appropriate. Route maps can be picked up from the Visitor Centre (near the Braid Rd entrance) which also offers a range of activities and information for younger visitors. It's worth taking a picnic as there are no catering facilities at the site. The area is popular with dog walkers so beware as there may be some mess.

Braidburn Valley Park

Located approx 1 mile south of Morningside junction, just off the A702 (at Comiston Road/ Pentland Terrace). The park is a well-maintained and calming open air space with great views up to the Pentlands. While there is no play park, there is ample grassy space for little ones to run around. There are periodic events held in the park, including an annual duck race in the Braid Burn.
Note: the Braid Burn runs through the centre of the park and is not enclosed. In addition, the park is popular with dog walkers and dogs are generally let off their leads.

Buckstone Park

Buckstone Circle
Edinburgh
EH10

A decent well-kept pre-school playground with a flat grassy park and wooded area nearby, ideal for hide and seek. Not much for children 7+ yrs. Park can be hard to find unless you know the area, basically keep going uphill through the Buckstone houses and the park is at the highest point, near the school. There is a footpath which gives access from Mounthooly Loan. Nearby links to wooded walks around Mortonhall.

Fairmilehead Public Park
(also known as Camus Park)

I wouldn't travel far to use this park as it's fairly basic and not particularly scenic, but a useful play park for those in the Fairmilehead area. Entrance from Camus Avenue, Comiston Road and Pentland View.

Falcon's Gardens Playpark

A pleasant, small play park tucked away from the road and a little off the beaten track, except for the pupils of St. Peter's Primary School next door who visit straight after school (so best avoided then if possible). Two toddler swings and two traditional swings, multiplay with small helter skelter, two other slides, rope climbing frame and small climbing wall. Small, steep grass area.
Entrances on the corner of Falcon Rd/Falcon Gdns beside St Peter's Primary School and on Canaan Lane opposite Woodburn Ter.

Swanston Village

Swanston Village is on the outskirts of Edinburgh and provides a pleasant stroll for all the family. We like to park up and wander past the village and the golf club to The Steadings for lunch. This is about a half mile walk, good for toddlers, but not terribly pushchair friendly although it can be done. Alternatively there are walks to the Hill End ski run or your children can say hello to the Highland cattle.

The Pentland Hills

Regional Park HQ
0131 445 3383

A beautiful range of hills spreading along Edinburgh's southern edge. Supported by City of Edinburgh, Midlothian and West Lothian Councils and Scottish Natural Heritage. The Pentland Hills regional park consists of two country parks, reservoirs (no swimming permitted), nature reserves and other private areas. Within the Regional Park there are several areas of interest to parents with young children. These include Glencourse, Hillend, and also Bonaly, Harlaw and Red Moss (listed under West).

Glencourse Reservoir

On the A702(T) Biggar Rd, 7½ miles from the city centre; turn right at the Flotterstone Inn.
An Information Centre with displays and maps can be found in the car park. The road up to Glencourse Reservoir is closed to public vehicles. Ideal for pushchairs and cyclists. As you leave the car park, on your left next to the burn is a barbecue and children's area - dog free. Further along, off to the left across a footbridge, is a wooded picnic area and another up the hill in woods on the right. Several paths fork off across fields and up into the hills. At the reservoir anglers in boats can often be seen. It is possible to follow the northern edge along to the end on a surfaced road. The water is fenced or walled off. Paths branch off to the right at intervals up to Castlelaw firing range and across the hills to Harlaw (unsuitable for youngsters). Lambs can be seen over the fences in spring.

Hillend Country Park

Follow the Biggar Rd out just beyond Lothianburn Golf Course on the right and turn up to Hillend. The No 4 bus stops on the main road and there is a long path up to the ski centre. There are picnic tables up to the foot. There is a notice board with maps and general information on the Pentland Regional Park. At the top of the road there is the Hillend Ski Centre and a large car park. A chairlift at the artificial ski slope here may be used by non skiers. It is open daily, but check (Tel: 445 4433) as it closes in poor weather. No pushchairs. There are several bench type seats so you can tuck tots in between adults, a bar comes down to lap and foot height and keeps you safely in. Very active toddlers should not use the chairlift. There is a stop half way up to get off if a child becomes frightened. The ride up is exhilarating, sailing over skiers below. At the top there is a viewfinder on a cairn and there are paths through the heather, which energetic tots or parents with backpacks could cope with. The weather can change quickly though so don't stray too far from the chairlift. At the top of the lift are cameras and a tannoy so that the operators can check everybody is safely in before moving. Toilets in the ski centre reception and refreshments are available.

Dalkeith Country Park

Dalkeith Country Estate
Dalkeith
EH22 2NJ
0131 654 1666
www.dalkeithcountrypark.com

This is a huge country park with a big adventure playground, picnic benches, barbecues for hire, cafe, and several sign-posted walks to follow.
Watch out for traffic, the road through the park is surprisingly busy.

Visit our website for updates:
www.efuf.co.uk

Vogrie Country Park
Near Gorebridge
Midlothian
EH23 4NU
01875 821990
www.midlothian.gov.uk
This is a lovely big park 4 miles from Dalkeith, with lots of big open spaces for kids to run and run, great playgrounds for all ages, forest areas perfect for playing hide and seek, and some giant chairs and bicycles to discover and climb on.

Vogrie House has some interesting displays on the natural heritage and history of the park. The Cedar Tree Cafe is in Vogrie House along with a small soft play for under 5s.

The park is largely traffic-free but look out for the occasional blue badge holder or ranger vans. There are two barbecue areas available to hire as well as an events field (book ahead on 0131 663 1103).

A Miniature Railway runs around the park most Sunday afternoons in summer, weather permitting.

Dawyck Botanic Gardens
Stobo
Near Peebles
EH45 9JU
01721 760254
Situated on the B712, 8 miles SW of Peebles. Signposted from A721.

The garden is part of the Royal Botanic Garden Edinburgh and entry here is free to members. Car park is free. No dogs, cycles or footballs allowed.

The gardens set on sloping hillside are lovely for children to run about in, with plenty of interesting features. A burn runs through the garden, the Beech walk provides grand views, the snowdrops in spring are spectacular, some trees are amazingly tall. Think about taking a picnic as the lovely tearoom can get busy. Gift shop and toilets, with nappy changing facilities, are in the main building.

Kailzie Gardens
Kailzie, Peebles, EH45 9HT
01721 720007
www.kailziegardens.com
Located 2½ miles from Peebles on B7062.

Pretty gardens with small river running through with walled garden and greenhouse. There's a Blue Tit and Osprey Watch (see below), as well as red squirrels, fish, badgers and swallows. Picnics can only be eaten outside gardens – watch out for hungry ducks! Also a 18-hole putting green and petanque pitch. Children will need close supervision at play area, especially on slide/climbing frame. Small gift shop. Nappy changing mat in restaurant toilet. Restaurant can be busy in summer months so may be worth booking.

Osprey Watch
Kailzie has an osprey centre, where you can watch live CCTV pictures of the ospreys, which may be seen from 10.00-17.00, daily from the end of March when the ospreys arrive until the end of Aug, when they fly off again.

Priorwood Garden and Dried Flower Shop
Melrose
08444 93 21 00
Located near the Abbey.

Specialist garden, run by the National Trust for Scotland, where the flowers grown are all ideal for drying. You can enjoy a walk through the orchard and take a picnic here in the summer. Gift shop sells large range of NTS merchandise as well as dried flower gifts.

Anything out of date?
Let us know -
info@efuf.co.uk

WEST

Saughton Park and Winter Gardens
Balgreen Road (car park entrance) EH11
The northern half from the Stevenson Dr side houses a sports centre with all weather facilities and a separate enclosure for football and athletics. The Southern half accessed from Balgreen Rd (car park) and Gorgie Rd contains the sunken Italian garden, specimen trees, a glassed Winter Garden with exotic plants, a garden of sweet fragrances for the blind and a rose garden with lovely wide pathways for pushing a buggy along. There is a very basic café in the glass house, which can be accessed from three sides. There is also a new skate park which caters for beginners right through to experienced skateboarders. The existing playpark will be getting overhauled now that the skate park is completed and will contain a large sandy area with a play structure for the younger children incorporating a slide. The remainder of the playpark is bark covered and will house a roundabout, caterpillar rope swing, two play structures with slides, a zip line ride, basket and normal swings, climbing wall and a large rope climbing frame amongst others. There will also be picnic tables. This will be a great park once all the work is completed as it caters for all age ranges and there is plenty of open space surrounding the playpark to kick a ball and the lovely gardens, which are always full of flowers, are just across the pathway. The water of Leith runs along the Gorgie Rd edge and is a good spot for feeding the ducks.

Stewart Terrace Park
Off Gorgie Rd
Enclosed toddler park which is bright, clean and inviting. There are two bucket swings, two springy animals, plus a multiplay which has tunnels, a slide and climbing structures. There are also grassy areas and benches.

Sighthill Park
Broomhouse Road
Playpark with two areas: toddler area equipment includes a sit-down roundabout, a multiplay and two bucket swings on a special low frame to help eliminate the disappointment of swing wrap round. The junior area includes a multiplay and more adventure style equipment, incl. a 'Space Climbing' net. Next to the playground on the surrounding grass there are two small goal posts and a skateboarding ramp area.

Murieston Park
Murieston Crescent
Playpark and some grass.

White Park
Gorgie Road
Situated opposite the Hearts Football Ground Gorgie Rd entrance. Playground plus grassy area.

Harrison Park
West Bryson Road/Watson Crescent
Fenced park with tree-lined walkway along the banks of the Union Canal. Set near tennis courts, playing fields and a bowling green. There are four bucket swings, a seesaw, a slide and a small climbing frame.

Fauldburn Park
East Craigs
Multiplay plus buckabouts. There are children's goal posts on grass next to the park.

Roseburn
Roseburn Crescent
Multiplay unit, situated next to open playing fields.

Corstorphine Hill Playpark
Craigcrook Road
Just north of Hillpark Green
Playground with four rocking animals, toddler multiplay with slide and rope climbing frame. Close to path leading up to Corstorphine Hill Local Nature Reserve.

Corstorphine Hill Local Nature Reserve

Panoramic views of the city and beyond are offered from the 531ft summit. Terrain is varied with large areas of woodland and also a steep rocky section (including a flooded quarry). At the summit is Clermiston Tower, built in 1851 to commemorate centenary of Sir Walter Scott's birth. Access to tower by arrangement with Ranger Service, or on Sundays in summer courtesy of Friends of Corstorphine. Between tower and Clermiston Rd is Walled Garden which has been restored by Friends of Corstorphine into a woodland walk for the community.

There are several routes to the summit: Clermiston Rd (3 paths; the one near the hotel is rough and steep), Queensferry Rd (steep and rugged), Craigcrook Rd (between new houses up a fairly steep but smooth path, some steps); Ravelston Dykes Rd (200 yds north of Murrayfield Golf Clubhouse) and from Cairnmuir Rd at junction with Kaimes Rd. The latter is easiest for pushchairs though muddy after rain and path follows the edge of the zoo.

Gyle Park
Wester Broom Place

This is a large expanse of grass and includes, playpark, football pitches, skate area and basketball court. Accessible via the Wester Broom/Gyle estates or via the road leading to the David Lloyd Leisure Club.

The playpark is securely fenced and consists of two frames, one suitable for toddlers and one aimed at 2+ yrs. There is also a flying fox, swings (baby and older) and on the ground a hopscotch area and paintings of ducks and frogs which you have to find throughout the park.

The only fault I can find for this park is that the protective ground surface has holes in places which could cause problems for little ones walking.I would highly rate this park as my son loved it, and could manage all the equipment.

The general green area is also in very good condition, with raised areas with trees. Perfect for a wee picnic and some playing in the park.

St Margaret's Park
Corstorphine High Street
EH12

Leafy playground and large, flat, grassy area. Playground fully fenced with three bucket swings, four swings, roundabout, large slide and toddler multiplay including slide. Also in park is Heritage Centre with café, putting green, tennis courts, football area and bowling green. Limited on-street parking in Orchardfield Av and Dovecot Rd.

Union Park
Carrickknowe Drive

Small playpark, within large green area used for rugby matches and general public use.

The play park itself is easily accessible from Carricknow Dr or via the main park, Its securely fenced on all sides with metal railings that are in good all round condition. The park itself consists of a climbing frame and a small metal train. The park is sadly lacking some swings which would improve it no end.

The climbing frame is suitable from around 18mths upwards, with supervision as not all aspects of it are suitable. It has a fireman's pole, a bridge, slide, and platform. Definetly one for the more adventurous toddler, and is in fact mostly used by primary age children. The train sadly serves very little purpose other than being a place for lots of muck to gather. I feel that a roundabout and a swing in this park would make all the difference. It is secure and clean from dog muck etc, but could probably do with more to keep active toddlers entertained. Also used often by kids playing football within the playpark which its not ideal for as its quite small.

Craiglockhart Dell

Beautiful wooded glens with the Water of Leith and its walkway running through the centre. Plenty of paths to explore, although those with pushchairs will have to search for flat routes. Cycling is only permitted on the main Water of Leith Walkway. Bridges for 'Pooh Sticks' and open grassed areas next to the river are ideal for picnics and games. Access includes Dell Rd, Colinton, Katesmill Rd, pathway from Lanark Rd near Dovecot Pk and behind the Tickled Trout pub on Lanark Rd at Slateford.

Craiglockhart Hill

Street parking is available at Craiglockhart Ter, Lockharton Cres and at Craiglockhart Sports Centre. Level paths from the sports centre and from Craiglockhart Ter are suitable for pushchairs and take you to the pond. The pond is home to swans, ducks, moorhens and coots, the nests of some of which can be seen in early summer. There is a map of the area at Craiglockhart Ter and at the pond. Many interesting and attractive plants have been established to improve the area for wildlife. Off the level path you'll find steep sections, some with steps, that go up through seminatural woodlands to the top of the hill. The highest part is open and gives impressive views of the city and countryside beyond.

Colinton Dell
Spylaw Street
Acres of waterside walks under the shade of trees. Perfect for a long stroll on a summer's day but can be muddy and slippy after heavy rainfall. Pushchairs can be taken, but can prove awkward to manoeuvre in places as where steep and/or muddy. Small children need close supervision as they can get right down to the waters edge. Picnic tables provided at intervals. Take binoculars to help you spot some of the wildlife that live here.

Colinton Mains Park
Oxgangs Road North
A large, flat space ideal for learning to ride bikes etc. Fenced playground including three bucket swings. There is pushchair-friendly access to the park from all sides.

Spylaw Park
Spylaw Street/Gillespie Road
One of Edinburgh's most beautiful parks, a hidden gem which can prove tricky to find on a first visit. Both entrances through woodland are sloping and can be quite muddy so can be a little taxing for pushchairs, but worth the effort. Fenced playground at the far end of the park is well shaded by trees. A path runs alongside the Water of Leith, so close supervision of small children is required. Best bits include meeting lots of friendly dog-owners (and dogs!) and watching kids play poohsticks from the bridge.

Wester Hailes

This area has very few large playgrounds, but it has benefited from a programme to create a number of small play centres within individual estates for children.

Curriemuir End Park
Off Wester Hailes Rd
This playground has to be approached on foot, using either the path that leaves Wester Hailes Rd close to the junction with Viewfield Rd, or the underpass beneath Wester Hailes Rd that links the Clovenstone estate to the park.
Playground with mainly wooden equipment. Surrounding park is grassy and hilly, and there are several picnic tables nearby.

Bloomiehall Public Park
Juniper Green
This park is situated at the end of Juniper Park Rd, and accessed from Baberton Ave (opposite the entrance to Baberton Golf Course). Pushchair access can be found on a track that goes round the edge of the park. This excellent playground, situated in large grassy area, has a range of equipment to suit all ages. The toddler area multiplay is based on a train theme with carriages, a station and a ticket office - all on a coloured track. To the side of this there are two bucket swings on rubber surfacing. The section for older children is behind this and separated by red metal fencing. It has a large amount of multiplay equipment with slides, rope climbing, bridges, balancing beams and a large tyre slide. For the more advanced there is a large rope pyramid structure. The park is encircled by a fence, has benches, and is generally well maintained.

Pentland View Park
Currie
Situated on the busy Lanark Rd, but it's fully fenced and the access gate doesn't lead directly on to the road. Playground contains two toddler multiplays, two bucket swings, plus four other swings. Two benches for adults.

Dean Park
Balerno

Situated next to Dean Park Primary School. Access by car via Dean Park Pl. Compact park with equipment which includes a toddler multiplay, a springy motorbike and tractor.

Bonaly

Where Bonaly Rd crosses the city bypass there is a fork in the road. The right turn, Torduff Rd (public vehicle access for only a few hundred yards and limited parking) leads up to Torduff Reservoir and is surfaced, but is a long push for pushchairs and small cyclists. At the reservoir you can turn left for a walk across to Bonaly Country Park – steps and a grassy path, but good views over the city. For pushchairs, a better walk is to follow the west side of the reservoir along to the end where there is a short push up to Clubbidean Reservoir, ¾ mile. Here there is more space for picnics and there are sometimes anglers in boats to watch. The path alongside Clubbidean is rougher for pushchairs but energetic parents with backpacks may like to continue on to Currie, 1½ miles.

Following Bonaly Rd, from the city bypass as far as it will go, brings you to a car park. This area is know as Bonaly Country Park and from here you can walk up into the hills. There is an information board with maps and a picnic area. Of the three paths up from here, the left is too steep for youngsters, the right takes you over Torduff Reservoir and up into the heather. The middle path, possible with pushchairs and for reasonable walkers, leads up through a plantation of trees to Bonaly Reservoir.

Harlaw and Threipmuir Reservoirs

Harlaw Reservoir car park is reached by leaving Currie on Kirkgate (follow signs for Currie Old Kirk) or Balerno on Harlaw Rd; turn off at Harlaw Farm. There is an information board here. At the gate, turn right and follow a surfaced road about 100 yards to the reservoir. The former waterkeeper's cottage and garden are open as a Ranger Centre with maps, displays and leaflets. Toilet available. Picnic benches and pond in the wildlife garden. The path around the south side of Harlaw Reservoir is ideal for pushchairs and bicycles. On the north side is a track (occasionally used by council vehicles), which can be reached by a small metal bridge or across the overflow in summer – fun for paddlers. The track (with paths off through the trees to explore), continues to the end of Harlaw Reservoir where it joins up with Threipmuir Reservoir by way of another overflow. To continue on around Harlaw, cross the footbridge here and turn left through the gap in the wall. The track follows the wall and over the bank on your right is Threipmuir Reservoir (not fenced). Turn left at the end of the wall to continue on around the south side of Harlaw. Those without pushchairs may like to negotiate the stiles further on for a walk back to the car park, along a lane across the fields.

It is possible to walk along Threipmuir from the overflow, keep to the right and do not cross the footbridge. This is an easy walk for pushchairs but you cannot link up with the car park at Red Moss as there are kissing gates at the other end. It is not possible to walk all around the Threipmuir Reservoir. A variety of birds can be seen on this walk, keep your eyes peeled for herons and cormorants.

Car parking available also at Threipmuir and Red Moss Nature Reserve. Take 1st left in Balerno Village after the High School. Follow the road for approximately 2 miles out of the village past the animal sanctuary to the car park.

Red Moss Wildlife Reserve and Bavelaw Bird Reserve
Balerno

Parking at Threipmuir – see Harlaw and Threipmuir Reservoirs. There is a picnic table here and information board with maps. A short footpath, unsuitable for pushchairs, leads down to Threipmuir Reservoir and along to Harlaw. With a pushchair the best route is to turn left out of the car park and follow the road along towards a bridge. On your right is the Red Moss Nature Reserve. This area is boggy so keep to the boardwalk. Continue over the bridge and up a steep tree lined hill. Bavelaw Bird Reserve is on your right and there is a bird hide on the shore, over a stile and along to a narrow boggy path. Note: the key is held at Balerno Post Office.
A signpost at the top of the hill gives walking options. Only the left continues to be suitable for pushchairs until you reach the stile opening onto the Pentland Hills. This walk is exposed and can be cold but worth it on a clear day for the views. There are sheep and cattle in the fields, waterfowl and fishermen on the reservoir below.

Almondell and Calderwood Country Park
01506 882254
almondell&calderwood@westlothian.gov.uk
Signposted off A89. The entrance is 2 miles south of Broxburn. Almondell North car park is nearest to the Visitor Centre. People with walking difficulties can park next to Visitor Centre.
This country park has lovely riverside walks, an aquarium, and displays/seasonal exhibitions in the visitor centre, which also serves hot drinks and snacks in a small seated area. The paths are suitable for both pushchairs and wheelchairs. There are also wilder tracks to explore.
The Rangers organise family events throughout the year and host playgroup visits. There is also a wooden play area and duck pond near the visitor centre, picnic tables and a barbecue site which requires booking in advance.
Calderwood has been left as a natural area to encourage wildlife. The paths are rough tracks, take a sling rather then pushchair. An area called Oakbank also connects with Calderwood. This is an old shale mining area, which has been planted with nitrogen-fixing plants to restore it to nature.

Beecraigs Country Park
01506 844516
mail@beecraigs.com
www. beecraigs.com
Located 2 miles South of Linlithgow. Drive through the town centre; turn south into Preston Rd and keep going, past all the houses and on up the road. It is well signposted. The 1st junction on your left leads you to the deer park, toilets, campsite and visitor centre. Alternatively, keep on and next left turn-off takes you into Balvormie area, where the play park, barbecues (for hire) and pond are situated.
Woodland walks, deer farm (with raised viewing platforms), trout farm, fishing reservoir, outdoor pursuit activities, caravan and camping site. Park Centre for information, refreshments, craft sales, farm shop and Countryside Ranger Service. Restaurant within the Park environs. Clean well thought out play area which suits a large range of ages. The walk up Cockleroy Hill is very rewarding (this is privately owned land, not part of country park) - good for rolling eggs on Easter Day.

Where would you suggest?
Tell us -
ed@efuf.co.uk

Muiravonside Country Park
The Loan
By Linlithgow
EH49 6LN
01506 845311

Take the A801 south from the M9, J4 (Lathallan Roundabout), then at roundabout follow the B825 towards Linlithgow and Whitecross. Country Park is signposted on the right. Free car park.

Set in 170 acres, while the mansion house is long gone there is a stepped garden on its site, with picnic benches and a barked children's play area, complete with a large spider-web climbing structure. While the chute is very high, and the swaying log-walk too advanced for most under 5s, the toddler playpark next to the barked area is much more accessible. There are swings (bucket-swings), a couple of animal-shaped buckabouts and a see-saw.

The main car park is sited next to Newparks Farm, where children can see an array of animals, including horses, Shetland ponies, guinea pigs and rabbits in abundance, sheep and goats, Tamworth pigs and a Highland bull. There are toilets at the farm site.

There are industrial relics of the estate's past scattered here and there, so don't be surprised if you come across rusting skeletal tractors.This is a lovely place for a stroll. However, the River Avon (said as to rhyme with Gavin) flows alongside some of the paths – and there is a weir and a mill lade, so keep a close eye on children if you take a walk along the lower paths.

There's a visitor centre: park in the small overflow carpark and walk along the road – there are a couple of parking bays for disabled drivers next to the visitor centre, which is in the old farm buildings of the estate. There are toilets (clean but basic, including those for disabled visitors) next to the centre, and there's a café on the opposite side of the courtyard. If you make the visitor centre your first port of call you can pick up a really clear map of the entire estate. Contact the Ranger Service on the number above for information and updates.

Polkemmet Country Park
Whitburn
01501 743905
polkemmet@westlothian.gov.uk

By car take M8, J4 then A705 through Whitburn, straight on along B7069 and then B7066 towards Harthill. Park is signposted to the right. There is one car park immediately off the road, but keep going to get to the car park by the stable block.

Polkemmet offers a variety of facilities, including signed riverside walks (leaflets available), picnic areas, golf course, driving range and a barbecue area (for hire). Some paths are suitable for pushchairs, some are too rough. Toilets in nearby stable block with a nappy changing bench. Block also houses a Countryside Ranger's information centre and shop in the courtyard where sweets, ice cream and drinks are sold. Accessible to pushchairs and wheelchairs. Tables outside in courtyard. The walk downstream the River Almond brings you to The Horn, a 24m high metal horn, part of the M8 Art Project, right by the M8 motorway.

Callendar Park
Falkirk
FK1 1YR
01324 503770

From M9, J5, turn left along the Laurieston Bypass. At the end, turn left, then right onto A803. Pass the grassy banking of the Antonine Wall and the park entrance is on your left, signposted, at a roundabout. For the House and Stables Tearoom, take 1st left past the high flats.

Large park with woodland walks and Castle Callendar – an enclosed, dog-proof play park for children of all ages and abilities, which features irresistible spiral slides, unusual tyre swings and a big sand-pit. Also seasonal crazy golf, putting, bouncy castle, electric cars. The boating pond is inhabited by many greedy birds. Kiosk selling ice-lollies, burgers, etc. For historical interest, you can run up and down the Antonine Wall, built by the Romans, which defines the park's northern boundary.

The museum is well worth a visit. The park also has a tearoom and the Park Gallery, a small contemporary art gallery with temporary exhibitions and an art activity box to create your own artwork.

Kings Park
Victoria Place
Stirling
FK8 2

The park has all sorts of landscape from open space to trees, rough grass and bush - there is lots to explore.

Watch out for the golfers as a large part of the park forms a golf course, although there are good walks round the boundary of the golf course. As well as the tennis courts, skatepark and pitches there is a fantastic playground. The playground includes toddler swings, a water and sand play area, giant swinging tyre and a flying fox, so it provides something for all ages. The park is some distance from the nearest shop so best to bring your own refreshments. In good weather there can be an ice cream van at the main gate.

PLANES, TRAINS & AUTOMOBILES

CENTRAL

Edinburgh Bus Tours
031 220 0770
info@edinburghtour.com
www.edinburghtour.com

The buses are all painted in distinctive colours. The four different city tours are: City Sightseeing Tour; The Edinburgh Tour; Mac Tours and The Majestic Tour. Some buses are fully open top, some part covered. So depending on the weather and the friskiness of your under 5 you can choose to be inside or outside.

The Forth Bridges Cruise Bus and Boat Tour provides a bus link from the city centre to South Queensferry for a boat tour out on the Firth of Forth aboard the Forth Belle. See www.forthtours.com or their leaflet for details.

The city tours, all approx 1 hr, depart regularly from Waverley Bridge. Tickets are valid for 24 hours and you can 'hop on-hop off' at designated stops along the city routes. While the tours are all run by the same company at present, they offer slightly different experiences, and take slightly different routes round the city. You can buy tickets from the tour bus drivers, Waverley Bridge ticket sellers, or from the Lothian Buses Travelshops at Waverley Bridge, Hanover Street and Shandwick Place. You can also buy tickets on-line which you must print yourself ready to use.

Some tours have recorded guided tours (in up to 9 languages) and provide your own personal headphone set for your journey. Others have real-life guides providing commentary over loudspeaker.

Tickets offer discounts on various other Edinburgh attractions. Ask the ticket seller or see their leaflets for details.

Trainspotting

There is a footbridge which connects West Princes Street Gardens to the lower ramparts of Edinburgh Castle behind the Ross Bandstand. Its mostly transparent sides provide a perfect viewing point for the small train enthusiast. The bridge crosses the 4 main railway lines into and out of Edinburgh Waverley station. The trains are of various types and run to numerous destinations both near and far. Drivers tend to be friendly and will usually blow their whistles and wave back to any children that are on the bridge.

A return ticket from the city to North Queensferry on a nice day means a trip across the Forth Bridge - a very pleasant way to spend train time with an enthusiastic youngster.

NORTH

Royal Yacht Britannia

2nd Floor, Ocean Terminal
Ocean Drive
Leith
EH6 6JJ
0131 555 5566
enquiries@tryb.co.uk
www.royalyachtbritannia.co.uk

A good, but pricey, afternoon out. A guided tour takes about 1½ hrs, handsets with audio description linked in to each exhibit are geared either to adults or under 10s, but these are taxing for younger children after the initial excitement of having their own talking phone. However, there is lots to see that shows a side of Royal life it is hard to imagine without seeing. There didn't seem to be a hands off attitude, so plenty of interesting things to handle and touch, and lots of photo opportunites. For younger children in pushchairs, it is pretty much a stroll about a boat, with no interactive entertainment aimed at toddlers. There is an adult atmosphere in the café, though there are colouring materials available on request, but no play area or toys. Staff were helpful and friendly, and the cakes in the café were good enough for a queen!

   £ S

Inchcolm Island

0131 331 5000
www.maidoftheforth.co.uk

By car follow the signs for the Forth Road Bridge, then the brown tourist signs for Inchcolm Abbey Ferry.

A fantastic little island in the middle of the Firth of Forth, often referred to as the Iona of the East. Several boats head out from both Newhaven and South Queensferry on a daily basis, though only the Maid of the Forth sailing from South Queensferry is suitable for under 5s. The Maid of the Forth offers a 1½hr cruise only option or a 3hr cruise with landing running from April to October with up to 4 sailings a day during peak times (this drops to two during October).

This boat trip is accessible with a pushchair and the crew are most helpful with getting on and off the boat, although a carrier would be easier. An interesting commentary is given whilst sailing with seals, guillemots and cormorants being spotted on our trip, however, it is rumoured that dolphins, puffins and porpoises may also be seen so you may want to bring binoculars.

The Island itself is home to Incholm Abbey and visitor centre. The ruins are fun to run around and the island has a host of paths to explore before the boat sets sail for the return journey, seagulls do nest on the far side of the island so please be aware during nesting season. The grassy area next to the pontoon has a couple of benches ideal for picnics whilst watching the seals play in the bay.

Visit our website for updates:
www.efuf.co.uk

Isle Of May
Anstruther Pleasure Trips
01333 310103
www.isleofmayferry.com
The May Princess sails from Anstruther Harbour once a day. The crossing takes 45mins including a cruise round the island to see the colony of grey seals basking on the rocks. Sailing times vary depending on tides. Tickets can be purchased from the Kiosk in Anstruther Harbour 1hr before sailing or pre-booked up to one week in advance. The boat has light refreshments but it is advisable to take your own too.

On most trips you can land and spend 2-3hrs ashore exploring. In the summer you are met by a warden who explains about the abundant wildlife including puffins, kittiwakes, guillemots, razorbills, terns and shags. The puffins were amazing!

There are marked routes, which allow you to visit all parts of the island, a small information centre with toilets, the remains of a 12th century monastery and the first lighthouse ever built in Scotland.

EAST

Myreton Motor Museum
Aberlady
EH32 OPZ
01875 870288
Take A1 to Haddington then A6137 towards Aberlady.
An interesting collection of bicycles, cars, motor cycles, and World War II military vehicles, among others. Also has displays of posters and toy cars and related memorabilia. Toilet, but no nappy changing facilities. Accessible to single but not to double pushchairs.

Museum of Flight
East Fortune Airfield
East Lothian
EH39 5LF
0131 225 7534
info@nms.ac.uk
www.nms.ac.uk/flight
A great day out, especially if the weather is good as there are acres of open space including an outdoor Assault Course, plus lots of hands-on activities to keep them amused indoors. Our kids loved climbing up the steps and going on Concorde (they were a little disappointed that they couldn't sit on the seats on board). Ample tables and chairs outdoors for a packed lunch or visit the Aviator Café. As everything is at ground level the whole site is easily accessible for wheelchairs and pushchairs. A free road train (the "Airfield Explorer") circuits the museum stopping at all the hangars and this is also a big hit with small children.

WEST

Union Canal
This runs from the Lochrin Basin in Fountainbridge, access from Gilmore Pk and Leamington Rd. Or there is a signposted car park before the bypass at Calder Gdns off Calder Rd, from where you can walk into the city or out into the countryside. Hermiston also provides a convenient place to park. Thanks to the Millennium Link project the Union Canal now runs right through to Falkirk where the Millennium Wheel carries boats onto the Forth & Clyde Canal, thus connecting Edinburgh and Glasgow. The towpath through the city is on the north bank and is suitable for pushchairs, obviously children need close supervision. From the centre of the city and industrial buildings the canal passes suburban gardens and parks, and nesting swans can be seen. You may also see oarsmen from the rowing club. The canal is carried by the 12 arch Slateford Aqueduct over the Water of Leith and a long flight of steps leads down to the Water of Leith Walkway. Beyond the bypass the canal offers an easy and delightful walk through open countryside, although you may have to negotiate steps to reach it.

The Water of Leith Walkway
The Water of Leith Trust
24 Lanark Road
0131 455 7367

A comprehensive guide to the walkway complete with map and historical notes is available from the trust. Edinburgh City Libraries stock a good selection of books on the Water of Leith.

The Water of Leith rises in the Pentland Hills and runs through the villages of Balerno, Currie, Juniper Green and Colinton and into the heart of Edinburgh before flowing into the Firth of Forth at Leith. In its 24 miles it flows through wooded dells, past abandoned mills, elegant Georgian terraces and new housing developments, before opening up into a broad river surrounded by the buildings of Leith docks. It is designated an Urban Wildlife Site by the City of Edinburgh Council. Look out for herons, especially near weirs.

The walkway runs along most of the river in the City and most parts are negotiable with a pushchair. Unfortunately access is not always so easy and we have tried to list alternatives to steps, where they exist. Some sections are well used by dogs too. Keep an eye on young cyclists as the banks can be steep and there are not always railings.

The brown water is due to peat. Giant hogweed a tall plant (up to 3m) with tiny white flowers has established itself on several stretches. Touching this plant or blowing through sections of its hollow stem may cause an allergic reaction and photosensitivity of the skin. These plants are routinely treated with weedkiller and hacked down but return each year. Along stretches of the river are raspberries and brambles which should be safe to eat, but remember that dogs may have been there before you – pick high!

The Water of Leith walkways are accessible in parts. Contact centre for further information.

Water of Leith Buggy Scheme

This is a scheme to provide disabled and other children who have limited mobility the means to access the countryside. The aim of the project is to enable users to enjoy previously inaccessible places, like the Water of Leith Walkway, visits to the countryside, beaches and hill-walking. It's a free service, registration is required. The 5 all terrain buggies come in three sizes, with one available in the small 'ranger' size – suitable for children up to 11yrs. They're kept at the Water of Leith Visitor Centre, Slateford, and Craiglockart Tennis Club. The parent/carer must first register by taking along 2 forms of identification (one photo ID and one with a home address). After a familiarisation session, which lasts about 15mins, you will be able to borrow a buggy. The buggies are available for half day, full day or weekend hire (subject to availability) and once you are a registered user all you need to do is call in advance to reserve your buggy for the day.

BALERNO TO JUNIPER GREEN

The walkway begins to the north side of Balerno High School, Bridge Rd and follows the track of an old railway, making it ideal for pushchairs and cyclists. There are a number of access points along the route to Currie, Waulkmill Loan is easiest for pushchairs. At Currie Kirkgate there are steps up to the walkway, next to the bridge. Here it is better for pushchairs if you continue under the bridge and up the road to Currie Baptist Church, where there is access to the walkway via an old goods yard; you can park here too. The walkway continues for approx 1½ miles to Juniper Green. Easiest access is at Kinleith Mill, through the industrial estate off Blinkbonny Rd. There are also steps up from the walkway to Blinkbonny Rd bridge. There is a section here where a 20 feet wall drops sharply down to the river below, so hold on to wandering tots. The path then crosses to the north side of the river again. Access in Juniper Green is from Baberton Loan, next to the Post Office where you can park.

JUNIPER GREEN TO SLATEFORD

Inc Craiglockhart Dell and Colinton Dell.
Along this attractive and peaceful section of the river the walkway continues on the old railway, passing under the city bypass and into a wooded dell, crossing the river several times. Good access next to Post Office in Juniper Green, West Mill Rd, Gillespie Rd by the bridge, or through Spylaw Park, Colinton where there is a good play area. Continuing on the walkway enters an old railway tunnel, dimly lit but not as long as it looks and a superb place for echoes. Look out for a silhouette on the wall of a Balerno pug, the small engine specially designed for the steep sided Colinton Dell. The path emerges way above the river with other paths below. From Dell Rd, Colinton, down past the church the walkway runs through the wooded Colinton and Craiglockhart Dells. This section is difficult for pushchairs as there are steps every so often. Access points include Katesmill Rd, at Redhall Mill and behind the Tickled Trout, on Lanark Rd at Slateford.

SLATEFORD TO ROSEBURN

The Water of Leith Trust (Tel: 455 7367) is located on the A70 Lanark Rd at Slateford opposite the Tickled Trout pub. It is open daily and admission is free. There is an exhibition where children can listen to the sounds of some of the wildlife they may see and look down onto a video of the river. Toilets and nappy changing facilities. There is limited parking at the centre.
A flight of steps leads up to the Union Canal from Slateford for those without pushchairs. A flat pathway runs from Slateford to Gorgie Rd and the river can be followed through Saughton Park. The section beside Murrayfield Rugby Ground and Ice Rink can be accessed from Baird Dr and Riversdale Rd and provides an easy walk for pushchairs.

ROSEBURN TO DEAN PATH

Access the path from Roseburn Cliff where shallow steps lead to a concrete path right next to the riverside. It is easy to follow to Belford Bridge - steps at the bridge so it is easier to leave the path by the back of the Belford Hotel. Also access to the Gallery of Modern Art via a steep/stepped path. From Belford Bridge the Dean Bank footpath is surfaced and runs on the riverbank, a precarious few feet above the water. Some sections have a handrail about 3ft high – useful for adults but small children can slip underneath quite easily. Access is from Dean Path, with steps a little way up the hill from Dean Village, or for pushchairs a better option is at the footbridge along from Sunbury Mews in a modern housing development. There is access from an alleyway beside Damside in Dean Village, but the cobbles can be slippy after wet weather and the walkway here is liable to flooding.

DEAN PATH TO STOCKBRIDGE

This well railed and paved section runs along the south bank from Miller Row in Dean Village, to Saunders St in Stockbridge. As the river gushes beneath the dramatic Dean Bridge it is hard to imagine the urban bustle only 10mins walk away at the West End of Princes St. The depth of the steep wooded valley is emphasised by the views of the backs of Moray and Ainslie Pl. St Bernard's Well, a Georgian statue and temple, is halfway along the path and there are several flights of steps down to paddling and fishing spots. There are upper and lower routes between St Bernard's Well and the bridge at Saunders St. A curved sloping path allows pushchair access direct to Saunders St.

STOCKBRIDGE TO WARRISTON

There are steps down to the Deanhaugh Footpath from Deanhaugh Street in Stockbridge. Easier access from Haugh St or Falshaw Bridge at the other end of the pathway. At Falshaw Bridge turn left and immediately right onto Arboretum Ave. At the end of Arboretum Ave you reach the Rocheid Path with views across the river of the Colonies. Easiest exit from this path is via Inverleith Terrace Lane onto inverleith Row. If you cross the river the path becomes rather overgrown and there are steps up to Canonmills.

Anything out of date?
Let us know -
info@efuf.co.uk

WARRISTON TO LEITH

To continue to follow the river take Warriston Rd and follow the riverbank at the bridge. It is possible to take a pushchair along this path but hard pushing is sometimes required. An easier but less scenic route is to access the Warriston Cycleway from the corner of Canonmills and Broughton Rd. The two routes join at Connaught Pl where you can continue along the old railway line and rejoin the river after 500 metres. Or take the flight of steps up to Newhaven Road, cross the road, turn right and walk towards town, and after 50m the walkway will take you across the river to Anderson Pl. Upon exiting at the road, turn left then right along West Bowling Green St and then rejoin the walkway where the sign indicates on the left side.

The scenery changes yet again as the now broad river enters the docks of Leith and you can treat yourselves to a well earned cup of coffee. There are plenty of buses to various destinations from the bottom of Leith Walk.

Edinburgh Canal Centre
27 Baird Road
Ratho
Midlothian
EH28 8RA
0131 333 1320
info@bridgeinn.com
www.bridgeinn.com

Follow 'Edinburgh Canal Centre' signs from Newbridge Interchange.

Although the canal boats only offer group cruises – with the exception of the Santa Cruises - the Centre is a pleasant place for a meal and a wander around. The tow-path makes for a good walk with pushchairs, though there are obvious water safety issues for those with tearaway toddlers. There are ducks and swans for children to look at as well as a rather old but functioning parent-powered carousel.

Toilets with nappy changing facilities are available in the Bridge Inn. Santa visits from his magical island during the festive season and boats can be hired for children's parties.

 Some of the entry points and most of the walkway areas of the Union Canal are accessible in the Edinburgh area. For more information on the canal walkways contact the Centre.
See also www.thewaterwaystrust.org.uk

The Bridge Inn, which incorporates the Edinburgh Canal Centre, is wheelchair accessible – unlike the canal boats! Children who use a wheelchair would have to transfer from their chair and be carried into the boat, where they would then sit in one of the standard seats. If you can manage this then the Santa Barge Trips may be an option. Staff will assist with transfers in and out of the boat (although transfer equipment is not in place) and should be happy to help you if you need any other assistance.

 £

Linlithgow Union Canal Society
The Basin
Manse Road
Linlithgow
01506 671215
info@lucs.org.uk
www.lucs.org.uk
Signposted from A803, sharp right turn at first railway bridge, then up and over canal bridge. The Basin is on the right.

Boat trips on the Union Canal over the Avon Aqueduct. Boats are available for private charter and there is another boat for self-drive hire. When Santa visits the Basin at Christmas, (usually on the 2 weekends prior to Christmas) there are barge trips and a gift for children.

The museum has an audio-visual presentation (perhaps more for interested parents than under 5s). The tearoom serves drinks and home-baking. The area is accessible to pushchairs and also wheelchairs. There are toilets, but there are no nappy changing facilities. It's an enjoyable outing for under 5s.

Looking towards the town from the Canal Society there's an old doocot with tended gardens in front of it – nice for a sit down or a picnic. If you walk further along the canal path to the West you can cut off the path. Go up and over the canal bridge and then walk down the first roadway lined with houses on your left. This will take you into the large Rosemount Park – perfect for a run around! Keep away from the canal end – there's no fencing. There are no toilets here, but you're about 10-15 mins walk from Linlithgow High Street and facilities at the Vennel.

Bo'ness & Kinneil Railway
Bo'ness Station
Union Street
Bo'ness
01506 822298 (Talking Timetables)
01506 825855 (Office)
www.srps.org.uk
Take Junction 5 off M9 out of Edinburgh. Follow the signs to Bo'ness on the A904. Or, take A90 out of Edinburgh, then A904 through Newton to Champany Corner. Turn right for Bo'ness. The railway is situated near the shore of the River Forth in the town centre and is signposted.

Steam train trips. A very pleasant outing for both children & carers. Special events are very popular e.g. Easter Egg Specials; Days Out with Thomas; Santa train trips in December. Special timetable and fares (incl. those for under 5s) apply for special events. Details from Scottish Railway Preservation Society - details above.

Fares are available which include Caverns of Birkhill Mine (great visit, but is a very long way back up carrying your kids). The Scottish Railway Exhibition at Bo'ness station has an interesting collection of locos, rolling stock etc. with a Scottish connection.

 Disabled parking is available close to the station, although may be popular at busy special events. If you're having difficulty, ask a member of staff for advice. There's a ramp up to the main building. On busy days expect long queues, although it may be possible to use the side ramped entrance instead of waiting in the queue. If your child has a special need that makes waiting in the queue a difficulty explain this to staff who should be happy to help. There is access from the platform to the train carriage via a ramp and a carpeted area in one of the carriages suitable for a child wishing to stay in their wheelchair, with a seat beside for a carer. The carriage for the disabled is not available on the Santa Steam trains, however, staff will be very happy to assist and wheelchairs may be stored and delivered back to you after the journey. Ask about a carer's discount. Toilet for the disabled provided.

Falkirk Wheel
Lime Road
Tamfourhill
Falkirk
FK1 4RS
01324 619888or 08700 500 208
www.thefalkirkwheel.co.uk
From Edinburgh take the M9 towards Stirling. Follow brown tourist signs for The Falkirk Wheel, but beware if travelling to the Falkirk Wheel from another attraction in Falkirk - few direction signs in the town itself!

Tickets for boat trips can be booked by phone in advance. Admission to visitor centre is free. Pushchairs are not allowed on the boat, nor is there a secure place to leave them in the visitor centre. On our visit some pushchairs had been left outside visitor centre beside boat, but the advice is to leave them in the car if possible.

The Falkirk Wheel is the world's first and only rotating boat lift. Built as part of the Millennium Link, the canal restoration project that reunited the historic link between Edinburgh and Glasgow. The trip on the Falkirk Wheel is made on a pleasure cruiser that departs from in front of the visitor centre. Once on board small children should sit where they can get a good view over the side of the boat as it moves upwards on the lift. At the top of the lift the boat crosses a short aqueduct before passing through a tunnel that is partially illuminated. The boat then turns round and goes back the way it came. The round trip takes about 1hr. On a hot day the boat's glass roof can make the trip a bit uncomfortable.

In the visitor centre there are several interactive displays. Younger children may need the help of an adult to work these properly. Remote control boats and playpark. Picnic tables. Nappy changing facility in the toilet for the disabled.

  £   S

RAILWAY PATHS & CYCLE TRACKS

Railway & Cycle Paths
Railways were developed through Edinburgh by rival companies. The remains of some of these tracks have been developed into a network of cycle and footpaths which supply flat walking, ideal for pushchairs and wheelchairs. Spokes, the cycling organisation, publishes a map which shows them all. Routes include the Water of Leith Walkway and the Innocent Railway, so called because horses not steam engines initially pulled the carriages. It runs from Holyrood Park (east of Pollock Halls) to Craigmillar, walled between Prestonfield Golf Course and Duddingston Loch Nature Reserve; then on through Bingham to Musselburgh, following the main East Coast railway line, approximately 6 miles.

Another former railway cycle track starts from Balbirnie Place in Roseburn where there is a map of the route. This metalled track crosses the Water of Leith with steep steps down to join the walkway and continues north to the old Barnton railway junction at Craigleith, where it divides. One branch goes to Davidson's Mains and the other branches again to Leith and Trinity. Here the cycle path passes along side St Marks Park which has a playground, and then through the centre of Victoria Park, which has two playgrounds.

Where would you suggest?
Tell us -
ed@efuf.co.uk

RAINY DAYS

MUSEUMS & ATTRACTIONS

CENTRAL

Brass Rubbing Centre
Trinity Apse
Chalmer's Close
81 High Street
EH1 1SS
0131 556 4364
Free entry, but there is a charge for the brass rubbing.

The Centre is tucked away in an old church building located between High St and Jeffrey St (look for it almost directly across from the Museum of Childhood). Access to the Centre is via a flight of several steps, so be aware if travelling with a pushchair. Inside, the Centre is bright, warm and welcoming, and contains a collection of replicas moulded from ancient Pictish stones, rare Scottish brasses and Mediaeval church brasses. There are several tables, chairs and stools available to do the rubbings, and all materials and instructions are provided. Several small gift items are also available for sale. Of more interest to the over 5s, but a mature under 5 might enjoy producing a small rubbing. There are no toilet facilities on site, however, there are toilets available at the Museum of Childhood.

S

Museum of Childhood
42 High Street
Royal Mile
EH1 1TQ
0131 529 4142
The first museum of its kind devoted to the history of childhood. A vast collection of trains, boats, planes, dolls, teddy bears and many more playthings of the past are displayed in five galleries. Hands-on exhibits and activities have recently been added to give children more things to do in the museum. Gallery 1 has a few coin-operated working models including a nickelodeon. Gallery 2 has a rocking horse and hands-on puppets, trains and optical toys for children to use. Gallery 3 has dolls and teddy bears on display with feely boxes, games, a doll's house and family activity sheet. Gallery 4 has board games, a reading corner and a Lego wall for children to use. Gallery 5 has several period room sets with sound effects and a dressing up box. The museum also has different temporary exhibitions running throughout the year.

It is encouraging to see some of the displays at low level, suitable for viewing by small children. However, small children may get bored, and some of the hands-on stuff, because it's well used, looks rather tired.

The museum is partly suitable for pushchairs and wheelchairs but there are many steps and pushchairs are best left downstairs. There is a lift between galleries 1, 2 and 3, ramps to gallery 3; public toilets are in gallery 4. There is a good shop at the entrance, which sells traditional small toys/gifts. Nappy changing facilities in the toilets for the disabled, access with a uniformed attendant by the lift to the basement.

S

Camera Obscura
549 Castle Hill
EH1 2ND
0131 226 3709
info@camera-obscura.co.uk
www.camera-obscura.co.uk

This is the oldest purpose-built visitor attraction in Edinburgh, and adults and children alike still find it fascinating. Over 3s would probably get a lot from a visit, and many of the exhibits are interactive - particularly in the "Magic Gallery" on Level 4. Under 3s usually enjoy the hologram exhibition on level 3 and the view from the rooftop terrace on level 5 more than the camera. There are small stools available throughout to help give small children a boost up to eye-level. It has to be very dark in the camera room, so be warned if your child is nervous of this, although the sight of the streets below may take up their attention! Has a narrow staircase with approximately 100 steps to the rooftop terrace, which is unsuitable for pushchairs. These may be left beside the reception desk. There is a toilet on level 1 with nappy changing facilities. Choose a bright day to visit!

£   S

National Museum of Scotland
Chambers Street
0131 247 4422
www.nms.ac.uk/royal

Membership of NMS is available, which offers a variety of benefits, such as free entry to charging exhibitions, shop discounts etc.

A fantastic sightseeing option, this is definitely much more than a rainy-day option! The National Museum of Scotland incorporates the interconnecting Royal Museum and the Museum of Scotland buildings and houses a vast array of object and artefacts to interest and amuse under 5s. Access to the building is easy for pushchairs and wheelchairs via the Museum of Scotland entrance and there are lifts to all floors. There are purpose built nappy changing facilities on the ground floor next to the shop and all adapted toilets on each floor have a pull down changing unit. The Tower Restaurant has more formal dining, but there are the two cafés situated on the ground floor of the Royal Museum building.

ROYAL MUSEUM BUILDING

This vast, awe-inspiring Victorian building houses international collections of Decorative Arts, Science and Industry, Archaeology and the Natural World. The main entrance involves a flight of steps but this access is to be modernised over the next few years. At present the steps can be avoided by using the Tower entrance to the Museum of Scotland next door

Of particular interest to children are fish ponds in the foyer, along with the Millennium Clock - the display of figures and music is fascinating to watch, for young and old alike. There are various temporary exhibitions throughout the year.

Remember to check out the Connect Gallery, where there are reaction speed games, robots which can spell out your name, a formula 1 driving simulator, Dolly the sheep, and a lot more.

There is a dedicated parent and baby room beside the ground floor female toilets which is clean and spacious and has chairs for breastfeeding.

MUSEUM OF SCOTLAND BUILDING

Although both buildings are choc-full of great displays, the funky modern Museum of Scotland building comes out trumps for us, but only because it's got wee hidey hole seats and arrow-slit style apertures on to other floors and exhibitions, and also because you can dress up like a Viking, a Mediaeval lady or gentleman, a Roman soldier (the chainmail is heavy!) and more, as you explore the various floors.

The Museum takes a journey through Early People, Kingdom of the Scots, Scotland Transformed and finally Industry and Empire, with Discovery Zones on the way, which are great for older under 5s. Other displays which may interest the under 5s include a thatched cottage, a coin store and the Silver Gallery – an entire room devoted to silver which sparkles when you walk in! There are model trains which have moving pistons, the gory Maiden of Edinburgh (a guillotine), fossils, habitat zones with the sounds of wolves and their prey, and so on. Lift to roof terrace for views of the city.

    M   S

The People's Story
Canongate Tolbooth
163 Canongate
EH8 8BN
0131 529 4057
A fascinating museum tracing the lives and work of ordinary people from late 1700s to present day. Includes a series of reconstructions – such as a fishwife, a servant cleaning a grate, prisoners in a cell, a tearoom and a washhouse. These are all enhanced by smells and sounds as well as photographs and displays of everyday objects which under 5s can appreciate, though it will probably be better appreciated by older children. A 22min video complements the story line. A lift allows pushchair access to 1st floor. The next level is just a few steps further up but the video room is reached by a spiral stone staircase. Pushchairs may be left at front desk. Nappy changing in roomy toilets for the disabled.

S

The Writers' Museum
Lady Stair's Close
Lawnmarket
Royal Mile
0131 529 4901
This museum contains memorabilia and manuscripts relating to three of Scotland's great literary figures - Robert Burns, Sir Walter Scott and Robert Louis Stevenson. Also regular programme of temporary exhibitions covering other Scottish writers. The Museum is housed in a 17th century building with spiral stone staircases, so is tricky for pushchairs. Nappy changing table in the ladies toilet which can be used by men on request. Best visited as parents of infants (perhaps in a papoose) as little of direct interest to under 5s, although there are plenty of visual items which older children will appreciate with a bit of parental interpretation - check out the trip step (a 17th century burglar alarm)! However, the close and the courtyard outside has carved paving stones with famous lines from some of Scotland's greatest poets, and provides an interesting shortcut from the Mound on to the Royal Mile.

NORTH

South Queensferry Museum
53 High Street
South Queensferry
EH30 9HP
0131 331 5545
museumsandgalleries@edinburgh.gov.uk
www.edinburgh.gov.uk/museums
The museum is dedicated to the local social history of Dalmeny and South Queensferry. There are displays on the Royal Burgh, aspects of life and leisure, the spectacular Forth Bridges and the unique local annual custom of the Burry Man. The shoreline of the Forth Estuary at South Queensferry provides a variety of wildlife, which can be explored using the museum's binoculars and the display showing the natural history of this area. Good views of the bridges, but not much else to appeal to under 5s. Access is not possible with a pushchair and there are no dedicated facilities for children or for mothers who wish to breastfeed. However, there is a table with crayons and colouring in sheets.

F

Kirkcaldy Museum & Art Gallery
War Memorial Gardens
Kirkcaldy
01592 412860
Situated 5 mins from Kirkcaldy railway station
This museum is lively, friendly and fully accessible to pushchairs and to disabled visitors with ramped access to main entrance and a lift to the first floor galleries. There is a local history display with some 'please touch' sections, galleries with temporary exhibitions and an outstanding collection of 18th to 20th century Scottish paintings. Gift shop. For further information, contact the Outreach Officer.

 S

St Andrews Museum
Kinburn Park
Doubledykes Road
St. Andrews
01334 412690

Small local museum in a park about ½ mile from the town centre. Previous researchers have described this as 'a great bolt-hole for a rainy day' – we arrived on a dreich day and would thoroughly agree! The exhibits are not wildly exciting for under 5s, but there is a basic activity room, for school parties (on 1st floor, lift available) which provided paper and crayons for under 5s to draw. Friendly and welcoming staff were another bonus to this visit. There is easy parking, a café in the museum, plus the surrounding parkland has putting in summer months, all-year tennis, and space to run about. The museum is totally accessible to pushchairs and wheelchairs: entry via a ramp located at the side of the building (you need to ask staff to open the side door). Nappy changing facilities and potties in both male & female toilets.

EAST

Our Dynamic Earth
112 Holyrood Road
EH8 8AS
0131 550 7800
www.dynamicearth.co.uk

Located by the Scottish Parliament. Limited onsite pay parking.   Alternative parking also available near-by.

Our Dynamic Earth is an interactive tourist attraction, which tells the story of the Earth and the elements. It's not primarily designed for under 5s and you're more likely to take a young child when visiting with older children. Be prepared for the fact that they may be scared when it is dark, with the flashes of light or when the floor vibrates in the volcano experience. However many under 5s will love it! Expect to spend around 1½ hrs, 'travelling' through time, though you can 'escape' earlier – but you might need to be shown a quick way out by a member of staff.

You can meet a life-sized pterodactyl, find out what volcanic tremors feel like, experience a tropical rainstorm and touch an iceberg! Everywhere is wheelchair and pushchair accessible, with lifts where necessary. Older children tend to crowd round interactive displays – so be prepared to get stuck in there if it's busy.

The "Ocean Commotion" Play Area is located in the gift shop, which is a dedicated soft play area (parental supervision required) for children 1-10yrs. There is a variety of special events during the year, some of which will be suitable for under 5s. Birthday parties are also available for 4+yrs.

Separate nappy changing facilities available. Chair suitable for breastfeeding in the nappy changing rooms.

 £ M S

Visit our website for updates:
www.efuf.co.uk

The Scottish Parliament
Holyrood Road
EH99 1SP
0131 348 5200
sp.booking@scottish-parliament.uk
www.scottish.parliament.uk

Although under 5s might not be too interested in The Parliament itself, it has a nice café which serves all of the usual lunch time offerings as well as kids' boxes. Home to a free state of the art public crèche facility with a fantastic range of toys and very friendly staff. Crèche is available to children 6mths-5yrs and for up to 4hrs at a time, so long as you remain within the Parliament. You can pre-book or drop-in (subject to availability). This can allow you to relax over lunch/coffee, take a guided tour or attend a meeting or debate. There are excellent facilities in terms of access for pushchairs and wheelchairs, disabled toilets, private breast feeding area and baby changing (M&F).

 F

SOUTH

Scottish Mining Museum
Lady Victoria Colliery
Newtongrange
EH22 4QN
0131 663 7519
enquiries@scottishminingmuseum.org
www.scottishminingmuseum.com

Located 10 miles S of Edinburgh on A7. From city bypass, at Sherriffhall Roundabout follow signs for Newtongrange – approx 3 miles.

A purpose-built visitor centre with two floors of exhibitions, displays, buttons to press and magic helmets, so while young children might not understand the exhibition, there's a good chance that they'll still enjoy it. Families can enjoy Scotland's biggest steam engine and a simulated coalface, plus an Operations Centre full of activities.

Café serves hot and cold meals throughout the day. Children's outdoor play centre with Victorian toys (e.g. skittles).

   S

WEST

Bannockburn Heritage Centre
Glasgow Road
Stirling
FK7 OLJ
01786 812664

Leave M9 at J9 services and take A872 Stirling, Bannockburn HC, N for 1 mile.

This heritage centre is built near the site of the Battle of Bannockburn, when the Scottish army led by Robert the Bruce defeated the English army and drove them out of Scotland. Displays, tableaux, model soldier layouts, and audio-visual presentation (lasts about 15mins) of the build-up to the famous battle and the battle itself. Some gory bits! On certain days there is an actor who gives a living history presentation for added enjoyment, although some of his weaponry and tales of bloody battles might alarm little ones.

Usually some simple craft activity on offer. Soldiers' helmets and period costumes (including very heavy chainmail for older ones and willing parents) available for dressing up as 14th century warriors and peasants! Nappy changing facility in toilet for disabled. Pushchair and wheelchair access.

The shop is well stocked with gifts, books and toys for all ages. Drinks, crisps and sweets also available. The hotel next door does have a bistro and a beer garden, however, and is open to non residents.

The heritage centre is surrounded by grassy parkland that is ideal for children to run about on. A march up to the nearby monument to Robert the Bruce completes the visit.

 NTS **S**

LEISURE CENTRES & POOLS

Swimming

Most babies love moving in water, although it can take a little while to get used to the sights, sounds and smells of a new environment. Swimming is an excellent way of exercising the body, and more and more parents are introducing their children to the pleasures of water early in life. Safety is obviously a motivating factor, living as we do in a country with many lochs, rivers and canals as well as the sea. Opinions vary as to when to start your child (classes are available from 4 mths), but whenever you start, here are a few things to remember:

- Have a healthy respect for the dangers of water.
- Always stay near your child when in or near water.
- Allow at least 1hr after a feed before entering the water.
- Respect your child's wishes. Do not force youngsters into the water if they dislike it; wait and try again in a week or so.
- Babies get chilled easily. Take them out of the water at the first signs of cold. 10 mins in the water is enough for the first few times, and no more than 30 mins at other times.

What to Wear

There are various companies producing reuseable swim nappies in a wide range of fun patterns and colours, ranging from 0-36mths. Sometimes you can find them at NCT Nearly New Sales. Disposable swim nappies are available, but probably less economical if you go swimming regularly. Ordinary nappies are not suitable.

Buoyancy Aids

Small arm bands are available. The type with 2 or more air chambers and non-returnable valves are the safest. The triangular type with a flat section next to the body will stop your child wobbling too much. Other buoyancy aids, such as body vests and inflatable ring seats, are available. You might find that these are more suitable for young babies and aids such as these also come in several sizes. Remember that arm bands and inflatable rings are not lifesavers, and can wear out, so check them regularly.

Classes

Early classes are intended to develop your child's confidence and pleasure in the water. They teach some of the basic skills leading towards learning to swim, and show parents how they can help their children. As regards a proper stroke, experts say that it is better to let under 5s develop their own way of swimming through playing regularly in water: perfecting a stroke can come later. In fact, the longer you leave it, the quicker they learn. There are many books available about teaching children to swim from bookshops or from local libraries.

Edinburgh Leisure follow the national standards in Scottish Swimming's 'Adult and Child' and 'Learn to Swim' programmes. Lessons are very popular and most must be booked in advance. Some Adult and Baby sessions and Adult and Child sessions do not need to be booked, but check with each pool for details.

Edinburgh Leisure Pools
www.edinburghleisure.co.uk

The pools in this section are all local authority run. Edinburgh Leisure's website gives lots of useful details about activities and classes (the activity and timetable search facility is useful but does not cover all pools).

- Edinburgh Leisure offers free swimming to all primary age children, except at Leith Waterworld.
- Adult prices vary according to type of pool.
(For adults Edinburgh Leisure have various membership schemes giving reduced admission rates to cardholders.)
- When visiting a pool for the first time it can be a good idea to ask the reception staff if there is anything you should know. They are usually very helpful – e.g. family changing, where to leave your pushchair, what coin needed for lockers, nappy changing, playpens etc.
- All pools have lockers (usually £1 or 50p refundable), showers and hairdryers (some are free, some coin-operated).
- In general you get unlimited swimming time. However, when pools are busy they may run sessions of limited duration, usually 40 mins.
- Most pools sell armbands, goggles, etc.
- Most pools without cafeterias have vending machines selling drinks and snacks.

- Spectators are allowed into all Council pools, free of charge.
- During school holidays and at weekends, most of the pools have fun sessions with toys, inflatables etc.
- Edinburgh Leisure guidelines for adult/child ratios in the water are: one adult can supervise maximum two children of 0-4yrs; one adult can supervise maximum 4 children of 5-8yrs; children 9+ yrs can swim unsupervised. These guidelines vary between different local authorities and can be quite rigorously applied, so do check when out with the city.
- At most pools you are required to wear blue plastic overshoes in the changing areas to help keep the area clean.
- Most pools have either a playpen, highchair, or wall-mounted seat to secure a roaming toddler while you get changed.

Private Swimming Pools
Some of the city's private gyms and hotels have pools that offer swimming classes and activities for children. These can be expensive but offer a more personally tailored programme.

♿ Remember to ask for a carer's discount! Under 5s and accompanying carers should get into any Edinburgh City Council swimming pool free of charge. If you're phoning in advance of taking your child swimming, it may be worth asking about equipment available (and whether it is clean and in working order!).

Equipment that can be helpful, if not vital for some families, includes: a height adjustable changing bed, a shower chair that doesn't couple as a toilet chair (that is, it doesn't have a large hole in the seat area), and a hoist for pool entry (although you may not choose to use this with younger children). While all such equipment will be geared towards disabled adults, it is often suitable for use with children too. While all swimming pools and leisure centres should have facilities for the disabled, equipment varies between venues with some pools not having a shower chair and others not having a working changing bed. Venues also differ with reference to cleanliness of facilities for the disabled. If a pool doesn't have a chair that your child can use to gain access to the poolside, do ask about taking a wheelchair in if your child needs to.

CENTRAL

Glenogle Swim Centre
Glenogle Road
Stockbridge
EH3 5JB
0131 343 6376
www.edinburghleisure.co.uk
Pay-and-display on street parking close to both entrances on Glenogle Rd and Saxe Coburg Pl. Lift access available from the Glenogle Rd entrance.

This beautifully refurbished Victorian pool is a very popular and friendly place to visit. Adult and Child sessions and children's lessons available. Changing cubicles are at poolside, one larger cubicle for family changing on left. Hairdryers available. Toilets are in the shower area and also upstairs.

The 23m pool has access steps at each corner. Water level is 30cm below poolside, but there is a bar all around to hold. Upstairs viewing gallery all the way around the pool with benches. Separate small seating area upstairs away from pool. Sauna and steam room at far end of pool with seating area for relaxation.

NORTH

Drumbrae Leisure Centre
30 Drumbrae Terrace
EH4 7SF
0131 312 7957
www.edinburghleisure.co.uk
A friendly and welcoming leisure centre.Facilities include a 25m swimming pool (with great view), gym, multi purpose sports hall, fitness studio and creche (you can book 7 days in advance). Range of swimming lessons to suit all ages and abilities, gym courses and Gym nippers (book ahead).
Pool changing area is mixed (single sex changing rooms are available opposite entrance to pool changing area) there are plenty of lockers and family changing rooms.There is not always a barrier up between the changing rooms and pool so keep an eye on any little ones.The pool has a moveable floor which can be altered to a 1m depth and there is a pool fun session at weekends (recommended for under 5s confident in water) ring reception to find out current times.

Blue badge parking bays near the door. Changing facilities are accessed by key, which you'll need to ask for at reception (you'll be required to leave a car key or similar as a deposit). The staff are very helpful so do ask if you need assistance. The disabled changing area is near the poolside. It is large and clean with lockers, adapted toilet and shower and a very good height-adjustable changing bed. A shower chair is also provided, however it couples as a toilet chair so may not be suitable for children – ask about taking your child's wheelchair onto the poolside if you need to. There's a small seat with a grab rail in the communal shower area beside the pool.

Ainslie Park Leisure Centre
92 Pilton Drive
EH5 2HF
0131 551 2400
www.edinburghleisure.co.uk
Modern centre with 25m swimming pool (usually split - lane swimming, lessons and free area), childrens' pool, jacuzzi/spa, two sports halls, gym, sauna, fitness studio and crèche facility. An extensive range of activities and coaching sessions.

The unisex changing areas located poolside consist of family and individual cubicles. Wall-mounted hairdryers, a playpen, changing tables, wall mounted highchairs and a giant body dryer. Due to the location of the changing area in relation to the pool care should be taken with over enthusiastic children. Showers are also located poolside.
The learner pool has a gentle slope leading into a very shallow area which is ideal for introducing small babies and toddlers to the water (although having said that the water often feels quite cold). Parent and baby sessions are held throughout the week. There are bookable and turn up on the day sessions available. Swimming lessons are also available but booking well in advance is recommended.

The small cafe in reception sells cakes, tea/coffee and this leads to a door where the spectator area is located. The crèche can be booked in advance but is quite pricey. The centre also has a range of childrens' parties on offer, including a bouncy castle party in the sports hall with exclusive use of the crèche room afterwards. Check with the Centre for full details.

Leith Victoria Swim Centre
Junction Place
EH6 5JA
0131 555 4728
Car parking, including parking for disabled, at the Bonnington Rd entrance. This Victorian swimming pool with sauna and gym is situated just off Great Junction St. Extended to include a huge gym and fitness facilities. Children's lessons available. Full details from the centre.
There is the choice of changing areas: separate male and female modern communal areas with communal and private showers; or you can use the original Victorian poolside cubicles, 1 family cubicle with fold down child seat and space to change nappies. Lockers in communal areas and at poolside, also small lockers for special valuables at reception). Changing room for disabled and poolside lift available. Pushchair corner with chain and padlock available at reception if you leave a deposit. Hairdryers available next to reception.
Beautiful balcony forr spectators accessed via stair at back of building or from poolside.

Leith Waterworld
377 Easter Road
EH6 8HU
0131 555 6000
www.edinburghleisure.co.uk

This is a swimming pool with a difference! Whether you're coming with a baby, a toddler, or a pre-schooler, you can be sure that you will find something to suit. If you are looking for a bit of adrenaline, head for the flumes or to big waves. If you are wanting more of a quiet time, let yourself float through the river run, or simply relax in the lagoons.

The water is usually warmer than in other local swimming pools.

The changing facilities are extensive and include large family cubicles as well as parent/carer and child cubicles.

 A favourite with many children. Parking is in the nearby car park shared with Scotmid. Blue badge parking bays are available but are in high demand at peak times. Changing facilities for the disabled are accessed by key, available from reception. Large family changing rooms are also available which might suit. There is no shower chair but wheelchairs can be taken close to the poolside and staff are happy to store a wheelchair securely while you are in the pool. There's a small seat in the communal shower area beside the pool. The sloping beach style entrance to the pool means non-swimmers can enjoy the waves too. Staff are helpful and experienced in accommodating disabled visitors.

Perth Leisure Pool
Glasgow Road
Perth
PH2 0HZ
01738 492431 or 492421
leisure@pkc.gov.uk
www.liveactive.co.uk

There is plenty of fun for all the family here. The very shallow Monkey Jungle area for under 8s has two slides, exotic birds, a crocodile and monkeys all spouting water; the lagoon is a shallow pool area with a slide and height restriction; there is also a wild water channel, bubble beds, flumes, and a popular outdoor pool which is accessed directly from the indoor pool. A separate children's teaching pool with slide can be used when free, armbands can be borrowed from the poolside, and there are plenty of large floats and foam rings to play with in the water. Six spacious family changing rooms are a great help.

10 blue badge parking bays and accessible entrance via an extensive ramp. Helpful reception staff and carers and under 5s get in for free. Lift access to changing area with family changing rooms large enough to accommodate a wheelchair as well as facilities for the disabled: adapted toilet, a shower with pull down seat and a changing bed. The changing area is on the poolside and you can request use of the shower chair to take your child to the poolside if needed. There is a separate pool area for younger children, which may suit children of limited mobility. There are a number of water features that children might enjoy, and an outdoor area (where the water should be quite warm).

There is also a park adjacent to Perth Leisure Pool – the Boomerang Play Area. This has been thoughtfully designed to include wheelchair access to the slides and may prove to be a hit!

Anything out of date?
Let us know -
info@efuf.co.uk

EAST

Portobello Swim Centre
57 The Promenade
EH15 2BS
0131 669 6888
www.edinburghleisure.co.uk
If going with smaller under 5s call the venue to make sure the small pool is open to the public as the main pool is too cold for babies. Swimming lessons are held most days for all ages, and the centre also offers a range of classes for under 5s, all classes are listed on the website. The crèche is lovely and friendly and is open five mornings a week. For adults there is a fully-equipped gym, Turkish Baths, and various fitness classes.

♿ Parking can be problematic in surrounding streets and is in high demand. The facilities for the disabled – shower area, adapted toilet and shower chair – are close to the pool. Staff are helpful and can take you through a short cut to the pool from the changing room. The shower chair can be taken to the poolside and a hoist is available if needed. There's a lift to access the upstairs level (where the café is) and ramps leading up to the automatic main doors of the venue.

Royal Commonwealth Pool
21 Dalkeith Road
EH16 5BB
0131 667 7211
www.edinburghleisure.co.uk
The pool closed in 2009 for a two year refurbishment. It will reopen with a new layout including:
- New 25m teaching pool with a moveable floor
- Improved 50m pool that can be split by a boom
- New 25m diving pool with a moveable floor
- New dry land training area for divers
- Larger gym with three fitness studios
- New changing village, including family changing
- New reception area and cafe
- New children's play area, with a party room
- New multi purpose rooms

During the closure all swimming activities including classes have been reallocated around the other nine Edinburgh swimming pools. This information is all available on the Edinburgh Leisure website.

Gracemount Leisure Centre
22 Gracemount Drive
EH16 6RN
0131 658 1940
Various lessons and classes run through the day so public swimming times vary. Check with centre for exact details.
This modern centre includes a 25m pool, sauna, gym, health and fitness studio and sports hall. Adult and Baby sessions, Adult and Child sessions and children's swimming lessons available. Full programme available from the centre. Nappy changing facilities (M&F). There is an area for private breastfeeding. Premises are accessible to double pushchairs. Lift access to upper floor. Café and internet cafe.

Musselburgh Sports Centre
Newbigging
EH21 7AS
0131 653 6367
Phone for current opening hours and charges. Run by East Lothian Council.
A modern sports centre, offering a wide range of facilities, such as a pool, health suite and café. Children's swimming classes, including lessons for under 5s, are available – contact centre for details. Centre also offers children's gymnastics classes. Centre accessible to double pushchairs.

♿ Car park with blue badge parking bays close to the entrance. The facilities for the disabled (adjustable changing bed, adapted toilet and shower area) are clean and shower chairs (2) are available. A hoist is available for entry to the pool and the shower chair can be taken right up to the poolside. The children's area of the pool (which is quite deep at 0.8m) may be busy at peak times or during swimming lessons. It can be a little cool in the pool. Staff are friendly and helpful. It's sometimes easier just to shower at the poolside rather than in the disabled changing area unless your child can transfer to the seat (without sides) provided in this area.

Dunbar Splash Leisure Pool
Castlepark
Dunbar
EH42 1EU
01368 86 54 56
Opening times vary considerably - phone to check. Lovely bright pool overlooking the harbour and castle, well worth the journey. Special features include a gently sloping beach area where the water gradually gets deeper - perfect for nervous toddlers. Also a bubble bed, flume, slide and geyser sprays, as well a wave machine which operates once or twice an hour. Soft play area adjacent to pool, also health suite with sauna, steamroom and gym. Café and spectator area on poolside. Crèche available. Changing area: mixed family changing on poolside, with two family rooms next to the showers.

Disabled parking bays provided a little distance from the entry to the centre, no larger than other bays so may prove tricky. One disabled changing area is provided next to two family cubicles on the poolside. Unfortunately the disabled cubicle seems to get used as an additional family cubicle and, indeed, doesn't provide any extra facilities. A shower chair is available, you need to ask for it. Benches in the changing area are quite small, with no changing bed provided. Pool has a ramp access and a beach style entry to the water, so non-swimmers can enjoy the waves too.
There is a variety of animal water features, a shallow bubble pool area and reasonably warm water. The spectating area is on the poolside so another adult not swimming may be able to assist if needed. A small soft-play area accessed from the poolside may be enjoyed by a child with limited mobility, or a child improving on crawling/early walking skills. Toys available in the soft play. Disabled toilet in the wet area beside the pool, as well as downstairs (lift access) in the dry area.

Where would you suggest?
Tell us -
ed@efuf.co.uk

SOUTH

Warrender Swim Centre
Thirlestane Road
Marchmont
EH9 1AP
0131 447 0052
Various lessons and classes run through the day so public swimming times vary. Check with centre for exact details. On street parking available within parking zone S1 (pay-and-display charges operate Mon-Fri). Area is generally very busy.
A refurbished Victorian pool with sauna and gym. Ramp access from street with lift to pool and changing area. Adult and Child sessions and children's lessons available. Full programme available from centre. You can choose to use the poolside cubicles or use the family changing area to the rear which has three large cubicles (gate between this area and pool). There are two larger cubicles with bench and nappy changing for family/disabled use further on beside the showers. Playpen near to showers.
Spectator balcony at shallow end overlooking pool, some toddler toys and books. No lift access.

Bonnyrigg Leisure Centre
King George V Park
Park Road
Bonnyrigg
EH19 2AD
0131 663 7579
Run by Midlothian Council. Adults may only supervise a maximum of two children (aged under 8) each in the pool. Pool available for private booking.
This modern centre includes a leisure pool, consisting of upper and lower lagoon, and special water features such as water cannons, geysers, spa pool, slides and water mushrooms. Swimming lessons available. Contact centre for full details. Centre also has 'Knights and Princesses' soft play area, and a games hall. Other activities include gymnastics, martial arts and mini kickers. Mixed family changing is available with nappy changing facilities. No spectating area.

Loanhead Leisure Centre

George Avenue
Loanhead
EH20 9LA
0131 440 4516

Opening times: vary - contact centre for current hours. Run by Midlothian Council. Adults may only supervise a maximum of two children (aged under 8) each in the pool.

This modern leisure centre has a 25m pool and an adjoining toddler pool with slides and a viewing gallery. Water tends to be nicely warm for children during parent and child sessions. Mixed family changing is available with nappy changing facilities.

The Penicuik Centre

Carlops Road
Penicuik
EH26 9EP
01968 664066
penicuik.lc@midlothian.gov.uk
www.midlothian.gov.uk

The Penicuik Centre is a state of the art swimming pool with leisure facilities. It is a 25 metre pool with a floating floor and boom wall. The changing facilities are clean and spacious. There is a mixture of sizes of changing cubicles which can easily accommodate families and/or a changing table/highchair. The range of activities include:

- Public swimming
- Adults only swimming
- Aquafit
- Lane swimming
- Inflatable fun sessions
- Swimming lessons

A comprehensive range of swimming lessons are available but require pre-booking. Classes are for parent and baby, parent and toddler, and pre-school. The teachers are in the water with the pre-school children making the lessons a huge success. The Centre also offers a range of fitness facilities and classes in the Technogym Wellness System equipped Tonezone.

A crèche is available if you want to take classes but this needs to be booked and paid for in advance (non refundable) to ensure your place.

WEST

Dalry Swim Centre

Caledonian Crescent
EH11 2AL
0131 313 3964

The centre has just one pool so is sometimes closed to public swimming while lessons or adult only sessions take place. Check with centre for exact details. On street parking available within parking zone S4 (pay-and-display charges operate Mon-Fri). Area is generally very busy.

Refurbished Victorian 23m swimming pool with sauna and gym. Ramp access from street. Centre offers Adult and Baby sessions, Adult and Child sessions and children's lessons. Full programme available from centre. The main changing facilities are upstairs, but facilities are also available downstairs at pool level. Upstairs the corner cubicles are larger than the rest. Nappy changing facilities and play pens upstairs and at poolside. Ample space for parking pushchairs by reception. Spectator seating at poolside accessed from reception area.

Disabled parking (2) at main entrance to reception and pool, both of which are at street level. Hoist available with staff trained to operate it. Toilet, changing and showering accommodation for people with disabilities is provided, as is a shower chair and smaller benches that may be suitable, depending on your child's needs.

Wester Hailes Swimming Pool

Wester Hailes Education Centre
5 Murrayburn Drive
Wester Hailes
EH14 2SU
0131 442 2201
www.whec.edin.sch.uk

Modern leisure pool with facilities for adults and children, including a 25m pool; a children's pool; and a diving pool with springboard and highboard. The children's pool is graded in depth, so small children can touch the bottom at one end. There is a frog house with slide into the water. Under 4s must be supervised on the slide. When the leisure pool is really busy it operates on session times. A comprehensive programme of swimming lessons is available for those 3+ yrs. Lessons must be booked in advance. Details on request from centre.

In the female changing area there is a separate facility which includes mats, play pen and high chairs, these items are available on request in the male changing area. Lockers lock automatically on closure, so beware of locking the key inside! There is a powder room with mirrors, and hairdryers. A lockable pushchair bay is also available. Nappy changing facilities available on the pool side. The staffroom may be used for breastfeeding. Pushchairs and wheelchairs allowed inside. Toilets by cafe.

SOFT PLAY

Soft play centres are a great way for youngsters to burn off energy when it is too wet or cold for the park and can be a good social activity too. They can vary greatly in terms of size and availability of areas for younger children – where some may have some great facilities for older brothers and sisters, under 3s may be confined to a ball-pit – ideal if they're happy, not so great if they're not. It might be wise to avoid planning your first visit to a soft play centre during school holidays, or on school half-days, as they can become extremely busy and the noise and general good-natured mayhem might overawe a young first-timer.

NORTH

Leith Waterworld Soft Play

377 Easter Road
EH6 8HU
0131 555 6000

A small soft play area, usually fairly quiet. Most suitable for a child with the ability to pull themselves to stand and to climb ledges to reach the upper level. The ball pool area is at the bottom of the slide so may not be suitable for a less mobile child. Adults sit very close to the play area, which may suit. There is a sensory facility for children with special needs that can be booked in advance. The sensory room is close to the soft play area and is a great facility for children who enjoy the multi-sensory experience. Call in advance to check availability.

Molly's

2nd Floor, Ocean Terminal
Ocean Drive
Leith
EH6 6JJ
0845 123 5593
info@mollys.co.uk

Large play structure that includes racing slides, corkscrew slide, various obstacles, climbing wall, tree house and a soft play/ball pool area for babies/toddlers and their parents/carers. There are staff on hand to help out with any less confident children. You register your child on entry and pay for the amount of time you've been in when you leave, so watch you don't lose track of the time! You can also put drinks, etc. on a tab and pay when you leave. Shoes are not permitted on the structure. Parents/carers are required to remain in the centre at all times. Once inside there are picnic tables with benches and a few sofas to sit on, but it often feels very cramped and is difficult to manoeuvre a pushchair around. There is a cafe counter selling basic food, including a children's meal deal – offers sandwich or microwave heated pizza choices. Drinks/food from outside are not permitted. The seating areas, carpet and toilets could do with refurbishment and the toilets aren't always the cleanest. All that aside, if you go for an hour on a rainy day, or to have a cuppa after shopping, it is good value at £3/hr.

There's a small area for the very young – this may not be suitable for a larger child due to the small access point. The main play area can offer stimulation and a lot of fun. There are three entry points – a steep rope net that may suit good climbers but be tricky to others, a sloped padded entry point for a crawling child who can manage steps, and a series of stairs inside the play tree. The stairs are wide, not too steep, and the unit has been designed so that a child can transfer straight from a wheelchair onto the bottom of the steps. A crawling child should manage these steps and access the long wave slides at the top. Adults are not allowed, although a child requiring extra support may be accompanied at most times. Staff have a positive attitude to inclusion and may assist children on a one-to-one basis during quiet times. Plenty of parking – level E is best for Molly's. A discount is available for children with disabilities.

Clown Around

Units 2&3
109 Restalrig Road
EH6 7NY
0131 553 7676
07976 053690
www.clownaround.me.uk

A soft play centre, which has the additional attraction of trampolines. There's a toddler area, which has a multi level soft play unit, along with soft shapes and interactive items, such as musical notes on one of the walls. The other multi level area is for 4-10yrs, and has rat runs, a slide, a large ball pit, moveable 'obstacles' etc. There's also a games console area. Nappy changing facilities available.

There are two locations with tables, from which you can see the play areas. There's a café, so you can have a tea or coffee while you watch the antics. Birthday parties catered for. The unit has access for disabled visitors, and a controlled entry/exit.

Different areas for different age groups. The 0-3yrs area may be enjoyed by children with limited mobility. Parents can go into this area and some thought has gone in to the provision of equipment for sensory experience, including low placed music notes that sound when pressed. There is a slide in this area, however entry is quite difficult and the slide isn't wide enough for an accompanying adult. In the main area, for 4-10yrs, the two entry points are difficult and relatively steep. Adults are not allowed in this area, a rule that is particularly enforced during busy times. There is an additional trampoline area with six trampolines with soft surrounds and covered gaps. Older children tend to jump between the trampolines and adults are not allowed to go on with their child (although may rescue them if needed!). The party room can accommodate children with additional needs and wheelchair access can be created at party tables, or chairs with sides provided. Similarly, in the café area, some tables will accommodate a wheelchair although space may be an issue. It may be necessary to call in advance to check how busy the centre is. There are no blue badge parking bays so parking can be difficult. The exit from the soft play leads directly onto the car park. No discount at the time of visit for children with disabilities.

Rainbow Room

Meadowbank Sports Centre
139 London Road
EH7 6AE
0131 661 5351
info.msc@edinburghleisure.co.uk
www.edinburghleisure.co.uk
Soft play room with climbing frames and softballs. Pretty basic and limited for under 2s. Space for several pushchairs and wheelchairs to be parked and for children to leave their coats and shoes. Entrance is by security code provided at reception. Minimum height for children is 75cm – maximum is 150cm. Available for party hire and group bookings - worth calling in advance to make sure it is not booked for a private party when you plan to visit.

Spacious soft play with a soft area for less mobile children to play, complete with soft shapes and some balls. Within the actual framework, lots of levels for children to explore and a large ball pool at bottom of slide. Children need to climb out of ball pool which may be difficult for children with mobility issues. Parents can sit nearby to supervise and could go inside to assist children who were 'stuck'. Some tables and chairs (but no high chairs) where you could sit for a snack/drink (vending machines available). Nappy changing available in small room accessed via soft play room. 11 parent and child spaces in the car park and 8 disabled blue badge spaces.

Make your business stand out from the rest

Place an advert in the next edition of EFUF

Visit the buiness section of our website for more information

or email business@efuf.co.uk

www.efuf.co.uk

Noah's Ark

Glendevon Farm
Weston Edge
Perth
PH1 1QE
01738 445568
A rather unprepossessing grey building in an industrial estate, but if you are near Perth, particularly on a rainy day, then do persevere. Inside is an excellent soft play with separate areas for the under 3s, under 5s and 5–12s. If this isn't enough excitement they also offer go karting, bowling and a ceramic pottery decorating experience.
The café provides inexpensive food, with burgers sourced from a local butchers and free papers are provided to read whilst your young whiz down vertical slides and chutes to their hearts content.

2 disabled spaces. Reduced entry fee for children with disabilities. There are three different areas for different age groups. The one for the under 3s may be enjoyed by children with limited mobility or children enjoying a less busy area. Adults can accompany and there is plenty of room and soft shapes to support sitting or to provide stimulation for crawling and limited climbing. The under 5s area offers more opportunity for the development of crawling and climbing skills – with a child who is able to crawl independently potentially able to access all the area without assistance. If assistance is needed, adults are allowed to accompany. The area for older children offers excitement and stimulation for more able-bodied children and may be useful for families visiting with older siblings. The café area is large, with seating beside the under 3s area, which may be useful for parents needing to keep an eye. Door handles are high to prevent young children escaping and doors have finger-safe hinges. Toilet for the disabled.
The karting may suit a child with sitting ability but the seats are deep and there is a seatbelt so a child with balance difficulties should still be able to ride. If you need help to get to the cart – do ask. The staff are very friendly and willing to help.

EAST

Jelly Club
Peffermill Road
EH15 5UY
0131 652 0212
www.jellyclub.co.uk

♿ No blue badge parking bays, although the car park is fairly large. Significant reduction on entry fee for children with disabilities. Different areas - the area for younger children is large with plenty to occupy crawling or walking children, and plenty of soft shapes that may be suitable for children needing sitting support. The tables next to this area may be useful for keeping an eye while allowing some independence. The two slides in this area are accessible by ledges that may be crawled up or accessed by a child with limited climbing ability (adult assistance is possible). The area for older children has a tube slide that may be accessible to a crawling child and may allow for some independence (and if necessary an adult can easily access to assist). The remaining slides have difficult access to them (rope ladders, steep inclines) and adults may not be able to accompany due to space restrictions. During quiet times, the bouncy castles may be suitable, although adults are discouraged from going on. Floor area between the different play zones may be dirty and unsuitable for a crawling child. Toilet for the disabled provided. The increased security at the entry/exit doors may suit a child prone to wandering off!

Portobello Indoor Bowls and Leisure Centre
20 Westbank Street
EH15 1DR
0131 669 0878 or 669 9457
www.edinburghleisure.co.uk

Welcoming and friendly staff give the centre a pleasant atmosphere. The softplay is a good sized room aimed at 0-5yrs. The room is a good size to hire for parties (accommodating twenty people). The centre also host numerous classes for babies and toddlers. Good access, nappy changing facilities and a cafe make this a great place to visit.

Clambers
21 Dalkeith Road
EH16 5BB
0131 667 7211
www.edinburghleisure.co.uk

Clambers closed in 2009 for the refurbishment of the Royal Commonwealth Pool. It will reopen in 2011 with a brand new layout.

Jamboree
Musselburgh Sports Centre
Newbigging
0131 653 6367

Multi level soft adventure play area. Very child friendly, secure and safe, padded for extra safety with bish bash men, an ideal place to introduce toddlers to soft play. The accompanying adult must remain in the soft play area at all times, but the centre does operate a crèche facility. Check for availability and times. Area can be hired for parties. Centre staff are friendly and helpful. Children must be over 4 mths but under 9yrs.

Happy Castle
Bankmill
Valleyfield Road
Penicuik
EH26 8LW
01968 675638

The Happy Castle is an alternative soft play area out with Edinburgh. On entering the building it looks very run down. The main play area is poorly lit and dark and is definitely showing that it is several years old. It also could be cleaner.

There are two sections – an under 3s which has a small climbing area and ball pool. The second section is for everyone else, including adults. This soft play reaches to the top of the roof and therefore provides great climbing opportunities. Included in this section are slides for all ages, ball pits and flying fox.

There are tables in the middle of the soft play, ideal for watching and enjoying a coffee. Like all soft plays this is particularly busy on wet days.

This soft play centre provides good stimulation for a child with reasonable ability to climb and for older/more able bodied children. The easiest entry point to the main area is by climbing a series of ledges, about half a metre high each. This may pose a good challenge for a child improving climbing skills, but may be a barrier to a child not able to pull him/herself to stand or climb. An adult must accompany children with special needs; adults are allowed in all areas. Slides are located at the upper level of the equipment and are large enough for an adult to accompany a child (and quite good fun!). In most areas, an adult may be able to assist a child with climbing due to the design. There is one blue badge bay and no discount for children with disabilities.

WEST

Monkey Bizness

Unit 6 Fountain Park
Dundee Street
EH11 1AF
0131 257 4412
edinburgh@monkey-bizness.co.uk
www.monkey-bizness.co.uk/edinburgh

Recently opened Edinburgh branch. Plenty of play areas to choose from with something for all ages (adults are encouraged to try out the frame too!). Offers opportunities to climb, go karts, ball cannons, ball pit, slides and more. Parents/carers are responsible for supervising children and ensuring the centre's 'code of play' is adhered to. We didn't see many staff during our visit - best to keep an eye on your little ones, particularly near the door area, if they are liable to try and escape. Separate toddler area, but we would advise avoiding peak times with under 5s where possible. Cafe provides a varied menu to choose from, though at busy times you may find it hard to find a table and food can take a while to appear if they are catering for parties. Party rooms and packages available.

Timetwisters

Bankhead Drive
Sighthill
EH11 4ES
0131 308 2464
www.timetwisters.co.uk

This is a large soft play space with an egyptian theme running throughout. It can be quite tricky to find, look out for the Topps Tiles sign. It has two play areas with tables and chairs situated between the two areas. There is no ball pit.

Over 3s may find the small play area too basic and the large frame to big too play on. There is an indoor football pitch which is useful when children become bored of the soft play. There is a toy cube on the floor near the under 3s play area with a bead frame and other activities on the sides. The under 3s play area has a slide and a tunnel and pieces of soft play shapes on the floor. The large play frame has multiple levels with various slides and a shooting gallery.

Food is very healthy with large portions and it's homemade so can accommodate food allergies. There is no separate café area so you can continue to supervise your children whilst you eat/have coffee at your table. There is additional seating upstairs, generally suited to those with older children who can play without supervision, although there is a view of and entry/exit points to the large frame. There are also two party rooms upstairs with thrones for the birthday child to sit on. There is no lift. Parties for disabled children can be accommodated at ground floor level.

There are no highchairs, but booster seats which are provided on request. I wouldn't recommend these for children who are less than 6mths old and you need to keep an eye on them to ensure that they don't fall sideways.

Egyptian themed soft play. Separate area for toddlers under 3, rest of the area is aimed at 4+ yrs.. Entry is by a wide ramp, there is a party room with disabled access and toilets for disabled. One blue badge space in car park.

Tumbles

Craiglockhart Sports Centre
177 Colinton Road
EH14 1BZ
0131 444 1969
www.edinburghleisure.co.uk

The soft play is based in the Tennis Centre and not the Leisure Centre (worth remembering if walking from the car park in the rain!). Younger children will love this self contained soft play as it is smaller in size and isn't too daunting. It's restricted to under 6s making it a gentler experience than some soft play facilities. The cafe seats are round the corner, so you may find yourself taking a seat on a comfy bean bag to ensure you can keep an eye on your children. Some supervised sessions during the week to allow parents/carers to attend classes at the centre.

The cafe offers a good selection of well priced options and a healthy children's lunch box. If it's busy you may need to share a table. Birthday celebrations catered for.

Scrambles at EICA

South Platt Hill
Newbridge
EH28 8AA
0131 333 6333
www.edinburghleisure.co.uk

Visiting the Ratho Climbing Centre can be an adventure in itself for the under 5s who love to press their noses against the glass fishbowl and watch the climbers scale the walls. If you and your children can drag yourself away from this entertainment Scrambles offers three separate areas for 0–18 mths, 18mths– 4yrs and 4– 9yrs, additionally there is a small wall with child friendly hand holds, so they can try climbing for themselves.

All the tables have a good view of the soft play which is a great bonus if your child likes to be able to see their parent/carer. There is a small café offering light refreshments, but the upstairs main café has a wider selection of soup and sandwiches.

Scrambles also offers birthday parties and it is worth ringing at weekends to ensure that your visit does not coincide as you may have to wait to go in.

Space Bugs

Linlithgow Leisure Centre
Kettlestoun Mains Road
Linlithgow
01506 775440

Drive through town until you come to the crossroads at Linlithgow Bridge. Take the left and continue along Mill Rd (B8029). Cross over at the roundabout.

A fun soft play area on two levels. Plenty of room to run about, slide, or swing on the ball-slide. Dark area, rollers and crawl tubes. Separate area for under 3s, with large soft shapes and ball-pit. When quiet adults can use structure which makes it more fun for all the family. Parental supervision required. Centre runs supervised sessions, ring for current timetable.

If you visit Linlithgow Palace, why not end the day with some soft play? Also good if you go to Beecraigs and it starts raining.

Tumble Zone

5c Grange Road
Houstoun Industrial Estate
Livingston
EH54 5DE
01506 444200
www.tumblezone.co.uk

Take Jct 3 off M8. Exit next slip road off the A899, at the roundabout take the first exit onto Houstoun Rd. Turn right into Grange Rd. Tumble Zone is situated on the left with parking to the front and rear

A fantastic trip for toddlers offering plenty of variety and space to burn of that excess energy ! Well worth a visit. Gigantic adventure centre with separate baby, toddler and over 4s areas. Parents are not allowed on the structures, but children can be easily watched. Well supervised by staff.

Mini go kart circuit and mini 5 a side football pitch. Plenty of seating available and café with a selection of meals, snacks and drinks. Available for party hire. The size of the centre makes it very easy for pushchairs and wheelchairs. Child friendly toilets with nappy changing facilities.

Edinburgh City Libraries welcome under fives!

Children love books and stories. We offer board and picture books, toys, story CDs, storytimes and rhymetimes. Babies and children are welcome at any age and it's all free!

Visit the library! It's fun!

LIBRARIES

www.edinburgh.gov.uk/libraries
Libraries welcome under 5s! In fact, libraries welcome everyone! There is lots for you and your child to enjoy at the library: a huge selection of books, books on CD, toys, games, magazines, comics, music CDs, computers with the internet as well as organised activities and events.

How to join
It's free to join and babies and children are welcome to join at any age. Just fill out a membership form for your child and they will be given their own library card on which they can borrow 12 items for up to 3 weeks. A welcome letter is sent to parents or carers describing the library service and asking carers to confirm the date of birth of under 16s; this is needed in case under 16s wish to borrow a video or DVD as these are age restricted.

It's also easy for adults to join. To get your library card just come along to any of our libraries, give us a few details: name, title, date of birth, address, phone number - and that's it! If you would like to borrow audiobooks, cds or dvds you will need to provide one form of proof of name and address, for example a recent utility bill. You can also join online by going to the 'How To Join' section at www.edinburgh.gov.uk/libraries and using the membership application form. Please email your completed form to eclis@edinburgh.gov.uk and your membership card will be sent to you by post.

Parents/careres are responsible for books borrowed on their child's card, and for returning them on time. There are no fines on overdue books borrowed on children's cards and it is free to reserve books. There are no charges for damage to board and picture books. Items borrowed can be returned to any Edinburgh City library.

Visit our website for updates:
www.efuf.co.uk

Books – and much more!
All libraries have designated children's areas. They all have kinderboxes with a great range of interactive fun board books, picture books and story books for babies and toddlers. There is also a wide selection of books on CD, cartoons, poetry books, books for beginner readers, books on sensitive topics, chapter books, stories for older children, information books and reference books which are great for homework. Through your library you have access to dual language picture books and books in large print. In all libraries children's books are arranged by subject, interest and reading level. Shelves are clearly marked and there is a leaflet available explaining the system. Staff are on hand to help.

Check out library services for under 5s at:
www.edinburgh.gov.uk/libraries/underfives

Children's Multilingual Picture Book Collections
Dual-language picture books are available in Arabic, Bengali, Chinese, Farsi, French, German, Gujarati, Hindi, Italian, Japanese, Polish, Portugese, Punjabi, Spanish, Turkish and Urdu. Single language books are available in Arabic, Bengali, Chinese, French, Gaelic, Japanese, Polish and Urdu. The Ethnic Services Library at McDonald Road Library has extensive collections. Smaller collections are available at some community libraries. For further information and for details of bilingual rhymetimes contact Ethnic Services on 242 8103.

Computers, internet and the council website
All libraries have computers with free internet access and word processing and you can call in advance to book time on them. There are PCs dedicated for children's use in all libraries. Most libraries have PS2s and a selection of games for children to use.

Local information
Library notice boards can be a great source of both local and general information and are well worth keeping an eye on. Some libraries keep a diary of forthcoming local events or folders with local information.

Access and Toilets

Standards of access vary; new and refurbished libraries usually have good all-round facilities. Every library, apart from the Music Library and Fine Art Library, has wheelchair access, but not all libraries have toilets for the disabled and a few – notably the Central Children's Library – do not have public toilet facilities at all. The library staff will allow use of staff toilets if possible. Many have nappy changing facilities.

Library Opening Hours

Full-time libraries

Central, Blackhall, Corstorphine, Leith, Morningside, Muirhouse, Newington, Oxgangs, Piershill, Portobello, Wester Hailes:
Mon, Tue, Wed, Thu: 10.00-20.00: Fri: 10.00-17.00: Sat: 9.00-13.00

Part-time libraries

Balerno, Balgreen, Central Children's, Colinton, Craigmillar, Currie, Fountainbridge, Gilmerton, Granton, Kirkliston, McDonald Rd, Moredun, Ratho, Sighthill, South Queensferry, Stockbridge :
Mon, Wed: 13.00-20.00: Tue, Thu, Fri: 10.00-17.00: Sat: 9.00-13.00

Libraries open all day Saturday and Sunday afternoons

McDonald Road, Muirhouse, Newington, Oxgangs, Portobello,Wester Hailes:
Sat: 9.00-17.00, Sun: 13.00-17.00.

Storytimes and Bookbug sessions

Every library in Edinburgh runs Bookbug sessions and many run storytimes for under 5s - check website for details. Bookbug sessions, aimed at 0-3 yrs and their parents/carers, incorporate action songs and rhymes, listening to stories and looking at books. They're great fun!

Bookbug

eclis@edinburgh.gov.uk
www.edinburgh.gov.uk/libraries

Bookbug (previously Bookstart) works with Health Visitors and Early Years services to put books into the hands of babies and their families across the city. Free Bookbug packs are gifted to children at 6 wks, 18 mths, 3 yrs, and in Primary One.

Bookbug sessions with rhymes and songs are offered in libraries and outreach venues across the city. Babies can also take part in Bookbug's Library Challenge. A stamp will be added to the Bookbug collector card at every visit, with children collecting a colourful certificate after 4 visits.

Bookbug in Edinburgh works closely with partner:
Craigmillar Books for Babies
Castlebrae Community High School
2A Greendykes Road
EH16 4DP
0131 621 2621
info@craigmillarbooksforbabies.org.uk
www.craigmillarbooksforbabies.org.uk

CENTRAL

Edinburgh Central Library

George IV Bridge
EH1 1EG
0131 242 8000

Comprehensive public reference and information services, major collections of local history material, a large stock of adult fiction and non-fiction, and the largest local collection of books about children e.g. parenting, play, education, problems etc. Books for young children are available to borrow from kinderboxes in the general lending department. Extensive Music, Fine Art and Scottish collections. A Kurzweil reading machine, media aids and PC access software for people with disabilities are available in the Resource Centre (Tel: 242 8135).
Toilets in basement, access by lift with stairs to negotiate. If the toilets are not open, a notice is posted at the top of the stairs.

Central Children's Library
George IV Bridge
EH1 1EG
0131 242 8027
Situated next door to the Central Library. Level access. Compact library. If your child needs the toilet you have to leave the building and use the facilities next door in the Central Library.

Stockbridge Library
Hamilton Place
EH3 5BA
0131 529 5665
stockbridge.library@edinburgh.gov.uk
Access by ramped entrance. Community room available for hire. Photocopier and fax. Learning Centre. Toilet and Nappy change unit.

NORTH

Blackhall Library
56 Hillhouse Road
EH4 5EG
0131 529 5595
blackhall.library@edinburgh.gov.uk
Ramp access and car park. The children's section is roomy. 'Family Collection' of books to support parents and carers. Photocopier and fax. PS2. Out of hours book return letterbox so you can return library items even when library is closed. Self-issue terminals so you don't have to wait in a queue! Toilet facilities for disabled. Nappy change unit.

Muirhouse Library
15 Pennywell Court
EH4 4TZ
0131 529 5528
muirhouse.library@edinburgh.gov.uk
Library with friendly staff and a good selection of books, CDs, and DVDs for all ages. Dedicated "Children's Zone" with a kitchen, sit-in car, and other toys to help keep children occupied. The Bookbug programme runs free sessions. Songs are led by Bookbug staff for the first ½ hour, then coffee/tea is available for parents/carers, while children can play with toys (provided) or take part in colouring or another activity. Male/female toilets, and nappy changing facilities on site. At times, tissue and running water/soap not available, so it's a good idea to have some wipes/hand gel packed in your bag. The North Edinburgh Arts Centre is located just behind the library, with a Café if you are looking for lunch or a snack after your visit. Community room, computers, learning centre, photocopier and fax all available.

Granton Library
Wardieburn Terrace
EH5 1DD
0131 529 5630
granton.library@edinburgh.gov.uk
Located in a residential area close to Granton Primary School. Library doesn't look the best from the outside but inside has a good selection of books, audio tapes/books, DVD's, magazines, and papers. There is **FREE** PC/internet access at several computers. Friendly and helpful staff. On street **FREE** parking. Bookbug essions with snacks for children and tea/coffee/biscuits for adults afterwards. Well run, interactive session with traditional and new nursery rhymes aimed at 0-3 yrs, usually a gate which sections off one half of the library to stop toddlers getting out but this quite often gets broken and takes a longtime to get fixed. Automatic door switched off during Bookbug sessions to stop toddlers escaping.

Anything out of date?
Let us know -
info@efuf.co.uk

Leith Library
28-30 Ferry Road
EH6 4AE
0131 529 5516
leith.library@edinburgh.gov.uk
Libraries are a fantastic FREE place for local parents to gather and make the most of the resources on offer. Leith has a dedicated 'Babies Corner' and Bookbug sessions - very popular so be early to get a good seat! There are no public toilets available although staff will kindly allow potty training children to use their facilities. Children who join the library recieve a certificate for every 4 times they borrow, plus a FREE book while stocks last!

McDonald Road Library
2 McDonald Road
EH7 4LU
0131 529 5636
mcdonald.library@edinburgh.gov.uk
Large and bright library with a good children's area with a wide selection of books and some toys. Books on tape, large print, cds and dvds and books and newspapers in different languages available. Ramp access and lift to all floors with an accessible toilet and nappy changing facilities. Computers available for games and internet access.

South Queensferry Library
9 Shore Road
EH30 9RD
0131 529 5576
southqueensferry.library@edinburgh. gov.uk
Excellent selection of books for under 5s. Play area with toys and games, and lots of seating for children. Staff very friendly and welcoming. Some reference books, e.g. latest copy of EFUF. Plans to use garden area at some point in the future. Bookbug sessions and plans to reinstate a Storytime session.

EAST

Piershill Library
30 Piersfield Terrace
EH8 7BQ
0131 529 5685
piershill.library@edinburgh.gov.uk
Friendly local library which holds Bookbug sessions for babies and toddlers and Story Time for older children. Lovely bright childrens area with seating for children and adults, a toy box and colouring table. Great selection of baby, toddler and childrens books and CDs. Level access and easy parking at the door, or in Morrisons carpark just behind. Toilet and nappy changing facilities at rear.

Portobello Library
14 Rosefield Avenue
EH15 1AU
0131 529 5558
portobello.library@edinburgh.gov.uk
The library is a good size with friendly, helpful staff. Fantastic and very popular Bookbug for babies and pre-school children, which is free. Turn up early to ensure entry. Pushchairs left on ground floor.

Craigmillar Library
7 Niddrie Marischal Gardens
EH16 4LX
0131 529 5597
craigmillar.library@edinburgh.gov.uk
Craigmillar Library is very welcoming with an enclosed picket fenced area especially suited for the under 3s. This brightly coloured area has 'grass' flooring, cushions, bean bags, soft toys and child sized furniture. Children can choose their books from the well stocked child height boxes. There is a Bookbug session for babies to 3 yrs.

Gilmerton Library
13 Newtoft Street
EH17 8RG
0131 529 5628
gilmerton.library@edinburgh.gov.uk
Ramp access and car park at rear of the building. Small but bright library. PS2. Community Room and computer centre. Photocopier and fax. Toilets. Nappy change unit.

Moredun Library
92 Moredun Park Road
EH17 7HL
0131 529 5652
moredun.library@edinburgh.gov.uk
Ramp access. Photocopier and fax. PS2. Toilets with nappy change unit. Disabled access. Car park.

SOUTH

Newington Library
17-21 Fountainhall Road
EH9 2LN
0131 529 5536
newington.library@edinburgh.gov.uk
Friendly, welcoming atmosphere in the library, with a well-stocked children's section. Free internet access available

Morningside Library
184 Morningside Road
EH10 4PU
0131 529 5654
morningside.library@edinburgh.gov.uk
The children's section is large and separate from the rest of the library so there is no pressure for extreme quiet. Great selection of books; story cds and tapes; colour-ins and toys to play with during the visit. PS2, PCs, Photocopier and Fax. There are currently no toilet facilities. Storytime and Bookbug sessions are held for under 5s.

WEST

Balgreen Library
173 Balgreen Road
EH11 3AT
0131 529 5585
balgreen.library@edinburgh.gov.uk
The library is small but friendly. There are no toilet facilities. There are a few toys in one corner along with a children's table to sit at. There is also another table with crayons and colouring in sheets. Bookbug sessions held. There are low bookholders holding the children's books so they are easily accessible to the children, one with books for the very young, up to around 2 yrs and another with books for slightly older children. Books for over 5s can be found on the shelves around the walls.

Fountainbridge Library
137 Dundee Street
EH11 1BG
0131 529 5616
fountainbridge.library@edinburgh.gov.uk
Murdoch Terrace entrance has ramp access. PS2. Community Room available. Photocopier and fax. Toilets with disabled access. Nappy change unit.

Sighthill Library
6 Sighthill Wynd
EH11 4BL
0131 529 5569
sighthill.library@edinburgh.gov.uk
Level access and automatic doors. Car park. Parent's collection of books, leaflets and magazines. Photocopier and fax. Two PS2s. Learning Centre. Toilets. Nappy change unit. Bookbug Sighthill project based at the library running Bookbug sessions and other events for children aged 0-3yrs and their parents and carers. Visit for more information or call the library.

Corstorphine Library
12 Kirk Loan
EH12 7HD
0131 529 5506
corstorphine.library@edinburgh.gov.uk
Children's section is roomy and includes a selection of toys to play with during visit. Ramp access, automatic doors. Photocopier, fax and PS2, internet access. Staff toilet made available for use. Bookbug sessions held.

Colinton Library
14 Thorburn Road
EH13 0BQ
0131 529 5603
colinton.library@edinburgh.gov.uk
The library provides a warm welcome to all ages and a well-stocked children's book section. Bookbug and Story Time (3-5yrs) sessions held. Highlights of our visits so far were a very crowded Bookbug in July (so many parents delighted to find that some activities still on during the long summer holidays!) and watching librarian Heather let my son date-stamp his own books.

Mobile Library Service
Service based at:
Access Services HQ
343 Oxgangs Road
EH13 9LT
0131 529 5683
access services@edinburgh.gov.uk
The Mobile Library Service visits about 60 locations in the Edinburgh area ranging from small villages such as Dalmeny, to large urban locations such as Wester Hailes. Other stops include East Craigs, Inch, Barnton, Juniper Green, Buckstone, Cramond, Clermiston, Prestonfield, Liberton and Gracemount. For a full list of stops contact Access Services (details above). A wide variety of books are available, including an ever-changing selection of children's books. All mobiles have stairlifts for easier access.

Oxgangs Library
343 Oxgangs Road
EH13 9LY
0131 529 5549
oxgangs.library@edinburgh.gov.uk
Level access. Community room with kitchen facilities available. Photocopier and fax. PS2. Toilets with disabled access. Nappy changing facilities.

Wester Hailes Library
1 West Side Plaza
EH14 2FT
0131 529 5667
westerhailes.library@edinburgh.gov.uk
Access with double pushchair. Community room available on first floor (lift access). Youth Library and Learning Centre. Photocopier and fax. Toilets with nappy change unit. Bookbug Wester Hailes based at the library running Bookbug sessions and other events for children 0-3yrs and their parents/carers. Visit for more information or call the library.

Currie Library
210 Lanark Road West
EH14 5NN
0131 529 5609
currie.library@edinburgh.gov.uk
Car park and access with double pushchair. Photocopier and fax, PS2. Toilet facilities. Nappy change unit.

Balerno Library
1 Main Street
EH14 7EQ
0131 529 5500
balerno.library@edinburgh.gov.uk
Ramp access. Small library, part of primary school annexe. PS2. Photocopier and fax. No public toilet.

Ratho Library
6 School Wynd
EH28 8TT
0131 333 5297
ratho.library@edinburgh.gov.uk
Access with single pushchair. Car park. Photocopier and fax. PS2. Toilet facilities and nappy change facilities.

Kirkliston Library
16 Station Road
EH29 9BE
0131 529 5510
kirkliston.library@edinburgh.gov.uk
Kirkliston Library is a modern library with excellent facilities for young children. There is a play area with plenty of toys and tables and chairs for little ones as well as a good selection of books for all ages. Nappy changing facilities in the toilets and baby music and story groups held.

Listening Books
www.listening-books.org.uk
Listening Books is a charity that provides a postal audio book library service to anyone who has an illness or disability that makes it impossible or difficult to hold a book, turn its pages, or read in the usual way. They provide audio books for both leisure and learning - providing important support for the National Curriculum at Key Stages 2, 3, 4 and A-level, as well as a large adult library. The service caters for those with physical disabilities, visual impairment and specific learning difficulties, including dyslexia, for which reading print is frustrating, even impossible. Their catalogues include many titles for children of primary 1 age that may be suitable for slightly younger children.

TOY LIBRARIES

As their name suggests, toy libraries are centres which lend toys to families, carers, and also to children with special needs. Most of them are run as drop-in centres, and as such guidance can be given on the toys best suited to your child.
There is generally a small joining fee, and depending on the centre, toys can be borrowed for little or no charge. It is wise to check with each individual project.
Opening times tend to miorror school terms, but some do stay open during the holidays.

The main contact is:

Playmatters
National Association of Toy and Leisure Libraries
0131 664 2746
natll.scotland@playmatters.co.uk
www.playmatters.co.uk

Contact the local centres for details of opening times. Services are inclusive of everyone, professionals, children and parents.

Casselbank Kids Toy Library
South Leith Baptist Church
5 Casselbank Street
EH6 5HA
0131 665 6682
07879 284375

Duncan Place Toy Library
Duncan Place Resource Centre
4 Duncan Place
EH6 8HW
0131 554 1509

Gorgie Dalry Toy Library
St Martin's Church
323 Dalry Road
EH11 2JG
0131 346 1179
www.gdtoylibrary.org.uk

Where would you suggest?
Tell us -
ed@efuf.co.uk

Oxgangs Toy Library
Oxgangs Surestart Project
1Firhill Loan
EH13 9EJ
0131 441 7318

Play Plus Toy Library
Inch Community Centre
225 Gilmerton Road
EH16 5UF
0131 664 2746

Toy Box Toy Library
Portobello Community Library
Rosefield Avenue
EH15 1AU
0131 529 5558

SPECIAL NEEDS TOY LIBRARIES

Barrie House Toy Library
Barrie House
Canaan Lane
EH10 4FG
0131 446 3120
A division of the Royal Blind School and as such is primarily inteneded for parents of children who attend the playgroup there, but the library welcomes other enquiries on behalf of children with visual impairment.

SPLAT Toy Library
Keycomm Resource Centre
1c Pennywell Road
EH4 4PH
0131 311 7130
For children from City of Edinburgh with special needs. Will also adapt families' toys.

FESTIVALS & EVENTS

There are some events which you only have one chance a year to enjoy. Some have a long history, others are more recently established events; some can provide a whole day's worth of entertainment, others can help pass a pleasant hour or so.
For more information the following websites may prove helpful:
www.edinburgh.org
www.edinburgh-festivals.com
www.edinburghguide.com

Numerous venues listed as 'Places To Go' have an annual calendar of events. Keep an eye out for adverts, sign up for newsletters or check individual websites for details of special themed events for Easter, Summer, Halloween and Christmas etc.

JANUARY-MARCH

The start of the year can be a bit of an anti-climax: Christmas is over, the lights are down in the city and the outlook and the weather can seem a bit bleak. However, there are events and attractions to go and see...

Pantomimes and Plays
The panto season extends through the Winter season. If you are thinking about going to one, why not wait until after Christmas, otherwise the outing might just become part of the exciting blur leading up to Santa's visit. While venues such as the King's Theatre and the Playhouse stage traditional pantos, other theatres such as the Royal Lyceum, North Edinburgh Arts Centre, Theatre Workshop and the Netherbow have offered more contemporary, or certainly less traditional shows, in recent years.
Although many of the pantos have famous names heading the bill, they tend to appeal to an older audience and are far too long for many under 5s. Plus remember that the jokes tend to become more adult in the evening performances!
Probably more suitable for under 5s are shows such as those from The Singing Kettle (www. singingkettle.com).

Snowdrop Day

Dalmeny House
South Queensferry
EH30 9TQ
0131 331 1888
www.dalmeny.co.uk

Still in private ownership, Dalmeny house is only open for 3 afternoons a week in July and August. However, the gardens are opened specially on a Sun during Feb/Mar for 'Snowdrop Day' The exact date depends on when the snowdrops come out! Impressive display on Mons Hill. Backpacks, wellies and warm socks recommended. Refreshments available in the tearoom.

This is a charity event and all funds raised benefit St Columba's Hospice, The Queen's Nursing Institute of Scotland and The Garden Fund of the National Trust for Scotland. Look online for current information.

Easter Event

Historic Scotland Ranger Service
Holyrood Park Education Centre
1 Queen's Drive
EH8 8HG
0131 652 8150
www.historic-scotland.gov.uk/index/
rangerservice/rsevents.htm

Organised Easter Event within the bounds of Holyrood Park. Events change annually so please check the website or info boards within the park. There are usually events specially suitable for under 5s, such as teddy bears picnics.

The Puppet Animation Festival

www.puppetanimation.org

From mid March. Various venues throughout Edinburgh and the UK each year.

APRIL-MAY

Parents Like Us

Leith Primary School
St Andrews Place
EH6 7EG
0131 553 2152
info@parentslikeus.co.uk
www.parentslikeus.co.uk

This 3-day festival, held on Leith Links, is aimed at parents and carers with under 5s and has family shows, activities, storytelling, interactive demos, live music, games, products and information. Admission to the main arena is free - as is almost half of everything on offer throughout the weekend. Also does reduced-rate therapies, fairground rides and a wide variety of child-friendly food. Very popular, so book early. Next PLU festival will be held in May 2012. Phone/email for a free brochure or see the website for more details.

Edinburgh International Science Festival

www.sciencefestival.co.uk

This is the largest science festival in the world. Various venues throughout the city, including the Science Play Centre at the Assembly Rooms. Programme becomes available at the beginning of March, with some fantastic events for 3+ yrs. Although the programme always looks as if there's loads for younger children there is much more for 5+ yrs, and while these children might have loads to do, you might find yourself (plus an under 5) pacing around waiting. Forewarned is forearmed! Pay on the door events may also charge additional fees for specific attractions. See programme for details of shows - pick one up from bookshops throughout the city or from The Hub. Best to book well in advance.

comic icons by Rosaly Johnston, Edinburgh

www.parentslikeus.co.uk

A 3-day festival for children aged 0-6 years (with lots for the 6-10s too)

science activities : storytelling : face painting : arts & crafts : music

therapies : information : sport : interactive demos : healthy food : products

puppet theatre : parent-with-child taster sessions : musical shows : creche

ADMISSION FREE

LEITH LINKS, EDINBURGH EH6 8BN - END OF MAY

for a free brochure tel. 0131 553 2152 or email
info@parentslikeus.co.uk or see www.parentslikeus.co.uk

Scottish charity no. 036841 Leith Primary School, St Andrews Place EH6 7EG

NCT Nearly New Sales
www.nctedinburgh.moonfruit.com
Edinburgh North and South Branches hold regular sales of nearly new nursery equipment, toys and children's and maternity clothes. A small percentage from the sale goes to NCT funds, the rest to the seller. First sale of the year is usually in Spring and sales are held approximately 8 times over the year, in different venues in the city. Check the website for dates and venues.

Balerno Children's Gala
www.balernogala.org
Usually held last week in May, the event starts with a procession of floats and the crowning of the Gala Queen. Many events held around the village during the week leading up to the gala day, including bike races for all ages and a pet show. There are children's races, bouncy castles, disco and puppet shows, as well as many stalls representing local clubs. Please check with organisers for specific details.

Imaginate
Scottish International Children's Festival
45a George Street
EH2 2HT
0131 225 8050
www.imaginate.org.uk
Held at various venues around the city for one week (Mon-Sun) May/June. This is Britain's largest performing arts festival for children. Weekend and afternoon shows with venues which are chosen for child friendliness.

Links Market
Town House
Kirkcaldy
www.fifedirect.org.uk (under 'Leisure')
Kirkcaldy Esplanade. This historic fair lasts 6 days, starting on Wed before 3rd Fri in April. Reputedly the longest street funfair in Europe - perhaps in the world, and April 2004 saw its 700th anniversary. Expect attractions along the lines of Medieval, craft or farmers' markets, stalls, a funfair, and falconry displays. Numerous rides and stalls for under 5s. Well worth the 40min drive across the Forth. Trains from Waverley and Haymarket.

JUNE - JULY

Tree Fest
Inverleith Park
www.edinburghtreefest.org.uk
Summer 'green' festival at Inverleith park, opposite the Botanics. Fantastic family event comprises many eco friendly stalls, workshops for kids, displays, demonstrations, axe throwing, tree climbing demo, renewable energy games, skate ramp, extreme mountain biking display, entertainment and refreshments.

Royal Highland Show
Royal Highland Centre
Ingliston
EH28 8NF
0131 335 6200
www.royalhighlandshow.org.uk
Thu-Sun 3rd week in June. Lothian Regional Transport usually operate a special bus service for the four days of the show. Picks up/drops off at the East Gate entrance to the showground.
There's a huge range of attractions available within the showground and the show does offer specific activities especially for children, although the very size of the place might be a little overwhelming for them at first. It makes no difference to children that the cattle, sheep, horses and poultry are the country's finest - it's fun just to see them up close! Each year there are unique attractions, so the show has an individual input every year. There's also usually an indoor activity centre, where children can try the likes of seed planting, willow weaving, etc.

Lifeboat Week
North Berwick Tourist Information
01620 892197
Take A198 to N Berwick. Regular bus and train services. North Berwick, last week in July. All kinds of fundraising - fantastic day if the weather is good!

Festival of Flight
Museum of Flight
East Fortune Airfield, East Lothian
01620 880308
www.nms.ac.uk/flight
Festival of Flight show in mid-July, with rare/ vintage planes, flypasts, air displays etc. Spectacular events for plane-mad under 5s and for anyone interested in aviation. Recent inclusions have included an evening event with flights choreographed to music. Peripheral attractions usually include stalls, bouncy castle and refreshments. A great day out but very noisy - the museum recommends ear plugs for young children. Only guide/hearing dogs permitted entry.

The Big Tent
Falkland
Fife
www.bigtentfestival.co.uk
Weekend environmental festival with lots to interest under 5s. Enjoy the whole festival and stay in the nearby campsite which has a dedicated family area. Music, children's activities, food village, stalls and more. Under 12s go free and further discounts are available if you go green

The Hopetoun Summer Fair
Hopetoun House
South Queensferry
0131 331 2451
www.hopetounhouse.com
Last Sun in Jul. The stately home's major fundraising event aimed at families, hosted on the house's West Lawn. Attractions include crafts marquees, environmental themed demonstrations and an arena programme.

Galas

Many local Galas that are held in the city and the Lothians take place in June. These may be the principal annual event that draws a community together and they are well worth supporting, although due to changing local demographics, insurance requirements, and funding difficulties many are finding it hard to continue. Keep an eye out for local advertising.

AUGUST - SEPTEMBER

August is Edinburgh's busiest month of the year, as people from all over the world descend upon the city. The city's population is said to double in August. There are breathtaking numbers of official events, and almost the same amount of street entertainers, although licensing is reducing their numbers year on year. Free snippets of acts can be seen on the main stage in Princes Street gardens during the day and evening. So hold on to your under 5s, turn up and enjoy yourselves!

♿ Due to the large number of venues throughout the city, it's not possible to list those that may be accessible or not. The advice would be to book directly with the venue if you can rather than through the box office (particularly for late bookings) – as booking with the box office may mean having to pick up tickets from a different location before heading to the venue. Check with the venue beforehand about access. Some buildings may have an alternative wheelchair access that you may need to arrange use of in advance. While most venues will have done their best to ensure accessibility, forward planning may still be needed. There may be a strict 'no pushchair' rule in small, busy venues so explanations may be necessary and staff should be able to accommodate your needs by allowing you to go into the show first with your child. This can be really helpful (and may even result in a sneaky detour backstage for ease of access!). If your child transfers out of a wheelchair for the duration of the show, the staff may store their chair in a safe place and should deliver it back to you at the end of the show.

Edinburgh Fringe
180 High Street
EH1 1QS
0131 226 0026
admin@edfringe.com
www.edfringe.com
Cited in the Guinness Book of Records as the largest Arts Festival in the world! A myriad of events, such as puppet shows, magic, drama and music at venues throughout the city. The programme lists events by age group. Programme free from the Fringe Office and other venues round the city - bookshops are the best bet for picking one up.

Fringe Sunday
as for Edinburgh Fringe above
Held in the Meadows. 2nd Sun of Festival. This is an exuberant melange of what's on offer throughout the Fringe: it's bright, loud and tends to reflect the essence of what the Fringe is about. It's also extremely busy, so hold on to small hands! There is normally a handy NCT feeding and changing tent.

Edinburgh International Book Festival
Scottish Book Centre
137 Dundee Street
Edinburgh
EH11 1BG
0131 228 5444 or 624 5050
admin@edbookfest.co.uk
www.edbookfest.co.uk
An annual event, held in an extensive tented village in Charlotte Square Gardens each August. Europe's largest book event and while the majority of sessions are aimed at children 3+ yrs, younger children may also enjoy them. (The programme indicates a recommended audience age.) There are workshops, storytelling from favourite authors and even visits by well loved characters. Tickets can be booked in advance or on the day, but popular events do sell out very quickly. Some events are free. Also has an excellent children's bookshop with a huge range of titles. The bookshop also incorporates an activity corner with chairs/tables for little ones and hands-on activities including art and crafts.
Cafes on site and an ice cream trike. Website has specific info about the Children's Book Festival. Nappy changing tent.

Edinburgh International Festival
The Hub
Castlehill
Royal Mile
EH1 2NE
0131 473 2015 or 473 2001
www.eif.co.uk
Held in venues throughout the city. The reputation has taken Edinburgh's name to all parts of the globe. Events include theatre, puppet shows, dance, opera and music - some shows may be suitable for under 5s, it all depends on the programme. Full programme available from end of March onwards. Check your nearest bookshop for a copy. What might be of more interest to youngsters are the Cavalcade and the Fireworks Concert.

Festival Cavalcade
Procession of floats, pipe bands, groups from Tattoo etc. on 1st Sun of Festival. Starts at Waterloo Pl at around 14.30, proceeds along Princes St and arrives at the Grassmarket at approx 16.00. Very popular, so arrive early - the castle rock provides a dramatic backdrop. For a seat at the concert performed by the Chamber Orchestra in Princes St Gardens book very early at The Hub (it's done by postal ballot and the closing date is in May). Small children may be wary of the loud noise and the crowds, which can be very heavy around Princes St, George St and The Mound. Quieter locations, still with great views, are around Bruntsfield Links and Inverleith Park - take a radio as at least one local station has coverage - so you can hear the music while watching.

Edinburgh Mela
info@edinburgh-mela.co.uk
www.edinburgh-mela.co.uk
The Edinburgh Mela is a long established weekend celebration of multiculturalism. Stalls, sculptures and artworks, music, puppet shows and performers. Children's workshops vary each year, but they are mostly best suited to older children. The fun is for all the family however and most events are free. Other events around the city in week running up to w/end. More information online.

Edinburgh Military Tattoo

Tattoo Office
32 Market Street
EH1 1QB
08707 555 118
edintattoo@edintattoo.co.uk
www.edinburgh-tattoo.co.uk
Held on Edinburgh Castle Esplanade during first 3 wks in Aug. Famous event including pipes, drums and massed bands, as well as international music, theatre and dance. There's a different theme each year. Performances start late, but there are additional early shows on Sat (book early as it's very popular). Quite an ambitious event to take under 5s to, due to the length of show and the bangs and crashes that can be part of the displays, but they go free if they sit on an adult's knee. Seating is hard and can be cold - take a cushion along! Tickets half-price at dress rehearsal. Blankets and refreshments advised.

Access for the disabled has been fully considered. for Mon to Fri performances a vehicle pass facility is operated so that drop-offs by taxi or private car can be made right up at the esplanade. If you need to bring your car, the nearest disabled parking is St Giles St at the top of the Mound (the disabled parking on Johnston Ter is restricted during Aug and it usually isn't possible to park there after 16.00). A carer will be free when accompanying a disabled adult or child. The North stand has wheelchair spaces with carer seats next to them on the ground level. Toilet for the disabled provided.

Festival Fireworks

These are impressive and usually very loud – so not for everyone! Parking for blue badge holders is available on Kings Stables Rd and this is the best entry point for wheelchair users (other entry points can be difficult to say the least). Remember that if you choose to sit at the east end of the gardens, it may be difficult to get back to the west end King's Stables Rd exit point once the fireworks finish. This entry/exit point tends to be closed earlier than the rest so you may find yourself without an easy exit (and a steep flight of stairs carrying a tired child, a wheelchair and the remnants of a picnic may not be what you fancy at midnight!).

Pleasance Kidzone

0131 556 6550
www.pleasance.co.uk/kids
The Pleasance Courtyard is a favourite venue for many during the festival. The great news is the offering just gets better - recent years have seen the inclusion of a wider variety of shows for under 5s, a child-friendly cafe, all manner of activities to keep little ones entertained between shows and a creche, so parents/carers can take in a show while their little ones are looked after.

Traquair Fair

Traquair House
Innerleithen
EH44 6PW
01896 830323
enquiries@traquair.co.uk
www.traquair.co.uk
1st w/end in Aug. Entertainment for all the family. Themed fairs have opened up a new dimension to this well-established event. Entertainment on offer includes the likes of theatre, live music, street entertainers, clowns, workshops, crafts etc. Children's entertainment includes well known children's musicians (Mr Boom, Jo Jingles etc), magicians, face painting, art workshops, a mini train and swing boats. Special entrance prices for this weekend, under 5s free and advance purchase discounts are available.

OCTOBER-NOVEMBER

Scottish International Storytelling Festival

43-45 High Street
EH1 1SR
0131 557 5724
info@scottishstorytellingcentre.co.uk
www.scottishstorytellingcentre.co.uk
Various venues throughout the Lothians, end Oct-mid Nov. A two week feast of storytelling from the oral tradition for all the family. Booking essential.

Fireworks Extravaganza
Meadowbank Sports Centre
139 London Road
EH7 6AE
Large well-organised display on 5 Nov, which is usually enjoyed by a capacity aduience. Popular with an older audience but may prove a bit overwhelming for under 5s. Smaller fireworks displays organised by local Scout or Round Table groups are advertised locally. See press for details.

DECEMBER

Edinburgh's Christmas
0131 529 4310
www.edinburghschristmas.com
End of Nov to 24th Dec. A varied programme of street theatre, a parade, shopping opportunities in the themed Christmas Market in Princes Street Gardens, and the switching on of the Christmas lights. Santa takes up residence in West Princes St Gardens where children have the opportunity to see reindeer, hop on board the Santa Express, hear magical storytellers, take part in fun workshops and post their letter to Santa. They may even get to meet the man himself! There's also a funfair in Princes St Gardens with children's rides, a huge Ferris wheel, and an ice-skating rink. See local press near the time for details.

HOGMANAY

Edinburgh's Hogmanay
hogmanay@edinburgh.gov.uk
www.edinburghshogmanay.org
Venues all over the city centre. 29th Dec-4th Jan. This event has become Britain's biggest (and busiest!) street party. Includes a carnival and funfair and other indoor and outdoor events, some ticketed and some free. There's also the torchlight procession, kids' Hogmanay, a food fair and live music. Events around Princes St and the High St on Hogmanay can be extremely crowded, require street passes (which are in limited number), and would probably prove too much for an under 5.

Sled Dogs
Holyrood Park
Takes place on the afternoon of 1 Jan. Wrap up warmly and take a trip to Holyrood Park where you can watch sled dog racing. The dogs themselves seem very attractive to young children. Maybe it's because of their eyes - many have blue or mis-matched ones. The races are for fun, and there's a relaxed, friendly atmosphere.

Ed's Crunch Busters.....

In the current economic climate we're trying harder than ever to make ends meet. With so much on offer for children you could easily find yourself panicking about how to afford all the things you want them to have. The good news is Edinburgh is well-blessed with an abundance of free/relatively inexpensive activities for children. Here are Ed's top tips for keeping your kids entertained and ensuring you still have some pennies in your purse (provided your little darlings haven't found it and tipped the contents into their piggy-banks!).

Enjoy the great outdoors - Edinburgh has plenty of beautiful outdoor spaces - parks, beaches and countryside are all within easy reach. Happiness is having plenty of space to run around, kick a ball, or ride a bike. It's great for us too when the effects of all that fresh air and exercise result in a good night's sleep. A real win-win.

Enjoy the great indoors - When the good old Scottish weather lets us down (as it does from time to time) never fear because Edinburgh is extremely well served for indoor activities for children that are free. Check out your local library for new stories to share, Bookbug or Story Time sessions; visit a museum or art gallery, or window shop in one of the big shopping centres.

Get to know local Mums - Visit a local toddler group for a great place to enjoy a cup of tea and a biscuit with fellow parents/carers. Your kids will get the chance to play with different toys and meet other childen. Meeting local families can also lead to play dates - an invaluable lifeline when your little ones are bored with your company and crying out for someone else to play with.

Recycle as much as possible - All kids outgrow toys and clothes faster than we can afford to buy new ones. Look around nearly new sales, local websites, school fairs and small ads in the local paper for bargains. Young children are happy enough with an item that is new to them, so don't feel guilty about not always buying brand new. You're also helping the environment - give yourself a pat on the back!

Invest in an all-weather survival kit - Buying a few small items to keep wee ones amused whatever the weather can really pay off in the longer term. Bats and balls, frisbees and kites, can all be bought for a few pounds and make a trip to the park so much more exciting. Invest in some indoor play items - play dough and cookie cutters; crayons and colouring books; card, paper, glue and stickers; and cake making ingredients. Cut out pictures from old magazines and glue onto coloured card for an instant masterpiece. An empty cardboard box can provide hours of fun.

Remember, less is more - With so much to do on offer in and around Edinburgh it's easy to sometimes get carried away and find that you're trying to do too much. Over-tiredness is one of the biggest causes of grumpy, uncooperative children and it can be wise to have a "chill out" day. Relax and allow the kids to lounge around in their pyjamas, watch a favourite DVD, draw pictures and read all those wonderful books you discovered at the library. Put a travel-rug on the floor and enjoy an indoor pic-nic (teddies welcome!). We all need some R&R, so enjoy it together.

Places To Eat

Places To Eat

Some new parents feel that once they have children, the type of bistro, café or restaurant they are welcome in alters. Out go the sleek bistros, in comes 'chips with everything'. Every style of eatery has its place, but you shouldn't feel pigeon-holed and the good news is that things are still improving in terms of dining out with children.

Everyone is different when it comes to the idea of a pleasant (or successful) meal out – we all have different tastes in food, different dietary requirements, different expectations, and so on. To reflect this, we have included a range of cafés, restaurants and bistros in Edinburgh and further afield, which have been tried and enjoyed by our researchers – because it's easy for an eatery to say they are child friendly, but it's quite another thing to turn up and put this to the test! We have tried to give a varied selection – from the 'family-friendly' restaurant chains, to independent bistros – and even some of Edinburgh's premier restaurants.

The experience of eating out with young children often lies somewhere between fun and enthusiastic chaos! Needs vary according to age and our researchers endeavoured to check all the various requirements. A newborn will be quite content in a car seat, but in a matter of months a high chair is a priority, then, before you know it, the location of the toilet is the first requisite for toilet training toddlers – the list goes on.

Some of the places listed may not be able to accommodate all ages of children, but where there has been a positive attitude towards dining out with a child, we have included them.

If you are choosing a meal for a special occasion you are always best to book first, mentioning that you will have children under 5yrs (and that you found the restaurant listed in this book). Check that the facilities you need will be available (high chairs may be reserved, for example). Several hotels and family restaurants have special promotions at the weekend, such as under 5s eating free or special children's entertainment, so it's worth checking.

Licensing

The Licensing (Scotland) Act 2005 came fully into force on 1 September 2009. Licensed premises must now decide whether to 'opt-in' to children accessing their premises. Licences are granted depending on whether the facilities are suitable, subject to appropriate hours and areas of access for children, and whether children are accompanied or not. It is now mandatory for nappy changing facilities to be accessible on licensed premises that allow access for young children. Venues should display their licence/children's certificate. You will also see some venues putting up signs confirming that children are not allowed on their premises as their licence does not allow for this.

Generally speaking children (under 14) are allowed in licensed premises where a children's certificate is displayed as long as they are accompanied by an adult (for the purposes of eating a meal on the premises). Children are usually permitted on premises until 8pm, but this can vary by venue and it is worth checking for any specific licensing restrictions in advance if you're planning an evening out.

You Tell Us

Please let us know of any other places where your family have enjoyed a meal, and of any good or bad experiences in places included here – management or staff changes can alter a venue for the better or for the worse. You can email us via our website www.efuf.co.uk.

It may be that you have a favourite restaurant or café that has always been great to visit because they are attentive and positive to families and individuals with young children, but they might not be in the book – not every venue we contacted wanted to be listed, for one reason or another.

We've listed the restaurants and cafés geographically - enjoy!

Key

£ - Good value
££ - Slightly pricier
£££ - For a special occasion

Veg - Sizable vegetarian menu

 - Accessible premises/facilities

EAT CENTRAL

Agua Restaurant
Apex City Hotel
61 Grassmarket
EH1 2JF
0845 365 0002
www.apexhotels.co.uk
Stylish restaurant with views over the Grassmarket. Children's portions taken from main menu. Nappy changing (F).

££

Always Sunday
170 High Street
Edinburgh
0131 622 0667
Airy, bright self-service café/restaurant with friendly and accommodating staff in a super location on the Royal Mile. Aims to give visitors 'that Sunday feeling' by offering a varied menu in relaxed surroundings. The wide choice ranges from full breakfasts to home baking via soups, salads and hot dishes and is particularly strong on healthy and vegetarian options. The imaginative fruit smoothies were a highlight on our visit. No separate children's menu but half portions available on request. Clear labelling for special diets. Space to park two or three pushchairs unfolded when quiet. Toilets in basement down a flight of steep stairs.

£   Veg

BHS Restaurant
64 Princes Street
Edinburgh
0131 226 2621
Large, spacious self-service café/restaurant. Level access from Rose St entrance but can also be accessed from main store via escalator to centre of eating area. Offers an extensive choice from snacks to lunches, including vegetarian dishes and carry-out items. Large children's menu and half portions available for under 12s. Children's meals come in decorative lunch/picnic bags. Baby food available, or will warm food brought in by parents. Toilets and feeding and nappy changing room (M&F) one floor up (3 flights of stairs).

£

Blue Moon
36 Broughton Street
Edinburgh
EH1 3SB
0131 556 2788
www.bluemooncafe.co.uk
Probably not the first place that springs to mind, but worth a visit. Staff are most welcoming and there is a highchair available. This is a particular favourite for breakfast/brunches. No changing facilities.

£   Veg

Cafe Camino
1 Little King Street
Edinburgh
EH1 3JR
0131 523 0102
info@cafecamino.co.uk
www.cafecamino.co.uk
This is the cafe and meeting space for St Mary's Cathedral (behind John Lewis, opposite The Omni). It's a fantastic place to have a coffee, sample the baking, or enjoy a light lunch. Kids lunchboxes now available too.

£   Veg

David Bann
56-58 St Mary's Street
Old Town
0131 556 5888
www.davidbann.com
Has to be the restaurant of choice in Edinburgh for vegetarian diners. What more can we say, except that staff are great and children are welcome.

££   Veg

Debenhams
4th Floor
The Castle View Restaurant
Princes Street
08445 616161
Table service restaurant with friendly staff and (as its name suggests!) stunning views of castle. Varied menu including hot food (with children's options cooked to order). Excellent range of cakes. Relaxed and spacious surroundings. Waitress service makes visiting a lot easier if you are on your own with youngsters.

££

Anything out of date?
Let us know -
info@efuf.co.uk

The Elephant House
21 George IV Bridge
Edinburgh
0131 220 5355
A useful café stop on the way into town from the Meadows. The Elephant House is a self-service friendly coffee house with a good range of coffees, baking and lunches. Staff happy are to accommodate children's tastes and will prepare a plain sandwich for a fussy eater! Wonderful display of all things 'elephant' to keep toddlers amused, especially the curtains. They also love the elephant seats at the front of the café. Magazines and children's books at the rear. Space may be limited at busy times.
Accessible toilets with nappy changing.

£   Veg

Empires
24 St Mary's Street
Old Town
0131 466 0100
www.empirescafe.co.uk
We enjoyed everything from the Turkish decor to the live music on our visit. The mezze platter allows you to choose a variety of dishes and are great for sharing (and for little ones keen on joining in). Our toddler loved helping to put sugar into the glasses of mint tea and he discovered a taste for the delicious Baklava on offer.

££   Veg

The Filling Station
235 High Street
Edinburgh
0131 226 2488
Children welcome in the eating area of this bar/restaurant. Car theme throughout, fun atmosphere, TV and video. American, Mexican and Italian food. Children's menu with the usual culprits – pasta options are good value but lack vegetables. Attentive, child friendly service, balloons and children's activity pack provided. Children will find the Filling Station a fun eating experience.

££

The Fruitmarket Gallery Cafe

Fruitmarket Gallery
45 Market Street
0131 226 1843
www.fruitmarket.co.uk
An arty venue, with great food, and where kids are welcome. Wonderfully varied menu from soup, to filled rolls and daily specials. The cakes and traybakes are particularly scrummy making this a great place for a coffee. The only downside is it can get busy, so best not to go at peak times.

£   Veg

Gennaro

64 Grassmarket
Edinburgh
0131 226 3706
Traditional, long-established Italian restaurant which welcomes families. Varied menu with children's portions available. No prams allowed, pushchairs must be folded. Seating outside continental style. If not too busy, waiters like to entertain children, allowing parents to enjoy their meal in peace. Carry-out food available.
Toilets and nappy changing (D) on the same level as the café.

££

St Giles Cathedral Café

High Street
Edinburgh
EH1 1RE
0131 225 5147
www.glenfinlas.com
Situated below St Giles Cathedral. The menu offers a great selection of local produce and home made fare. No specific children's menu, but a good selection of soft drinks, fresh presse and smoothies. The toilets are down four stone steps and there are two heavy doors. Although there is plenty of room there is no nappy changing facility. Disappointing that the facilities are not more child-friendly, however this would not stop me from going back if I was in that part of town.

£   Veg

Henderson's @ St John's

St John's Terrace
3 Lothian Road
Edinburgh
0131 229 0212
www.hendersonsofedinburgh.co.uk
A more recent venture for the well known Henderson's of Edinburgh. Great vegetarian food in a central location. The picnic tables outside are a perfect spot on sunnier days. Well worth the visit whether it's for a meal or just coffee and cake.

£   Veg

The Hub

Castlehill
Edinburgh
EH1 2NE
0131 473 2067
thehub@eif.co.uk
www.thehub-edinburgh.com
Relaxed friendly cafe at the top of the Royal Mile. Child friendly, spacious and uncluttered (with table service). There is a seperate children's menu and small portions of adult meals too. A good variety of sandwiches, home cooked soups and very nice cakes. Pushchairs can easily be taken in unfolded, the toilets and changing facilities are accessible and nearby. A stylish relaxed getaway, while remaining child-friendly.

£

The Lot

4-6 Grassmarket
Edinburgh
EH1 2JU
0131 225 9924
www.the-lot.co.uk
Quirky bistro inhabiting a converted church below Edinburgh Castle in the Grassmarket. Lovely and relaxed atmosphere that welcomes children. Delicious children's menu available. Great choice for a coffee, lunch, or an evening meal.

£   Veg

Metro Brasserie
Apex International Hotel
31-35 Grassmarket
Edinburgh
EH1 2HS
0845 365 0002
www.apexhotels.co.uk
Chic brasserie in the centre of the city. Open daily for lunch and dinner and snacks in the bar area. Children's portions taken from main menu. Changing facilities (M&F).

££

Monster Mash
20 Forrest Road
Edinburgh
EH1 2QN
0131 225 7069
www.monstermashcafe.co.uk
Relaxed restaurant serving British classics with sausage and mash the house speciality. A specials board announces the daily flavour options sourced from Crombies as well as the mash of the day. Other childhood favourites such as shepherd's pie and macaroni cheese can be found on the adult and children's menu alike. Puddings are similarly comforting and substantial. The staff are friendly and helpful. No nappy changing facilities.

£   Veg

Pani Solinska
73 Broughton Street
Edinburgh
EH1 3RJ
0131 557 6900
edinburgh@panisolinska.com
www.panisolinska.com
Polish restaurant with a family atmosphere, serving meat, sausage and cheese goodies from the deli counter and Polish home cooking, including pierogi dumplings, goulash, baked cheesecake and pancakes. Children enjoy the fairy lights and cheerful decor, and are offered a babycino of frothy milk.

££

The Piazza Open Air Cafe
West Princes Street Gardens
0131 225 5533
Handy spot to grab a coffee, soft drink, or snack near to the playground.
Large groups can be catered for by prior arrangement.

£

The Queen Anne Café
Edinburgh Castle
Castle Rock
Edinburgh
EH1 2NG
0131 225 9846
www.historic-scotland.gov.uk
Situated in Crown Square.
Emphasis on Scottish produce and recipes. Coffees and lighter snacks available all day. Organic baby food available free of charge.

££

Redcoat Café
(Edinburgh Castle - as above)
Next to the One O'clock Gun.
Range of main meals and carvery items. Offer an 'Edinburgh Castle' lunch box, as well as children's hot meals. Organic baby food available. There are toilets, but they are down two short flights of stairs.

££

Scottish Storytelling Centre Café

43-45 High Street
Edinburgh
EH1 1SR
0131 556 9579
reception@scottishstorytellingcentre.com
www.scottishstorytellingcentre.co.uk
This is a great place to come for coffee or lunch. Kids will have plenty of scope to entertain themselves in the big open space of the café/exhibition space. Crayons and paper are available for lots of drawing fun. The central feature is the Story Wall made up of lots of story boxes to be explored and discovered. It will interest and delight people of all ages!

£   Veg

No 28 Charlotte Square

28 Charlotte Square
Edinburgh
EH2 4ET
0844 493 2272
information@nts.org.uk
www.nts.org.uk
This café is located in the National Trust for Scotland Headquarters in Charlotte Square. It might be quite easy to overlook it from the outside as it is in an old New Town building but inside it is spacious with several rooms given over to the café. Many of the clientele are older or tourists but we have always found a very warm welcome there even from when our daughter was just a few days old. We have tended to leave our buggy in the reception area though this is not large and therefore it might not be best suited to large groups of mums and tots if pushchairs or prams are in tow. Lovely light meals such as soup, sandwiches etc are served as well as breakfasts (before noon) and a limited selection of main meals. There is also usually a very tempting array of cakes and biscuits. One observation we would make is that part of the café walls in one of the rooms are lined with books and other items for sale and so might be best avoided if your under 5 is mobile and curious!

£

Bar Roma

39a Queensferry Street
Edinburgh
0131 226 2977
Friendly and spacious Italian restaurant. Children's portions are available, plus crayons. It can be very busy at lunchtimes. Friendly staff who love children. Gluten free pasta available.

££

Bella Italia

9/11 Hanover Street
Edinburgh
EH2 2DL
0845 201 7891
www.bellaitalia.co.uk
Popular city-centre eatery. Good value children's menu of Italian favourites, dessert and unlimited juice. Crayons and colour-in mat provided and children's seasonal pictures may be displayed. Pushchairs can be taken in and stored.
Nappy changing facility (F) in upstairs toilet,

££

Browns Restaurant and Bar

131-133 George St
0131 225 4442
Spacious restaurant at the West end of George St that has become a firm favourite with many families. Owing to licensing laws children are not allowed in the bar area, but under 5s are welcome in the restaurant. The children's meals are excellent quality and the price includes a main course, ice cream and drink. A dining experience that doesn't compromise on adult appeal, while remaining child-friendly. Attentive and friendly staff, keen to accommodate children.
When the restaurant is busy you may need to fold your pushchair.
Nappy changing facilities (M&F) in ground floor toilet

££

Café Andaluz

77b George Street
Edinburgh
EH2 3EE
0131 220 9980
This place has a fantastic interior that complements the tasty tapas on offer. Whether it is tapas, a sandwich, or cake and a coffee, Cafe Andaluz is well worth a visit. Staff are very welcoming and happy to encourage younger diners.

££   Veg

Café Rouge

43 Frederick Street
Edinburgh
EH2 1EP
0131 225 4515
www.caferouge.co.uk
Very friendly, welcoming and attentive staff. Children receive a helium balloon, colouring book and pencils. Very efficient and quick service, though we did visit on a quiet Wednesday lunchtime. Good range of food on children's menu. Would say this is more of an adult restaurant but that they make children very welcome, and all babies and toddlers were seated in the same part of the restaurant where the waiter was obviously well-used to dealing with children.

£

Centotre

103 George Street
Edinburgh
EH2 3ES
0131 225 1550
info@centotre.com
www.centotre.com
Spacious centrally located Italian restaurant. The owners have made a special effort to welcome children to this location. Children receive a party bag to help keep them (and their parents) entertained. The focus here is on 'fresh, simple, Italian', and the menu does not disappoint. Children can choose from a taster menu especially for little tummies. A great place to bring the family for a more special experience!

££   Veg

Garfunkels

29-31 Frederick Street
0131 225 4579
www.garfunkels.co.uk
Comfortable, table-service restaurant serving a wide range of American-influenced food. Friendly helpful staff. Also offers a children's menu. All children under 10 receive a bag containing 'goodies'.
Toilets downstairs in basement.

££

Gurkha Brigade

9a Antigua Street
Edinburgh
0131 556 6446
Friendly Nepalese restaurant welcomes families at all times. Children's snacks and meals such as chicken salad, fish and chips also available, but the menu, unsurprisingly, concentrates on Nepalese cuisine: Chinese and Indian influences, but with an emphasis on coriander, ginger, chilli, and garlic. Garden at rear for summer visits. Chef welcomes children in the kitchen to see food being prepared. Space for pushchairs.

££

Where would you suggest?
Tell us -
ed@efuf.co.uk

Gusto

135 George Street
Edinburgh
0131 225 2555

This eatery aims to combine great food, cool surroundings and a positive attitude towards families. Popular with people without children too, the restaurant manages to cater for all ages. There is a children's menu, although half portions of the main pasta dishes always go down well, and they can draw while waiting for their food (crayons and paper provided).
Nappy change surface (M&F).

££

Hard Rock Café

20 George Street
Edinburgh
0131 260 3000

Busy and informal family restaurant, with a focus on US and Tex/Mex food. There are small booths available for family gatherings or if you prefer some privacy for breastfeeding. Colour-in books, crayons and balloons for children, also plasma screens and fairly loud music to keep them amused. Staff friendly, very attentive, and welcoming to children. Very little room to accommodate pushchairs, but staff will make every effort to find space – can be parked in the shop area.
Nappy change facilities (M&F).

££

Henderson's of Edinburgh

94 Hanover Street
Edinburgh
EH2 1DR
0131 225 2131
mail@hendersonsofedinburgh.co.uk
www.hendersonsofedinburgh.co.uk

Family run vegetarian restaurant, deli and bistro. Canteen style self-service. Healthy, varied selection of meals, snacks, teas and coffee. Live music and talks in the evenings.
Need to carry pushchair down steep steps to restaurant. Member of staff will help if you ring from the top of the stairs. Further steps and alcoves present pushchair obstacles inside, but generally accessible.
Alcoves provide (some) privacy for breast feeding. Some toys also available.
Access to upstairs deli easier, as there are only a couple of steps, but seating is limited and is unsuitable for toddlers (bar stools and no high chairs).

£   Veg

Howies

1a Alva Street
Edinburgh
EH2 4PH
0131 225 5553
westend@howies.uk.com
www.howies.uk.com

Four Howies restaurants in Edinburgh to choose from. The Alva Street restaurant is in a basement down a steep flight of stairs, with a relatively compact layout. They have highchairs and the manager has a toddler of his own, so welcomes families. However you may find other Howies venues more accessible.

££

(Other Howies located at: 208 Bruntsfield Place, 10-14 Victoria Street, and 29 Waterloo Place.)

Pizza Express

32 Queensferry Street
West End
0131 225 8863
www.pizzaexpress.co.uk
Pizzas with all sorts of toppings (including sultanas!) and dough balls and ice creams that are just a little bit different. Crayons, paper and balloons are available to distract impatient young diners. Children's menu available. Restaurant can cater for children's parties if given prior notice.

££

A Room in the Town

18 Howe Street
New Town
Edinburgh
0131 225 8204
www.aroomin.co.uk
Although high chairs (in the form of boosters) are available there is no separate children's menu. Staff are friendly and welcoming to children but perhaps best to go with a small baby who will sleep while you eat!

££

The Scottish Café & Restaurant

Weston Link
The National Gallery of Scotland
The Mound
Edinburgh
EH2 2EL
0131 226 6524
info@thescottishcafe.com
www.thescottishcafeandrestaurant.com
New Scottish Café and Restaurant to the left as you enter the Link from Garden level. This eatery serves delicious food with a Scottish flair so expect to see Cullen Skink, scones, butteries and locally sourced food as well as lovely cupcakes, main courses and a large selection of teas, coffees and cocktails. It is owned by the family who run Zanzero and Centotre so the space is family oriented with pram/pushchair access, highchairs and baby changing facility in the disabled toilet. Comfy chairs facing the windows looking east are a great place to get comfortable and relax with a hot drink.

Opening hours will vary according to season – call if you wish to dine out of Weston Link opening hours.

££   Veg

Tony's Table

58a North Castle Street
Edinburgh
EH2 3LU
0131 226 6743
info@tony'stable.com
Not an obvious choice for a family meal, but well worth the visit. Delicious food with a menu that changes on a daily basis. No children's menu, but a small portion of an adult meal makes little ones feel very grown up. Staff couldn't be more friendly and go out of their way to ensure even the youngest diners are happy. We had great fun playing 'spot the pigs' on our visit.

££

Wannaburger
7/8 Queensferry Street
West End
Edinburgh
EH2 4PA
0131 220 0036
westend@wannaburger.com
www.wannaburger.com
A very family-friendly restaurant serving quality burgers and milkshakes, as well as a tasty breakfast menu with bottomless filter coffee for those mornings where you really need a caffeine-kick! Vegetarian options are available and include bean, portabella, and haloumi burgers. Best of all, Wannaburger actively accommodates and welcomes children of all ages. Staff will make room for your pram/pushchair at the table, highchairs are provided for younger children, and older children are given a colouring placemat and crayons. A special kids menu offers (among other choices) beef, chicken or bean burgers served with chips and salad sticks, and kid-size versions of shakes, very thoughtfully served in a lidded cup with a straw to help avoid spills! Staff are very patient and friendly with children, and willing to accommodate their requests. When our 2 year old announced he wanted something from the breakfast menu at tea-time we were told this was no problem and a potential tantrum was avoided! For under 5's with not quite enough teeth to eat a burger, staff will happily heat food for you. A good-value, fun place to eat that will keep you coming back time and time again (join the loyalty scheme for a discount!)

£

Zizzi
42 Queensferry Street
Edinburgh
EH2 4RA
0131 225 6937
A very welcoming place for little ones. Children get colouring pencils and a menu of their own. Staff were very attentive. Access is good and there were no issues with taking a pushchair. Nappy changing facilities easy to negotiate too.

£   Veg

Atholl Dining Room
The Howard Hotel
34 Great King Street
Edinburgh
EH3 6QH
0131 557 3500
www.thehoward.com
The Howard is a very smart but very friendly hotel and although high tea is a formal affair, children are welcomed with open arms and well catered for. The service is absolutely impeccable and when one of my sons developed an urge for non stop mini Dundee cakes, the staff were all too happy to provide an endless supply. The tea comprises of finger sandwiches, light as air scones and jam and a wonderful selections of cakes and patisseries. A definite recommendation for a special occasion.

££   Veg

blue
10 Cambridge Street
Edinburgh
0131 221 1222
www.bluescotland.co.uk
Upstairs from the Traverse Theatre you'll find blue and all it has to offer. As well as brasserie meals you might be surprised to find this is a great venue for a coffee or a light meal with the kids. It's very relaxed and children are made to feel very welcome.

££   Veg

Cafe Montagu
12 Montagu Terrace
EH3 5QX
0131 551 5359
Provide a warm welcome to under 5s. A bright space with good coffee, cakes and other goodies on offer. There is a large playroom at the back, stocked with toys and books. Also has good nappy changing facilities.

£

Chop Chop
248 Morrison Street
Edinburgh
EH3 8DT
0131 221 1155
A fantastic Chinese restaurant that has recently enjoyed national fame. Highly recommended and children are made to feel most welcome. Don't miss trying the dumplings - children get their own smaller version. Take advice from the staff who will help you make sense of the menu and portion sizes. The only difficulty you'll have is choosing what to try as everything sounds yummy.

£   Veg

Circle Café and Bakery
1 Brandon Terrace
0131 624 4666
brysonscatering@hotmail.co.uk
This table-service café has a relaxed and very welcoming atmosphere. Menu is changed regularly, but always contains larger lunch plates, deli items, with vegetarian options and light snacks. They also carry a breakfast and an afternoon tea menu. Offers a range of coffees and soft drinks, plus cakes. All food is made to order.
Friendly and efficient staff provide half portions of some items (soups, sandwich plates, salads) on request. Circle is happy to provide hot water for heating baby food & bottles; free babycinos for youngsters when accompanying adults have coffee.
Phone ahead if there's a group coming and they can organise space for you, usually at the front of the café. The toilet is small and has no changing table.

£   Veg

Dionika
3-6 Canonmills Bridge
Inverleith
0131 652 3993
www.dionika.com
Typical Spanish food served up with a warm welcome. Children are made to feel at home in a truly relaxed Spanish restaurant. A varied menu of tapas and dishes to choose from - our toddler enjoyed trying just about everything. You'll often find Juan the owner on hand to ensure everyone is well fed and happy.

££

Espresso Mondo
116 Lothian Road
Edinburgh
EH3 9BE
0131 228 3990
Handy place if you want to meet centrally for a coffee or light bite. Not specifically geared to children, but there are nappy changing facilities and we were made to feel welcome.

£

Filmhouse Cafe Bar
88 Lothian Road
Edinburgh
EH3 9BZ
0131 229 5932
cafebar@filmhousecinema.com
www.filmhousecinema.com
Relaxed yet vibrant atmosphere with an informal approach means young children are made welcome. Wide range of dishes steering a path away from standard 'chips with everything' to provide a great variety. Especially good choice for vegetarians.

£   Veg

The Gateway Restaurant
John Hope Gateway Centre
Royal Botanic Garden
Arboretum Place
Inverleith
0131 552 2674
www.gatewayrestaurant.net
A much grander dining venue than the Terrace Cafe with prices to match. Great views of the Botanics with plans in the summer to offer outdoor tables on the terrace. Offers breakfast, lunch, and afternoon tea menus. Good children's menu available too.

££

Glass and Thompson
2 Dundas Street
Edinburgh
EH3 6HZ
0131 557 0909
A bright and modern deli style café where we were welcomed to its relaxed atmosphere. Whilst there are a number of savoury options on the menu (a good selection of those vegetarian) there are no hot main meals available. The café also doubles as a takeaway for fine cheese, meats and other luxury and local food produce. There is no children's menu or options but whilst Glass and Thompson is not somewhere you would take children specifically for their lunch, the owner would be able to give a smaller portion on request. The cheese and meat platters are easily something you could share with your children.
Watch out for toilets, they are very small and have no nappy changing facilities. The manager has a change mat which you can use and there is a small section of the restaurant that is more private.

£ Veg

 Don't forget to let businesses know you saw them in the EFUF book!

Hamilton's Bar and Kitchen
Hamilton Place
Stockbridge
0131 226 4199
info@hamiltonsbar.com
A gastropub which has a dining area away from the bar thoroughfare – up a couple of steps. Menu has a range of influences and always has a range of vegetarian options. Offers a set lunch menu or a la carte options. Portions tend to be large – as are the wedge cut chips! Staff have always been friendly and accommodating during our visits.
Toilets on ground floor.

£ Veg

John Lewis - The Place to Eat
St James' Centre
Edinburgh
0131 556 9121
Large, busy self-service restaurant and espresso bar on level 4. Fantastic views over the city from large windows. Vegetarian dishes available, as well as children's portions and children's lunchboxes. Small selection of baby food available to buy. Plenty of room for pushchairs. Staff will assist with getting trays to tables. Bibs, bowls and spoons available if required. Easy access from lifts. Also easy access to fantastic baby facilities, 'the loos with the views' for the under 5s. Children made most welcome everywhere, but the smaller espresso bar with its temptingly low furniture and glass walls is probably more suitable for babies and older children than lively toddlers.

££

Lazio Restaurant
95 Lothian Road
0131 229 7788
Families are welcome at this restaurant. Varied menu, children's portions available. Folded pushchairs only. Crayons and pencils supplied. Toilets on ground floor.

££

The Olive Tree Cafe
St. George's West Church
Shandwick Place
0131 225 7001
st-george-west@btconnect.com
In addition to great value hot meals and cakes, you will find toys/books to entertain and a warm welcome. Access also by lift at side entrance on Stafford St. Space for multiple push chairs, no need to fold them up.
Nappy changing surface (F).

£

Pizza Express
1 Deanhaugh Street
Stockbridge
0131 332 7229
Pizzas galore in stylish surroundings by Water of Leith walkway. Restaurant is on two levels, and the lower area is complete with an outside terrace for al fresco eating on sunny days - best if you don't have a pushchair to lug down the stairs. Crayons and paper usually materialise on the table pretty quickly if you have a toddler, and balloons sometimes are a 'goodbye' gesture. There are seasonal variations to the menu, and a special children's menu. Friendly staff. Toilets with changing facilities downstairs – only accessible via a flight of stairs.

££

Terrace Café RBGE
Royal Botanic Garden
20a Inverleith Row
Edinburgh
EH3 5LR
0131 552 0606
www.rbge.org.uk
An excellent place to meet for a coffee before/after a walk through the garden, although somewhat pricey. The Café offers a good selection of hot and cold food, including yummy cakes! Take a seat outside to enjoy fresh air and the stunning views of the city skyline, while the kids run around on the lawn. The kids play area inside is a good idea, but unfortunately rather neglected. The nappy changing area is not always as clean and tidy as you might wish it to be, and a stool for little people to reach the sink in the grown-up loos would be welcome.

£   Veg

Traverse Bar Café
10 Cambridge Street
0131 228 5383
Centrally located, a large, open bar café with friendly and welcoming staff. Wide range of vegetarian dishes and home baking. Children's portions are available. Lift to café, bar and theatres. There's a good wine list and American and continental beers are available at the bar. The atmosphere is very relaxed making it an ideal place for parents with young children to enjoy a drink, a coffee and something to eat. Space for pushchairs.

£   Veg

Vincaffe
11 Multrees Walk
Edinburgh
0131 557 0088
A contemporary, stylish setting for relatively formal dining, which manages to be child friendly at the same time. Under 5s are welcome, with Sundays a particularly good day for family dining. Children's menu with healthy, appetizing Italian dishes that children are sure to love. Friendly staff, although you may have to avoid peak times for quick service. Paper and pencils provided for children. Pushchairs can be taken in. Dining is on the ground and first floor, with lift access. Also outside seating.

££   Veg

Zanzero
14/16 North West Circus Place
Edinburgh
EH3 6SX
0131 220 0333
info@zanzero.com
www.zanzero.com
Large, open, bright restaurant focusing on fresh wholesome foods, and which openly welcomes (and encourages!) children of all ages. Children are made to feel like special guests and are given goodies on arrival. Great children's menu and an excellent selection of Italian food for grown-ups too.

£

EAT NORTH

Café Citron
14 Marischal Place
Edinburgh
EH4 3NJ
0131 539 7977
Sandwiches, soup and baking. A lovely little stop for a coffee and/or a bite to eat. We're always made to feel most welcome. Space is limited, but staff have managed to accomodate us (pushchairs and all).

£

Café Newton Dean Gallery
Belford Road
0131 624 6200
enquries@nationalgalleries.org
Art deco style ground floor café, with good coffee and lovely cakes! And there's also a tasty and interesting lunch menu with a dish of the day and a variety of vegetarian dishes. Half portions available for children. Toilets in basement – very colourful decor. Lift access.

£   Veg

Cafe Revive
Marks & Spencer
Unit 1B Craigleith Retail Park
40 South Groathill Avenue
Edinburgh
EH4 2LN
0131 343 3641
A lovely spot to take a break from shopping or just enjoy a coffee. Child friendly with lunchbags and babycinos on offer.

£

Channings
12-16 South Learmonth Gardens
Edinburgh
EH4 1EZ
0845 202 6177
restaurant@channings.co.uk
www.channings.co.uk
Tucked away this is a restaurant for a special family meal where the children will be well catered for. It offers good food in a relaxed setting.

££   Veg

The Cramond Brig
Cramond Bridge
Edinburgh
EH4 6DY
0131 339 4350
enquiries@cramondbrig.com
www.cramondbrig.com
Two restaurants, one of which has been relaunched as The Brig Family Restaurant. There is a play room with plenty of toys to choose from. Extensive children's menu on offer and plenty of activities to entertain - makes this an ideal place to take the family.

£

Holiday Inn – Edinburgh North
Queensferry Rd, Blackhall
0131 311 4903
Inventive children's menu provides plenty of choice; healthy options/ 'build' your own dinner/ kids cocktail list. There is an outdoor play area for use at Sunday lunch times with climbing frame and see-saw.

££

Lauriston Farm Restaurant
69 Lauriston Farm Road
Edinburgh
EH4 5EX
0131 312 7071
www.tobycarvery.co.uk
Large and spacious restaurant, part of the Brewer's Fayre chain. Carvery menu for children and adults. The tables outside are great for sunny summer days.

££

The Gallery Café
Scottish National Gallery of Modern Art
72 Belford Road
Edinburgh
0131 332 8600
Access by lift to self-service café in basement. A firm favourite for delicious home-cooked soups, hot meals, salads and great cakes. Also vegetarian meals. Baked potatoes, soup and filled rolls available for children. Outdoor terrace for fine weather, where children can enjoy the garden. The only downside is that it can be very busy during lunchtime.

£   Veg

Maxi's
33 Raeburn Place
Stockbridge
EH4 1HX
0131 343 3007
maxiscafe@hotmail.com
Well established café on Stockbridge's 'high street'. Deli-style food with plenty of sandwich fillings to choose from, as well as a small selection of hot options. They also do generous servings of soup and bread. Cakes, tray bakes and a range of drinks on offer. There's room for a couple of unfolded pushchairs, but if you can, it's best to fold them. The café has a double door, which can open to allow a wider access.

£   Veg

Where would you suggest?
Tell us -
ed@efuf.co.uk

Brewers Fayre with Fun Factory

51-53 Newhaven Place
Edinburgh
08701 977093

Large 'family-themed' restaurant near the Travel Inn on Newhaven Harbour. Generally child-pleasingly loud and lively. Operates system of ordering and paying, then table service is provided - handy if you need to take the children out quickly! Children's menus for under and over 5s. Children's meal can include visit to the ice cream factory to choose their own sweets to top the ice cream, but Brewers Fayre have also introduced fruit salad options. Baby food available to buy. Large choice for adults, including a daytime snack menu and special meal deals.The restaurant is on one floor. One area adjacent to the bar is a 'child free zone', but with a 'Fun Factory' (soft play) on site there is plenty to keep young children occupied.

££

Loch Fyne Restaurant

25 Pier Place
Newhaven Harbour
0131 559 3900
www.lochfyne.com

A particular favourite for those who love fish and shellfish, with daily specials available. Related to the original Loch Fyne Oyster bar, you will of course find Loch Fyne oysters on the menu. Not such a great choice for those who aren't seafood fans, but as child-friendly places go it's a good venue for a family meal.

££

Anchor Café

Leith Community Centre
New Kirkgate Centre
Leith
EH6 6AD
0131 554 4750
info@leithcommunitycentre.com
www.leithcommunitycentre.com

Once you find the lift access (next to Superdrug) a whole new world opens up above the New Kirkgate Centre. You would never guess there was room for two halls (one large and one small), four general purpose rooms, a room suitable for crèches, a photograph dark room and a Café up there. From support groups to dance classes, the list of activities is endless. The café may not be that flash but it is very easy on the pocket and has a fantastic view across the old cemetery. Best to contact the centre for up to date class details as the website can be out of date.

£

Baxters

Ocean Drive
Ocean Terminal
Leith
EH6 6JJ
0131 553 0840

With a fantastic view of the Forth and such big coffees and slices of cake, this is definitely a good place to head to recharge at Ocean Terminal. The food is straight up and simple with soup, sandwiches, baked potatoes and pancakes. There are also other hot meals available too. The cafe does draw an older crowd though so if the kids are on the noisy side, it might be best to save this for another day!

£

Britannia View
Debenhams
Ocean Drive
Ocean Terminal
Edinburgh
EH6 6JJ
0131 555 5683
With an amazing view through the Royal Yacht and across the Firth of Forth, this aptly named café is using its unique selling point to its advantage. With a good range of choices on the children's menu and a selection to fill up your snack box with, children are really made to feel welcome here. There are highchairs for young babies and ones who can sit as well, a microwave and hot food containers so you can heat your own food without making a mess. Paper and crayons plus a big table for the kids to eat and draw at are all strong pulling points. Unfortunately the toilets could really do with an upgrade.

£

Café Fish
60 Henderson Street
Leith
EH6 6DE
0131 538 6131
info@cafefish.net
www.cafefish.net
This is a classy new restaurant and bar near the shore. They specialise in Scottish seafood, but also offer steaks and vegetarian dishes on their daily menu. It is a very friendly place, equally good for a relaxed lunch or a special evening out. The open kitchen is fascinating to watch and the décor of the whole place is really well done. They are happy to accommodate little ones at any time – and weren't at all put out by the amount of mess ours made! Instead of a children's menu, they offer a half portion of anything on the menu for half price.

££

Café Revive (M&S)
Ocean Terminal
Leith
0131 225 2301
Small Marks and Spencer café located within the Simply Food store on the first floor, with additional seating out on the concourse. Café serves coffees, cakes and light lunches as well as juices for the kids.

£

The Cairn Cafe
Tiso Outdoor Experience
41 Commercial Street
Leith
EH6 6JD
0131 555 2211
www.thecairncafe.co.uk
Delicious foods and baking from those clever people at Porto & Fi - need we say more. The cafe offers the option of sitting in or take-away.

£

Chop Chop
76 Commercial Street
Leith
www.chop-chop.co.uk
We can't recommend Chop Chop in Morrison Street enough and this is the new sister restaurant that is just opening as we go to print. It promises to offer the same great food, but in more spacious surroundings and with a little more grandeur.

£   Veg

Costa Coffee

Ocean Terminal
Leith
0131 555 5124

Extremely accessible, this café opens out on to the ground floor of Ocean Terminal. Self service style, you can choose from a selection of sandwiches, cakes and coffees, the usual Costa fare. Can be a bit tight to negotiate around the tables with a pushchair but if you sit at the edge there is plenty of room. You can also get coffee etc to take away.

£

Daniels Bistro

88 Commercial Street
Edinburgh
0131 553 5933
danielsbistro@hotmail.com
www.daniels-bistro.co.uk
Accessible

Unpretentious French food served in relaxed, informal surroundings. Children are made very welcome with toys and crayons to keep them occupied. Excellent range of food options for adults and children. The children's menu steers clear of burgers and chips offering crepes and moules among the choices. The lunchtime set menu is particularly good value. Staff are exceptionally friendly and accommodating.

££

Dr Bell's Family Centre

15 Junction Place
Leith
EH6 5JA
0131 553 0100

A great little café - a real godsend for parents of young children looking for somewhere relaxed and affordable to go. There is always a generous homemade soup of the day, a selection of sandwiches and baked potatoes and a particularly tasty chocolate biscuit cake. The café can fill up between 12 and 1pm and is unfortunately closed on a Friday.

£

Drill Hall Arts Cafe

34 Dalmeny Street
Leith
0131 555 7100
www.outoftheblue.org.uk

If you're looking for somewhere to go with a bit of space for little ones to stretch their legs (or even so you know there will be room for pushchairs) try the Drill Hall. It's a great space where lots of interesting things are happening. The food is yummy and very reasonably priced.

£ Veg

E:S:I

46 Queen Charlotte Street
Leith
EH6 7EZ
0131 555 3103
info@esibrasserie.com
www.esibrasserie.com

This new restaurant is in a nice quiet part of Leith and offers a relaxing and spacious venue for lunch or dinner. The owners (an Englishman, a Scotsman and an Irishman – hence the name) are friendly and helpful. The menu is varied, offering everything from a bowl of soup to a fillet steak. The cuisine is modern and international, with an emphasis on fresh ingredients.

££ Veg

Visit our website for updates:
www.efuf.co.uk

La Favorita
325-331 Leith Walk
Edinburgh
EH6 8SA
0131 554 2430
info@la-favorita.com
www.la-favorita.com
Spacious family owned and family friendly Italian restaurant specialising in log-fired pizzas and interesting pasta dishes, with all dietary requirements catered for. Portions are big and the desserts are lovely. Staff are very welcoming to families and young children, providing balloons, high-chairs and special 'kids eat for £1' menu at the time of review, as well as small portions from the main menu as requested. Good place for a coffee and a cake during the day. There is plenty of room for pushchairs and noise level is high so our energetic toddler fitted right in!

£   Veg

Guilty Lily
284 Bonnington Road
Edinburgh
EH6 5BE
0131 554 5824
www.guiltylily.com
Beautifully refurbished bar on the corner of Newhaven and Bonnington Road. The inside is comfortable and friendly, with plenty of soft armchairs and sofas, as well as traditional tables and chairs. There is a standard children's menu, choice of pasta, cheese on toast and such like, and ice cream for pudding. A tad limited, but sufficient. The adult menu has a selection of burgers, chips, sandwiches, and mezze, as well as some more substantial specials with fish, meat and vegetarian main courses, and a few tasty puddings. It is bright and airy, friendly, clean and comfortable. A nice place for a stop off.

£

Giuliano's on the Shore
1 Commercial Street
Leith
0131 554 5272
Children very welcome in this attractive, lively Italian restaurant where they can even make their own pizzas, but grown-ups are well catered for too! Half portions available and they promise they can cater for any diet. Crayons and books are also available. Access is good and the restaurant has its own parking, although you may need to look slightly further afield at busy times. Toilets on ground floor.

££

Leith Lynx
100-102 Constitution Street
Leith
0131 538 4796
www.leithlynx.co.uk
A little off the beaten track but worth the trip. This modern restaurant offers an interesting menu and you might find it difficult to decide what to have. No specific menu for children, but staff are very accommodating and will offer small portions to suit.

£

Malmaison Brasserie
1 Tower Place
Edinburgh
0131 468 5000
Friendly hotel by Leith Docks. Helpful and welcoming to children, but posh enough to please the adults. Varied menu with good choice for vegetarians. Half portions available. Good access. Space for pushchairs.
Nappy changing table (D).

££

Anything out of date?
Let us know -
info@efuf.co.uk

Newhaven Connections Community Cafe
Craighall Road
Edinburgh
EH6 4ND
0131 551 3931
newhavenconnections@n-c.org.uk
The Café serves a good selection of home baking and light lunches. Staff are very friendly and accommodating to children and they ensure that the café has a relaxed atmosphere. A microwave is provided to warm baby food and plenty of high chairs are available. Food includes home made soup, rolls, toasties and baked potatoes and some really delicious cakes. Children and families are made very welcome.

£

Ocean Kitchen Bar & Grill
Ocean Drive
Ocean Terminal
Leith
EH6 6JJ
0131 555 6068
Large canteen style café in the centre of Ocean Terminal with fantastic views over the Forth from the floor to ceiling windows. A large tv screen shows cbeebies for the little ones and there is ample seating and space to fit pushchairs and shopping. Choice of sofas for lounging with coffee, or chairs along the windows for eating lunch. Soups, salads, sandwiches and more substantial meals available, as well as coffees and cakes.

££

Pizza Express
38 Waterview House
The Shore
Leith
EH6 6QU
0131 554 4332
Pizzas that are just a little bit different from other pizza chains, with views overlooking Water of Leith and The Shore. Nice desserts, which do have an ice cream theme going on. Having said that, the cheesecake is great! Crayons and paper usually materialise on the table pretty quickly if you have a toddler, and balloons are sometimes a 'goodbye' gesture. Friendly staff. Toilets on same level as restaurant.

££

Porto & Fi
47 Newhaven Main Street
Edinburgh
EH6 4NQ
0131 551 1900
enquiries@portofi.com
A busy hive of delicious food and baking. Cafe, deli, come bistro that welcomes families. A great children's menu on offer that includes fish goujons and cheesy pasta. While for adults the chocolate beetroot cake is a must. This is a popular place and you may want to phone ahead or risk being disappointed.

£ Veg

Potters
Ocean Terminal
Leith
0131 555 6700
This large bright and modern family themed restaurant is on the top floor of the centre and serves a broad all-day menu of char-grilled dishes, pastas, salads and burgers. Children's menu available. Large open space great for children and pushchairs and lovely views from the tables at the back. Balloons for the kids.

££

Prezzo

25 Pier Place
Edinburgh
EH6 4LP
0131 552 4356
www.loveprezzo.co.uk
Prezzo overlooks Newhaven Harbour and is the ideal place to enjoy a pizza, the views of the Forth and the boats in the harbour. The restaurant is housed in a renovated warehouse building so is very spacious and airy and there are also tables outside. The staff are friendly and there is no problem in bringing a pushchair to your table. Although the service is a little leisurely, the food is delicious and there is a good choice of pizza and pasta and a small selection of other meals. A children's menu is available and kids are provided with an activity pack when ordering from this menu. Every two kids must be accompanied by an adult ordering from the main menu to be able to benefit from the children's menu. You can walk off those carbs with a walk round the harbour to the little lighthouse or further round the bluff to watch the ships travelling down the Forth.

£

The Raj on the Shore

5-91 Henderson Street
Leith
EH6 6ED
0131 553 3980
www.rajontheshore.com
Welcomes children of all ages with their friends and family. Waiters will advise parents on the suitability of dishes and size of portion. They will offer platters of different milder dishes more suitable to younger palates (priced as starters or side dishes). Lunch, express lunch and dinner menus available.
A free soft drink/bottled water or ice cream is offered to each child diner.
No nappy change or high chairs, so better for older under 5s!

££

Rocksalt Café Deli

46 Constitution Street
Edinburgh
EH6 6RS
0131 554 9873
Fantastic café and deli. A very friendly place to eat with small children, plus a good range of menu options. Staff were happy to give information on ingredients and to adjust portion sizes to suit small appetites (children get half portions of adult meals, but this was too big for our under 5 and our over 5!). Good clean facilities. The seating is well spaced and there is room both for prams/pushchairs and for children to move about. An ideal place to go for lunch or a relaxing coffee and cake. Would also be a good place to meet up with friends or to pass a quiet hour on your own.

£   Veg

A Room in Leith

1c Dock Place
Edinburgh
EH6 6LU
0131 554 7427
www.aroomin.co.uk
This atmospheric bar and restaurant serves a range of Scottish food, from their warming "Mug Menu" to delicious steaks and fish dishes. On a sunny day, sit outside by the Water of Leith on their large picnic tables, and in the winter curl up on the comfy leather sofas inside. The owners and staff are very friendly and will do anything they can to help with small children. Facilities are spotless. Children are allowed at any time, though they may recommend you avoid particularly busy times as it can get quite crowded.

£

Roseleaf Cafe Bar
23-24 Sandport Place
Leith
EH6 6EW
0131 476 5268
info@roseleaf.co.uk
www.roseleaf.co.uk
Appears quite ordinary from the outside, but step inside and you will be amazed. There is a friendly, very child friendly atmosphere, but interesting and arty at the same time. The bar area can seat children until 5pm, the side café room until 8pm, but worth phoning ahead to make sure there is space. The menu is exciting, with a great choice on both the kiddie menu and adults, plus a specials menu and bargain lunch deals. Fantastic selection of freshly squeezed juices available. Their motto is to use free range, organic and locally produced food wherever possible, which shows through in the food, which is tasty, healthy, and devilishly good. Service is friendly, a tad on the slow side, but always helpful, and colouring pens and paper were produced on arrival without prompt. A very positive and delicious experience.

£   Veg

Royal Yacht Britannia Cafe
Ocean Drive
Ocean Terminal
Leith
EH6 6JJ
0131 555 5566
enquiries@tryb.co.uk
www.royalyachtbritannia.co.uk
On the top floor of the Royal Yacht, with a panoramic view over the Forth, to the Forth bridges and Fife, this is a lovely place for a treat. However you have to pay an entrance fee to the Royal Yacht to use the café, so it is not somewhere you can pop into to meet up with friends, unless you all happen to be visiting the yacht together. The food on offer is limited, but delicious. Savouries are restricted to soups and sandwiches. There is a selection of fine teas and coffees, and the most delicious cakes, prepared freshly on board each day. These are cakes fit for a queen.

£

Tapa Barra y Restaurante
19 Shore Place
Leith
0131 476 6776
www.tapaedinburgh.co.uk
A lively and entertaining venue that makes for a great family meal out. Before we could blink a selection of toys appeared on the highchair table to keep the little one entertained. Staff were so friendly and made sure everyone was happy. Plenty on the menu to choose from with tapa providing plenty of interest and variety with something to tempt even the fussiest of eaters. During our visit there was even live music to really make the evening go with a swing.

£   Veg

The Water of Leith
52 Coburg Street
Leith
EH6 6LQ
0131 555 2613
www.waterofleithcafebistro.com
When you visit this fresh new bistro in the heart of Leith you just know that the owners are parents. They really have thought of everything - the big buggy parking space, the spacious layout, the comfy corner with sofas and a big box of toys, the well stocked baby changing area and the healthy children's menu. On top of all that it is the relaxing décor, huge south facing windows and delicious home cooked food and cakes that will make the adults want to keep going back. Newly opened in September 09, this deserves to become a favourite hangout for Leith parents – and is worth a journey for anyone else who would like to join us!

£   Veg

 Don't forget to let businesses know you saw them in the EFUF book!

The Yard

2 Bonnington Road Lane
Leith
EH6 5BJ
0131 554 1314
info@theyardleith.com
www.theyardleith.com

With experience of running Molly's Play Centre these owners know about entertaining kids. The Yard, a restaurant and bar, has something for all the family. Enjoy a coffee, brunch, food or drinks. When the sun shines on Edinburgh this place really comes into its own with plenty of outside space and toys to keep little ones entertained.

£

Zizzi

Ocean Terminal
Leith
EH6 6JJ
0131 555 1155

Children and parents couldn't be more welcome with pencils and crayons, highchairs and a kids meal deal on offer. The menu offers the usual Italian fare and staff are attentive to children's needs. Staff are more than happy to carry pushchairs down to the lower level or you can use the ramp at the opposite end of the food terrace and they will open the gate for you. This is a great place to enjoy the views and the high ceilings swallow up the kids' noise!

£   Veg

The Finishing Line Café

Meadowbank Sports Centre
139 London Road
Edinburgh
EH7 6AE
0131 661 5351

Bright and airy café overlooking the athletics track with plenty of room for pushchairs and a toddlers corner with a few toys. Food and drink is basic but reasonably priced and a children's snack plate is available. The only drawback are the heavy doors which are difficult to open and manoeuvre a pushchair through.

£

Joseph Pearce's

23 Elm Row
Edinburgh
EH7 4AA
0131 556 4140
www.bodabar.com

Situated on Elm Row by Valvona & Crolla, Joseph Pearce's is a friendly, laid back and stylish place to meet with small children. There is an excellent baby and toddler corner upstairs which provides comfy seats for parents and toys for the children. There is a microwave area for food and bottles and nappy changing faciilities in the toilets. Staff are more than happy to help you up the steps to the children's area and provide table service to make life easier. The upper area is made safe with a stair gate. A full menu is available and also snacks such as Organix crisps and the messy favourite, Tunnocks Teacakes! Children are allowed in the bar from 11am to 5pm when the area is turned back into an adults area.

£

Vittoria Restaurant

113 Brunswick Street
(Leith Walk)
0131 556 6171

Friendly Italian restaurant happy to serve anyone anything from a coffee or a glass of wine to a full meal. Pizza and pasta available, vegetarian options, burgers, chips, sandwiches and ice creams. Children's menu and half portions available. There is space for pushchairs outside (where you can sit out to eat when the weather is good) or folded if inside. Fully accessible entrance and toilet. Parties hosted.

£

Craigie's Farm Deli and Cafe
West Craigie Farm
South Queensferry
Edinburgh
EH30 9TR
0131 319 1048
john@craigies.co.uk
www.craigies.co.uk

This is a great set-up with outdoor tables and play area and fabulous views across to the Forth, Edinburgh and the Pentland Hills. Craigie's offers delicious and imaginative food freshly prepared with local and seasonal produce, all excellent value. The staff are very friendly and accommodating, a definite bonus. Be sure to allow time to browse around the shop, it is full of wonderful treats. This is a must for anyone who enjoys seeing where their food comes from!

£

Orocco Pier
17 The High Street
South Queensferry
EH30 9PP
0870 118 1664
info@oroccopier.co.uk
www.oroccopier.co.uk

This is a trendy bar/restaurant and therefore we were not sure what kind of welcome we would receive with two under two's in tow but all credit to Orocco Pier we were impressed. Having popped in to see if a table was available for a birthday lunch we found our table all set up with highchairs by the time we had parked the car and walked back. Our waiter was happy to move furniture around to accommodate a sleeping child in a pushchair and fill up sippy cups with water. We did not need to ask about food for our wee ones but they do have a good and fairly healthy children's menu which includes two courses and a drink. They also seemed very helpful in terms of heating up food and milk. A more casual café/bar area has recently been added to this venue which does not have table service but does have more sofas and comfy chairs so if a coffee or quick sandwich is more what you are after, you would be catered for this now too.

£

Picnic
5 Mid Terrace
South Queensferry
EH30 9LH
0131 331 1346
picniccoffeeshop@aol.com
www.picniccoffeeshop.com

This is a little café that we found by chance during a rain storm. Although it is quite small we were given a warm welcome as a family and noticed that they even had a small play table positioned in one corner. We ordered their excellent fresh coffee and cakes but snacks such as soup and sandwiches were on offer too and takeaway was an option. The café also functions as a gallery and has local artwork for sale on the walls which adds interest. Rain or not, next time we are in South Queensferry we will be popping in again!

£

Stables Tearoom
Hopetoun House
South Queensferry
EH30 9SL
0131 331 2451
www.hopetounhouse.com

While the Stables Tearoom looks quite formal, everyone was very friendly when we visited, and there are food options which would suit children, plus snacks such as scones and muffins. Drinks include milk and still fruit drinks. Modern toilets with nappy changing surface.

££

Where would you suggest?
Tell us -
ed@efuf.co.uk

Deep Sea World Cafe

Battery Quarry
North Queensferry
KY11 1JR
01383 411880
info@deepseaworld.co.uk
www.deepseaworld.com

Bright, spacious café which serves a range of snacks, teas and coffees. Children's lunch boxes and meals available.
Nappy changing facilities and ramp access except for the Under Sea section.

££

The Boathouse Bistro

The Pier
Kinross
(follow signs for Lochleven Castle)
KY13 8UF
01577 865386

A spacious and friendly cafe/bar serving hot daily specials, baked potatoes, sandwiches, toasties and soup. Situated on the shores of Loch Leven, and marking the start of the new, 8 mile Loch Leven Heritage Trail (which is pushchair, bike and wheelchair friendly), the Bistro also has an information point with leaflets and some displays on local wildlife and walks. The cafe shares a building with Lochleven Castle's ticket office and giftshop but is not owned by Historic Scotland.

£

Hill of Tarvit Tearoom

01334 653127
www.nts.org.uk

Pleasant tearoom selling light lunches and home baking, where staff are friendly and accommodating. Children's lunch options available. You can also hire a picnic hamper from the tearoom, choose what you'd like to put in from the menu, pick up an estate map and enjoy lunch alfresco. Hamper hire is £5 (refunded on return of hamper).

££

Loch Leven's Larder

Channel Farm
Milnathort
Kinross
KY13 9HD
01592 841000
www.lochlevenslarder.com

The restaurant/café at Loch Leven's Larder is located in a spacious wing of the main building (which also houses an extensive deli/farm/gift shop and kitchen showroom) with lovely views out over Loch Leven and beyond. There are a large number of tables inside and plenty outside too which are often needed as it can get busy. They serve soup, paninis, baked potatoes, quiche and salad, as well as a few more substantial meals usually advertised on the specials board. There seemed to be lots of high chairs and we found it easy enough to negotiate round the tables with a pushchair. They have provided a few toys and paper/crayons, but if you want to ensure a peaceful meal you might do well to bring some of your own, especially if the toys are in high demand! Staff seemed friendly and helpful and conveniently it is table service. One point to note is that there is an area between the shopping area and the café which is intended as a quiet room and families with children are discouraged from sitting there. The small outdoor play area was a big hit with our family and we also enjoyed wandering along the path that leads down to Loch Leven itself, spotting farm animals on the way. We plan to return soon in order to use the farm as a base to cycle the 8km path round the loch and investigate the nature trail.

£

Castle Campbell Tearoom

At the head of Dollar Glen
FK14 7PP
01259 742408

Small tearoom with vaulted ceiling which is open seasonally, serving soup, paninis, sandwiches, baked potatoes and home baking. Children's portions available.

£

Fife Animal Park Restaurant
Auchtermuchty
01337 831830
Handy stop for a bite to eat or refreshments if visiting the animal park. Hot meals, baking and sandwiches, with children's half portions available. Play area and nearby soft play (entry fee).

£

Muddy Boots
Balmacolm
Fife
FK15 7TJ
01337 831222
muddyboots@live.co.uk
A lovely light and spacious café that is very family friendly. Seating area with additional sofas around a wood burning stove – perfect for relaxing and reading the paper. Choose from the menu, and then order and pay at the counter. Service is very good and fast. Food is reasonably priced, healthy and tasty with farm grown and local ingredients used extensively. Lovely homemade soups and asparagus crepes were a highlight. Menu also includes sandwiches and quiches. Delicious homemade cakes on offer too.

£

Spill The Beans Cafe
6 Cathedral Street
Dunkeld
PH8 0AW
01350 728111
Lovely little cafe for a light lunch or to sample the tempting home-baking. Special menu for under 5s with delightful bear-shaped sandwiches!

£

Cafe Biba
40 Atholl Road
Pitlochry
01796 473294
www.thepancakeplace.net
This is a great place if you're visiting Pitlochry and looking for somewhere to eat. Children get crayons and pencils to colour with at the table. The children's menu provides plenty of variety and the staff couldn't be more helpful. You have to try the pancakes.

£

Blasta
Main Street
Newtonmore
PH20 1DA
01540 673231
www.blasta-restaurant.co.uk
If you're in this neck of the woods (not far from The Highland Wildlife Park) and looking for somewhere to dine then Blasta is worth a visit. No children's menu, but smaller portions from the adult menu available. Very child friendly. Phone in advance to be sure of a booking.

££

Ord Ban Restaurant Cafe
Rothiemurchus Centre
By Aviemore
01479 810005
ordban@googlemail.com
www.ordban.com
Delightful place to stop for refreshments or something more to eat. Little ones are well catered for with a lunchbox that you can take away with you if they can't quite manage to finish it all at once.

££

Anything out of date?
Let us know -
info@efuf.co.uk

Brechin Castle Centre Coffee Shop
Brechin
Angus
DD9 6SG
01356 626813
enquiries@brechincastlecentre.co.uk
www.brechincastlecentre.co.uk
Large, airy coffee shop selling a range of snacks and hot food – the portions were huge when we were there. Nappy changing (M&F)

££

EAT EAST

Café at the Palace
Palace of Holyrood House
0131 524 1032
Friendly café situated in the grounds of the Palace of Holyrood House, access beside the shop. Large selections of cakes and coffees/teas available as well as more substantial meals of sandwiches and baked potatoes. Spacious dining area so plenty of room for pushchairs if you choose a table at the side. Easy access as café and toilets (with nappy changing) are all on the ground floor.

£ Veg

Cafe Turquaz
119 Nicolson Street
Edinburgh
EH8 9ER
0131 667 6664
cafeturquaz@ymail.com
Great place for coffee lovers looking for a friendly place to sit and enjoy a cup. If you fancy something to eat, there are some particularly fine mezze on offer.

£

The Engine Shed Café
19 St Leonard's Lane
Edinburgh
0131 662 0040
Run by Garvald Community Enterprises, the café houses a bakery, as well as a bright, organic vegetarian café on the 1st floor, accessed by the lift or stairs. Reasonably priced menu changes daily and children's portions are available. All the food is made on the premises. Carry-out service, delivery within the city and outside catering available. Children made very welcome. Relaxed atmosphere and friendly staff.
Toilet for the disabled on the ground floor and toilets adjacent to café. Moveable nappy changing unit suitable for use in (F) or (M).

£ Veg

Karen Wong's
107-109 St Leonard's Street
Newington
Edinburgh
EH8 9QY
0131 662 0777 or 662 0772
karen_wong@hotmail.co.uk
www.karenwongchineserestaurant.co.uk
Karen's larger than life personality and helpful team of staff make this a delight of a restaurant to visit. We couldn't have been made to feel more at home, even when the little one was doing his best to break all known decibel records. Children's menu available.

£ Veg

Spoon Cafe Bistro

6a Nicolson Street
Edinburgh
EH8 9DH
0131 557 4567
spooncafe@btinternet.com
An old favourite that has recently moved to a new location opposite The Festival Theatre. The new venue offers more space and incorporates a play area. Staff are welcoming and willing to help you. Meals and snacks are cooked to order, vegetarian options always available with an emphasis on fresh seasonal produce. Staff will try to accomodate fussy eaters, and when all else fails will produce a slice of toast. Well worth a visit.

££   Veg

Ti Amo Restaurant

16 Nicolson Street
EH8 9DH
0131 556 5678
www.tiamorestaurant.com
Families are welcome in this Italian restaurant before 19.00. Books, crayons, paper, toys and lollipops available and children can help to make their own pizza. The fishpond is an additional attraction!

££

Beach House Cafe

Bath Street
Edinburgh
EH15 1EA
0131 657 2636
the-beachhouse@hotmail.co.uk
Lovely spacious cafe on Portobello Promenade. Great views of the sea with friendly and helpful staff. Delicious home-baking, take-away tea and coffee available if you're out for a walk along the beach.

£   Veg

The Espy

62-64 Bath Street
Portobello
EH15 1HF
0131 669 0082
Friendly, accommodating staff, fresh, well-cooked food and a warm family-friendly atmosphere meant we enjoyed a pleasant and relaxed Sunday lunch at this seaside pub. With big squishy sofas, scrubbed wooden floors and quirky furnishings, one half is dedicated to drinking and dining, the other to drinking only (no children in this section). The menu features burgers, nachos, salads and fish pie, plus daily specials ranging from seafood or cottage pie to special salads. Sounds like a standard bar menu, but it's not: everything is freshly prepared and well-presented in huge portions. The children's menu is a mini version of the adult one plus some old favourites such as cheese on toast and sausage and beans. Colouring books and crayons available plus Twister if the adults get restless!

£   Veg

Kitchener's Deli

127-129 Portobello High Street
Portobello
EH15
0131 669 9290
Had good experiences at non busy times. Deli has small seating area and not much space for pushchairs. There are no nappy changing facilities and the one unisex toilet is very small and narrow. Staff are friendly and helpful.

£   Veg

Visit our website for updates:
www.efuf.co.uk

Mums Catering

Portobello Swim Centre
57 The Promenade
Portobello
EH15 2BS
01875 611338
www.mumscatering.com
This is a nice bright cafe with lovely views over the beach and a tasty selection of home-baking. It's perfect for a coffee, plenty space for pushchairs and a good-sized play corner with a toy kitchen and toys and books.

£

Portobello Indoor Bowls and Leisure Centre Cafe

20 Westbank Street
Portobello
EH15 1DR
0131 669 0878 or 669 9457
www.edinburghleisure.co.uk
Friendly 2nd floor café serving the users of the Leisure Centre. Extremely geared to children and babies with a play area and many highchairs. The café holds a Healthy Living Award and hot food is freshly prepared on the premises. Very friendly staff who tolerate messy babies. Plenty of tables to sit at, a couple of sofas and a balcony to sit with older kids. Very spacious café with a sea view. Well used by mums and children. The play area is ideal for toddlers.

£

Reds

254 Portobello High Street
Edinburgh
EH15 2AT
0131 669 5558
contact@reds4families.com
www.reds4families.com
Reds is one of the few genuinely child-friendly restaurants I have eaten at. What makes it more special is that it's adult friendly too. With entertainment for the children in the form of a softplay area, pleasant decor and good food, it adds up to a meal out that can be enjoyed by the whole family. The children's menu features old favourites – spaghetti bolognaise, fish and chips, chicken goujons – all freshly made with no nasties added and in hearty portions. You can also order child-sized portions from the adult menu. Everything is well thought out, from the child-sized toilet seats to the rounded edges on child-height tables. The owners have children themselves and know what they like – somewhere to burn off their energy and interesting things to eat. They also appreciate that if your children are entertained and well fed then you'll enjoy yourself too. Definitely worth taking a trip to – with the beach and swimming pool around the corner it could be part of a great day out.

£   Veg

Gabbro Restaurant

43-45 Salisbury Road
Edinburgh
EH16 5AA
0131 667 1264
info@the-salisbury.co.uk
www.the-salisbury.co.uk
This is a particularly good cafe bistro choice for a fair weather day as there is a child-friendly walled garden for outdoor eating (keep an eye out for the light well at the bottom of the garden though). Close to the Commonwealth Pool. A wide choice of food at a reasonable price.

£

The Garden Café
The Thistle Foundation
Niddrie Mains Road
Edinburgh
EH16 4EA
0131 661 3366
This community cafe is not so easy to find (follow signs to The Thistle Foundation) but well worth the effort. A large bright airy room with two walls of windows looking onto a patio garden. It is very reasonably priced and has a children's menu. There is also a children's corner with books, soft toys, oven, blackboard, children's table and chairs, and colouring in sheets and pens. (This kept my 2 yr old fully entertained for our entire visit!).
Breakfast is served from 10–11.30 and lunch from 11.30-14.30. With great value homebaking and fair-trade coffees/teas, you'll be giving the big coffee chains a miss!

£

Rhubarb
Prestonfield House Hotel
Priestfield Road
Edinburgh
EH16 5UT
0131 225 1333
www.prestonfield.com
Prestonfield is pretty much a grown up experience and therefore children's activities and facilities are limited.
Rhubarb is a very glamorous, stylish and richly decadent restaurant set in the restored Prestonfield House Hotel. It is owned by James Thomson, better known for the Witchery and Tower restaurants. You are offered a drink and the menu in one of the hotel's bars before entering into Rhubarb. After dinner you are served coffee in one of the drawing rooms in front of a log fire.
The venue is very much aimed at the luxury market and though children would not be excluded you might want to keep this for an adult only treat!
On a child-friendly side the grounds Prestonfield sits in are much more attractive for children. There are gardens, a putting green and a woodland walk with bird feeders as well as the famous peacocks and Highland cows.

£££

IKEA Café
Straiton Mains
Straiton
Loanhead
EH20 9PW
0131 440 6600
www.ikea.com
Extensive café/restaurant with self-service and very amiable staff. Unsupervised children's play area with a good selection of toys. Menu with snacks and main courses including vegetarian and Swedish options. Children's meals or lunch box available. Jars of organic baby food available, with micowaves and bottle heaters available. Plenty of highchairs available. Hard to find somewhere that is more family friendly.

£

Brunton Theatre Bistro
Ladywell Way
Musselburgh
EH21 6AA
0131 653 5250
www.bruntontheatre.co.uk
A very friendly bistro situated within Brunton Theatre in Musselburgh. Free car park to the back of theatre, designated disabled parking in front of theatre. Main entrance to bistro from foyer. Pushchairs have to be left in foyer.
The bistro serves home-made tasty snacks, cakes and lunches, as well as 2 or 3 course pre-theatre suppers. It serves themed theatre suppers for certain shows as well. Half portions offered to children. Also serves a tasty babycino!
Bistro has a wonderful play corner tucked in the back to keep your little ones amused with a children's table and chairs, toys, books and a writing board.
Booking is advisable, especially at lunch time as it is popular with locals, and in the evenings, for pre-theatre dinners. You can book your show tickets and pre-theatre meal as a package through the Box Office.

£

Lanna Thai Restaurant

32 Bridge Street
Musselburgh
EH21 6AG
0131 653 2788
info@thaifood-scotland.com
www.thaifood-scotland.com

Families are welcome at this small ground floor Thai restaurant in the heart of Musselburgh. Situated on the main street, just opposite Brunton Theatre. Open at lunch time and in the evening. Serves pre-theatre menu as well (Sun-Thurs, 17.30-19.30). Children's lunch menu available. Would happily warm up bottles. Toilet and nappy changing facilities are on the same floor, in the back of the restaurant.

Booking is advisable especially at lunchtime as it is popular with local parents, and at weekends. Take-away is available as well.

£

Luca's

32-38 High Street
Musselburgh
0131 665 2237

An East Coast institution. As well as the famous ice-cream to eat in or take out, the café serves a full menu from toasties and panini to pizzas and all day brunches. And who could resist a knickerbocker glory for dessert? Children's portions available. Easy pushchair access to ground floor and lovely helpful staff. Kids love it!

£

The Village Coffee House

10 Rosebery Place
Gullane
East Lothian
EH31 2AN
01620 842509

A great place to come for a bite to eat or a good old-fashioned cream tea after a day out at Gullane beach. Very child-friendly with books to keep younger ones amused and half size portions at half the price.

£

Aviator Café

National Museum of Flight
East Fortune Airfield
East Lothian
EH39 5LF
0131 225 7534
info@nms.ac.uk
www.nms.ac.uk/flight

Café outlet based within National Museum of Flight. A range of hot and cold snacks are available in addition to children's lunchboxes, homemade soup and cakes. My 4 yr old especially enjoyed his aeroplane shaped shortbread biscuit!

£

Merryhatton Garden Centre Coffee Shop

East Fortune
North Berwick
EH39 5JS
01620 880278
info@merryhatton.co.uk
www.merryhatton.co.uk

Café style coffee shop within Merryhatton Garden Centre. Bright and airy with open outlook across fields to the railway. Lovely selection of home-cooked hot food, filled rolls and home baking. Half portions available for children. Welcoming children's play area in the corner is decorated with some of the lovely gift items available to buy in the shop. A nice touch is the "priority" for parents/carers signs on the tables adjacent to the play area. The café is owned and run by friendly people who are themselves parents of young children and have clearly used their own experiences to provide a welcoming environment for under 5s and their carers. Both male and female toilets have nappy-changing facilities and were very clean. Best bit had to be lingering over my third cup of Earl Grey tea and huge slab of Maltesers cake whilst the kids played happily in the corner! The garden centre itself sells a lovely range of children's books and baby gifts. All in all a very welcoming family retreat on the way to or from the many places of interest in East Lothian.

£

Scottish Seabird Centre Cafe
The Harbour
North Berwick
East Lothian
EH39 4SS
01620 890202
www.seabird.org
If you're visiting the Seabird Centre or having a day out in North Berwick consider eating here. It's a lovely cafe with a good menu to choose from. There's also a children's menu on offer. If you're a member of the centre you get a discount in the cafe. As a registered charity you'll also be supporting education and conservation programmes.

£

Smeaton Tearoom
Smeaton Estate
Preston Road
East Linton
EH40 3DT
01620 860 501
mail@smeatonnurserygardens.co.uk
www.smeatonnurserygardens.co.uk
From the A1 take the East Linton A199 exit. Follow signs for Preston Mill through East Linton, turn right on Preston Road. Smeaton Estate is signposted. The walled gardens are at the top of the drive. The Nursery and Tearoom are set in a beautiful old walled garden. The tearoom has been transformed from the original greenhouse and apple store into a wonderful place to eat, drink and relax. It has a traditional feel and plenty of old features inside and a view of fantastic lush gardens outside. Very child-friendly and popular with parents and toddlers during the week. Serves tasty snacks and lunches. The home-baked cakes are highly recommended! The outdoor seating area allows you to appreciate the nursery and plants around, and gives your little ones a chance to explore.
This is a real gem, and definitely worth a visit.

£

Tea in the Park
East Links Family Park
Dunbar
East Lothian
EH42 1XF
01368 863607
www.eastlinks.co.uk
This cafe offers a good range of reasonably priced hot and cold filled rolls, baked potatoes, soups, toasties, snacks, baked goods, drinks, teas, and coffee. It can get busy, and the tables are close together, so it is best to park your pushchair outside (highchairs available). Bottle warming and baby food heating facilities are available. The café is open to the public if you happen to be in the area, and want to drop in for lunch or a snack. Toilet and nappy changing facilities are located in the café. This is a good place to fuel up during your day exploring the park, or to have a relaxing cuppa and a treat after a full day out with the kids!

£

EAT SOUTH

Café Lucia
Edinburgh Festival Theatre
13/29 Nicolson Street
0131 662 1112
This self-service café offers light snacks and half portions for children. It is part of the theatre and has show material displayed like 'Playdays' and 'The Singing Kettle'. Toilets and nappy changing room (M&F) are one floor up. Lift available.

£   Veg

Butterflies Cafe
Marchmont St Giles' Church Centre
1a Kilgraston Road
Edinburgh
EH9 1TZ
0131 447 4359
butterflies@marchmontstgiles.org.uk
www.marchmontstgiles.org.uk
Popular cafe in light airy space serving freshly prepared, home-made food at reasonable prices. Excellent children's menu for 'little' and 'junior people', including puddles of soup, breadsticks, cream cheese & raisins plate, sandwiches and fresh fruit plates, served with lovely touches such as a little fresh fruit with the sandwiches, and plastic plates and cutlery. A main dish of the day available, which can be served as a small portion, such as salmon bake and beef casserole. Machine to squeeze your own orange juice provides entertainment and a good dose of Vitamin C! At the end of the cafe there is space for pushchairs to be left unfolded and for children to play with the selection of toys provided. Also access to a pretty little garden at the rear, if not too cold to have the door open.

£

Earl of Marchmont
22 Marchmont Crescent
Edinburgh
EH9 1HG
0131 662 1877
www.renroc.co.uk
Formerly a somewhat dingy pub, the Earl has been vastly improved by a recent facelift and is a very welcome family-friendly addition to the Marchmont area. Run by the same owners as Café Renroc, they serve a limited but decent range of traditional bar foods. Plenty of room for pushchairs inside or at outdoor tables. There is a changing mat but not much space in the female toilets. License allows children until 18.00.

£   Veg

Elephants and Bagels
37 Marshall Street
0131 668 4404
www.elephant-house.co.uk
Sister café to The Elephant House, Edinburgh's first and foremost bagel shop, serving a variety of bagels with all kinds of fillings, as well as other light snacks. Crayons, pens and paper provided. Children's art exhibited – and there's a large collection of elephants. Space for pushchairs. Additional seating outside in the summer. Toilets are downstairs. Children's parties by arrangement.

£

Hellers Kitchen
15 Salisbury Place
Edinburgh
EH9 1SL
0131 667 4654
info@hellerskitchen.co.uk
www.hellerskitchen.co.uk
A smart, calming interior makes this bistro a great place for a quiet evening meal if you can find a babysitter, but it's also a buzzing, child-friendly venue by day. The toilets are downstairs, which isn't ideal, but a nappy changing unit is available. In the restaurant itself there are highchairs, children's portions available, and hot water provided for bottle warming. Staff are very friendly and keen to help.

£   Veg

Toast
146 Marchmont Road
Edinburgh
EH9 1AQ
0131 446 9873
www.toastedinburgh.co.uk
A friendly café serving drinks, light snacks and meals throughout the day. Can get very busy at weekends. Children's portions and bottle/food warming are available. Room inside for folded pushchairs only. An eclectic selection of artwork on the walls and a huge selection of magazines and newspapers to keep all the family entertained. Helpful staff compensate for the small space.

£   Veg

Victor Hugo
Continental Delicatessen
26/27 Melville Terrace
Edinburgh
EH9 1LP
0131 667 1827
info@victorhugodeli.com
www.victorhugodeli.com
Not a lot of space to manoeuvre inside, but a great place to get a sandwich to enjoy over the road in The Meadows. If you do decide to eat in, smaller portions of hot dishes are available - just ask. The chocolate brownies are highly recommended. This is also a handy place if you are unlucky enough to be resident at The Sick Kids and are looking for a bite to eat/opportunity to get some fresh air.

£

Braid Hills Hotel
Buckstone Bistro
134 Braid Road
0131 447 8888
Families are welcome in the Buckstone Bistro. Children's menu available. A wide choice of food in lovely surroundings without being too costly. Waitress service. No pushchairs.

££

Café Blush
219 Morningside Road
Edinburgh
EH10 4QT
0131 447 1012
www.cafeblush.co.uk
Café Blush is a bright, busy café in the centre of Morningside. It offers a good selection of paninis, toasties and salads as well as waist band expanding all day breakfasts. For children there are babycinos, a small inexpensive children's menu and a tempting array of cakes and tray bakes. The quality of the food is excellent and the bread accompanying the soup is delicious. The staff are eager to help if you have any specific requirements, and will cater for gluten free diets.

£   Veg

Café Grande
184 Bruntsfield Place
Edinburgh
EH10 4DF
0131 228 1188
info@cafegrande.co.uk
www.cafegrande.co.uk
A café by day and a bistro by night. A well-established and popular place with a good atmosphere. Children are welcome and catered for. Ideal for breakfast, coffee and cake, lunch and evening meals. Best to book tables for lunch and dinner as it gets busy. Children's menu for under 10s with favourites such as pasta dishes and sausages, etc. Colouring-in books and a computer are available to keep kids occupied. Jazz on Sunday nights 19.00 – 21.00. Artwork on display and for sale. Space for nappy changing is limited to a mat on the floor of the ladies toilet.

£

Anything out of date?
Let us know -
info@efuf.co.uk

Loopy Lorna's Tea House

370-372 Morningside Road
Edinburgh
EH10 5HS
0131 447 9217
www.loopylornas.com
Loopy Lorna's Tea House offers a warm welcome to all and children love to look at the brightly knitted tea cosies and admire the cake displays. There is a good selection of delicious breakfast and lunch items on offer for everyone, not to mention the many variety of teas.
Babies are well served with free heated baby food if parents are eating, as well as free nappies if required. Although there isn't loads of room for pushchairs staff will do their best to fit them in.

£   Veg

Luca's Morningside

16 Morningside Road
Edinburgh
EH10 4DB
0131 446 0233
www.s-luca.co.uk
A family-friendly place to eat and of course to enjoy some delicious ice cream. There are a couple of small tables on the ground floor, but if you wander up the spiral staircase there is a much larger dining area with plenty of tables. You can leave pushchairs at the bottom of the stairs. The menu offers a good range of items including an all-day breakfast. For ice cream lovers, the real stars of the menu have to be the ice cream treats however! Milkshakes, sundaes, and ice cream cones in a range of flavours are a must while eating here. Luca's welcomes children, and a children's menu is available with smaller portions of some dishes. Staff will provide hot water for heating bottles, and will heat baby food for you. Wooden high chairs are available. Be warned! If you are visiting with your "under 5s" (or you simply have a sweet tooth!) it is difficult to get past the fantastic selection of sweets, quality chocolates, and ice cream on the ground floor without being tempted to take a little something home with you! You can also order ice cream cakes for birthdays and special events.

£

Stables Tea Room and Bistro

The Stable Yard
Dalkeith Country Park
EH22 2NA
07974 027585
www.stable-bistro.com
Spacious cafe selling tea, coffee, good selection of home baking and ice creams. Also a small range of sandwiches and soup of the day.
Cafe is in a lovely big traffic-free courtyard with picnic benches so you can take your drinks outside if the weather is nice. Welcoming and friendly staff.

£

Cedar House Café

Vogrie House
Vogrie Country Park
EH23 4NU
01875 823695
www.cedartreecafe.co.uk
This is a spacious, bright and friendly cafe in the middle of Vogrie Country Park.
As well as the main indoor cafe area, there is a conservatory and there are picnic tables outside. There are lots of open spaces around for children to play while you drink your coffee. The cafe has toys, books and crayons for kids to play with, and some magazines for adults who are lucky enough to get five minutes to read them.
The menu has a good selection and the kids menu includes a tasty snack plate with sandwiches and fruit. The staff are very friendly and endlessly patient with small children who can't quite make up their minds.

£

Kailzie Gardens Restaurant

Kailzie
Peebles
EH45 9HT
01721 722807
www.kailziegardens.com
Nappy changing mat in restaurant toilet. Restaurant can be busy in the summer months so may be worth booking.

£

Floors Castle Terrace Cafe
Near Kelso
Roxburghshire
TD5 7SF
01573 223 333
Serves soup, meals, cakes and pastries, with a menu prepared by the castle's chef. Situated to the west of the castle, next to the Garden Centre, the beautiful walled garden and the playground.

££

Jedforest Deer & Farm Park Cafe
Jedburgh
01835 840364
www.jedforestdeerpark.co.uk
The café is self-service and provides sandwiches, soup and cakes. M&F nappy changing facilities. Prams and pushchairs can be parked inside the premises. All facilities on ground floor.

££

Stables Tea Room
Paxton House
Berwick upon Tweed
TD15 1SZ
01289 386291
info@paxtonhouse.com
www.paxtonhouse.com
Serves home-cooked meals, plus snacks, including home baking. Some tables are set into old horse stalls, so provide some privacy for breastfeeding. Best to take cash for the tea room.

££

1745 Cottage Restaurant
Traquair House
Innerleithen
01896 830323
enquiries@traquair.co.uk
www.traquair.co.uk
Seating inside and out, so if it's a nice day you can sit in the walled garden or on the patio. Serves children's lunch-boxes and has a children's menu option. Light meals, salads, panini and home-baking. Nappy changing facilities.

££

Ed's Eats.....

Craigie's Farm Deli and Cafe

Drill Hall Arts Cafe

Joseph Pearce's

La Partenope

Luca's

Pizza Express

Porto & Fi

Reds

Tapa Barra y Restaurante

Zanzero

EDINBURGH FOR UNDER FIVES

Where is your favourite place to eat?
Tell Ed
email ed@efuf.co.uk

EAT WEST

St. Bride's Centre
10 Orwell Terrace
0131 346 1405
Café offering hot meals and home-baking at great prices. There is a large soft play area, reading corner and toys for children. Plenty space for pushchairs. Mother/toddler group - all welcome. Programme of children's activities. Call for details.

£

The Caley Sample Room
42-58 Angle Park Terrace
Edinburgh
EH11 2JR
0131 337 7204
info@thecaleysampleroom.co.uk
www.thecaleysampleroom.co.uk
This is a nice quiet place to go with under 5s but I would only recommend it for coffee as the children's menu is more suited to older children. Sausages, fishfingers, chicken nuggets all with chips or beans on very thick toast and you have to ask as there is no printed children's menu. The food is all served on adult sized plates with adult sized cutlery. The food is gastro pub with a daily specials board making use of seasonal ingredients. They do Sunday lunch which is popular with families. Staff are very friendly. There are plenty of seats and although half the pub is set-up for dining you can eat anywhere. There is plenty of space to park a pushchair but the pub still retains a cosy atmosphere.

£

La Partenope
96 Dalry Road
Edinburgh
EH11 2AX
0131 347 8880
www.lapartenope.co.uk
La Partenope is a Neapolitan Italian restaurant. They serve excellent Italian food made with fresh ingredients and provide a good set lunch menu Tues to Friday. Dinner offers can be found on their website. They are extremely welcoming to children, with very friendly staff, who sometimes even magic up toys to entertain the children.
Although they don't do a children's menu, they do accommodate pushchairs and so this is an ideal restaurant to pop into with very small children. Bring their food with you while you enjoy the delightful grown up Italian cuisine. For older toddlers and children, the food may not be to all children's taste but there is pizza and pasta to choose from and of course bruschetta and if that is not to their liking then they will probably be happy with the desserts.

££

Timetwisters
Bankhead Drive
Sighthill
EH11 4ES
0131 308 2464
www.timetwisters.co.uk
Very generous portions of very tasty healthy food e.g. pasta, chicken strips, dips and strips, baked potatoes, soup and children's lunch bags. All food made on site and they always have home-made scones and also cakes if they have had time to make them. Coffee and tea and healthy drinks for children.
There are no highchairs but staff will provide a booster seat on request. These are slightly longer than the average seat and can be used from 6 months but you do need to keep an eye on your baby so that they don't fall over sideways.

£

Visit our website for updates:
www.efuf.co.uk

Verandah Restaurant
17 Dalry Road
Haymarket
0131 337 5828
A friendly Indian restaurant with a varied menu including vegetarian options. Special lunch menus available. Children's portions served, and crayons and colouring books provided to keep little ones amused. Carry-out food available. Free home delivery service.

££

Brasserie at Norton House
Norton House Hotel
Ingliston (opposite showground)
0131 333 1275
Contemporary styled restaurant with large conservatory overlooking the hotel grounds. Children's menu available.

££

Brasserie Restaurant
Apex European Hotel
90 Haymarket Terrace
Edinburgh
EH12 5LQ
0131 474 3456
reservations@apexhotels.co.uk
www.apexhotels.co.uk
Staff couldn't be more welcoming to families, and crayons and paper are provided for small children. Menu available for children is suitable for both big and small kids. Look out for good value 'Fixed Price' meals.

£

The Dower House
St Margaret's Park
Corstorphine High Street
EH12
0131 316 4246
Café selling tea, coffee and baking. Very friendly and welcoming. Extra seating upstairs. No highchairs or changing facilities

£

Jungle Cafe
Edinburgh Zoo
134 Corstorphine Road
Edinburgh
EH12 6TS
0131 334 9171
info@rzss.org.uk
www.edinburghzoo.org.uk
Large self-service cafe, serving fish and chips, jacket potatoes, hot dogs etc. Good range of sandwiches all freshly made. Children can choose from a range of sandwiches, drinks and crisps in a cute zoo lunch pack. Has a great soft play area. Children can play while the adults have a drink and a cake. Just outside is a huge lawn and plenty of picnic tables/outdoor seating.

£

Mansion House
Edinburgh Zoo
(as for Jungle Cafe)
Beautiful mansion house in the centre of Edinburgh Zoo. Bar downstairs serves the usual pub lunches and a children's menu. Upstairs has a lounge serving light snacks, with a small children's menu, ideal for a quick snack to recharge your batteries while you enjoy the beautiful views over the zoo and Pentland Hills. Tends to be a more relaxed atmosphere than the other cafes in the zoo.

£

Penguin Coffee Shop
Edinburgh Zoo
(as for Jungle Cafe)
Perfect for a quick coffee or for refreshments to take-away and enjoy in the sunshine. Picnic tables available outside with a great view of the penguin enclosure.

£

Rumblin' Tum
235 St John's Road
Edinburgh
EH12 7XA
0131 539 7008
Children are made welcome. Café offers breakfast to early evening meals and light bites, and coffee. Children's menu includes sausage and chips, macaroni cheese and beans on toast.

£

Stripes
Edinburgh Zoo
134 Corstorphine Road
Edinburgh
EH12 6TS
0131 334 9171
info@rzss.org.uk
www.edinburghzoo.org.uk
Large self-service cafe, serves a variety of hot foods such as fish and chips, sausages, burgers and snacks all day.There is a children's menu and you can get lunch packs where children can choose from a range of sandwiches, crisps and drinks and put them in a cute zoo bag. Can get very busy.

£

The Kilted Pig
101b Colinton Road
Edinburgh
EH14 1AL
0131 444 1911
oink@kiltedpig.co.uk
www.kiltedpig.co.uk
Friendly pub offering all day food. Children's portions and highchairs are available. Friendly staff are very accommodating and welcoming to children, offering books and crayons on arrival. A nice touch is the displaying of children's artwork on the pillars. A great place for breakfast or lunch when the pub is not too busy. A favourite haunt of mothers and toddlers during the week. Best bit was munching through my "hangover breakfast" (despite not having a hangover!) whilst my 3 yr old son ate his way through four sausages!

£

The Bridge Inn
27 Baird Road
Ratho
EH28 8RA
0131 333 1320
info@bridgeinn.com
www.bridgeinn.com
This spacious pub offers large helpings of basic pub grub with an Italian slant. Children have their own menu with a reasonable choice of semi healthy offerings although no vegetables provided with either the adults or kids fish and chips.
The main attraction for this location is the canal and barges. There is an outdoor seating area with a good view, but food is only served inside. Most toddlers would enjoy looking at the barges and feeding the ducks, but will require close adult supervision due to the proximity to the water. Santa cruises are available in December.

£

Whitmuir The Organic Place
Whitmuir Farm
Lamancha
West Linton
EH46 7BB
01968 661908
www.whitmuirtheorganicplace.co.uk
Lots going on at Whitmuir. Lovely menu of fresh, organic food with a "Little Piggies" menu for younger diners. The restaurant was only opened at the end of 2009 and already it's becoming a firm favourite. Great for children - offers toys to play with, nappy changing facilites and farm animals. Fantastic range of goodies on offer in the shop too.

£

The Park Bistro & Eating House
Park Farm
by Linlithgow
EH49 6QY
01506 846666
Situated on the east side of Linlithgow. Located along the Philipstoun turnoff from the B9080, just after Kingscavill.

Close to the Union Canal and the enclosed outdoor tables and children's play area allow you to make the most of pleasant views over the surrounding fields. Pedal cars keep under 5s happy. You can watch barges and boats sailing by on the canal.

Large portions of freshly cooked favourites and daily specials. Fixed price children's menu. Nappy changing (M&F), plus the toilets have toddler seats.

££

Morag's Milk Bar
Almond Valley Heritage Centre
Millfield
Livingston
EH54
01506 414 957
info@almondvalley.co.uk
www.almondvalley.co.uk
Wipe your hooves, park your pushchair at the door, and visit Morag's Milk Bar! This is a very child-friendly tea room with a good range of hot and cold lunch options, as well as (very tasty!) baked goods, teas, and coffees. Morag's Milk Bar is "proud not to serve chips", and has earned the Healthy Living Award. This means healthier options are readily available – just look for the green apple on the menu. "Old favourites" such as bacon rolls and beefburgers are also available. For those with smaller appetites, children's portions and "Munchboxes" are offered. Though you are unable to bring picnics into the Milk Bar, there are picnic tables and a covered picnic barn on-site. There is a bottle warmer and microwave available for heating baby food. The tea room is attached to "Morag's Meadow" (extra cost) and some tables are located in view of the soft play. This is the perfect place to enjoy a hot lunch on a cool day, or to fuel up for a busy afternoon exploring the rest of Almond Valley.

£

Five Sisters Zoo
Gavieside
West Calder
West Lothian
EH55 8PT
01506 872924
enquiries@fivesisterszoo.co.uk
www.fivesisterszoo.co.uk
Small cafe with a basic selection of sandwiches, toasties, soup etc. Staff are very flexible and happy to provide a roll and jam for fussy eaters.

£

Callendar Park Stables Tearoom
Falkirk
FK1 1YR
01324 503770
In Callendar Park, near Callendar House, by the east car park.

The tearoom is small and friendly and serves children's portions of most dishes. The garden at the rear is accessible via a lane to the left hand side of the Park Gallery and through a gate. Unfortunately the tearoom itself can't cope with pushchairs. Sit outdoors in the herb garden in summer and watch the swallows as they fly around the picturesque ruined tower. Nooks and crannies in the garden for exploring! A pleasant place to spend time.

££

Corrieri's Café
7/9 Alloa Road
Causewayhead
Stirling
FK9 5LH
01786 472089
A family run and family orientated café/restaurant beside the roundabout on the way to the University and the Wallace Monument. Italian food (pizza and pasta) but also great Scottish breakfasts, snacks and vegetarian food throughout the day. Very friendly ad fun place to eat with small portions for children. Quick service and fast cooking adds to the appeal for parents of under 5s! Ground floor access with room for pushchairs. On-road parking along Alloa Rd. Wide range of ice creams. Can be very busy at weekends.
If you just fancy an ice cream , why not buy one and go to the playpark just along the road. There's a tyre swing, a tyre balance, and a multi-level sandpit and climbing frame. There are bucket swings and a double covered tube slide. Next to the playpark is a basketball/football court. Plenty of grass to run on too.

££

Unicorn Cafe
Stirling Castle
Stirling
FK8 1EJ
01786 450 000
www.historic-scotland.gov.uk
Large café offering a range of sandwiches, soup, salads and baked potatoes. Kids' lunchboxes available. Castle has various toilets here and there, with various facilities, but there's a good one hidden away within the Great Hall, complete with a nappy changing unit.

££

Activities & Classes

Activities and Classes for children

There are a plethora of options available for taking your little one(s) to activity sessions and classes. Classes will vary from blocks of sessions booked in advance to activities where you are free to drop in when it suits you. In a lot of cases there will be an opportunity to attend a taster session or try the first class for free before committing to a regular booking.

These activities can also be good for parties and it's always worth asking whether the teacher would be interested in a private booking.

ARTS & CRAFTS

Although they are not numerous, there are art and craft classes available for under 5s in Edinburgh, outside a nursery environment. The following venues run classes for younger children.

First Impressions Art Classes
07951 137218
jbdawson@tesco.net
Art classes for little ones 4+ yrs.

The Imagination Workshop
136 Marchmont Road
EH9 1AQ
0131 466 0148
nicki@theimaginationworkshop.co.uk
www.theimaginationworkshop.co.uk
Offer craft workshops for 2+ yrs. Arty parties also available.

Messy Art Class for Mums and Toddlers
Ratho Community Centre
1 School Wynd
Ratho
0131 333 1055
Contact the venue for full details of the class.

Messy Monsters
0131 656 6758
sarah.smith@messymonsters.co.uk
www.messymonsters.co.uk
Messy Monsters art club is primarily a parent and toddler group that allows children, accompanied by their parents or carers, to spend one hour of quality time in messy, creative activities. Classes are available for children from 6mths and are held in various venues, typically community centres and church halls. Also available for birthday parties and other special occasions.

BABY CLASSES

Baby Sensory
edinburgh@babysensory.co.uk
www.babysensory.co.uk
Award winning baby development class.

Baby Massage Classes
07986 527947
info@beautiful-daze.com
www.beautiful-daze.com
Learn to massage your baby. Courses and one-to-one sessions available. Also offer sessions in your own home and pamper parties.

Baby Music
0131 229 3667
info@birthresourcecentre.org.uk
Action songs, rhymes and lullabies for babies up to 1yr and for 1yr to toddlers. Class includes time for tea/coffee and socialising with other parents. These are very popular classes, so please call for venue, times, cost and to reserve a place. Concessions are available.

Birthlight Baby Yoga
0131 557 1255
cleary_gfm@yahoo.co.uk
Classes provide a relaxed environment to learn baby yoga, helping to build confidence and trust between parent and baby. Songs and rhymes are used alongside simple yoga sequences to make this a very special time to share with your baby. Baby yoga can also help alleviate common baby ailments including colic, crying and poor sleep patterns. Classes to suit from birth to 3yrs.

Hullabaloo Kids
07738 078317
emmawhyley@hullabalookids.co.uk
Activites to stimulate little minds, exercise little bodies, promote bonding and enjoy. From birth.

Sing and Sign
0131 664 0355
deearmstrong@singandsign.co.uk
www.singandsign.com
Classes are for babies and toddlers 7-18 mths and run in a course of 10 wks (during term times). Signs are taught through songs and rhymes which are specially written or adapted to target signs relating to babies routines and interest. Musical instruments, props, puppets and pictures are used to capture the babies' attention and the aim of the classes is to enhance parent-baby communication by using signs (as well as having a bit of fun along the way).

Yoga for Baby
Avril Berry
0131 225 2012
avril@yogaforbaby.com
www.yogaforbaby.com
An excellent way to introduce your little one to yoga and you don't need any previous experience yourself. Provides a great opportunity for you and your baby to socialise in a relaxed and supportive environment. Classes suitable from 6wks until toddling (see Yoga for Toddlers).

Yoga With Babies
Andrea St.Clair
0131 229 9035
andrea@alexandertech.freeserve.co.uk
Friendly and relaxed classes for babies from 4 wks to 10 mths. Gentle ways to tone, strengthen and ease yourself and movements for the baby to enjoy with you.

BALL SPORTS

Coerver Football Coaching
01506 414449
Gordon.craig@coerver.co.uk
www.coerver.co.uk
Classes run at various locations – after school, weekends, and holiday camps. For pre-school.

Edinburgh Accies Mini-Rugby
minis@edinburghaccies.com
www.edinburghaccies.com
Mini-rugby for 4+ yrs.

Enjoy-A-Ball
08452 26 26 94
office.team@enjoy-a-ball.com
www.enjoy-a-ball.com
Sports coaching programme for 3-9yrs. No more than 10 per class. Classes are held in local sports, church and community centres throughout Edinburgh and Lothians. Also available for parties, contact as above.

Visit our website for updates:
www.efuf.co.uk

Golf
0131 652 2178
www.edinburghleisure.co.uk
Coaching for 3+ yrs at Craigentinny golf school.
Coaching camps and individual lessons on offer.

Mini Kickers
0131 652 2178
www.edinburghleisure.co.uk
Mini Kickers classes for 3-5yrs from Edinburgh
Leisure. The mini kickers football programme
enables the children to learn and enjoy the basics
of football through a range of fun practices and
games. The classes, delivered by SFA coaches,
will help develop good coordination and build upon
their communication skills.
Also at Bonnyrigg Leisure Centre: 0131 663 7579.

Play2Learn Sports Coaching
07952 147577 or 07766 143918
shane@play2learn.info
www.play2learn.info
Football and multi-sports sessions for nurseries and
playgroups across Edinburgh and the surrounding
areas. Also offer holiday camps and parties.

Playball
0131 652 2178
www.edinburghleisure.co.uk
Edinburgh Leisure classes based on fun, movement
and play. Allows children 3-5yrs to try a range of
sports including Basketball, Football, Rugby, Golf
and Tennis.

Rugbytots
0845 313 3252
kirsty@rugbytots.co.uk
www.rugbytots.co.uk
Rugbytots is a weekly play session for boys and
girls 2-7yrs. All classes are led by SRU qualified
coaches. Sessions available in Edinburgh, Lothians
and the Borders. Classes cover all the motor
skills by using rugby as a medium with the main
emphasis on fun. Book online.

Socatots
0131 473 2335
07923 005534
b.robertson@socatots.com
www.socatots.org/edinburgh
Socatots is a soccer-specific physical play
programme for children for 6mths - 5yrs. Sessions
are held in various venues in Edinburgh and East
Lothian and feature parent/carer participation.

Tennis
0131 444 1969
www.craiglockhart.totaltennis.net
Craiglockhart tennis and sports club offer tennis for
all abilities and age groups. From 2yrs.

Tots Tennis
0131 652 2178
www.edinburghleisure.co.uk
Edinburgh Leisure runs tots tennis classes for
children 3-5yrs. Classes teach young children
basic hitting, movement and co-ordination skills
for tennis. The coaching is by qualified and
experienced coaches in a fun and encouraging
environment. Parents/carers must accompany
children during the session.

Waverley Tennis Club
0131 667 9517
Waverley@waverleysports.co.uk
www.waverleysports.co.uk
Offers a thriving Juniors section with excellent
coaching from 4yrs.

Wee Dribblers
0131 652 2178
www.edinburghleisure.co.uk
Parent and toddler sessions run by Edinburgh
Leisure. Fun play with all types of balls as an
introduction to football.

DANCE

Classes for younger children (i.e. 2-4yrs), usually teach music and movement. This may include nursery rhymes and simple dancing: hopping, skipping, toe-pointing, mime and moving in time to music. Socialising, learning to wait your turn etc, are key elements in all dancing classes. Footwear is sometimes light shoes, available from any decent shoe shop, more often ballet shoes. There are many local dance classes, some of which are listed here, others may be found through friends, recommendations, ads in local libraries, community centres, shop windows and the local press.
Choosing the right class for your child can be difficult; it's worthwhile investigating the teacher's qualifications, class content, studio facilities etc.

The Royal Academy of Dance
0207 326 8000
www.rad.org.uk
The RAD has a registration system for teachers - contact them for a list of local registered teachers.

Angela Watson School of Dance
0131 661 9590
Angela4dance@yahoo.co.uk
Ballet, Modern and Tap classes in Colinton. From 3yrs.

Baby Loves Disco
www.babylovesdisco.co.uk
Monthly disco for children (from 6mths) and parents. Classic disco music, chill-out area, snacks and a bar for adults.

Boogie Babies
0131 652 2178
www.edinburghleisure.co.uk
Hip Hop and Pop dance classes for under 5s at Edinburgh Leisure Centres.

Buckstone Youth Dance
0131 445 3892
Ballet (RAD) from pre-school year. Modern and Tap (ISTD) from Primary 1.

CeilidhKids
0131 667 898
ceilidhkids@ceilidhkids.com
www.ceilidhkids.com
Fun and fitness for you and your child. For children 3-5yrs and their parents or carers. Book a block of classes or pay-as-you-go. CeilidhKids also offer family ceilidhs for celebrations, parties or fundraisers.

Creative Dance
0131 652 2178
www.edinburghleisure.co.uk
Creative Dance classes for 3-6yrs with Edinburgh Leisure.

Dance Base
14-16 Grassmarket
EH1 2JU
0131 225 5525
dance@dancebase.co.uk
www.dancebase.co.uk
Scotland's National Centre for Dance - fully accessible building offering state-of-the-art facilities, with four dance studios. Lots of classes on offer, including drop-in sessions. Toddler music and movement classes, pre-school and primary dance sessions.

Dance for All at the Theatre School
106 St Stephen Street
EH3 5AQ
0131 226 5533
jennylewis@danceforall.freeserve.co.uk
www.danceforall.co.uk
2-4yrs. General nursery dance; a fun introduction to dance steps, rhythm and co-ordination, mime, songs and creative dance. 4-5yrs pre-Primary Ballet; a gentle introduction to more structured dance steps and sequences, alongside free expression and creative dance, rhythm and co-ordination exercises. Tap Dancing classes and Jazz classes from 4yrs.
After-school classes and all day Saturday. Phone for full details.

The Edinburgh Dance Academy
4-6 Coltbridge Avenue
EH12 6AH
0131 337 3402
edinburghdance@aol.com
www.edinburghdanceacademy.co.uk
Ballet from 3yrs. Classes are held in venues throughout Edinburgh and the Lothians. Contact for current details, venues and requirements.

EH Dance
07976 585479
Ehdance@gmail.com
www.ehdance.co.uk
Classes in ballet, tap and jazz in the Craigmount and Granton areas. Classes start from 3yrs where the emphasis is placed on fun and the children are encouraged to learn the basics of balance, movement and interaction with other children. Phone for current prices.

Fit-n-Little
0131 337 2774
info@manukahealth.co.uk
www.manukahealth.co.uk
Classes combine music, dance and a lot of imagination, energizing children and making exercise fun. Along with healthy movements children learn the basics of healthy living, play games making exercise easy and develop their confidence socially. Such fun even the adults want to jump up and down!

Lothian Dance Academy
0131 669 9073
Pre-school ballet, tap, jazz and creative music classes for 3-5yrs, and also for older children. The main studio is in Portobello but classes are also held in various other locations throughout the city. Phone for current prices and locations.

Manor School of Ballet
0131 334 0399
enquiries@manorschoolofballet.co.uk
www.manorschoolofballet.co.uk
Music and movement for ages 2-4yrs. Ballet, Jazz, Tap and Highland classes. Venues across Edinburgh. The youngest pupils wear normal clothes, plus ballet shoes, which the school sells at a reasonable price. Children start to wear leotards from 3yrs. The school employs several teachers who are all RAD, ISTD and UKA registered.

Mhairi Hogg School of Dancing
0131 449 3035
Tap, Highland, and Modern Dance Classes for all ages held in Colinton Mains Community Centre and Oxgangs Neighbourhood Centre. Nursery Tap classes are held for 3-5 yrs. A class leotard is worn, plus Highland, tap, ballet or jazz shoes.

Mini Movers
07724 494522
minimovers@gmail.com
Dance and play for under 5s. Through a blend of creative movement and developmental play Mini Movers sessions channel children's inner drive to move, explore, bounce, skip and jump, helping them build the foundations for a good start in life. They also stimulate children's imagination which helps them to develop social and cooperative skills in a fun way. Teachers are all specially trained, hold liability insurance and are Enhanced Disclosure Scotland checked. Classes are run in playgroups and nurseries, or individually and can also be booked for children's events and parties.

Morag Alexander
moragalexander@btinternet.com
www.moragalexander.co.uk
Classes in East Lothian and Midlothian. Ballet, Jazz and Tap. From 3yrs.

Morningside Dance Academy
0131 668 4977
morningsidedance@btinternet.com
Ballet, Tap, Modern and Jazz dancing from 3yrs. RAD and BTDA syllabus to Examination Standard.

Pointworks Dance Classes
07772 504958
Ballet, tap, and modern dance. From 3yrs.

Steps School of Dance
0131 339 2315
Alex55555@btinternet.com
Ballroom, Latin, Disco, and Rock'n'Roll. From 4yrs.

Tap and Ballet with Mrs P Allam
01259 742973
Nursery Ballet from 3yrs. Classes, accompanied by a pianist, are held in Blackhall. Fully qualified staff.

DRAMA

The Drama Studio
0131 453 3284
info@thedramastudio.com
www.thedramastudio.com
Drama workshops for 3+ yrs in various venues across Edinburgh. Also run holiday workshops and birthday parties.

Edinburgh Acting School
0131 225 1444
enquiries@edinburghactingschool.com
Drama classes for 4-6yrs. Contact school for further information.

Helen O'Grady Drama Academy
0131 667 0939
midscot@helenogrady.co.uk
www.helenogrady.co.uk
Kindy drama programme for 3-5yrs. Story telling, dramatic play, creative movement, songs and language development activities.

Lyceum Playtime
Royal Lyceum Theatre Edinburgh
0131 248 4848
www.lyceum.org.uk
Creative Learning programme offers fun drama workshops for parents and children aged 2-4yrs. Times and dates vary. Please see Lyceum website or call for more information.

Orcadia Creative Learning Centre
3 Windsor Place
Portobello
0131 669 1075
www.orcadia.smartchange.org

Creative movement for children 4+ yrs with special needs and learning disabilities. Dance, creative movement, music, mime, mask and puppetry are all on the agenda.

Sparkle Arts
07717 706778
info@sparklearts.co.uk
www.sparklearts.co.uk
A fun mix of drama, dance and music with professionally-qualified teachers. Work with local nurseries. Also offer parties tailored to your child's age group. 2+ yrs.

Stagecoach Theatre Arts
0131 449 9507
edinburghnorth@stagecoach.co.uk
www.stagecoach.co.uk
Classes and holiday workshops at numerous venues in Edinburgh. Stagecoach teaches acting, dancing and singing.

 Anything out of date?
Let us know -
info@efuf.co.uk

GYMNASTICS

Gymnastics classes are popular for the under 5s and classes accommodating this age group are generally available in Edinburgh. When choosing a class convenience is usually the prime consideration. However, it is well worth checking on the teacher's qualifications for teaching pre-school children, the facilities available and their insurance cover.

All British Amateur Gymnastics Association (BAGA) coaches will charge a set amount to all children who attend their classes. This is paid to the Association for insurance purposes. This sum will be paid irrespective of the cost of the course. Anyone working with young children, ie nursery groups etc, might be interested in taking the Scottish Gymnastics Coaching Award for pre-school gymnastics and movement.

Unlike Glasgow, Edinburgh doesn't have a gymnastics-style class specifically for disabled children. The best advice we can give, if you want your child to try out a mainstream gymnastics class, is to speak to the coach to get an idea of how your child might best be included and what they might gain from the class. It may be best to organise a trial session to ensure that the club activities will be suited to your child's needs.

Scottish Gymnastics Association
www.scottishgymnastics.com
Contact the association for information on coaching awards, a copy of the syllabus, and advice on gymnastics classes.

Gymbabes
www.tumbletots.com/edinburgh
www.tumbletots.com/edinburgh-west
Programme to develop physical skills of agility, balance, co-ordination and climbing. For 6mths to walking. Gymbabes is for children who are crawling but not yet confident walkers - play, exploration and learning in a safe environment. Holiday programmes and parties also available. See Tumble Tots opposite for more information.

Gymini
0131 334 3657 or 447 7859 or 443 1390
gymini@hotmail.co.uk
www.gymini.co.uk
Gym classes for children from 12mths. Venues throughout Edinburgh. Classes are taught by multi-sport qualified coaches and provide a good basic foundation for sport.

Gymnippers
0131 652 2178
www.edinburghleisure.co.uk
Edinburgh Leisure gymnastics classes at centres across Edinburgh. Parent and toddler sessions for 18mths-3yrs and a pre-school music and movement class for 3-5yrs.

LoGy Centre Gymnastics and Trampoline Classes
0131 440 4495
info@logy-centre.co.uk
www.logy-centre.co.uk
Classes from 2yrs. Also offers Jungle Gyms summer play schemes and parties.

No specific class for children with additional support needs, but the centre is happy to discuss options. Parent & Toddler classes include simple gymnastics and trampolining classes for 3-5yrs to build on motor skills and extend the range of gymnastics/trampolining.

Ready Steady Play
0131 664 8894
Deborah@readysteadyplay.co.uk
www.readysteadyplay.co.uk
Physical activity classes for children 18mths-3yrs. Classes last 45 minutes and begin with a warm up followed by various activities, such as: ball play; hula hoops; running; relay games; balloon play; tug of war; creative movement and fun dancing. Activities end with a cool down and children receive a weekly reward sticker as they leave the class. Children are given a sports bib to wear during the class.

Toddler Gymnastics
Wester Hailes Education Centre
5 Murrayburn Drive
0131 442 2201
Classes for 3-5yrs. Block booking - a waiting list applies. Contact the centre for more details.

Tumble Tots
www.tumbletots.com/edinburgh
www.tumbletots.com/edinburgh-west
The Tumble Tots specially designed programme helps develop co-ordination, balance, agility and climbing skills. Follows on from Gymbabes from walking to 5yrs (Gymbobs sessions for 5+ yrs). Supervision is by specially trained staff. Tumble Tots for children from walking confidently to 2 yrs, 2-3yrs and 3-5yrs. Sessions are based around activity stations.

Edinburgh East
Contact: Jo Letelier-Lobos
01875 819966
joletelier.lobos@virgin.net
Covers Morningside, Fairmilehead, Haddington, and Marchmont.

Edinburgh West
Contact: Julia Kerr
0131 444 2444
Julia.kerr@tumbletots.com
Covers Trinity, Murrayfield, Corstorphine, Linlithgow, Cramond, Ravelston, and Livingston.

Although there is no class specifically for children with additional support needs, children are welcome to attend a class suited to their developmental stage. If your child is happy to attend a class with younger children, then this might suit.

HORSE RIDING

Edinburgh and Lasswade Riding Centre
Kevock Road
Lasswade
EH18 1HX
0131 663 7676
lasswaderiding@btconnect.com
www.lasswadestables.com
Half hour pony treks for under 5s. Small Shetland ponies and older, quieter ponies are used with this age group. For children from 2yrs - as long as a child is happy to sit on the pony s/he can be taken on a small trek. The ponies are on leads and one person is allocated to each child. Children should wear wellies/boots. The Centre also hosts children's parties and these include a pony trek, the opportunity to feed and groom a pony and then party food and grassy play area.

Riding for the Disabled

Horse-riding for people with disabilities, including young children 3+ yrs. All conditions except severe epilepsy (not controlled) or arthritis would be eligible.
There are several centres in Edinburgh and the Lothians:
Drum Riding, Gilmerton
08452 41 43 65

Muirfield Group, East Lothian.
08452 41 63 61
www.muirfieldrda.org.uk

Ravelrig Group, Balerno.
08454 50 67 25
www.rda-ravelrig.org.uk

Thornton Rose Group, Midlothian.
08454 50 69 22
www.thorntonroserda.com

West Lothian Group.
08454 50 69 52
www.westlothianrda.org.uk

Don't forget to let businesses know you saw them in the EFUF book!

Each centre's contact number is through to the contact for the organisation's home. Waiting lists can be extremely long so consider putting your child's name down as soon as you possibly can – but the wait can be well worth it. You will need to complete a medical information form and have it countersigned by a medical professional who knows your child. Volunteers are friendly, enthusiastic and dedicated. Your child may gain a lot from the experience of regular riding. Places are in high demand and the level of support offered to cater for a child's needs is commendable.

LANGUAGES

Allemann Fun
01383 824308
Group meeting at Gillespie's High School for children 3+ yrs who are bi-lingual in German. Child must have a German speaking parent.

Eveil Musical En Francais
Intitut Francais d'Ecosse
0131 225 5366
culture@ifecosse.org.uk
For children from 3-6yrs. French language taught by a qualified French music teacher. Children listen to and create music using the voice and percussion instruments.

Gaelic Parent & Toddler Group
0131 529 2415
For 0-3yrs. Groups meet in Corstorphine and Fountainbridge.

Le Petit Monde
07910 045743
info@lepetitmonde.co.uk
www.lepetitmonde.co.uk
Puppet shows, classes and workshops in French and English for schools and nurseries. 3+ yrs. Other venues considered.

MARTIAL ARTS

The Edinburgh Judo Club
0131 554 8330
edinburghjudo@aol.com
www.edinburghjudo.com
Evening and weekend classes from 3yrs.

Judo
0131 652 2178
www.edinburghleisure.co.uk
Full contact martial arts class from 4yrs. Learn throwing and holding movements with Edinburgh Leisure classes.

Junior Judo
0131 555 4578
george@juniorjudoclub.co.uk
www.juniorjudoclub.co.uk
Classes start from 4yrs. Highly experienced and long-running judo tuition for youngsters.

Shishi Kai Judo
0131 447 7859
jim@shishikai.co.uk
Judo classes for children aged from 4yrs. All coaches qualified, registered and child protection vetted. Contact club for prices and more information.

MUSIC FUN

Young children love music. However, in most cases under 5s are not able to specialise in a particular instrument - their hands are not big enough, they don't have the lung power etc. Most of the music classes mentioned below, therefore, teach listening skills and moving in time to music. It is highly advisable to book in advance for all classes.

The Boogie Bunch
01506 418 940

Lothian Downs Syndrome Association runs several clubs for children with Downs Syndrome and their brothers and sisters. Contact for more details.

Colours of Music
07783047848 or 0785842446
coloursofmusic@hotmail.co.uk
www.coloursofmusic.co.uk
Classes for children 18mths-7yrs based on a popular and effective method proposed by German composer Carl Orff. Children listen and dance to classical music, learn action songs and play instruments from different regions of the world. Classes are held by two experienced teachers in various locations, including clients' houses. They also offer entertainment for children during parties.

Daisy's Music Time
0131 661 2106
betty@ednet.co.uk
Fun music sessions for babies and toddlers aged 3mths-3yrs in the Trinity area. Singing, rhythm activities, movement, listening and playing percussion instruments. Lots of props. Classes run during school term time by an experienced teacher. Phone for current times and further information.

Children with additional needs are welcome. The parent/carer stays with their child for the session. Venues are accessible and have toilets for the disabled.

Dough-Doh Music Club
0131 332 4540
Educationally motivated music club for 2-5yrs. Established 1994, this club is taken by Carol and Laraine, two experienced teachers. Meet the Dodo family! Listen, learn and move to unique Dodo stories, tongue twisters, rhymes and songs. Children develop natural rhythm through use of percussion instruments.

Edinburgh Young Musicians
0131 226 3392
admin@e-y-m.org.uk
www.e-y-m.org.uk
Musical play classes for children, starting in their final pre-school year (from 3yrs), leading to instrumental tuition, choirs, orchestras, chamber groups and theory and aural classes for older children. Pre-school classes provide a general introduction to music, developing the child's sense of rhythm, sense of pitch, listening skills, co-ordination and imagination. Classes are held at James Gillespie's High School on Saturday mornings.

Hullabaloo!
01875 341679 or 07966 434591
charlotte_mcmillan@sky.com
Music classes in Pencaitland and Haddington for 4mths-2yrs and toddlers to pre-school. Singing and movement to popular rhymes and songs.

Jack and Jill
0131 667 9664
jill.reeves@blueyonder.co.uk
Lap rides, finger plays, action songs, dancing, playing simple percussion instruments, and listening to live music - interactive musical fun and learning for tots (18mths-5yrs) and their accompanying adults. Classes run by qualified and experienced music teachers. Classes are held in Marchmont.

Children with special needs are very welcome at these music fun classes. Jill, a qualified teacher and music therapist, has a very positive attitude to inclusion and will work to make sure no children are left out of the activities. These classes come highly recommended.

Jo Jingles
www.jojingles.com

Music and movement classes for various age ranges from 6mths to 5yrs. Includes action songs, nursery rhymes and playing of musical instruments. Some songs are familiar, others are new, so there's something to keep the participating parent/carer on their toes. Also available for Birthdays. Classes held in various venues throughout the city.

Edinburgh East & Mid Lothian
Contact: Susan
0131 620 3282
jojingles@thejamesons.co.uk

Edinburgh West & West Lothian
Contact: Joanne
0131 443 4196
jojingles@goodall5.co.uk

Kindermusik with Monica
0131 308 0582 or 07903 420061
monica@musicandgiggles.co.uk
www.musicandgiggles.co.uk

Kindermusik is an innovative music and movement programme for children from newborn to 7yrs. Each class is a world of discovery and adventure, using language skills, literacy, listening, problem solving, social skills, self-esteem, and musicality. And it happens within a nurturing environment full of energy, imagination, music, dancing, and playful delight. Classes are held in various venues across the city - contact Monica for current times and further information.

St Mary's Music School
0131 538 7766
info@st-marys-music-school.co.uk
www.st-marys-music-school.co.uk

Music classes for children in their final pre-school year (4+ yrs), including musical games, singing, listening, and use of simple percussion instruments. Classes are on Saturday mornings.

Mini Minstrels
0131 441 3750

Music sessions for 3-6yrs. Singing, musical games, instruments, and development of musical skills through fun.

♿ Children with special needs are welcome. There are three steps up to the property. Parking is unrestricted but you may wish to get there early as the street can become a little busy when classes are on. Hazel has experience of working in a special needs environment.

Mini Music Makers
National Youth Choir of Scotland
0141 287 2943 or 07799 414 329

Music sessions at St Mary's RC Cathedral in Edinburgh. Classes for 0-18mths and 18mths-3yrs. Open up the world of music for you and your child with singing games and rhymes.

Monkey Music
www.monkeymusic.com
Award winning classes that nurture a child's love of music so that it will last a lifetime. Weekly music classes that are entertaining and educational, based on an innovative and progressive curriculum. Classes are tailor-made to encourage children to learn through catchy songs, rhymes, games and fun with percussion instruments.

Edinburgh South
Contact: Alison
0131 669 6004
Alison.rankin@monkeymusic.co.uk

Edinburgh North/West
Contact: Rachel
0131 260 9667
Rachel.huggins@monkeymusic.co.uk

Morningside School of Music
0131 447 1117
morningside@polarflamemusic.com
www.morningsideschoolofmusic.com
Private and group instrument lessons from 4yrs.

Music for Little People
0131 440 2362
Ann.heavens@googlemail.com
www.musicforlittlepeople.co.uk
Offers parents/carers and children the opportunity to explore the foundations of music in a fun and interactive way. Classes for 2-3yrs and 3-5yrs.

Music with Mummy
07751 699084
Lively approach to music for children up to 3yrs. Structured programme that encourages listening skills, sense of rhythm through music and games - and having fun! Has been running since 1992. Weekly sessions - please phone for current times.

Music for Fun
0131 620 0685
Fun rhymes, songs, games and percussion playing for children from 3yrs to school age. A fun time for your child and a chance for you to meet other parents in relaxed surroundings.

Musical Minis
0131 552 1120
jenni@musicalminis.co.uk
www.musicalminis.co.uk
Fun musical group for children from 6 mths. Sessions introduce children to music and percussion, with an emphasis on rhythm, song, sound and music. Includes action songs and nursery rhymes. The range of music is diverse, from classical to modern. Musical Minis also runs specialised nursery classes and is available for birthday parties.

Portobello Music School
0131 669 1120
info@portobellomusicschool.com
www.portobellomusicschool.com
Portobello Music School is an exciting music initiative offering comprehensive music education to children from pre-school to primary school age. Classes take place at Towerbank Primary School, Portobello on Saturdays. Creative music classes, group instrumental instruction, junior choirs, and children's composition classes.

Song Circle
0131 332 7067 or 07919 954334
stockbridgemusic@blueyonder.co.uk
Singing sessions for under 5s. Class for babies and a session for 2-5yrs old. Nursery rhymes, action songs, poems and lullabies.

Wriggle, Rattle and Rhyme
07899 087883
wrigglerattlerhyme@hotmail.co.uk
www.wrigglerattlerhyme.vpweb.co.uk
Run by a professional actor with many years experience of running song and rhyme sessions for babies and toddlers. Share songs and rhymes in a friendly environment and have fun with percussion instruments as you explore rhythm and movement.

SPORTS

Athletics
0131 652 2178
www.edinburghleisure.co.uk
Coached Edinburgh Leisure classes from 3yrs. Focuses on the fundamental skills of running, jumping and throwing.

Edinburgh Leisure Holiday Camps
0131 650 1001
www.edinburghleisure.co.uk
Edinburgh Leisure run camps during school holidays at various centres across Edinburgh. Activ5 programmes for under 5s offer sports activities and arts & crafts too.

Edinburgh Southern Orienteering Club
0131 225 7771
www.esoc.org.uk
Events for families with children of all ages. Visit website for details.

Ice Skating
Murrayfield Ice Rink
0131 337 6933
info@murrayfieldicerinkltd.co.uk
www.murrayfieldicerinkltd.co.uk
Beginners learning to skate classes and private coaching available from 4yrs.

Learnabikes
0131 652 2178
www.edinburghleisure.co.uk
Edinburgh Leisure course teaching children balance and co-ordination on bikes. Suitable from two and a half yrs when children can be introduced to 'balance bikes'.

SWIMMING CLASSES

Edinburgh Leisure offers classes in their pools and there are a number of private swimming teachers who run classes at various venues throughout Edinburgh. Many of these have long waiting lists and have preferred not to be listed in this guide.

Depending on your child's needs, you may be able to access one of the many mainstream swimming classes on offer.
Council-run classes for children who require one-to-one support are not available at present, although class sizes are reduced in those classes aimed at children with additional support needs. In these classes, the instructor is not usually in the water. These classes are offered at a variety of venues – call the venue before booking the class to make sure they have the facilities you need; not all swimming pools have shower chairs and some have very long walks to the pool side! It may be advisable to arrange a trial session to check that the class will be suitable for your child's needs.

Adult & Child Water Activities Programme
0131 652 2178
www.edinburghleisure.co.uk
Edinburgh Leisure classes at venues across the city. Adult and Baby for 4-12mths. Adult and Child for 12-40mths.

Learn To Swim
0131 652 2178
www.edinburghleisure.co.uk
Edinburgh Leisure pre-school classes at venues across the city. Learn To Swim classes for 3-5yrs.

Lothian Waves Swimming Club
Classes held at Braidburn School
107 Oxgangs Road North
0131 445 2987 or 312 2320

♿ This swimming club aims to provide the opportunity for children with physical disabilities and/or visual impairment to: have confidence in water, learn to swim to the best of their abilities and desire and to progress or move on to another more appropriate club as they wish. Children learn to swim in a fun, safe and enjoyable environment.

The club works with children on a one-to-one basis and welcomes children of all abilities. A team of dedicated volunteers work with the swimming teachers to encourage each child to develop their swimming ability as best they can. Parents don't go in the water with their child, but sit close by (and chat!). The swimming pool is warm and the changing facilities geared towards additional needs. This swimming club comes highly recommended! Contact as above for more information.

Swim Easy
0131 466 0764
info@swimeasy.co.uk
www.swimeasy.co.uk
Classes start with Swimtots, from 3yrs with adult. The main programme starts with 4-5yrs for pre-school non-swimmer and beginner stages. Teachers work in the water applying minimum manipulation to aid confidence. Call or check the website for further details.

Swimming Nature
08700 949597
bookings@swimmingnature.co.uk
www.swimmingnature.co.uk
Classes held in venues throughout Edinburgh. Class sizes are small and instructors work in the water following a modular programme that can be easily followed by children and their parents. Fun, games, stories and rewards are used to encourage and stimulate the children to love the water. Intensive courses offered in school holidays. Call centre for information and to make a booking.

Water Babies
0131 554 6682
woggle@waterbabies.co.uk
www.waterbabies.co.uk
Classes for babies from birth onwards. Fully qualified STA instructors teach water confidence and safety techniques with babies swimming above and below the water's surface. Classes are small and held throughout Edinburgh in private, warm-water pools. Contact Waterbabies for information about prices and course times.

TUITION

Explore Learning
www.explorelearning.org.uk
After school and weekend learning sessions for children of all abilities from 4yrs.

First Class Learning
0131 552 9253
Edinburgh@firstclasslearning.co.uk
www.firstclasslearning.co.uk
Maths and English after school classes from 4yrs.

Kumon
www.kumon.co.uk
After school classes from 3yrs. For all levels of English and Maths abilities.

Whizzkidz
0131 447 5893
gillian@whizzkidz.co.uk
www.whizzkidz.co.uk
Fun and educational computer classes for children aged 3+ yrs. Computer based activities are used to teach pre-school children basic language and maths skills. Classes are held on an individual or small group basis and are booked in monthly blocks.

YOGA

Yoga for Children
Aditi Yoga Centre
5 Alva Street
EH2 4PH
0131 226 2601
info@aditiyogacentre.com
www.aditiyogacentre.com
For children 2-5yrs. Classes are a blend of active and passive poses, and are a combination of playful yoga postures, animated breathing exercises and imaginative relaxation and meditation activities.

Yoga for Toddlers
Avril Berry
0131 225 2012
info@yogaforbaby.com
www.yogaforbaby.com
Follows on from Yoga for Baby classes with Avril. Suitable from toddling to 3yrs. Parents/carers are fully included as the classes include yoga practice for you and your toddler. Experienced yoga teacher who clearly enjoys working with under 3s.

Yoga Stars
0131 652 2178
www.edinburghleisure.co.uk
A yoga-based class from Edinburgh Leisure for 3-5yrs. Aims to develop co-ordination, balance, creativity and self-expression. Uses songs, stories and relaxation techniques.

MISCELLANEOUS

Cooking Mania
1 North West Circus Place
EH3 6ST
0131 336 2012
www.cookingmania.co.uk
The primary objective of this school is to make cooking fun. They run themed workshops for Halloween, Christmas, Valentines and Easter. They can also organise Chef For A Day birthday parties, where the kids cook and bake for their own party.

Community Courses
Balerno High School
5 Bridge Road
Balerno
EH14 7AQ
0131 477 7733
Offers a variety of activities for 3-5yrs. Includes fun with food cookery, drama and dance, and green tots environment course. Contact the Community Manager for further information.

Relax Kids
0131 539 2006 or 669 6772
relaxkids@theseaoftranquility.co.uk
www.relaxkids.com
Classes from pre-school (4+ yrs) where children learn how to use various relaxation techniques in a fun way.

YOUTH ORGANISATIONS

Although many children cannot join youth organisations until they are over 5 it is often sensible to find out about local groups before they are 5 as there may be long waiting lists for places.

Edinburgh Leith and District Boy's Brigade

0131 551 1200
office@thebb-edinburgh.org.uk
www.thebb-edinburgh.org.uk
Uniformed organisation for boys. Four main age sections covering a variety of ages. Youngest section are Anchor Boys – from 6yrs. 35 local groups in and around Edinburgh. Contact for further details.

Edinburgh Scouting

0131 229 3756
info@southeastscotlandscouts.org.uk
www.southeastscotlandscouts.org.uk
Uniformed organisation for both boys and girls, with five main sections covering a variety of ages. Youngest are Beavers - 6-8yrs. Contact for further details of the various groups meeting throughout Edinburgh.

Girlguiding Edinburgh

0800 169 5901 or 0131 225 4154
admin@girlguiding-edinburgh.org.uk
www.girlguiding-edinburgh.org.uk
Youth organisation for girls, four main sections covering a variety of ages. Youngest section are Rainbows - 5-7yrs. Groups meet throughout Edinburgh and the Lothians. Call or email to have your details passed onto the local contact.

Girlguiding Scotland

0131 226 4511
www.girlguidingscotland.org.uk
Contact for details of opportunities out with Edinburgh (i.e. Mid/East/West Lothian and further afield).

Girl's Brigade Scotland

Edinburgh: Jenny Paton 07929 467664
Midlothian: Jill Williamson 0131 660 6875
West Lothian: Lorna Robinson 01506 853475
www.girls-brigade-scotland.org.uk
Uniformed organisation for girls. Three main sections covering a variety of ages. Youngest section are Explorers for primary 1-3 age group.

St Andrew's Ambulance

0131 229 5419
Youth training for first aid - Badgers 5-8yrs. Contact office for details of local groups.

Ed Says.....

Baby Sensory

Adult & Child Water Activities Programme (Edinburgh Leisure)

Enjoy-A-Ball

Gymini

Music (Jo Jingles or Monkey Music)

Sparkle Arts

Rugbytots

Tots Tennis

Tumble Tots

Water Babies

EDINBURGH FOR UNDER FIVES

What would you recommend?
Tell Ed
email ed@efuf.co.uk

Activities and Classes for Adults

Making time for yourself as well as for your children is very important, for everyone involved.

The aim of this section is to provide you with some starting points and ideas of the types of community classes and groups, education and training opportunities, and sports facilities in the area. Many of the centres listed have creche facilities and it is always worth checking with the venue.

There are many possibilities open to parents with young children, thanks to evening classes, open/flexible learning opportunities and a wealth of community-based initiatives to help parents extend their horizons and have a break from childcare. If the venues are unable to provide childcare, there are a range of private crèches/nurseries. For full listings, see Pre-school Play and Education.

COMMUNITY EDUCATION CENTRES

These centres provide a broad range of formal and informal activities and classes. There are opportunities to study for qualifications, keep fit, or learn a new craft or skill. Many provide a crèche. The majority of these centres are schools, community schools or resource centres.

Community Education Head Office
0131 469 3250
Many centres run programmes under the management of the City of Edinburgh Council's 'Adult Community Education Programme'. Classes start in September, January and April. Contact the head office above for further information on classes, or contact you local centre direct:

Burdiehouse & Southhouse Community Centre
25 Burdiehouse Street
EH17 8EZ
0131 664 2210

Cameron House Community Centre
Cameron House Avenue
EH16 5LF
0131 667 3762

Carrickvale Community Education Centre
2 Saughton Mains Street
EH11 3HH
0131 443 6971

Castlebrae Family Centre
Castlebrae Community High School
2a Greendykes Road
EH16 4DP
0131 661 1282

Clovenstone Community Centre
54 Clovenstone Park
EH4 3EY
0131 453 4561

Craigmount Community Wing
Craigmount High School
Craigs Road
EH12 8NH
0131 339 8278

Craigroyston Community Centre
1a Pennywell Road
EH4
0131 332 7360

Craigroyston Early Years Centre
Craigroyston Community High School
Pennywell Road
EH4 4QP
0131 477 7801

Drummond High Community High School
41 Bellevue Place
EH7 4BS
0131 556 2651

Duncan Place Resource Centre
4 Duncan Place
EH6 8HN
0131 554 1509
www.duncan-place.org.uk

First Step Community Project
37 Galt Avenue
Musselburgh
EH21 8HU
0131 665 0848
firststep1@btconnect.com

Fort Community Wing
North Fort Street
Leith
EH6 4HF
0131 553 1074

Gilmerton Community Centre
4 Drum Street
Gilmerton
EH17 8QG
0131 664 2335

Goodtrees Neighbourhood Centre
5 Moredunvale Place
EH17 7LB
0131 672 2629

Inch Community Centre
Inch House
225 Gilmerton Road
EH16 5UF
0131 664 4710

Lasswade High School Centre
Eskdale Drive
Bonnyrigg
Midlothian
EH19 2LA
0131 663 8170
www.lasswade.info

Lochend YWCA
198 Restalrig Road South
EH7 6DZ
0131 554 3400
lochend.ywca@care4free.net

St Bride's Centre
10 Orwell Terrace
EH11 2DZ
0131 346 1405

South Bridge Resource Centre
Infirmary Street
EH1 1LT
0131 557 5478

South Queensferry Community Centre
Joint Sites:
Community Centre
Kirkliston Road
and
Rosebery Hall
South Queensferry
0131 331 2113

Southside Community Centre
117 Nicolson Street
EH8 9ER
0131 667 0484
www.southside.edin.org

Stevenson College Edinburgh Community-Based ESL Section

Duncan Place Resource Centre
4 Duncan Place
EH6 8HW
0131 535 4630
Community-based classes (held in schools and community centres all over the city) for adults permanently resident in Edinburgh who speak English as a second language.

Tollcross Community Education Centre

Tollcross Primary School
Fountainbridge
EH3 9QG
0131 221 5800
www.tollcross.edin.org

Wester Hailes Education Centre

5 Murrayburn Drive
EH14 2SU
0131 442 2201

YWCA Roundabout Centre

4b Gayfield Place
EH7 4AB
0131 556 1168 or 557 4695
www.ywca.scotland.org
This is a women's community centre committed to the elimination of racism and to empowering women to develop their full potential.

EDUCATION & TRAINING

Edinburgh offers a huge variety of education, training and 'new direction' courses. There are also opportunities to learn a practical skill, craft or sport through the Community Learning and Development Programme run by the City Council at schools throughout the city. Creches available at some venues – contact them for further details.

If you're not sure what you are looking for, why not try contacting the council. If you do this online, you'll find that their site is huge, but use the following link as a starting point:
www.edinburgh.gov.uk/internet/ learning/learning_for_life/

Community Learning & Development

City of Edinburgh Council
Waverley Court
4 East Market Street
EH8 8BG
0131 200 2000

COMMUNITY COURSES & PROJECTS

Adult Learning Project

Tollcross Community Centre
Fountainbridge
EH3 9QG
0131 221 5800
Stan.Reeves@educ.edin.gov.uk
Courses, programmes, projects and events. Linking adult education and social action, including social and national politics, history, women's studies, language and writing, multicultural work and literacy.

The Number Shop

188-190 The Pleasance
EH8 9RT
0131 668 4787
maria.mccathie@educ.edin.gov.uk
www.numbershop.edin.org
The Number Shop is part of the City of Edinburgh Council's Community-Based Adult Education Service and provides free help with arithmetic and maths. Tuition is available to adults who want to improve their numeracy skills and to feel more confident with numbers for everyday use. Just drop-in or phone for an interview with a member of staff.

Women Onto Work (WOW)

137 Buccleuch Street
EH8 9NE
0131 662 4514
mail@womenontowork.org
WOW provides courses for women over the age of 21, who have been out of employment for 6mths or more, and who live in an eligible area. WOW can also help women look at options for employment or further study.
WOW also provides courses for women from an ethnic minority or with a disability. Full childcare provided. Courses in Craigmillar, greater Pilton, Wester Hailes, South Edinburgh and citywide.

COLLEGE & UNIVERSITY COURSES

Edinburgh College of Art

Lauriston Place
EH3 9DF
0131 221 6000
www.eca.ac.uk
College offers courses via its centre for Continuing Studies. Courses in around 20 disciplines, including introductory courses. Part time courses available. Some twilight and evening classes available, plus there are summer school options.

Edinburgh University Settlement

Community Learning Centre
Building 3
New Parliament House
5-7 Regent Road
EH7 5BL
0131 550 6807
www.eus.org.uk
Courses for adults with few or no qualifications who want to return to work or find a new direction for their lives. Courses include certificated and non-certificated SQA modules in communications, numeracy and IT. Courses in child development, parenting, behaviour and play (all SQA) also available. Other venues at Craigmillar, Wester Hailes, Pilton and South Edinburgh.

Edinburgh's Telford College

350 West Granton Road
0131 559 4000
mail@ed-coll.ac.uk
www.ed-coll.ac.uk
Wide range of courses in general education, vocational skills and general and recreational interest suitable for preparing to go back to work or wishing to maintain skills and interests. Large open learning programme and a range of other attendance patterns - ask if shorter hours are possible. Some subject areas have 'drop-in' facilities which increases flexibility. This college has an on-site nursery (contact for information: 559 4080).

Heriot-Watt University

Riccarton Campus
EH14 4AS
0131 449 5111
enquiries@hw.ac.uk
www.hw.ac.uk
Established university with excellent reputation in science, engineering, mathematics, computer science, management, finance, languages and built environment. Check website for details of courses available at undergraduate & postgraduate level. Pinocchio's Nursery is located at Heriot-Watt.

Anything out of date?
Let us know -
info@efuf.co.uk

Jewel and Esk Valley College

Milton Road Campus
24 Milton Road East
EH15 2PP
or
Eskbank Campus
Newbattle Road
Eskbank
Dalkeith
EH22 3AE
08458 50 00 60 (information services)
info@jevc.ac.uk
www.jevc.ac.uk
Wide range of educational, vocational and leisure courses. A range of courses, including full-time, part-time and evening courses, plus Scottish Wider Access Programmes for mature students moving on to higher education. Swimming pool and gymnasium at Milton Road. Open learning options available.

Moray House School of Education

University of Edinburgh
Old Moray House
Holyrood Road
EH8 8AQ
0131 651 6138
www.education.ed.ac.uk
Courses leading to qualifications in teaching, community education and sport and leisure. Undergraduate and postgraduate courses available. University has nursery provision.

Napier University

Craiglockhart Campus
EH14 1DJ
08452 60 60 40
info@napier.ac.uk
www.napier.ac.uk
Full-time undergraduate, postgraduate and part-time courses. Prospectus available from the Information Office. Flexible learning, as well as open learning facilities and courses, summer school and a wide range of short courses. Campuses throughout the city.

The Office of Lifelong Learning

University of Edinburgh
11 Buccleuch Place
EH8 9LW
0131 650 4400
oll@ed.ac.uk
www.lifelong.ed.ac.uk
Offers a Return To Learning programme. Courses specifically designed for adults or those who fall into the 'mature student' category: course structures include 'New Horizons' for people who like the idea of studying but are not sure what's involved. There is also a 5 week 'Learning Afresh' course which provides the first steps back into study. Evening classes on a wide range of subjects also run - contact centre for prospectus and information.

The Open University in Scotland

10 Drumsheugh Gardens
EH3 7QJ
0131 226 3851
Scotland@open.ac.uk
www.open.ac.uk/scotland
The OU offers a wide range of courses, diplomas, degrees and professional qualifications. With the support of a personal tutor, you study by part-time open learning, which fits around your family and work commitments. For many OU courses, you don't need to have any previous qualifications. Contact the Course Choice Team for further information and a prospectus.

Queen Margaret University

Queen Margaret University Drive
Musselburgh
EH21 6UU
0131 474 0000
admissions@qmu.ac.uk
www.qmu.ac.uk
A range of full-time, part-time, distance learning, post-registration and continued professional development courses. Undergraduate and postgraduate degrees are available in the areas of healthcare, theatre arts and cultural management, communication and information, business and management and social sciences.

Scottish Wider Access Programme (SWAP)

0800 731 0949
www.scottishwideraccess.org
Local office:
SWAP East
25 Buccleuch Place
EH8 9LN
swapeast@ed.ac.uk

Wide range of access courses to prepare adults, over 21, who do not have the standard entrance qualifications for study in further or higher education. Successful completion of an access course at an appropriate level guarantees a place at a range of colleges and universities. Part-time and flexible programmes may be available.

Stevenson College of Further Education

Bankhead Avenue
EH11 4DE
0131 535 4700
info@stevenson.ac.uk
www.stevenson.ac.uk

Offers a wide range of courses on a full-time, part-time, evening and flexible learning basis. Courses are designed to help achieve your ambitions whether they involve returning to work or education, gaining formal qualifications or developing your career. Student support team can help arrange childcare and may be able to help with fees for after schools clubs, nurseries and childminders. Contact the information centre on the above number for further information.

University of Edinburgh

Old College
South Bridge
EH8 9YL
0131 650 1000
communications.office@ed.ac.uk

Special prospectus for mature students. Entrance qualifications for degree courses may differ for mature students. See also the Office of Lifelong Learning, above. The University offers childcare facilities see Pre-School Play and Education for more information.

INFORMATION & SUPPORT

Beeleaf Consulting

07954 433659
www.beeleafconsulting.co.uk
Specialise in supporting women in the workforce. Offers support through workshops, coaching and provides advice on returning to work and flexible working.

Careers Scotland

0845 850 2502
www.careers-scotland.org.uk
Information on careers, education and training. Individual career counselling services for employed and unemployed adults. There are various premises throughout the city. Some, especially those in libraries, are only information points. Others, listed below, offer a full range of services. See the website for more information.

Local offices:

79 Shandwick Place
EH2 4SD

22 Hailesland Place
Wester Hailes
EH14 2SL

Adam Ferguson House
Station Road
Musselburgh
EH21 7PQ

20 Croft Street
Dalkeith
EH22 3BA

Learn Direct Scotland

0808 100 9000
www.learndirectscotland.com
Offers careers advice and course information. Advisors can give objective course information and subjective advice over the phone. LDS also provides details of other similar organisations and can forward individuals' details regarding the Scottish Executive's Individual Learning Account (see www.ilascotland.org.uk), and can advise and explain about other sources of course funding.

NISUS Scotland

121 Giles Street
EH6 6BZ
0131 554 5656
info@nisusscotland.org.uk
www.nisusscotland.co.uk
Full-time courses, including the Edinburgh Women's Training Course, which is a part-time course in computer technology for women with no, low, foreign or outdated qualifications. Course includes nationally recognised SQA units and the European Computer Driving Licence (ECDL). Course is funded through the European Social Fund, the City of Edinburgh Council and Edinburgh's Telford College. Assistance is provided with childcare and travel expenses.
NISUS also offers:
Quaytech Training - cost-effective IT skills training to both voluntary and private sectors, which is open to men and women. Flexit - a drop-in IT training programme in hourly blocks for men or women with disabilities or health concerns, and their carers. Skilltech - provides IT and personal development training for black and minority ethnic people, refugees and asylum seekers.

Play Scotland

Midlothian Innovation Centre
Pentlandfield
Roslin
Midlothian
EH25 9RE
0131 440 9070
info@playscotland.org
www.playscotland.org
A charitable organisation which provides advice and information to both its members and the public about play, funding opportunities, play provision and play training. Also acts as a pressure group to persuade others that play is important for children and young people and conducts and stimulates research into play provision in Scotland.

Scottish Pre-school Play Association (SPPA)

Head Office
45 Finnieston Street
Glasgow
G3 8JU
0141 221 4148
www.sppa.org.uk
SPPA provides practical help with all aspects of running a pre-school group. It provides information and advice on setting up and running your group, competitive group insurance, and a range of under 5s publications and training opportunities. For membership information contact SPPA Centre.

SPPA office covering City of Edinburgh:
111 Union Street
Glasgow
G1 3TA
0141 227 3922
joyce.waddell@sppa.org.uk
Local support service for playgroups, toddler groups, under fives groups and nurseries.

Visit our website for updates:
www.efuf.co.uk

Supported Employment Team

Waverley Court Business Centre 1/7
4 East Market Street
EH8 8BG
0131 525 8040
Primarily for individuals with disabilities or health problems looking to return to work. Services include interviews to discuss job aspirations, work preparation, job matching and practical assistance to take on employment through the Open Employment Scheme.

Workers' Educational Association (WEA)

Riddles Court
322 Lawnmarket
EH1 2PG
0131 226 3456
hq@weascotland.org.uk
www.weascotland.org.uk
Scotland-wide voluntary adult education organisation which works locally to encourage access to learning through life. Free, friendly and informal courses in confidence building, returning to learning, social and political studies, and the arts. Courses can be tailored to meet needs of groups.

SPORT & LEISURE

The sports centres that are run by local councils offer reasonably priced facilities, membership and regular crèches. In addition to local authority centres there are a number of privately-owned health, fitness and sports clubs around the city. These usually charge a joining fee, and thereafter have a monthly payment scheme. Full details can be found in the Yellow Pages. It's worth checking local press for up-to-date information, or indeed phoning around, as this market is very competitive and many clubs run short-term special offers for new memberships.

Check the crèche facilities - there have been past examples of crèches running only for a short time, as an incentive for new membership, and then being closed down: if documentation mentions a crèche is 'planned' proceed with caution. However, many private clubs do have established crèche facilities which are as popular as those run within the centres run by local councils: always book your crèche place in advance.
At the end of the section is some information on private dance, yoga and Pilates centres offering interesting classes for adults.

Leisure Access Scheme

Edinburgh Leisure, which runs sports and leisure facilities for the City of Edinburgh Council, offers this scheme, giving access to a wide range of benefits and discounts to all Edinburgh Leisure facilities, including sports, swim and golf centres. There is an annual one-off payment for an adult Leisure Card, with concessionary rates available. There are different rates for activities for cardholders and non-cardholders at peak and off-peak times. Cardholders get 25% of activities at 14 gyms, 9 swimming pools, and over 500 fitness classes each week across Edinburgh. Children always pay the lowest price available. You do not need a Leisure Access Card to use facilities but if children (under 18s) or adults want to book in advance they must have one. Application forms are available from all sport and swim centres, local libraries and Edinburgh Leisure Head Office. Parents and carers who are Leisure Card holders are entitled to use on-site crèche facilities at reduced rates. All centres provide information about their prices, current activities and the coaching they offer. Programmes do tend to vary throughout the year, so it is advisable to check details in advance.

Edinburgh Leisure Head Office

54 Nicolson Street
0131 650 1001
Contact for more information and/or Leisure Card application forms. For information about the crèches contact the Crèche Co-ordinator.

Edinburgh Leisure's Sports and Service Development Section
Based at Meadowbank Sports Centre
0131 652 2178
Provides an information point for sport and recreation opportunities within Edinburgh, and will advise on classes, crèche facilities etc.

SPORTS & LEISURE CENTRES

The 'Places To Go' section lists the main sports and leisure centres that offer sports activities for families. We have not included those already listed here (please refer to 'Places To Go'). The following are additional leisure suggestions that you might find useful:

Balgreen Bowling
Pansy Walk
0131 313 5097

Braid Hills 1
Braid Hills Approach
0131 447 6666

Princes Golf Course (9 holes)
Braid Hills Drive
0131 447 3568

Carrick Knowe Golf Course
Glendevon Park
0131 337 1096

Countryside Ranger Service
Hermitage House
Hermitage of Braid
69a Braid Road
Morningside
EH10 6JF
0131 447 7145
ranger@cecrangerservice.demon.co.uk
www.cecrangerservice.demon.co.uk
Guided walks and special events programme based on various themes for all the family all year round. Phone for information and programme - rangers are very helpful. Details of women's walks programme advertised in local notice boards and local press - especially 'Herald and Post'.

Crags Sports Centre
10 Bowmont Place
0131 667 3334

Craigentinny Golf Course
Fillyside Road
0131 554 7501

Craiglockhart Tennis & Sports Centre
177 Colinton Road
EH14 1BZ
0131 443 0101

EICA Ratho
South Platt Hill
Newbridge
0131 333 6333

Gorgie Dalry Community Association
22 McLeod Street
EH11 2NH
0131 337 3252
Formed from an amalgamated sports centre/ community association - activities include football, basketball, tennis, hockey, badminton cricket, self-defence and general keep-fit classes. Can also host one-off social and community events. Call centre for full details.

Inch Community Education Centre
255 Gilmerton Road
EH16 5UF
0131 664 4710
Exercise classes and crèche facilities.

Jack Kane Sports Centre
208 Niddrie Mains Road
EH16 4NB
0131 669 0404

jogscotland
0131 539 7341
membership@jogscotland.org.uk
www.jogscotland.org.uk
Great at encouraging new runners. Contact for details of local jogging groups and events.

Kirkliston Leisure Centre
Kirklands Park Street
EH29 9ET
0131 333 4700

Lasswade High School Sports
Eskdale Drive
Bonnyrigg
Midlothian
EH19 2LA
0131 660 1933
Facilities include main sports hall, 2 squash courts, weight training room, fitness suite, activities studio, gymnasium, lounge, cafeteria, outdoor facilities, indoor football and rugby. Also a variety of daytime/ evening classes for adults. Creche facilities available.

Leith Links Bowling
John's Place
0131 669 0878

Meadowbank Sports Centre
139 London Road
EH7 6AE
0131 661 5351

Meadows Tennis Complex
East Meadows
0131 443 0101

Port Edgar Marina
Shore Road
South Queensferry
0131 331 3330

Portobello Golf Course (9 holes)
Pavilion
Stanley Street
0131 669 4361

Powderhall Bowling
Broughton Road
0131 669 0878

Queensferry High Recreation Centre
30 Ashburnham Road
South Queensferry
EH30 9JN
0131 319 3222

Ratho Community Centre
1 School Wynd
Ratho
EH28 8TT
0131 333 1055
Keep-fit classes with crèche facilities.

Saughton Sports Complex
Stevenson Drive
Balgreen
EH11 3HB
0131 444 0422

Silverknowes Golf Course
Silverknowes Parkway
0131 336 3843

St Margarets Park
(bowling and tennis)
Corstorphine High Street
0131 669 0878

Victoria Park Bowling
Newhaven Road
0131 669 0878

DANCE & EXERCISE

The Activities for Children section lists numerous dance organisations. As well as offering classes for under 5s, several including Dance Base, The Edinburgh Dance Academy and Manor School of Ballet offer sessions for adults too.

Aditi Yoga Centre
5 Alva Street
EH2 4PH
0131 226 2601
info@aditiyogacentre.com
www.aditiyogacentre.com
Complementary therapies, Hatha yoga, Meditation, mum and baby yoga, Pilates, postnatal yoga, and yoga for pregnancy. Please contact centre for current timetable and costs for all classes.

Astanga Yoga Centre
25 Rodney Street
EH7 4EL
0131 558 3334
reception@astangayogacentre.com
www.astangayogacentre.com
Pregnancy Yoga. Classes welcome complete beginners to those women who are experienced in yoga. The emphasis is on gentle postures, breathing and relaxation. While the classes may benefit postnatal women, no babies can be brought to the classes.

Attic Salt Pilates Studio
50 Thistle Street North East Lane
EH2 1DA
07765 068136
jo@jomunro.co.uk
www.jomunro.co.uk
Run Pilates classes for pregnancy and mother and baby pilates classes.

Babies and Mums
41 Commercial Street
EH6 6JD
0131 553 2646
www.babiesandmums.co.uk
Offer a range of classes for pre and post natal women and a range of classes for babies and toddler. Classes include pre and post natal yoga, yoga for mums and babies, baby massage.

BabySteps
0131 337 2774
info@manukahealth.co.uk
www.manukahealth.co.uk
BabySteps is designed to give new mums and their babies (from 6wks-2yrs) a fun and safe way to exercise, using your pushchair, your baby and a creative outdoor gym! The hour-long session includes energetic walking with pushchairs, toning, strengthening and stretching exercises to target those major 'mummy muscles'. Classes held in across Edinburgh.

Bea Alexander Pilates
07951 686322
classes@beaalexanderpilates.co.uk
www.beaalexanderpilates.co.uk
Post Natal Pilates classes to re-train your abdominal muscles and offer some relaxation to new Mums.

Dance/exercise for Mums
0131 337 2774
info@manukahealth.co.uk
www.manukahealth.co.uk
Classes and 1-2-1 private tuition in hip-hop and jazz dance, giving your mind and body a good work out. Suits all levels.

Pilates
0131 337 2774
info@manukahealth.co.uk
www.manukahealth.co.uk
Antenatal and Postnatal Pilates - Classes or 1-2-1 private tuition. Postnatal Pilates classes focus on regaining correct posture after the birth of your baby, retraining and toning the muscles back to the strength and the shape you were before you became pregnant. Learning safe and effective exercises, which can be practised at home and used to maintain a strong and healthy body.

The Pilates Place
3 Queen Charlotte Lane
Leith
EH6 6AY
0131 555 6423
info@thepilatesplace.org.uk
www.thepilatesplace.org.uk
Regular Pilates classes and workshops (including mother and baby) from this specialist studio. Highly skilled instructors who work with small class sizes to offer maximum attention.

Pilates Works
0131 334 1113
Edinburgh@pilates-works.co.uk
www.pilates-works.co.uk
With two studios in Edinburgh and a variety of matwork venues across Edinburgh there is plenty on offer. Post natal classes also available.

Skye Reynolds
07855 855570
Experienced and fully qualified Pilates Foundation UK teacher. Private/studio, pregnancy and post-natal classes available.

Union Yoga
0131 558 3334
www.unionyoga.co.uk
Studio specifically designed and used for yoga and meditation. The studio offers a space where you can switch off from the outside world. Range of courses available, including plenty of beginners classes.

Yoga Body
41 Commercial Street
EH6 6JD
0131 553 2646
reception@yoga-body.co.uk
www.yoga-body.co.uk
Offer a variety of yoga classes from Ashtanga to Iyengar, Hatha and yoga for pregnancy.

Yoga Stable
Montgomery Street Lane
EH7 5JT
0131 556 9526
info@yogastable.com
www.yogastable.com
Ante-natal yoga and post-natal mother and baby yoga.

Ed Likes.....

Beeleaf Consulting

Jog Scotland

Pilates (Pilates Place or Pilates Works)

Southside Community Centre

Yoga (Aditi Yoga Centre)

EDINBURGH
FOR UNDER FIVES

What would you recommend?
Tell Ed
email ed@efuf.co.uk

Shopping

Shopping

Shopping when pregnant or with small children requires a completely different approach from shopping you may have been used to. Browsing at leisure can become a distant memory, you have to discover good sources of maternity, baby and children's equipment and clothing, and you may also find that planning, timing, and toilet stops become of the utmost importance – for you and your child!

In this section, we've tried to offer some ideas for where to shop, plus information for planning a less stressful shopping experience (why not look at Places To Eat too).

Due to High Street competition and legal requirements regarding access, as well as any sense of customer care, large shops are increasingly family and child friendly.

Automatic doors, lifts, and in-store nappy changing facilities are just some of the things which have become of standard contents of department stores, as has the presence of a café or restaurant which has high chairs, may offer a bottle and a baby food warming service, and recognises the requirements of people with young children.

Some other things don't change: large stores do alter their layout fairly often, so always check information against a store guide. If you have something to return, ask as soon as you enter the store for the correct procedure: you may be directed to a Customer Service Desk, which may save you a trek to the wrong department.

Feeding and changing rooms are now considered a standard requirement in large department stores and shopping centres. They are available to male and female carers, although if you encounter a combined feeding/changing room, and you are male, it might be prudent to ask an assistant to check the room (some breastfeeding mothers may feel uncomfortable with a male stranger sharing the facility). Some stores have anticipated this, and have secondary rooms for male carers. These rooms should be separate from customer toilets, but it is an advantage to be near toilets, especially if you have an older child with you. The standard of parent and baby rooms in the centre of Edinburgh is generally high, but should you find them lacking in facilities, or not clean, it is worth mentioning this to a manager or supervisor (some rooms have a comments book), as it is only through such information that store managers are aware of customer requirements.

Most city centre shops have late night shopping on Thursday. Some stores use Tuesday and Wednesday mornings for staff training and open later. Tuesday or Wednesday is usually half-day closing in the outlying areas. Many city centre shops have Sunday trading hours (usually opening at 11.00 or mid-day). Sunday trading in suburban areas is almost standard practice. A lot of stores now open longer in the summer and during the Festival, as well as the run-up to Christmas.

Generally speaking stores have procedures in place for responding to lost children. The first rule is try not to panic, then contact a member of staff as soon as you become aware of the disappearance of your child/ren. Describe what your child was wearing and where you last saw them. Think of anything that may have attracted them on the way round the store or shopping centre. Try to carry some ID that identifies you as the child's carer; a recent photograph is useful. In shopping centres, stores always contact the centre's security. If you can, try to teach your child to approach a member of staff in a shop if they become lost.

HIGH STREET STORES

Argos & Argos Extra
www.argos.co.uk
Easy shopping. Stores carry a range of home goods. Stores also have clothing catalogues. All catalogues free to take away and choose purchases at leisure. Some items on display in-store.
Fill in catalogue no. on a slip and hand it to the cashier: goods are collected from the stockroom for you. You have 16 days to return goods if not satisfied. Argos also offers a ring and reserve service, if you have a catalogue at home and want to check that your store has what you want before you make the journey. Good value.
Branches at: 11-15 North Bridge, Kinnaird Park, Craigleith Retail Park, and Pentland Retail Park.

BHS
0845 8410180
www.bhs.co.uk
Stocks children's clothes – have ranges for 2-6yrs and 6-13yrs: these tend to follow fashion colours and trends. Good range of everyday wear for babies and children, at reasonable prices. Casual wear, outdoor wear, underwear, footwear and special occasion clothes. Home department stocks special children's bedding range, with accessories in various bright colours and character ranges. Night lights too.
Branches at: 64 Princes Street, Cameron Toll Shopping Centre and Ocean Terminal.

Boots the Chemist
wwww.boots.com
www.wellbeing.co.uk
Good selection of products for babies, children and families. Ranges vary by store, but generally stock personal care items, beauty products, baby toiletries and equipment, and baby food. Range of own brand (Mini Mode) baby and children's clothing, up to 6yrs. Clothes tend to be pretty hardwearing. Many in 100% cotton. Also do baby range for sensitive skins and a range of clothing for low birth weight babies ('up to 2.3 kg' and 'up to 4.5 kg').
Good for toys and provides useful photographic and pharmacy services.
Branches at: 101-103 Princes Street, Gyle Shopping Centre, Craigleith Retail Park, Fort Retail Park and Straiton Retail Park.

Debenhams
08445 616161
www.debenhams.com
Wide range of clothing for babies and children including own-brand ranges (Trader, Casual Club and Maine) and designer names (including Jasper Conran, Babbleboom, Tigerlily, Baker Boy and Girl and Rocha.little). Has a reasonable range of lingerie, which includes maternity ranges. VIP Baby Service in their restaurants. Customer Order, Home Shopping and Personal Shopper Services available.
Branches at: 109-112 Princes Street and Ocean Terminal.

Frasers
145 Princes Street
EH2 4DL
0870 160 7239
www.houseoffraser.co.uk
Ladies' fashion, including maternity wear and nursing bras. Lingerie fitting service available. Beauty, menswear and home wear departments also available. Restaurant and café with nearby feeding and nappy changing facilities.

Harvey Nichols
30-34 St Andrews Square
EH2 3AD
0131 524 8388
www.harveynichols.com
Store carries children's wear by various designers. The store's very chi chi, but unfortunately it has to be said it's probably best visited without little ones in tow. It's a toddler's dream of shiny, feathery, sleek (and expensive) things to grab at. They often have great window displays, so you might find yourself spending some time outside the store while your child's imagination is taken up with the displays.

IKEA
Straiton Mains
Straiton
Loanhead
EH20 9PW
0131 440 6600
www.ikea.com
Take the Straiton exit from the bypass on to the A701 and follow the signs. Various bus stops nearby. There are parent and child parking bays, but these can be busy: it's best to try and go at off-peak times if you want to avoid congestion in the car parks and the lifts.

Unsupervised play area for older toddlers outside and supervised crèche at main entrance. Shop for an hour while your child/ren (from 3yrs) play with the soft play, art materials, play music or enjoy the books on offer. Play areas dotted throughout the store and plenty of toys to try before you buy in the children's section.

Cots, beds, changing tables, chairs, tables, highchairs, furniture and storage available. Range of smaller items including cutlery, crockery, cups, bath time accessories, bath and bed linen. Most items reasonably priced.

Supermarket-style trolleys available, but these are not allowed in the car park – if you have bulky items, cars must be brought to the pick-up point and your purchases loaded from there. You can take your child/ren to the car and leave the trolley in one of the secure lock-up points (£1 coin, refundable) - but be warned, they don't always work: however, we've always found that staff will 'mind' a trolley while you fetch your vehicle.

John Lewis
St James' Centre
EH1 3SP
0131 556 9121
JL_Edinburgh@johnewis.co.uk
www.johnlewis.com
Large department store providing a wide range of goods and services. Store stocks prams, pushchairs, cots, car seats, baby carrying slings and backpacks, highchairs, accessories, as well as a range of babies' and children's clothing (own brand, plus branded items).

John Lewis offer a free personal nursery advisor service to help you understand and choose what you might need. Contact the store or website, to make an appointment and set up a list. The list operates in a similar way to a wedding list, where friends and family can buy items from your list.

Fabric & Haberdashery: wide choice of fabrics, from cheap and cheerful prints to sumptuous velvets. Stock sheeting, quilted fabrics, braiding, ribbons, buttons, motifs, lace etc. Craft materials such as beads, felt, fur fabric, tapestry and embroidery yarns, craft and needlework kits including samplers. Dolls' house kits, knitting wools and patterns, sewing and knitting machines and craft books.

Soft furnishings: Some great children's patterns, plus 'blackout' curtain lining, blinds. Also wipe-clean fabric for e.g. tablecovers.

As well as a great selection of toys and books John Lewis offers a range of climbing frames, swings, slides, bikes, sandpits and other outdoor toys. These can be delivered (free delivery on orders over £100). Samples usually on display in the summer months, however, the full range can be viewed via catalogue/web.

Feeding and changing room available with an automatic door to ease access. The breastfeeding area has views out over North Edinburgh and over to Fife. While there's a partition wall, there isn't a screen between the entrance door and the breastfeeding area, so if you need a bit of privacy, settle yourself at the window side of the room.

Marks and Spencer

www.marksandspencer.com

Womenswear, menswear, childrenswear, home furnishings and food hall. Good range of durable baby and children's clothes, many in 100% cotton. Underwear, sleepwear, leisure wear, and party clothes, as well as clothes for outdoors and school. Also stock seasonal dressing up outfits and costumes related to recent film releases. Range of padders, pram shoes and shoes (up to sizes 39/40). Baby range starts from newborn, with clothing for low birth weight babies.

Larger stores include some nursery equipment and toys. Lingerie departments offer nursing bras and an in-store bra-fitting service. Café outlets and nappy changing facilities make stores very child-friendly.

Branches at: 54 Princes Street, Gyle Shopping Centre, Craigleith Retail Park, Fort Kinnaird Retail Park.

Mothercare World

www.mothercare.com

Stocks clothes (Mothercare brand) and maternity wear. Large selection of own brand clothes for children, from newborn to 10yrs, including underwear, sleepwear (including sleep gowns), casual and fancy outfits, shoes and outerwear. Also carry a selection of low birth weight clothing. Stocks a range of nursery goods & bedding (own brand), car seats, pushchairs (various brands) and toys. Convenient parking. Stores also offer nappy-changing facilities and private breastfeeding area.

Branches at: Hermiston Gait Retail Park and Fort Kinnaird Retail Park.

SHOPPING CENTRES

Edinburgh has a good selection of shopping centres, both in and out of town, if you prefer to have a range of shops available under one roof. Many of the shopping centres offer hire of small pushchairs and toddler straps.

Almondvale Shopping Centre

87 Almondvale South
Livingston
EH54 6HR
01506 432961

Accessible from M8-A71 (parent/child parking) or by bus from St Andrews Square.

Variety of high street shops and places to eat. Mothercare has a good feeding and changing room located at the back of store. The nappy changing area is locked (key from assistant).

Situated on one level so it's easy to navigate. The toilets are located near Boots and Symingtons Jewellers. There are two nappy changing areas, a shopper's crèche and bottle warming facilities available from the cafes and restaurants. There are also various coin-operated children's rides around the centre.

Bruntsfield

www.bruntsfieldplace.com

Not technically a shopping centre, but the Bruntsfield area is a good one for shopping with plenty of interesting shops to choose from. There is also a local reward card scheme and you can pick up your Bruntsfield 'B' Card from any of the participating retailers. The card promises offers, discounts and perks throughout the year. Lots of the Bruntsfield shops listed in this section participate in the scheme.

 Visit our website for updates:
www.efuf.co.uk

Cameron Toll Shopping Centre
Lady Road
Edinburgh
0131 666 2777
Two large car parks serve both front and rear entrances. Can be very busy on Fridays and at weekends. Keep a tight grip on small children in car parks.
Pedestrian access from Lady Road but closely set bollards and a roll bar designed to prevent shoppers from taking trolleys out mean large prams and pushchairs need careful manoeuvring.
Self-opening doors and a variety of trolley designs to accommodate various ages of babies and small children, although many smaller shops do not allow trolleys inside.
A variety of shops on the main shopping floor and on the 1st floor there's the foodcourt. The centre usually hosts activities for Easter, Mother's Day etc, such as puppet shows, magicians and other children's entertainers.
Toilets on ground and first floor. There's a separate nappy changing room with two changing units and enclosed area for feeding.

Craigleith Retail Park
South Groathill Road
Compact shopping centre with good parking.
Range of shops including Sainsbury's supermarket, Boots, Mamas & Papas, TK Maxx, Next, Costa Coffee and M&S.   Parent and child spaces available. Several of the outlets offer good nappy changing facilities (Sainsbury's, Boots and M&S).

Fort Kinnaird
Newcraighall Road
0131 669 9242
Access from A1, and from Craigmillar and Newcraighall. Around 55 outlets set around three large car parks (watch the arrows on the roads – the negotiation around the car parks can be quite tight).
Huge variety of shops, cafes, and eating outlets. Mothercare has a good feeding and changing room, Boots also have nappy-changing rooms, and the Early Learning Playstore has an excellent nappy changing and children's toilet facility, and a baby 'dining-room' with seats for breastfeeding and bottle warmers.

Gyle Shopping Centre
Gyle Avenue
South Gyle Broadway
0131 539 9000
Entrance is situated off the South Gyle roundabout. Large colour coded car park, with parent and child parking, and parking for the disabled at all entrances. Single and double pushchairs and child reins available to hire free (ID required) at Customer Services Desk inside opposite main entrance. Small outdoor play areas with climbing frames etc.
Self-opening doors and a variety of trolleys to accommodate various ages. Around 60 shops all on one level. Lift and escalator to upper level where the 500-seater Food Court offers a range of snacks, meals and drinks. There are bottle/baby food heating facilities. Situated on the 1st floor is a fully-equipped Baby Room. Toilets also available on the ground floor beside the main entrance and also on the 1st floor – both include facilities for disabled visitors.

Hermiston Gait Retail Park
off A720 City Bypass
Take 1st exit marked Glasgow off A720 City Bypass coming from South Gyle. Do not follow sign to Glasgow, go straight on which will take you to traffic lights. Turn left and follow signs for Retail Park.
Large car park: keep a close eye on mobile youngsters – as the car park is usually quite quiet, drivers have a tendency to cut across parking bays rather than using the road layout. Feeding and nappy changing facilities available in Mothercare World.

Anything out of date?
Let us know -
info@efuf.co.uk

McArthur Glen Designer Outlet Livingston
Almondvale Avenue
Livingston
EH54 6QX
01506 423 600
J3 off M8 – follow signs to Designer Outlet Centre. Regular buses from Edinburgh – bus station is directly in front of the Centre.
Various car parks (there's 2000 spaces in all) although easiest access seems to be Centre West.
Large shopping centre on two levels. Mixture of designer and casual clothes shops, other shops include ELC and The Toyworld Store. With various options for food on the ground floor and an 8-screen cinema on the 1st level there is plenty to do. Two nappy changing areas with three changing units in each, plus closed feeding area available. One is located opposite Gap and the other one is in the Boulevard.

Meadowbank Shopping Park
London Road
near Meadowbank Stadium
Large car park with parent and child parking. Toilets and nappy changing facilities in Sainsbury's.

Newkirkgate Shopping Centre
Off Great Junction Street
Leith
Large car park. Some shops around open square, others in the covered mall.

Ocean Terminal
Ocean Drive
Leith
EH6 7DZ
0131 555 56
www.oceanterminal.com
1600 parking spaces – two multi-storey and one surface car park adjacent to Debenhams, with direct access to mall on all three floors, and stair or lift access on all.
Spread over three levels, with wide walkways and plenty to take youngsters' attention, whether it's the huge propellers on display, or the sight of boats in the River Forth from the eateries. As well as the more usual high street names Ocean Terminal offers a selection of clothing and lifestyle stores. Some particularly child-friendly outlets including Molly's and The Bear Factory. Parenting suites available on two of the three floors, with nappy changing facilities and seating for breastfeeding mothers.
Offers a wide range of places to eat and is home to the Vue Cinema.

Princes Mall
Princes Street / Waverley Bridge
0131 557 3759
Built on three levels with six entrances (two with access ramps; Waverley Bridge and Princes St, next to Waverley Steps, which leads to the small, busy lift which serves all floors). Busy shopping centre with the Tourist Information Centre located on the rooftop (access ramp from Princes St available).
There are over 50 shops and outlets.
Washrooms beside the Food Court. Free nappy changing room and toilet for the disabled to the right of the washrooms beside the food court (easy access with pushchair). Toilets with a separate nappy-changing room inside the ladies' toilets through a set of doors market 'Exit' at the other end of Princes Mall.

St James' Centre
Princes Street / Leith Street
0131 557 0050
www.stjamesshopping.com
Large shopping centre with shops that include the Early Learning Centre and John Lewis.
The eating area, Food on 1, is on the upper floor, along with the toilets for the disabled and the nappy changing facilities. This is accessible via a lift near the Princes Street end of the mall. John Lewis has an excellent changing/feeding room with a separate male changing/feeding room (on the store's 2nd floor, near to The Place to Eat). There are also cookie and juice stands. St James operates a pushchair hire service, which can be booked at the customer Information desk, or on phone number above.

Westside Plaza Shopping Centre
Wester Hailes Road
0131 442 3123
Large car park, plus railway station, bus terminal and taxi rank nearby.
Indoor shopping centre on two levels with lift and escalators. Shops include a variety of food, gift, toy, hardware, newsagent and charity shops, plus an indoor market on the ground floor. Toilets are located on the ground floor with a separate nappy changing area.

BOOKS

Even in these days of Amazon and online book sales there is nothing quite like looking around a real bookshop. Internet suppliers and supermarkets can tend to focus on bestselling titles and so it is often only by browsing in person that you spot that quirky, unusual or unjustly overlooked tale that will become a favourite with your under 5. No matter whether you are looking for new, second-hand, or a title from your childhood, Edinburgh is well provided for.

Admittedly, conditions are not always ideal: small spaces crammed with bookshelves that seemed so appealing when you were childless suddenly become more of an obstacle course when you are pregnant or have children. On the whole, however, booksellers try to accommodate children – and those shops with trained (or willing!) staff will always be prepared to fetch a title for you.

Most shops now have some sort of distraction for toddlers and young children, such as boxes of toys, tables and chairs or reading books. Better stores have staff who are well-trained, specialise in children's books and can give invaluable advice and recommendations.

If you cannot find the book you require, most bookshops will be happy to order it for you at no additional charge. You may find that the smaller stores can order it in for you just as quickly as the larger chains. In addition to books and audio books, you can also order large print books and books in languages other than English via bookshops, should you require them.

Despite television, DVDs and all the other distractions, books are still extremely popular with under 5s. Books can be introduced at the baby stage, where the focus is on bold patterns, pictures and robust pages. By 9mths most babies will be happy to sit on your knee and look at a book, for at least a few moments. The bedtime story for a toddler is an ideal way to wind down after a hectic day and to spend 10 mins or so talking with your child. Books introduce children to words and language they would not normally hear in normal conversation (or on television!) and greatly increase language development. They can also help introduce children to concepts, ideas and situations out of their normal, everyday life, so helping to stimulate their imagination. There are also titles which can help young children to come to terms with some of the more traumatic aspects of growing up, such as going to hospital or the loss of a grandparent. If you are looking for such titles, ask in your bookshop – the education dept can be helpful if it has one.

There is a tremendous choice for under 5s, superbly illustrated in many different styles, which are entertaining for parent and child alike – though be prepared for the 'favourite' book; you may find yourself reading it several times in a row, several times per day!

We have tried to list the best stocked and most friendly bookshops. Children's books are also sold in supermarkets, department stores, toy shops, some stationers and also via mail order (see Shopping from Home).

New books may seem expensive, but they compare very well with the price of toys and videos and they offer excellent value for money; well-loved books can be handed down through families in the same way as toys etc. You could also ask for Book Tokens for gifts for your children at Christmas or birthday time: ask for National Book Tokens, which can be used in most UK bookshops, rather than shop-specific ones. From the age of around 3+ a child will enjoy choosing their very own book!

Look out also for charity shops, NCT Nearly New Sales, church book sales, second-hand and jumble sales. Libraries also host sales, and sometimes you can pick great bargains, such as '10 for the price of 1'! Look out for any storytelling or author sessions during holidays in your local library or bookshop.

A few children's books have an Edinburgh theme. There are many on the subject of Greyfriars Bobby, and there is also the famous 'Maisie' series. While they have good illustrations, many of them are unfortunately rather too text-heavy for small children. That said, they are often popular choices for gifts. Note that some of the 'Maisie' series titles are also available in Gaelic.

As a child Robert Louis Stevenson lived in Heriot Row, in Edinburgh and in his 'A Child's Garden of Verse', the poem 'The Lamplighter' is about the man who lit the lamp outside his home – the lamp is still there, though it's electric now. And for older children's interest, JK Rowling wrote the first Harry Potter novel in Edinburgh and has held promotional events for subsequent novels in some Edinburgh locations, including Edinburgh Castle.

OUT OF PRINT BOOKS

Some bookshops offer a free search service for out of print titles. Others may be able to guide you towards companies which specialise in searching and locating out of print titles – it's always worth asking! Alternatively, start trawling the second-hand bookshops, where you can still find hidden jewels.

Blackwell's
53-62 South Bridge
EH1 1YS
0131 622 8222
Edinburgh@blackwell.co.uk
www.blackwell.co.uk
Bright, extensive children's department with play table and programme of events (ring for details). Scottish Books section, audiobooks, recommendations and reviews. Specialist school department with school texts and revision guides: knowledgeable and friendly staff. All areas pushchair accessible. Lift with room for pushchairs gives easy access to the rest of this large bookshop, where you'll find loads of books for adults and comfy sofas for relaxed browsing. Public toilet with nappy changing facilities in children's department. Café with high chairs.

The Children's Bookshop
219 Bruntsfield Road
EH10 4DH
0131 447 1917
www.fidrabooks.com
Edinburgh's only specialist children's bookshop is run by the independent publishing company, Fidra Books. A wonderful selection of children's fiction and non-fiction available for all ages. Also some books for adults relevant to being a parent/carer.

 Don't forget to let businesses know you saw them in the EFUF book!

Waterstone's
www.waterstones.com

Stocks a wide range of books, categorised by age and with separate sections for favourite characters, film and tv tie-ins, audio books, reference books etc. Excellent selection of hardback and paperback titles. Regular activities for children. Happy to donate posters and publicity material to teachers. Lifts available which can be used for prams and pushchairs.

Branches at: 13/14 Princes Street (East End), 128 Princes Street (West End), 83 George Street, Cameron Toll Shopping Centre and Ocean Terminal.

WH Smith Books
Gyle Shopping Centre
EH12 9JR
0131 339 8855
www.whsmith.co.uk

Bright store with friendly staff, carrying a wide range of fiction and non-fiction books. The children's section is at the rear of the store and, as it's all on one level, is reasonably pushchair-friendly. The shelving is brightly coloured and there is seating for small children to encourage family browsing. Books are categorised by age range and there is also a good range of reference and gift books, plus audio books, pre-school/education books and film/tv tie-ins. WHSmith's stationery store a few moments walk away carries the usual range of magazines, stickers, box games etc.

CAKES & COOKERY

3D Cakes
20 Roseburn Terrace
Edinburgh
EH12 6AW
0131 337 9990
enquiries@3d-cakes.co.uk
www.3d-cakes.co.uk

An award winning cake designer. 3D Cakes will create amazing designs to bring any of your child's favourite characters to life.

The Cake and Chocolate Shop
12 Bruntsfield Place
0131 228 4350
freshuk@cakeandchocolateshop.co.uk
www.cakeandchocolateshop.co.uk

Will make cakes to any design (the only limit is your imagination) and there are lots of books of photographs to give you ideas.

The Finishing Touch
17 Patrick's Square
0131 667 0914

Over 40 novelty tins to hire, plus numbers, letters, squares, hexagons, etc. Good instructions. Also every imaginable utensil and ingredient for cake decorating. Lots of party paraphernalia too including party toys, masks, wigs and an extensive range of ribbons.

Lakeland
55 Hanover Street
EH2 2PJ
0131 220 3947
www.lakeland.co.uk

A wealth of cookery goodies and lots more besides.

Real Foods
37 Broughton Street
0131 557 1911
and
8 Brougham Street
0131 228 1202
info@realfoods.co.uk
www.realfoods.co.uk

Local independent retailer of healthy ethical foods. Huge range including free-from foods for special diets. Operates a local vegetable box delivery scheme too.

Studio One Cookshop
71 Morningside Road
0131 447 0452
studioonecookshop@yahoo.co.uk

Lots of cake tins (letters, numbers, hearts, squares, etc.) and kitchen utensils for baking your own.

CLOTHING

Most department stores, an increasing number of larger supermarkets, and some chemists stock baby wear, children's clothes, and maternity ranges (see sections for High Street Stores and Supermarkets). Not all are listed here, as we have tried to include those with a good range, exciting stock, competitive prices, or those which have something special to offer.

Apart from the problems of finding the right style, fabric and colour at the right price there are two main bugbears when shopping for children's clothes: the lack of a standard sizing system and seasonal availability.

The large department stores and major brand names all have different sizing systems. Most are still based on the now out-of-date British Standard, with manufacturers adding their own allowances for growth, comfort etc. The age range given to sizes is therefore only a rough guide. Also, if using real nappies, it is worth buying the next size up in vests and trousers.

Some of the smaller shops in this section will make-to-measure, at little or no extra charge for children with specific needs.

Clothes for low birth weight babies (from about 3lbs) are available from some department stores or by post (see Shopping from Home), although more stores are now stocking such ranges. For children's ski wear, see Outdoor and Ski Shops.

This section also includes details of dancewear (although many dance teachers do sell leotards, shoes etc), kilts, school wear and shoes.

More and more stores are offering maternity clothing which can reflect your usual dress sense: no longer are mums-to-be forced to wear tent dresses or smocks or to buy 'normal' clothes in extra-large sizes. You can have anything from sleek suits to leopard print trousers and all points in between. Maternity clothes now tend to be comfortable, fashionable and even flattering, with ingenious adjustable waists allowing them to 'grow' as you do. Even after the birth, you may find that you want or need to keep wearing some of your maternity clothes while your shape is changing, so you may well get more than 9 months' wear out of them. Some stores also now stock tops specifically designed for breastfeeding mothers.

The range of clothes and goods available may, of course, vary according to the size of individual stores; if in doubt, phone ahead.

Blessings & Blossoms
132 St Johns Road
EH12 8AX
0131 334 8322
www.blessingsandblossoms.co.uk
This Aladdin's cave stocks quality traditional and designer clothes and shoes for casual day wear or special events. Everything from flower girl, bridesmaid, party and communion dresses plus page boy outfits can be made to order or you can choose from the wide range in the shop. There are also christening outfits plus wonderful ideas for baby gifts. The shop is small and there are a couple of steps to navigate, but well worth a visit. There are even toys to keep the little ones occupied while you browse.

Where would you suggest?
Tell us -
ed@efuf.co.uk

Bliss

5 Raeburn Place
EH4 1HU
0131 332 4605
and
111a Broughton Street
EH1 3RZ
0131 556 3311
Bliss_edinburgh@talktalk.net
Small but lovely range of dresses, tops, t-shirts, sleepsuits etc. Also stock Oriental-style slippers, bags, purses etc. Ranges include Daisy Roots, Pesky Kids, Birkenstock etc. Also stock a range of toys and gifts.

The Disney Store

0131 557 2772
Selection of clothing for under 5s featuring Disney characters, including sleepwear. Also stock Disney character costumes and dressing up wear.
Branches at: 18-19 Princes Street and Gyle Shopping Centre.

Gap, Gap Kids & Baby Gap

Offers fashionable baby wear 0-4yrs, with extensive newborn collection. Also stock daywear for 2-13 yrs. Range changes regularly.
Branches at Fort Kinnaird, Gyle Shopping Centre, 131-133 Princes Street, and Ocean Terminal.

JoJo Maman Bebe

9 Multrees Walk
St Andrew's Square
0870 241 0560
www.jojomamanbebe.co.uk
Newly opened store from this online/mail order favourite. Offers a range of modern-styled maternity clothing (incl. work wear, casual and evening collections), and lingerie. Also offer children's wear and home accessories.

NCT Bra Fitting

Frankie 0131 664 3710
Naomi 0131 332 2191
NCT offer a wide range of breastfeeding bras. Two local trained fitters can measure and fit you in the comfort of their own home.

Next

Babies' (0-2yrs), boys' and girls' clothing from 3-10 yrs. Contemporary, hard-wearing separates and casuals in vibrant colours. Underwear, footwear, outdoor wear, many in 100% cotton. Also stock party wear and some dressing up outfits. School wear available via home shopping by catalogue or online.
Branches at: 107-109 Princes St, Fort Kinnaird, Gyle Shopping Centre, St James' Centre, Craigleith Retail Park and Straiton Park Way.

Nippers

131 Bruntsfield Place
Edinburgh
EH10 4EB
0131 228 5086
mail@nippersforkids.com
www.nippersforkids.com
Designer children's wear – knitwear, t-shirts, shoes, hats and winter wear, including Nippers own designer fleece collections. Clothes and gifts for 0-6yrs. Also stock slings, blankets, soft toys and much more.

Pine and Old Lace

46 Victoria Street
0131 225 3287
Phone to check if you are making a special trip, as this is a one-woman shop. Stock always includes antique Christening gowns. Shop not accessible to double pushchairs.

Polarn o Pyret

(Jenners)
48 Princes Street
EH2 2YJ
0131 260 2324
www.polarnopyret.com
Popular Swedish brand of clothing which is functional as well as stylish.

Pretty Pregnant

4 Howe Street
Edinburgh
EH3 5LG
0131 225 9777
ppedi@prettypregnant.co.uk
www.prettypregnant.co.uk
This is a relaxed boutique providing a wide selection of maternity and nursing wear. Offers a specialised bra fitting service too.

The Royal Edinburgh Repository and Self Aid Society

23a Castle Street
0131 220 1187
The Society encourages people, particularly those in low income groups, to work in their own homes, using skills such as knitting, sewing, toy-making etc. The Edinburgh shop sells a unique collection of handmade articles, including beautiful baby and toddler hand-knitted items, handmade smock dresses etc, as well as toys. The shop also sells traditional old-fashioned items such as shawls and sleeping gowns. Special orders can be taken. All the money from the sale of goods is returned to the society members.

Vanilla Bloom

6 William Street
Edinburgh
EH3 7LW
0131 220 2502
www.vanillabloom.com
Ranges include stylish maternity wear, adorable baby wear and beautiful gifts for babies and toddlers. Also offer gift vouchers and wish lists. Just moved to their new address as this edition goes to print. The new store promises even more choice.

SCHOOL UNIFORM

Many department stores and supermarkets stock skirts, pinafores, shorts, trousers, blazers, shirts and socks in traditional school colours. Their stock is extensive in May, June and July but most have a reduced stock through the other months. Other suggested retailers are:

Aitken and Niven

234 Queensferry Road
EH24 2BP
0131 467 8825
and
6 Falcon Road West
Morningside
EH10 1AQ
0131 477 3922
Long-established Edinburgh retailer, which stocks school wear and sportswear including uniforms for Edinburgh's independent schools. Also stocks school shoes.

Clan House

45 Grove Street
EH3 HAF
0131 229 6857
and
28-30 Morningside Road
EH10 4DA
0131 447 3414
www.clanhouseofedinburgh.com
Stockists of uniforms, sportswear and equipment. Also stocks most Edinburgh school badges to sew on.

SPECIALIST CLOTHING

Some of Edinburgh's department stores stock dance or keep-fit wear. Some may only have a basic stock, while other may have quite a selection – especially of ballet-related products (John Lewis always has a pretty good range). However, as with all things, it does pay to shop around. Some dance teachers also sell shoes and/or leotards, so it's worthwhile asking if your child is starting a class.

Dancewear

182 Rose Street
EH2 4BA
0131 226 5457
sales@dancewear-edinburgh.co.uk
www.dancewear-edinburgh.co.uk
This shop provides a patient and knowledgeable service for children of all ages. Competitive prices for ballet shoes (satin and leather), tap, Highland, Irish and jazz. They specialise in point toe fitting for all ages. They also sell leotards, tights, catsuits, salsa wear, flamenco wear, ballet skirts, crossover cardigans, tu-tus and ballet giftware. Online catalogue - no online ordering though.

Dancia International

42 South Clerk Street
0131 668 9444
Full range of dancewear for children, covering all specialities, and also all types of shoes. Full fitting service.

Edinburgh has several good options when it comes to shopping for kilts. There are specialist shops, although shops such as Aitken and Niven, Ortak, and John Lewis stock kilts, tartan wear and/or accessories.

Proper kilt pleats should fold back behind the previous pleat: this is what gives that wonderful swing, but it also makes them rather heavy and very expensive, as so much fabric is used. However, if you do choose to buy a full kilt, you will have a family heirloom, which can be handed down the generations. A reasonable alternative is a 'half kilt', in which not all the pleats are full, but it still swings well and looks good. Many shops also sell kilted skirts off the peg. Small kilts can have straps or a bodice to hold them up, and you can get jabot shirts with elastic around the waist to cover this up.

Shops which sell made-to-measure kilts usually have books of tartan (you may need to choose a tartan with a small set for a small kilt). These stores can usually help you link your surname to a specific sept or clan. They can also give the kilt a good 'wrap around' and a generous hem to let down. Some will change the wrapover side for different sexes.

You can really go overboard with the accompanying regalia, such as: jackets, shirts (with jabot or bow tie), sporran, shoes, socks, flashes – and for teenagers and adults, a sgian dubh. A kilt can also look good with a Fair Isle, Arran or Shetland jumper, or just a plain white shirt and socks. As your children get older, you may find teenagers turn to the trendy alternative look of big boots, pushed-down socks and t-shirts!

What is worn under the kilt is anyone's guess (except toddlers can't resist showing everybody!!). If you only need a kilt for your child (or other family members) for a special occasion, a good alternative is to hire one.

Davison Menswear
Dress Hire Shop
31-33 Bruntsfield Place
0131 229 0266
sales@qualitykilts.co.uk
www.qualitykilts.co.uk
Kids kilt hire from 6mths.

Hector Russell
95 Princes Street
Edinburgh
EH2 2ER
0131 225 3315
HectorRussell@princesstreetstore. freeserve.co.uk
and
137-141 High Street
Edinburgh
EH1 1SG
0131 558 1254
These stores stock boys' kilts and trews and girls' kilted skirts, as well as: kilts, socks, sock flashes, belts, sgian dubh, shirts, and shoes. Stores also offer a made-to-measure service for children and dancers. Hector Russell do not currently hire children's outfits, but they do sell a range of off-the-peg outfits, such as kilts, trousers etc. Online mail-order service also available.

Highland Laddie
6 Hutchison Terrace
EH14 1QB
0131 455 7505
Complete outfits sold. All accessories available, jackets, shirts, brogues and shoes, sporrans etc.

CYCLING EQUIPMENT

Child Seats and Equipment
Most shops will fit a child seat for nothing, or for a minimal charge, if you have purchased it at their store. Do not lose any of the nuts and bolts, as some are unique and irreplaceable.

The addition of a child seat will obviously affect the handling and stability of your bike, as well as placing a greater strain on it, so keep it well maintained, especially the brakes and the wheels.

Rear Child Seats
The best rear child seats are made from high-impact, rigid moulded plastic, with headrests to support a child who has fallen asleep. They should also have the following items: a safety harness, footguards and straps to prevent feet getting caught in the rear wheel. If you have a sprung saddle, it makes sense to either cover or replace it, so that little fingers do not get caught. Suitable for children from around the age at which they are able to sit unsupported (usually 6mths) until they get too heavy for the seat. This aspect varies with manufacturer recommendation, but it's usually 22kg, approx. up to 3-4yrs.

Front Child Seats
These are not recommended. The child feels colder than would be the case in a rear-mounted seat, shielded by your body. Also, if a child falls asleep in a front mounted seat, you must use one arm to support the child and ride one-handed, which is unsafe.

Child Trailers
These are two wheeled pushchairs that attach to the rear fork of adult bike. The fixing device allows the adult bike to be laid on its side without tipping the trailer up, but it is a good idea to fit a stand to the adult bike. Most can carry two children from 9mths-5/6yrs, with the limiting factor being the weight of the children – the maximum combined weight is usually 50kg. A very young child can also be carried when strapped into a child seat, although this will leave no room for a second child. Most trailers also have a luggage space at the back. Trailers usually come with a rain-and-sun cover and a visibility flag. The best also have quick release wheels and can be folded down for easy carriage in trains, buses and cars. They are fairly expensive, but they do tend to have a high resale value. They also make useful luggage or shopping carriers, long after families have grown up! Makes include: Adams, Burley, Bike Trax.

Compared with a child seat, the child misses the view, feels the bumps more and is right at exhaust height on any road. However, a single adult can take two young children at once, the balance of the adult bicycle is less affected and the trailer may stay upright if the adult bicycle falls over.

Trailercycles
Also known as Tag-A-Longs, these consist of a special frame, without front wheels and with forks, which attach to an adult bike (or tandem), either at the seat post or rear rack. The child can help with the pedalling, but braking and steering are left to the adult. They are excellent for taking children out cycling in situations where either it would not be safe to let a child cycle independently, or where a child wouldn't be able to cope with the distance or hills. It's also a great way for a child to learn about observing traffic, signalling and road positioning while being safely in the control of an experienced adult. Some models have gears so children can learn how to change gear without having to worry about steering at the same time. The great advantage of trailercycles is their versatility. You can buy a 'seconds' tow hitch, which allows the trailercycle to be quickly swapped between adult bikes. A trailercycle can also be carried easily on trains by simply detaching and storing alongside the adult bike in the cycle storage area.

Visit our website for updates:
www.efuf.co.uk

Trailer bikes are suitable for children from 3 or 4 yrs. up to around 9yrs. Makes include: Bike Trax, Adams, Ally Cat.

Trailgator

A special bar which attaches to an adult bike and converts a regular child's bike to a trailercycle by lifting up the front wheel. Obviously, these are much cheaper, but are really only suitable for small bikes. Larger kid's bikes tend to fall over too easily.

Tandems

A 'Junior back' style tandem has a frame designed for an adult 'pilot' at the front and a child 'stoker' at the back. A potentially good solution if you are to do a lot of cycling, but they're not very versatile. Makes include: Dawes, Orbit, Thorn, Swallow.

Ordinary tandem are fitted with 'kiddy cranks' or crank shorteners. More versatile than a junior back tandem, as it can easily be converted back to an ordinary tandem again.

The advantage of a tandem over a trailercycle is that a few of them can also be fitted with a rear child seat to carry a very young child, in addition to the older child that is pedalling. The disadvantage is that they are not easy to store or to carry on trains.

Tricycles

A tricycle fitted with one or two child seats at the back can also be a good way of getting the family on the move. Suitable for children from 12mths to 5yrs.

Cycling solo

Balance bikes or 'runners' are becoming more popular. These bikes without peddles (available with and without brakes) are a great way to get little ones cycling and learning to balance. Most of the bicycle shops listed have a least one type of balance bike for sale. Try them out for size, probably suitable from 2-3yrs of when children can sit on the bike and reach the ground with the balls of their feet. Wooden versions are also available from toyshops. Otherwise check out children's bikes with stabilisers or tricycles, especially those with a handle that lets adults push/control the trike comfortably.

Helmets

Though not legally compulsory yet, a helmet should be an essential piece of equipment for all cyclists. It is important to take your child to the shop to have them fitted properly so they don't wobble. Look for one which has a European or American standard, preferably both as these standards have superseded the British one. To make them more acceptable for children, go for the coolest looking one you can afford! Children who are putting a lot of effort into pedalling will also appreciate one with plenty of ventilation. Makes include: Met, Hamax, Cateye, Specialized, Giro, Bell. Helmets are all 'first impact' so should be replaced, after a serious bash, or if they are damaged.

General Safety

Under no circumstances should you cycle with a baby in a backpack or sling.
Keep children's shoelaces short and tucked away. The same applies to scarves and other loose clothing. Dress children in brightly coloured clothing, so that they are visible to motorists. Think twice before carrying a very restless child. Beware of very cold and wet weather. Make sure that the adult bike is kept in good mechanical order. Especially ensure that the brakes are always working well to cope with the additional weight that the bike will be carrying.

A Good Tip!

It's a good idea to try out some of the more expensive items like trailers or trailercycles before you buy, to make sure that you are happy with the handling and that it's the right bit of gear for you. Try and borrow from another family, or consider hiring for a weekend – you could save yourself an expensive mistake! Go to a bike shop specialising in trailer bikes or tandems for advice on the best and most suitable equipment to buy.

BICYCLE SHOPS

Alpine Bikes
48 Hamilton Place
0131 225 3286
www.alpinebikes.co.uk
Adult and child bikes, child seats and helmets, trailer bikes and child trailers. Also stock Gore bikewear, Altura clothing and panniers. Bike spares and repair service with 24 hour turn around. Hires out trailer bikes, child trailers and mountain bikes. Also stock demo bikes.

BG Cycles and Blades
48 Portobello High Street
0131 657 5832
www.bgcycles.co.uk
Adult and child bikes, trailer bikes, child seats and helmets. Also in-line skates. Also repairs and spares – can uplift and deliver bikes for repair or service within a 15-mile radius for a small charge.

Bicycle Repair Man
111 Newington Road
EH9 1QW
0131 667 5959
www.bicyclerepairman.biz
Adult and child bikes, child seats and helmets, trailer bikes and child trailers. Bike spares and same day repair service.

The Bicycleworks
29-30 Argyle Place
0131 228 8820
Or at:
The Triathlon Centre
57-59 South Clerk Street
0131 662 8777
A repair and wheel building shop with a wide range of spares and accessories. Also sells child seats. Instant puncture repairs or tyre replacement. Fast turn around on all other repairs/servicing.

Bike Trax
11 Lochrin Place
EH3 9QX
Tel: 228 6633
info@biketrax.co.uk
www.biketrax.co.uk
Adult and child bikes, child seats and helmets, trailer bikes, child trailers and folding bikes. Dawes, Ridgeback, Trek, Brompton etc. Free after sales service. Bike repair shop will repair any make of bike, including children's bikes. 24hr turn around where possible. Free estimates. Free advice on cycle matters, local cycle routes, etc. Also hires out bikes and equipment. Hire before you buy, hire charge deducted from purchase price.

Dave's Bicycle Store
39 Argyle Place
0131 229 8528
Used bikes for adults and children. Trade-ins welcome.

Edinburgh Bicycle Co-operative
5-9 Alvanley Terrace
Whitehouse Loan
EH9 1DU
0131 228 3565
www.edinburghbicycle.com
A fantastic range of children's bicycles, trailers, trailer bikes, child seats, helmets, reflectives, accessories and clothing: all selected with the same attention to detail that the Bike Co-op lavish on their famed adult range. The child-friendly staff will happily offer advice to ensure your child gets fitted with, for instance, the correct size of helmet and the right size of bike.

Edinburgh Cycle Hire & Cycle Safaris
29 Blackfriars Street
0131 556 5560
info@cyclescotland.co.uk
www.cyclescotland.co.uk
Sells adult and child bikes, child seats, trailer bikes, child trailers, tandems. Repairs and servicing. Also hires out large selection of adult and child bikes, tandem, trailer bikes, child trailer, child seats etc. Also organises cycle tours, holidays and days out.

Freewheelin'
91 Slateford Road
0131 337 2351
Adult and children's bikes, child seats and helmets. Can also order trailer bikes, child trailers and tandems. Spares, servicing and repair service with same/next day turn around.

Great Bikes No Bull
276 Leith Walk
0131 467 7775
www.greatbikesnobull.com
Adult and children's bikes. Full range of safety accessories including child seats and helmets. Hire before you buy, hire charge deducted from purchase price. In basement, Recycling (0131 553 1130) offers reconditioned adult and child bikes guaranteed for 3mths.

Halfords Stores & Superstores
www.halfords.com
Good selection of children's sit-and-ride toys, trikes, pedal cars and bikes - Apollo and Raleigh. Child seats, spare parts and accessories. Free after sales service. Usually repair bikes bought here, but may occasionally do small outside repairs. Major repairs in-store. Free fitting of child seat if bike bought at Halfords.
Branches at: Hermiston Gait Retail Park, Seafield Road East, and 11 Straiton Mains.

Leith Cycle Co.
276 Leith Walk
EH6 5BX
0131 467 7775
www.leithcycleco.com
Also at:
1 Cadzow Place
EH7 5SN
0131 652 1760
Adult and children's bikes plus helmets, seats, car racks, and accessories. Extensive hire and repair services available.

MacDonald Cycles
26-28 Morrison Street
EH3 9BJ
0131 229 8473
Or at:
35 High Street
Musselburgh
EH21 7AD
0131 665 1777
www.macdonaldcycles.com
Good selection of children's trikes and bikes, cycle parts, child seats, children's helmets, children's cycle capes, spare parts and safety accessories. Free after sales service. Will repair any bike, if parts available. Usually 24hr turn-around, sometimes quicker. Will fit child seat free if both bike and seat are bought here.

Theraplay Ltd
www.triaid.com
0141 876 9177

For foot pedal tricycles, hand crank tricycles, gait trainers and toileting/shower chairs. The tricycles may be particularly popular with children who need additional support for cycling – the Imp tricycle comes in colours that appeal to children (including pink!) and suits children from about 2½ yrs. Adapted tricycles can be quite expensive – if you're applying for funding to buy one for your child remember the SNIP fundfinder service!
A rep will be able to come to your home to assess the kind of trike your child needs. You could also consider trying out a tricycle before you buy – the special needs toy library may have one available for loan or you could visit the Scotland Yard Adventure Centre and try one of the trikes they have.

Velo Ecosse
25-27 Bruntsfield Place
EH10 4HJ
0131 477 2557
veloecosse@freeuk.com
www.veloecosse.freeuk.com
Children's and adult bikes, child seats and helmets. Trailercycles and trailers and large range of cycle clothing. Spares and accessories. Repairs and servicing done within 24-48hrs. For serious cyclists, they stock Giant, Pinarello and Shimano.

FAIRS & MARKETS

Edinburgh Farmers' Market
Castle Street
www.scottishfarmersmarkets.co.uk
0131 652 5940
A selection of stalls selling fruit and veg, meat, poultry, game, fish, dairy, and more. The stall-owners are the primary producers, so they know their stuff. Much of what is on offer is organic, and you can sign up for home delivery of vegetable boxes at some stalls. There are also stalls selling delicious baking, jams and chutneys, beverages, soaps, and some knit-wear. The range seems to grow every week, and changes somewhat depending on the season. There are often samples available at many of the stalls (a good way to find out if your child likes what you're about to buy!), and you can purchase drinks and snacks such as wild boar and ostrich burgers, and roast suckling pig rolls. For non-meat eaters, there are also freshly cooked crisps, as well as hearty (and healthy!) porridge to buy. There are a few tables and chairs set up to eat at, but it does tend to get busy and difficult to manoeuvre pushchairs at times.

Garvald Bazaar
www.garvaldedinburgh.org.uk
This is held in the Gorgie Road workshop premises usually on the last Saturday in November or the first Saturday in December depending upon when the first Advent Sunday falls.

Steiner Christmas Fair
www.steinerweb.org.uk
The Christmas Market at the Edinburgh Rudolph Steiner School is a great day out. Lots of lovely stalls, great food and plenty of fun to be had by all.

Anything out of date?
Let us know -
info@efuf.co.uk

West End Art
Craft and Design Fair
www.3d2d.co.uk
Seasonal Event (usually runs for three weeks in August during the Edinburgh Festival).
An open air art, craft and design fair in the grounds of St. Johns Church at the corner of Lothian Road and Princes Street. Free entry and a good variety of stalls selling unique, handcrafted, good quality clothes, accessories, toys, art, pottery, jewellery, etc. There are ramps constructed so you can get around with a pushchair, but it does tend to get busy (especially weekends), so it may be slow-going at times. Hendersons Café underneath St. Johns Church offers drinks, snacks, and hot food. Other craft events during the year hosted at The Assembly Rooms in George Street.

HAIRCUTS

Having a haircut can be traumatic for a young child. Some love it – enjoying the attention – while others need a little more persuasion. If you already use a hairdresser regularly, it is worth asking if they would cut your child's hair, and how much they would charge, although what suits you might not be the best for your child: you need someone who is relaxed with children, is patient, and has a calm approach.

Many hairdressers have special seats so that children can sit at the right height, and have books and toys to keep them amused while they are waiting. A few even have videos to show, which is one way of getting your child to keep his or her head still. If your child is shy, it might be worth asking if they can sit on your knee while their hair is being cut.

Timing of the haircut can be critical, both for your child and the hairdresser. Choose a time when your child is usually on good form, perhaps early in the morning or after a nap. If it's possible, try to choose a quiet period at the hairdressers; there's likely to be a quieter atmosphere, as well as a shorter waiting time.

If it is your child's first visit to a salon, you will probably find it better to make the appointment in person, giving your child the chance to see where s/he is going and what it will be like. It may also help to take your child along if you are having a haircut yourself – though this plan is best put into action only if you have someone who can take your child away for a little while, as an adult cut can change from fascination to boredom pretty quickly!

If you are looking for a new hairdresser for your whole family, why not have a haircut first yourself. It will give you the opportunity to chat to the stylist and find out how keen s/he is to cut your child's hair, or if one of the salon's stylists specialises in children's cuts. Some salons offer reduced rates for children when a parent has a haircut too. Check out local salons – there may be no need to trail across the city with your toddler for a good cut.

Another option if you find it difficult to get out, or you find that your child is intimidated by the surroundings of a salon, would be to have a hairdresser come to your home. Check out Yellow Pages, www.yell.com or local press – or why not ask around at any group you attend. You may find that haircuts at home are a practical solution for your family, and an exciting afternoon for your small child!

While most salons are happy to cut and style children's hair, the following specialise in children's haircutting:

Kids' Stop
36 Morningside Road
EH10 4DA
0131 446 0123
Extremely child-friendly salon, which also welcomes adults! Special children's seat provided (horse, rabbit, bike), video while having a haircut, play area with toys, video and books. Sliding scale of rates, dependent on child's age.
Toilet and nappy changing facilities available. Appointments not always necessary. Make-over parties also available – please call salon for more information.

Kute Kutz
4 Meadowbank Avenue
0131 661 1339
A new kids hair salon. Fun for kids with a choice of chairs. DVDs and television to keep little ones entertained while they get their hair cut.

Fully accessible and hairdresser has experience of children with special needs and sensory difficulties.

Mizzumi
73-75 High Street
Musselburgh
EH21 7BZ
0131 665 1212
www.mizzumi.co.uk
A stylish salon for adults which also has a dedicated kids area painted in bright colours with televisions showing tv and videos to entertain little ones while they have their hair cut. Call the salon for more information.

MAKE YOUR OWN

Edinburgh has an excellent choice of wool and fabric shops, and you always end up with an 'exclusive' outfit. The shops listed below are those which we feel have something special to offer, and those which are more 'out of the way'.
John Lewis (see Department Stores) and The Cloth Shop probably have the largest choice of pattern books and paper patterns. In these tomes, you'll find everything from maternity wear, to pyjamas, dressing gowns and dressing up outfits. 'Teen' dolls can also have an extensive wardrobe to match your own, and there are usually popular soft toy patterns available.
There are many wool shops scattered around the suburbs and most stock baby wools. Pingouin and Rowan have children's knitting patterns in up to the minute designs and Pingouin also has a baby/toddler magazine. Paton's have a wide range of knitting patterns for small babies, starting at 14".

The Cloth Shop
169 Bonnington Road
EH6 5BQ
0131 554 7733
Large warehouse-style shop, with a fantastic selection of dress, curtain and upholstery fabric, and all the haberdashery that goes along with it. Stencil kits and cushion pads available, along with some great tulles and seasonally printed fabrics for dressing up clothes. Small customer toilets near the children's play area. Car parking.

David Drummond
77-81 Haymarket Terrace
Edinburgh
0131 539 7766
Sewing machines, including service and repairs. Haberdashery and wool. A treasure trove and well worth a visit.

The Dress Fabric Company
38 Bruntsfield Place
Edinburgh
EH10 4HJ
0131 221 0464
gp@dressfabric.info
Stocked full of lovely fabrics – the hard part is deciding which one to choose.

The Grassmarket Embroidery Shop
19 The Grassmarket
Edinburgh
EH1 2HS
0131 226 3335
www.grassmarketembroidery.co.uk
Fantastic range of threads, canvas, fabrics and more. As well as embroidery supplies this outlet offers classes and workshops.

Kiss The Fish
9 Dean Park Street
Stockbridge
0131 332 8912
www.kissthefishstudios.com
Sell children's craft kits and a range of arts and crafts materials. Also sell a range of cool gifts.

Mandors
131 East Claremont Street
EH7 4JA
0131 558 3888
www.mandors.co.uk
Stock good range of dressmaking fabrics, for everyday wear through to bridalwear, faux fur etc etc. Plenty of fun fabrics for children's projects and fancy dress outfits. There's also a good stock of haberdashery, such as ribbons and finishings. Mandors stock a selection of patterns. Staff are happy to welcome children and will provide a box of material to play with.

McAree Brothers
19 Howe Street
Edinburgh
EH3 6TE
0131 558 1747
Bountiful supplies of knitting and haberdashery goodies. Staff are only too happy to help and offer advice.

NURSERY EQUIPMENT

Many shops in Edinburgh sell well-known brand name equipment. If you decide to buy second-hand or an uncommon make, you must satisfy yourself as to its safety. Second-hand equipment can be in very good condition, but it may not conform to current safety standards. Cot and Moses basket mattresses should always be bought new: never buy a second-hand one. The same applies to car seats: you can't be sure if the seat has been in a traffic accident – there may be stress damage that you can't see, but which could endanger your child.

After sales service should be an important consideration when making your choice of equipment; ask about servicing and repairs before you buy. Most of the outlets that we have listed will do both to the brands they sell, and most will consider lending you a temporary replacement if the repair will take some time. It is a good idea to retain your receipt for a long time, as this is usually required as proof of purchase before repairs will be undertaken. Talk to friends before you buy – you only discover the pros and cons of equipment once you have lived with it for a while.

Shops usually keep one demonstration pram in stock. Ordering your style and colour can take from 6-20wks! No shop will make you buy a pram if you discover you do not need it (if you discover you're having twins, for example) and most will store it until you need it. All other equipment is usually held in stock.

Which? Magazine and Practical Parenting often have reports on nursery equipment and it is worth checking back numbers in the library, even if it's just to see what to look out for. See also 'Hiring', further on in this section.

High Street stores listed above are worth visiting for nursery equipment. Other stores to consider are:

Corstorphine Pram Centre
115-117 St John's Road
0131 334 6216
Wide selection of prams, pushchairs, cots, travel cots, backpacks, car seats and other equipment. Also a large selection of nursery décor ranges and furniture.

The Foam Centre
176 Causewayside
Newington
0131 667 1247
Different foams cut to any size and shape. Can be made to fit cots, Moses baskets, booster seats, etc. 'Beans' to top up or make your own beanbags. Maternity wedges, lumbar supports also supplied.

Mamas and Papas
Craigleith Retail Park
EH4 2LN
0870 830 7700
www.mamasandpapas.co.uk
Selection of own brand prams, travel systems, car seats, cots, etc. Also stock ranges of co-ordinating nursery equipment and accessories including bed and bath time linen. Stylish baby clothing from newborn. Outfits and separates, all in subtle colours. Small range of contemporary designed maternity wear. Now offering a gift list service too.

National Childbirth Trust Sales
0870 112 1120
www.nctsales.co.uk
A wide range of nursery equipment, furniture, car seats, slings, pushchairs and accessories available from the catalogue and website.

Ed's NCT.....

There's a lot on offer -

- **Antenatal Classes**
- **Breastfeeding Support**
- **Breast Pump Hire**
- **Bumps and Babies**
- **Edinburgh for Under Fives**
- **Helplines**
- **Nearly New Sales**
- **NCT Bras**
- **Postnatal Services**
- **Valley Cushion Hire**
- **www.nctsales.co.uk**

Visit our website for more information about the NCT in Edinburgh:

www.nctedinburgh.moonfruit.com

OUTDOOR & SKI SHOPS

For those parents wishing to take their children outdoors in Britain, our weather can always prove unpredictable. Keeping the small members of the family warm and dry is essential to everyone's enjoyment of an outing. There's a good selection of dedicated outdoor shops in Edinburgh, and many offer clothing and equipment for under 5s.

Babycarriers (or backpacks) allow you to go off the beaten track with your child safely away from mud, wet grass, sheep droppings, and all the other delights a small child can find in the countryside. These carriers can be equally useful in town, allowing negotiation of busy streets without many of the problems associated with pushchairs, such as other people (!), getting through doors and using escalators. The big drawback is the potential strain on your back – so the adage 'try before you buy' is essential, as with any piece of outdoor clothing. Remember, you and your partner may be carrying the pack considerable distances. Also, think about your intended use: if you want something for walking in the country, you'll probably want something which is reasonably rugged as well as comfortable. However, if the pack is more for 'urban' use, take this into account. If both parents are going to use the backpack, and are different heights, make sure you buy one which is easily adjustable.

As with most things, with outdoor equipment and clothing, you get what you pay for. So, keep your primary usage in mind, and keep comfort as a priority.

Blacks Outdoor Leisure Ltd
24 Frederick Street
EH2 2JR
0131 225 8686
www.blacks.co.uk
Or at:
13/14 Elm Row
EH7 4AA
0131 556 3491
Stores stock Vango baby carriers, children's boots and socks. Ski wear only available at Frederick Street store.

Millets
12 Frederick Street
EH2 2HB
0131 220 1551
www.millets.co.uk
The store is on 2 floors, stair access. Main children's department at rear of ground floor. Clothing (from 12mths), boots (from size 10), rucksacks, camping gear all available in a variety of styles and patterns. The 'Kids Eurohike' range of children's outdoor explorer equipment, e.g. Compasses, torches, binoculars, etc., is fun and can make your trips out easier for everyone.

Nevisport
19 Rose Street
EH2 2PR
0131 225 9498
www.nevisport.com
Stocks Macpac and Littlelife baby carriers for babies from 6mths. Also has a good range of waterproof clothing for toddlers upwards, fleeces, lightweight boots and children's rucksacks. For skiers there is a range of clothes and equipment for children. Skis from 70cm up, boots from size 16' (mondopoint sizing). Staff toilet available for emergencies. Access through doorway big enough for tandem pushchair but children's department is located on 1st floor. No lift access but ask staff for help in getting up stairs.

Snowlines
14/15 Bruntsfield Place
EH10 4HN
0131 229 2402
www.snowlines.co.uk
Stocks specialist clothing and footwear for running, skiing, snowboarding and outdoor pursuits. Offers a free instore video gait analysis. Operates an instore discount scheme, details of which can be found on the website.

Sports Warehouse
24-26 Coburg Street
EH6 6HB
0131 553 6003
www.sportswarehouse.co.uk
This sports and outdoor supplier has boots from size 11, baby and child size sleeping bags, swimming aids, Pentland waterproof cagoules and trousers from 3+ yrs. Also a good range of child-sized wetsuits in summer.

Tiso
123-125 Rose Street
EH2 3DT
0131 225 9486
www.tiso.com
The store is located over four floors with ski and children's departments on 1st floor. Clothing includes ranges of fleeces and waterproof jackets, suits and overtrousers including Berghaus, Northface, Togz and own-label Wild Rover. Wellingtons (from size 4) and walking boots (from size 10). Babycarriers from Macpac and Littlelife. Blues Ski Shop has children's clothing and equipment.

Tiso Edinburgh Outdoor Experience
41 Commercial Street
Leith
EH6 6JD
0131 554 0804
This store, the largest of its kind this side of the country, is situated on one level with car park available for 60 cars or you can easily take the bus. 'Outdoor Experience' is an interactive shop with everything from a boot path and carrymat test bed to a test climbing wall, as well as a large range of clothing and equipment. Comfy sofas available to rest your feet. Cairn Café at rear of shop. Customer toilets.

Trespass
27/29 Frederick Street
EH2 2NF
0131 225 7456
www.trespass.co.uk
Good range of outdoor clothing and boots for children 2+ yrs. Wellingtons from size 7, walking boots from size 10. Summer stock includes shorts, t-shirts but fewer waterproofs; winter stock extends to include more substantial waterproofs and ski wear. Store is on 2 floors, children's department at rear of ground floor. Easy access for pushchairs.

PHOTOGRAPHY

Department stores such as Boots and Debenhams and shopping centres such as Cameron Toll or The Gyle Centre often have visiting companies which specialise in photographing young children. Look out in the Herald and Post for details of these companies. The Herald and Post also has details of firms which are willing to video or photograph your party or Christening. The following companies have experience in working with under 5s.

Dimple Photos
100 Northfield Crescent
Willowbrae Road
EH8 7QB
0131 661 5031
07946 518 244
Portraits@dimple-photos.co.uk
Established in 1985, servicing maternity hospitals. Photographs of newborns. Specialists in baby portrait packs.

Helen Pugh Photography
07837 533 051
info@helenpughphotography.com
www.helenpughphotography.com
Portrait photography at home or on location.

Klaklak Photography
0131 346 8415
www.klaklakphotography.co.uk
Award winning children's photographer. Also offer birthday party photo shoots.

Leo Friel Photography
07778 639 787
info@leofriel.co.uk
www.leofriel.co.uk
Fun, natural children and family portraits at your home, family event or special location.

Moments-Preserved
68 St Stephens Street
Stockbridge
EH3 5AQ
0131 226 3589
sales@moments-preserved.com
www.moments-preserved.com
Studio sessions for individuals or groups and even pets are welcome. Happy to photograph babies from just a few days old and will do all that they can to make your portrait experience an enjoyable one.

Nipper Snappers
07515 521957
info@nippersnappers.co.uk
East Lothian based photographer who specialises in children's portraits.

Photo Express
7 Melville Terrace
EH9 1ND
0131 667 2164
info@photo-express-edinburgh.co.uk
www.photo-express-edinburgh.co.uk
Specialises in children and family groups. Portraits taken in studio. Toilet facilities available. Roadside metered parking.

Picture House
0131 553 1177
www.picturehousestudios.co.uk
Award-winning photographers specialising in child and family portraits.

Don't forget to let businesses know you saw them in the EFUF book!

Sarah Elizabeth Photography
Midlothian Innovation Centre
Roslin
EH25 9RE
0131 448 0111
sarah@sarahelizabeth.co.uk
www.sarahelizabeth.co.uk
Specialists in baby and children portraiture - contemporary portraits in the studio, single portraits or wall montages. Female only photographers. Baby changing facilities and free parking.

Venture
Meadowbank Retail Park
17 Earlston Place
EH7 5SU
0131 652 8130
www.thisisventure.co.uk
Experienced in photography of babies and children. New generation photography, which means the poses are not your static, traditional portraiture. Venture frames the resultant photographs. Studios, preview rooms, nappy change facilities.

PORTRAITS
Gemma de Luna
0131 538 0052
Freelance artist and portraitist, experienced in drawing children, including as part of street entertainment during the Edinburgh Festival.

Genuine European Portraits
Freepost SCO3533
EH10 0BR
0131 229 7556
www.portraits.org
Specialises in hand drawn portraits on a sale or return basis for nurseries, playgroups, toddler groups etc, which receive commission for each portrait, so it's a good fundraiser. Individual drawings from photos can be ordered through the website.

Pencil Portraits
07773 398749
Gardiner.aimee@yahoo.co.uk
www.aimeegardiner.co.uk
Pencil portraits by artist Aimee Gardiner. Portraits of children created from photographs.

REUSABLE NAPPIES

Modern cloth nappies are not only very fashionable, they're easy to use too: no pins, no boiling, no complicated folds and, if you use local nappy laundry services, no washing either. Cloth nappies are effective, comfortable and convenient. They can save you money and they're good for the environment too – we all know that disposable nappies are causing major problems in land-fill sites. Cloth nappies, on the other hand, can be used again and again, and if you have another baby you could even make greater savings.

The Real Nappy Project
Changeworks
36 Newhaven Road
EH6 5PY
0131 555 4010
realnappies@changeworks.org.uk
www.changeworks.org.uk
Contact the experts at The Real Nappy Project to help you choose real nappies for your baby. Parents living in Edinburgh and the Lothians can apply for a lending kit or trial pack. The lending kit provides a variety of nappies with enough to use for a two week loan period and the trial packs provide a taster of good quality real nappies. In addition, low income families can apply for a £30 voucher towards the cost of either a trial pack or a lending kit, and use the remainder to buy real nappies. Free information and advice is available via phone, email or at regularly held events.

Time for a Nappy Change?

The experts at the Edinburgh and Lothians Real Nappy Project can provide FREE help and advice plus the chance to try real nappies on your baby.

Talk to us

Call us or come along to a Nappuccino. Venues in Leith, Musselburgh, Bonnyrigg, Livingston and Linlithgow. Check our website for details.

Try them

A lending kit or trial pack can help you make an informed decision. Each cost £12 + delivery. Available to Edinburgh and Lothians residents*.

Low income families can apply for a £30 voucher to buy real nappies from selected retailers*.

*Conditions apply. Limited numbers available. One application per household. Charity No. SC015144

For further information contact Changeworks
T: 0131 555 4010
E: realnappies@changeworks.org.uk
W: www.changeworks.org.uk

Department stores and other stores including John Lewis, Mothercare World, the Musselburgh Pram Centre and SeeSaw stock a selection of nappies and accessories. Selected branches of Boots, Tesco, Sainsbury's and Waitrose also stock a limited range of cloth nappies and accessories too.

Earth Matters
67 High Street
North Berwick
EH39 5NZ
01620 895401
www.earthmatters.co.uk
Stocks a wide range of eco-friendly baby products and clothes.

Babykind
Sandra Vick (Midlothian)
07789 007 274
nappies@sandravick.co.uk
www.babykind.co.uk
BabyKind are committed to offering the most convenient cloth nappies at the lowest price. Free advice and no obligation demonstrations to find a nappy that suits you and your baby. Redeems the Real Nappy Project Voucher.

Dulce Cor
Jude Thomas (Edinburgh)
07751 673693
enquiry@dulcecor.com
www.dulcecor.com
Offers a wide range of real nappies and accessories. Free advice, demonstrations and group nappuccinos. Offers gift vouchers and online gift lists so family and friends can help with the cost of nappies. Second-hand sales service and special offers also available.

Lollipop
Fay Purves (Edinburgh and Midlothian)
0131 478 1831
07971 406 809
faypurves@hotmail.com
www.teamlollipop.co.uk
Offers free mother-to-mother advice on all types of real nappies. Stocks many different types of nappies and accessories. Redeems the Real Nappy Project Voucher.

SHOES

Many parents think that retailers put children's shoe departments in basements or on 1st floors simply to irritate them and to add to the overall hassle of the shoe buying trip. In fact, it is for safety - to ensure that junior does not take a trip straight out the door into the street when asked to take a few steps to see if the shoes fit! Many stores now operate a ticketing system: it's best to take a ticket before looking around. Try to avoid Saturdays and school holidays if possible, as these departments tend to be particularly busy.

Don't be shy where your child's feet are concerned. If you don't think a shoe fits, ask to have it checked by another more senior fitter. Several shops which sell nursery equipment also sell soft shoes for babies and toddlers. You could also try Aitken and Niven for school shoes and John Lewis who stock children's shoes.

The Children's Foot Health Register
PO Box 123
Banbury SO
OX15 6WB
01295 738726
www.shoe-shop.org.uk
The CFHR lists shops which are committed to the highest standard of shoe fitting for young, growing feet. To protect such standards members guarantee to provide comprehensive training for staff and offer children's shoes in whole and half sizes and in up to four width fittings. You can contact the Register directly if you need to.

trust us to find the right fit

With quality shoes from Startrite, Angulus, Ricosta, Ecco and Lelli Kelly (to name a few), we have styles to suit all shapes and sizes of feet - as well as every season and occasion.

Our staff are expertly trained to find the perfect fit, from cruisers right up to size 41 (UK size 7) - we can even find shoes for mum.

Our footwear is funky and stylish as well as being durable and beautifully crafted. Invest in the future of your child's feet, with us.

maddie & mark's

***** shoes *****

BLACKHALL: 1 craigcrook place edinburgh eh4 3ng ✳ tel: 0131 315 3322
BRUNTSFIELD: 205 bruntsfield place edinburgh eh10 4dh ✳ tel: 0131 447 9779
BUCKSTONE: 14 buckstone terrace edinburgh eh10 6pz ✳ tel: 0131 445 4425
www.maddieandmarks.co.uk
email: info@maddieandmarks.co.uk

Photography by: www.klaklakphotography.co.uk

Clarks Shoes Shops

A good selection of pre-walking shoes, available in sizes 3-4, and width fittings E-H. Also has an 'odd shoe service' available once your child's feet have been accurately measured, you select a suitable shoe (most styles are available). This information is then sent to head office and a pair is sent to the shop in approximately 3 weeks. These shoes cost 25% more than a standard pair. For entertainment there are various toys to keep the under 5s amused.

Kids shoes are found at: 79 Princes Street, Craigleith Retail Park, Cameron Toll Shopping Centre, Fort Kinnaird and Gyle Centre

Maddie and Mark's

205 Bruntsfield Place
EH10 4DG
0131 447 9779
or
1 Craigcrook Place
EH4 3NG
0131 315 3322
and their new shop at
14 Buckstone Terrace
EH10 6PZ
0131 445 4425
sales@maddieandmarks.co.uk
www.maddieandmarks.co.uk

Fantastic selection of shoes available. Offer a wide range of shoes for all shapes and sizes of feet. Staff are very helpful and extremely patient - all fully trained. Plenty of toys to keep little ones entertained while waiting. Plus, Maddie and Marks provide a cute framed picture when your child gets their first shoes.

Appointment service is available at busy times if required.

Russell and Bromley

106 Princes Street
EH2 3AA
0131 225 7444

Extensive range of children's shoes. Staff are fully trained in fitting. Stocks Clarks, Start-rite, Kickers and many more makes. There are both stairs and an escalator up to the first floor; pushchairs can be parked on the ground floor next to the cash desk. The colourful carousel horses always attract under 5s attention. Back to school periods are best avoided as it can be extremely busy.

Shoos

8 Teviot Place
0131 220 4626

Start-rite main stockist with a comprehensive range of shoes and boots in up to 6 width fittings, starting from baby size 2. Also stock slippers, wellies, sandals, canvas shoes and leather trainers in width fittings. Fully trained staff, with a member of the society of shoefitters usually present. All on ground level with toilet facilities. Start-rite odd shoe service is available.

Wee Masons

90 High Street
Haddington
EH41 3ET
01620 825600
www.mason-shoes.co.uk

Small, friendly shop with experienced staff and hardly any queues! Toys and videos to amuse other children while another is being fitted. Good range of Start-Rite, Elephanten and Doc Marten's. Ballet shoes, gym shoes and wellies also available.

W L Morrison

213 High Street
Linlithgow
EH49 7EN
01506 842923
wlmorrison@hotmail.com

SUPERMARKETS

No one would say that doing a big supermarket shop with young children is easy, but for many it's a necessity. Most stores have car parks and many offer 'Parent and Child' spaces, usually near to those for disabled drivers. These are usually situated near to the store entrance - unfortunately however, not everyone respects their role!

Check with Customer Services before you start your shop if you are likely to need a hand with your shopping to make sure help is available. Then ask at the check-out desk if you need assistance with transporting bags to your car.

Always follow the safety instructions for trolleys - these are often found on the bar or handles. Always use the restraints and report any faults to the store manager. As a general guide, baby cradle types are suitable for babies up to 9 kgs (20 lbs) and toddler types are suitable for up to around 3 yrs. Some stores have introduced trolleys which are suitable for use with your own car seat - helpful when transporting a sleeping baby!

If you're finding it difficult to get out to the supermarket, you can do your shopping online with many stores. There is usually a charge for this (in the region of £5) which may vary according to time and day of delivery. Alternatively, if you can make it to the supermarket, but just can't manage all your shopping home, many stores offer home delivery, also for a charge.

If your local supermarket doesn't already have a 'disabled child' trolley then you could request that they purchase one; this has been known to work in the past. These trolleys will usually be kept within the store as apparently they disappear easily!
The most common type of disabled child trolley is one that has a single large box seat, with some soft padding for comfort, fitted with a five point harness; your child will face towards you once seated and should be able to reach some produce if they want to help with the shopping. If your child needs extra seating support then this kind of trolley may not be suitable.

There are trolleys that have seats for disabled children who need extra seating support (car seat style) but these are a rare species!

Those supermarkets that do not have disabled child trolleys may offer a member of staff to accompany you as you shop. Avoid Saturdays for this service, which is less likely to be available at peak times.

With the number of stores available we have not listed all the details here in full. Please check websites for more information.

Asda
www.asda.co.uk
Branches at: 100 The Jewel, Chesser Avenue and Newhaven.

M&S Simply Food
www.marksandspencer.com
Branches at: Lower Straiton Retail Park, Morningside Road 212-216 and Ocean Terminal.

Morrisons
www.morrisons.co.uk
Branches at: Ferry Road, Gyle Shopping Centre, 30 New Swanston (Oxgangs), and 4 Piersfield Terrace.

Sainsbury's
www.sainsburys.co.uk
Branches at: 185 Craigleith Road, Meadowbank Retail Park, 39 Westfield Road (Murrayfield), Straiton Retail Park, and Cameron Toll Shopping Centre.

Scotmid Cooperative Society
www.scotmid.co.uk
Branches at: 56-60 Hamilton Place, 136 Lothian Road, 187 Whitehouse Road, 37-39 Raeburn Place, 1 Rannoch Terrace, 37-41 Boswall Parkway, 137 Granton Road, 49 North Fort Street, 207 Leith Walk, 76 Duke Street, 113 Ferry Road, 160-162 Restalrig Road South, 370 Leith Walk, 112-120 Easter Road, 126 Marchmont Road, 34 Warrender Park, 132 Bruntsfield Place, 236 Gorgie Road, 116 Polwarth Gardens, 283-289 Calder Road, 145 St. John's Road, 1 Drum Brae Avenue, 140-144 Saughtonhall Drive, 236-240 Crewe Road North, 6 Bath Street, 25 Northfield Farm Avenue, and 5-19 Leven Street.

Somerfield
www.somerfield.co.uk
Branches at: 114 Dalry Road, 100 Gorgie Park, 43 Pennywell Road, and 49 Shandwick Place.

Tesco
www.tesco.com
Branches at: 7 Broughton Road, 14 Colinton Mains Drive, 15 Drumbryden Road, and Corstorphine Road.

Waitrose
www.waitrose.com
Branches at: 38 Comely Bank Road and 145 Morningside Road.

TOILETRIES & COSMETICS

It's sensible to take time to pamper yourself, especially when pregnant. It keeps your own sense of identity and it's a great excuse for some 'you' time!

Where would you suggest?
Tell us -
ed@efuf.co.uk

Remember though, don't use essential oils while pregnant, and if you are thinking about massage oils etc, current advice is to avoid nut oil bases. This also goes for baby massage/pampering products – you'd be surprised how many have almond oil bases, and how many assistants don't recognise almonds as being nuts!

In general, the only 'safe' essential oils to use on young children are lavender and camomile; if in doubt, seek professional advice.

The Body Shop
www.thebodyshop.co.uk
Body Shop range includes all kinds of lotions, gels and pampering items for mums and mums-to-be, including cooling leg gel, massagers, and moisture-rich body creams, which intensify your skin's moisture content (might reduce stretch marks!) As well as their tried and tested cocoa butter stick, the African Spa range is rich in cocoa butter and has no essential oils in it.

Selection changes throughout the year – there are usually special offers around holiday times.

Branches at: Gyle Centre, Ocean Terminal, Princes Mall, 90a Princes St and Fort Kinnaird.

Crabtree and Evelyn
4 Hanover St
0131 226 2478
www.crabtree-evelyn.co.uk
Stepping into the shop, you're greeted by the sweet aroma of soaps, shampoos, bath gels and oils for mums in the tub. Creams, lotions, brushes and combs for after. The range includes traditional fragrances as well as more contemporary blends. There's also a range for dads. Small selection of soaps, bubble bath, lotions and creams for children, beautifully packaged and available in gift sets. Also sells room fragrance products.

Lush
44 Princes Street
EH2 2BY
0131 557 3177
www.lush.co.uk/edinburgh
Gorgeous handmade cosmetics with a conscience. Great for gifts and have delightful 'Ickle Baby' products too.

TOYS, GIFTS & CARDS

Make sure you always satisfy yourself as to the safety of toys, particularly if you are buying from an unorthodox source. When buying for playgroups, etc it is always worth asking whether discounts are available. Many shops expand their range and extend their hours in the run up to Christmas. Other shops that offer a selection of toys include Argos, Asda, BhS, The Disney Store, IKEA, John Lewis, Mothercare, and Sainsbury's (see previous entries).

Bohemia
33a Morningside Road
EH10 4DR
0131 447 7701
And
17 Roseneath Street
EH9 1JH
0131 478 9609
info@bohemiadesign.co.uk
A myriad of gorgeous things to choose from, including clothes, books, stationery, toys and gifts.

Build A Bear
119 Princes Street
0131 226 5780
and
Ocean Terminal
0131 554 8377
www.buildabear.co.uk
Lovely bears and soft toys that your little ones can help to make. Also offer Build-A-Party service where everyone gets to make a furry friend.

The Cinnamon Stick
36 Howe Street
Edinburgh
EH3 6TH
0131 225 4228
Great mix of cards and gifts for adults and children, including new born gifts and pocket money toys.

Clementine

141 Bruntsfield Place
Edinburgh
EH10 4EB
0131 477 2237
info@clementinehomeandgifts.com
www.clementinehomeandgifts.com
For a beautiful selection of gifts and goodies.

Cloudberry Gifts

193 Whitehouse Road
Barnton
EH4 6BU
0131 538 0168
www.cloudberrygifts.co.uk
A great new boutique-style gift shop offering lots of choice for everyone. Fabulous stuff for kids and a dedicated play area to keep them entertained while you shop.

Digger

35 West Nicolson Street
0131 668 1802
Small shop up 2 steps. An Aladdin's cave of handmade and traditional wooden toys. Wooden framed mirrors, bookends, clocks decorated with teddies, stocking fillers and party goods. Small selection of baby toys.

Early Learning Centre

www.elc.co.uk
For toys that are educational, safe and robust, with a focus on younger children. Also stock a range of outdoor toys including climbing frames, slides, swings, sandpits and trampolines. The Fort Kinnaird store is the largest, and therefore carries an extended range. The Fort Kinnaird location has a huge play area which allows children to 'try before you buy'.
Branches at: Gyle Shopping Centre, 61 St. James' Centre, and Fort Kinnaird.

Edinburgh Doll and Teddy Bear Hospital

Geraldine's of Edinburgh
42 Glendinning Road
Kirkliston
EH29 9HE
0131 333 1833
www.dollsandteddies.com
www.dollshospital.com
Dolls and soft toys can undergo repair for injuries caused by the ravages of time or over-exuberant play at this dolls hospital which now operates from a residential location. Items in need of rescue or surgery can be posted. The www.dollsandteddies.com website sells unique handmade dolls, teddy bears, as well as accessories and clothing.

Eero & Riley

7 Easter Road
EH7 5PH
0131 661 0533
info@eeroandriley.com
www.eeroandriley.com
Lots of funky toys and baby clothes. Great place for gifts. Winner of the best newcomer in Scotland at the 'Greats' Gift Retail Awards 2010.

Everyone's Designs

213 Bruntsfield Place
Edinburgh
EH10 4DH
0131 447 1504
You'll be spoilt for choice with the huge range of greetings cards on offer. Also stocks a range of gifts and stationery, including christening keepsakes.

Flux

55 Bernard Street
Leith
EH6 6SL
0131 554 4075
www.get2flux.co.uk
Lots of lovely, quirky, and beautiful gifts.

Halibut & Herring
108 Bruntsfield Place
Edinburgh
EH10 4ES
0131 229 2669
www.halibutandherring.co.uk
Trendy gift shop

Harburn Hobbies Ltd
67 Elm Row
Leith Walk
0131 556 3233
sales@harburnhobbies.com
www.harburnhobbies.com
Specialises in model railways, Scalextric and stocks the entire Hornby Thomas the Tank Engine range. Also stocks the Take-a-long Thomas die-cast toys by Racing Champions. Also stocks Britain's farm animals and tractors, as well as a range of the French company Papo's forts, knights and fantasy figures. Harburns have a large stock of colourful wooden dolls' houses and furniture, including the Swedish Lundby dolls house range. As well as this, they have a vast array of die-cast cars, buses and lorries.

Helios Fountain
7 The Grassmarket
EH1 2HY
0131 229 7884
info@helios-fountain.co.uk
www.helios-fountain.co.uk
This store stocks a good variety of arts and crafts from jewellery-making supplies to feathers and buttons. There is also a range of traditional wooden toys and cuddly (and unusual) soft toys, as well as a wide range of picture and story books.

Instore/Poundstretcher
Budget/value stores stocking a selection of inexpensive toys, including some educational toys, small bikes and stationery.
Branches at: 42 Shandwick Place, 10 West Harbour Road, New Kirkgate Centre, 100/106 South Bridge, Fort Kinnaird, 245-249 Gorgie Road, Meadowbank Shopping Park and West Side Plaza (Westerhailes).

Oh Baby!
120 Logie Street
Dundee
DD2 2PY
01382 666111
Great place for that extra special gift.

One World Shop Edinburgh
St John's Church
Princes Street
EH2 4BJ
0131 229 4541
info@oneworldshop.co.uk
Sells a wide range of toys, clothing, books and lots more. This is a leading fair trade retail company with lots of great gift ideas.

The Owl and the Pussycat
166 Bruntsfield Place
0131 228 4441
gilliecom@aol.com
Wide selection of teddies and other soft toys, stylish cards and gifts. Local artist Alison has a range of teddy drawings and prints.

Pinocchio's
96 West Bow
Victoria Street
0131 225 6547
www.pinocchiotoys.co.uk
This shop specialises in traditional, educational (and fun!!) large and small wooden toys from across Europe such as jumping jacks, rolling toys, and rocking horses. They also carry a wide range of games, soft toys, puppets, marionettes, toy theatres, kites, music boxes, jack-in-the-boxes, and, of course, Pinocchio's!

The Smart Stork
165b Bruntsfield Place
Edinburgh
EH10 4DG
0131 629 9424
www.thesmartstork.co.uk
Luxury gifts, christening wear, traditional toys, and clothing. Also a gift list service.

Studio One
10-14 Stafford Street
0131 226 5812
Down steps to basement shop with selection of traditional and wooden toys, including those by French manufacturer Djeco. Also stocks arts and crafts, books, etc. Good selection of pocket-money toys, stocking fillers, novelties, Christmas decorations etc.

Toys Galore
193 Morningside Road
EH10 4QP
0131 447 1006
and their new shop at
13 Comely Bank Road
Stockbridge
Good choice of toys for all ages with some to try out while you browse. Most major brands stocked: for example Galt, Crayola, Lego, Playmobil. Many others from pocket-money range upwards.

Toys'R'Us
Kinnaird Park
Newcraighall Road
EH15 3RD
0131 657 4121
Huge range of pre-school toys, soft toys, dolls, games, Lego, Playmobil, outdoor toys and so on. A store directory points to the different areas and there is a pick-up point for bulky items and electrical toys. Climbing frames, chutes, swings, sandpits and Wendy houses available with samples on display.
There is no play area and as such a vast array of toys may prove tempting, parents may find it easier to shop without their offspring.
Huge store which sells more than just toys. The Babies'R'Us area stocks baby food, toiletries, and nappies in bulk quantities, as well as nursery equipment. Reward card scheme.

Wonderland
97-101 Lothian Road
0131 229 6428
sales@wonderlandmodels.com
www.wonderlandmodels.com
Specialises in radio controlled cars, boats, planes and helicopters, as well as in model-making kits and railway sets. Stocks Scalextric. Good range of die-cast cars, buses and trucks. Doll's houses kits or ready assembled, plus accessories. Will order in specific models for customers. Easy access for all pushchairs. Also stock fantasy/graphic novel figures, so good for parents/carers too!

 Don't forget to let businesses know you saw them in the EFUF book!

SHOPPING FROM HOME

Shopping from home can be much easier than a shopping trip with young children. Most big-name companies have an internet site these days, but speciality shops are also reaching a far wider audience by being available on the world wide web. Most sites these days have secure online ordering – and remember it's still more secure to enter credit card details on the web than it is to hand your credit card over to a waiter in a restaurant who takes it out of your sight! Some sites allow you to order a catalogue if you prefer to browse through that and then order. This is a quick, easy and 24-hour way to shop, and now you can also get hold of things that you maybe couldn't get locally.

The Internet is fast becoming the way of researching and buying baby and toddler clothes and equipment. The following are just a few of note, but you can find many, many more if you look at one of the Internet search engines, or one of the internet children's directories, such as www.ukchildrensdirectory.com. If you are interested in green or ethically sound products, try www.thegreenshoppingguide.co.uk or www.ethicalsuperstore.com.
This section also includes mail order contact details.

BABY EQUIPMENT

Amazon
www.amazon.co.uk
Yes, Amazon has a baby store – with its own separate tab at the top. Fantastic resource for buying absolutely anything for delivery to your door.

Babies'R'Us
www.babiesrus.co.uk
Babies' equipment section of Toys'R'Us. Babies'R'Us has its own catalogue available in store, and you can order online. Very useful if Toys'R'Us are out of stock in your local store: it can be faster to order online than ask the store to reserve something for you next time it gets into stock.

BickiePegs
01224 790626
www.bickiepegs.co.uk
A long-established Scottish firm (trading since 1925). Teething biscuits for babies available from Boots and all leading chemists. Small mail order brochure in pack. 'Doidy' children's training cup and finger toothbrushes too.

Boohoo Baby
0845 224 1480
www.boohoobaby.co.uk
Edinburgh based company offering everything from prams, to pushchairs, nappies, high chairs and clothes.

Glasgow Pram Centre
www.pramcentreonline.co.uk
Great website, good range and discounted prices.

The Great Little Trading Company
124 Walcot St
Bath
BA1 5BG
0990 673008
www.gltc.co.uk
Practical products for parents and children. Wide range of helpful and interesting products. Also sells children's clothes. No quibble returns policy.

Groovystyle
www.groovystyle.co.uk
All types of baby equipment, with a lot of stylish items included.

Little Green Earthlets Ltd
Units 1-3 Stream Farm
Chiddingly
East Sussex
BN8 6HG
08450 724 462
sales@littlegreenearthlets.co.uk
www.earthlets.co.uk
Amazingly wide range of environmentally friendly and ethically sound baby equipment, products, nappies and clothing.

Kiddicare
www.kiddicare.com
Online baby superstore offering a wide range of products and accessories.

Safetots
01438 728 888
info@safetots.co.uk
www.safetots.co.uk
For a range of safety equipment.

Slingjax
08700 424 028
info@slingjax.co.uk
www.slingjax.co.uk
For sling sales and hire.

Totseat
0131 226 6064
happy@totseat.com
www.totseat.com
The totseat is a great 'highchair' for little ones from 8-30mths. Made of fabric and fits into a travel pouch. Couldn't be handier.

BABY EQUIPMENT HIRE

Busy Bee Babies
0131 552 9961
07926 536389
info@busybeebabies.co.uk
www.busybeebabies.co.uk
Provide baby and toddler equipment for hire in Edinburgh.

Tom Thumb Baby Equipment Hire
0131 667 9292
07910 929650
tomthumbhire@yahoo.co.uk
www.tomthumbbabyequipmenthire.co.uk
One-stop shop for the hire of essential items for babies and pre-school children.

CARDS & CRAFTS

Duff Doodles
www.duffdoodles.com
Supply greetings cards and illustrations. Commissions taken for any occasion.

Joyful Junie Stationery Co.
16 Craig-Na-Gower Ave
Aviemore
PH22 1RW
Contact: June Armstrong
01479 811527
Offers a unique range of hand-made, personalised Birth Announcement & Thank You cards, Christening and Party invitations. The range features delightful ink and wash illustrations. Speedy service guaranteed. Call for mail order catalogue.

Tryst Crafts
Contact: Lesley Protheroe
0131 445 5789
Handmade cards and gifts for any occasion. Can be personalised.

Phoenix Trading Greeting Cards & Giftwrap
This company is the UK's leading direct card selling business. Their aim is to sell cards and giftwrap at sane prices, and so they are much cheaper than most high-street stores. Very wide range of greetings cards, invitations, thank you notes and giftwrap at up to 50% less than shop prices. Call for a free brochure or order online (delivery is free).
Contact: Jane Ziemons
07584 135766
janeziemons@hotmail.com
www.phoenix-trading.co.uk/web/janeziemons/Store.php
or
Contact: Julia Grindley
0131 449 6331
www.phoenix-trading.co.uk/web/juliagrindley
Julia is also available for coffee mornings, parties, fairs and fundraising events.

CHILDREN'S BOOKS

Barefoot Books
0800 328 2640
www.barefootbooks.com
Books about our planet, cultures and ourselves. Creative and imaginative stories your little ones will enjoy.

Books For Children
4 Furzeground Way
Stockley Park
Uxbridge
UB11 1DP
08701 650299
www.booksforchildren.co.uk
Fifteen catalogues per year. Editor's recommended selection for each of five specific age groups sent automatically. Covers books from 0-12yrs.

Custom Books Ltd
01249 812375
www.custombooks.co.uk
Personalised children's books where your child becomes the star of the story. Books can also contain friends' names, home town, pet names, etc. Available in different languages.

Green Metropolis
customersupport@greenmetropolis.com
www.greenmetropolis.com
A great idea – recycling books in a sustainable way. Find your books a new home and get some fresh stories for your own. You help the environment and money from every book sold goes to the Woodland Trust.

The Red House Children's Books
0870 1919980
www.redhouse.co.uk
Mail order and online children's book shop. Hardback and paperback books, audiotapes, CD-Roms, videos, games and activities plus character merchandise.

CLOTHING ONLINE

Many of the shops already listed have an online shop as well as any local outlets. In this section we list a few other suggestions covering children's clothes, dressing up outfits, and maternity wear.

Baby Care by Dollycare
2 Winchester Ave
Blaby Bypass
Blaby
LE8 4G2
0116 278 3336
Clothes, nappies and soothers made especially for small and premature babies from 1+lbs (500g).

Babipur
01766 515240
shop@babipur.co.uk
www.babipur.co.uk
The name is Welsh for 'Pure Baby'. Babipur offers ethical and environmentally friendly clothing and baby products.

Babyjr
01732 455947
www.babyjr.co.uk

Manufacture unique front opening wrap vests for babies designed for easy changing – no need to pull over the head so may suit a child on oxygen therapy. Call or visit website for more information.

Bishopston Trading Company
193 Gloucester Road
Bishopton
Bristol
BS7 8BG
0117 924 5598
www.bishopstontrading.co.uk
Clothes for adults and children from birth-14yrs. Made from natural fabrics, mostly organic cotton. The company is a workers cooperative set up to create employment in a South Indian village. Catalogue and online ordering available. They also sell their stock through One World in St John's Church on Princes Street/Lothian Road.

Blooming Marvellous
020 8391 0022
Orderline: 0870 751 8944
www.bloomingmarvellous.co.uk
Colourful children's clothes 0-3yrs. Mix'n'Match range. Range of clothing for mothers-to-be. Casual and formal wear, plus hosiery, lingerie, sleepwear, swimwear and accessories such as breast pads.

Blue Peach
0131 467 4911
07834 418374
info@bluepeach.eu
www.bluepeach.etsy.com
Quality children's wear hand made in Scotland.

Boden
020 8453 1535
www.boden.co.uk
Mini Boden is logo-free, very good quality and stylish clothes for children up to 12yrs, made mostly of natural fabrics.

Bright Sparks
Upper Murthat Cottage
Nr Beattock
Dumfriesshire
DG10 9PJ
01683 300648
Sheila.brightsparks@tiscali.co.uk
www.brightsparksknitwear.co.uk
For handknitted children's wear.

Cambridge Baby
01223 572228
helenandnick@cambridgebaby.co.uk
www.cambridgebaby.co.uk
Natural clothing, fairly traded and eco-friendly.

Clever Togs
01578 750673
info@clevertogs.com
www.clevertogs.com
Fun and educational, hand-embroidered babies' and children's appliquéd t-shirts. Eco-friendly and fair-trade!

Clothkits
01243 600301
ww.clothkits.co.uk
Funky outfits and accessories supplied in kits for you to make. Easy to follow instructions.

Cotton Moon
020 8305 0012
www.cottonmoon.co.uk
100% cotton clothing and accessories for boys and girls from 6mths. Free returns.

CozyBear Kids
0843 289 4910
info@cozybear.co.uk
www.cozybear.co.uk
Colourful baby, toddler and children's fleece clothing and gifts.

CuteToots
07794 886672
cutetoots@hotmail.co.uk
www.cutetoots.co.uk
Brilliant bandana bibs handmade here in Edinburgh. Not only do they look great, they're eco-friendly too.

Fabric of the Universe
0131 258 9221
info@fabricoftheuniverse.co.uk
www.fabricoftheuniverse.co.uk
Based in Edinburgh selling gorgeous organic ethically-made baby wear.

Formes
08689 2288
e-shopping@formes-uk.com
www.formes.com
Browse and buy the clothing available in the boutiques without leaving home. Offers urban wear, leisurewear and nightwear.

Frugi
01326 221 930
info@welovefrugi.com
www.welovefrugi.com
Lovely organic clothing for children and babies.

Greenfibres
01803 868001
www.greenfibres.com
Organic cotton and wool clothes for babies and children, washable nappies, organic cotton toys.

Joules
0845 606 6871
www.joulesclothing.com
Style, colour and quality for little ones.

Kitschy Coo
general@kitschycoo.co.uk
www.kitschycoo.co.uk
Edinburgh based clothing for children. Unique and funky clothes – every item is a one-off.

La Redoute
0500 777 777
www.redoute.co.uk
Fashionable children's clothes at reasonable prices, along with teenage and adult ranges. Personal account option. Orders can be taken on website – there are often 'free p&p' options if orders are placed online. Free returns.

Little Green Radicals
0845 130 1525
info@littlegreenradicals.co.uk
www.littlegreenradicals.co.uk
Childrenswear that is organic and fair-trade. Ranges for babies and children.

The Natural Collection
01225 442288
www.naturalcollection.com
Organic cotton clothing, bedding and washable nappies as well as many other eco and/or ethical-friendly products.

NCT (Maternity Sales) Ltd
0870 112 1120
www.nctsales.co.uk
Baby clothes, accessories, gifts, books, leaflets and videos. Also stocks maternity clothing, sleepwear and a good range of maternity/breastfeeding bras in a wide range of sizes.

Nordic Kids
020 8736 0580
cs@nordickids.co.uk
www.nordickids.co.uk
Supply funky baby clothes and cool childrens' clothing.

Rainbow Babies
020 7099 5705
info@rainbowbabies.co.uk
www.rainbowbabies.co.uk
Trendy, simple, colourful and affordable clothing.

Stuck for Words
0131 332 1998
www.stuckforwords.co.uk
Hand-painted children's clothes, created in Scotland. A mail order company offering a range of 100% cotton clothes for children from birth to 10 yrs. Current products include t-shirts, sleepsuits and baby vests, all of which can be decorated with one of their striking and child-orientated designs. All items are also available tie-dyed in a range of colours.

Tatty Bumpkin
01732 812212
sales@tattybumpkinshop.com
www.tattybumpkinshop.com
Specialists in organic and bamboo kids clothing.

VertBaudet
0844 842 0000
www.vertbaudet.co.uk
Sizable catalogue selling babies', children's and maternity clothes and nursery goods. Also have a range of bedding and children's bedroom accessories. Personal account facility. Free returns. Also stock small range of low birth weight baby clothing.

Where would you suggest?
Tell us -
ed@efuf.co.uk

DRESSING UP CLOTHES

Hopscotch Dressing Up Clothes
0208 674 9853
www.hopscotchmailorder.co.uk
Dressing up outfits 18mths-9yrs. Cloaks, clowns, princesses, animals, astronauts, etc.

The Magic Wardrobe
Dressing up Clothes for Kids
0131 667 4813
cherryledlie@blueyonder.co.uk
www.magicwardrobe.ik.com
The Magic Wardrobe is a local recycling project which turns used and unwanted fabrics into dressing up clothes for children. All profits go to the NCT in Edinburgh. Costumes can be bought from the Magic Wardrobe stall at various School Fairs, or direct any time. Check the website for details of upcoming stalls, or phone to discuss a commission or private viewing. Ideal Christmas and birthday presents for imaginative kids. Donations of fabric, trimmings, old dress patterns, etc always welcome!

FOOD & DRINK TO YOUR DOOR

Babylicious
01494 432 902
www.babylicious.co.uk
Wholesome frozen babyfood.

The Chocolate Tree
07790 214 280
freddymatthis@gmx.de
www.the-chocolate-tree.co.uk
Hand crafted organic chocolate. Yum. Need we say more?

East Coast Organic Boxes (ECOBox)
24 Boggs Holdings
Pencaitland
EH34 5BD
01875 340227
07971 209081
ecobox@eastcoastorganics.freeserve.co.uk
www.eastcoastorganics.co.uk
Organic vegetable boxes as well as organic fruit, eggs and bread. Free delivery service available – phone or check website for details. Collection points throughout Edinburgh or collect direct from farm.

Ian Miller's Organic Meats
Jamesfield Farm
FREEPOST
EH3582
Newburgh
Fife
KY14 6BR
01738 850498
www.jamesfieldfarm.co.uk
Organic meat, poultry, bacon, fish, haggis, venison, speciality sausages and stuffing. This famous farm shop and restaurant near Perth now has its own online store.

Mama Tea
info@mamatea.com
www.mamtea.com
From the morning mama to combat morning sickness, via the ready mama for labour and birth, to the new mama for breastfeeding – mama teas have something for everyone. Based in Edinburgh.

Pillars of Hercules Organic Farm
By Falkland
Fife
01337 857749
www.pillars.co.uk
Organic vegetable boxes as well as organic fruit and eggs. Free catalogue available. Delivery to Edinburgh and Fife areas.

So Baby
01829 772555
yourthoughts@so-baby.co.uk
www.so-baby.co.uk
Menu of meals suitable for every stage of weaning and feeding from ages 6mths-2yrs.

The Whole Shebag
South Cobbinshaw
West Calder
West Lothian
EH55 8LQ
01501 785436
bags@thewholeshebag.com
www.thewholeshebagcom
Delivers fresh and tasty organic fruit and vegetables throughout the central belt every week. Great selection and bag contents can be adapted to suit your tastes. Each bag contains a newsletter with handy recipe suggestions.

HOLIDAYS

Access Travel
01942 888844
www.access-travel.co.uk

Provides holidays for disabled people. They can arrange wheelchair accessible properties, special aids, nursing and care services, and adapted vehicles.

Baby-friendly Boltholes
08454 890140
www.babyfriendlyboltholes.co.uk
Great recommendations for baby-friendly holiday accommodation to take the stress out of travelling with babies and toddlers.

The Calvert Trust
01434 250232
www.calvert-trust.org.uk

Specialises in outdoor activity holidays for people with disabilities. There are sites at Kielder, Keswick and Exmoor. They also have a bursary fund for financing holidays to Kielder.

Holiday Care
0845 124 9971
www.holidaycare.org.uk

Holiday Care is the UK's central source of travel and holiday information for disabled people, their families, friends and carers. They have information on hundreds of accessible hotels and visitor attractions in the UK and a range of information sheets on overseas destinations.

Special Families Homeswap Register
01752 347577
www.mywebpage.net/special-families

Set up for physically disabled people of all ages to enable them to swap homes in a two-way or one-way swap for holidays or breaks at any time of the year.

Trefoil House
0131 339 3148
www.trefoil.org.uk

Trefoil House is a specially adapted mansion in Edinburgh that provides holidays for adults and children with all levels of disability.

Visit our website for updates:
www.efuf.co.uk

MOBILITY

The City of Edinburgh Council produce a booklet with details of all the equipment you can get free without the need for an occupational therapy assessment (although your child should also be assessed by an occupational therapist if they need to be). All you have to do is fill in the form included in the book, send it to the council and they will send or deliver the equipment to you. You can get a free copy of the booklet, called "Equipment for use at home: simple solutions that you can choose" by calling 0131 313 2435.

The following are providers of equipment and/or advice that you may also find useful. Remember that even if you're buying a toy or a piece of equipment privately it's worth speaking to your child's physiotherapist or occupational therapist, who should be able to offer advice on what would be suitable.

If your child may need a wheelchair they should be referred to ETC – Enabling Technology for Children, for assessment. Speak to your child's physiotherapist for more information. ETC are based in the RES department at the Eastern General Hospital, Seafield Street, Edinburgh, EH6 7LN. You can contact them on 0131 536 4681.

The Association of Wheelchair Children
0870 121 0050
headoffice@wheelchairchildren.org.uk
www.wheelchairchildren.org.uk
Specialist national charity providing expert mobility training and advice to wheelchair-using children and their families across the UK and Ireland. They teach children useful, practical skills, such as the management of kerbs, slopes and steps enabling them to move safely and confidently about their homes and neighbourhood. All courses are free of charge and are in a variety of locations throughout the UK (including Scotland).

Cyclone
0800 180 4850
www.cyclonemobility.com
Manufacture an attractive sports style child's wheelchair.

DCS Joncare
01505 702 403
www.dcsjoncare.freeserve.co.uk
A company dedicated to mobility for disabled children offering a range of equipment including powered and self-propelled wheelchairs, standing and seating systems, and trikes.

Disabledaccessories.com
01480 494 417
0800 389 5534 (24 hr Orderline)
www.disabledaccessories.com
A range of aids and equipment, including paediatric aids and equipment.

The Disabled Living Foundation
0845 130 9177
www.dlf.org.uk
The website contains a huge amount of information and resources on equipment for people with disabilities. There are also fact sheets available for download – including fact sheets on choosing equipment for children.

G & S Smirthwaite
01626 835552
www.smirthwaite.co.uk
For furniture and equipment for special needs and conductive education. Wide range of products.

Anything out of date?
Let us know -
info@efuf.co.uk

Hug it
www.hug-it.co.uk
Manufacture seat harnesses for 12-28mths to be used on pushchairs, highchairs and wheelchairs to ensure better tightening of straps. It can also be used on adult seat belts to improve positioning. It's designed to stop young children 'escaping' their shoulder straps and may be especially useful for children with special needs as it offers extra support for the upper body. See website for more details. Offer 10% discount to NCT, NCMA and TAMBA members.

JCM Seating Solutions Ltd
01775 766664
www.jcmseating.co.uk
Paediatric equipment including seating systems, sleep systems and car seats. They have friendly, trustworthy reps who travel to Edinburgh on a regular basis.

Lomax
01382 503000
www.lomaxmobility.com
Independent wheelchair manufacturer based in Dundee. They manufacture wheelchairs for children and adults (their Kidactive chairs come in a variety of colours – including pink!)

Nottingham Rehab Supplies
0845 120 4522
www.nrs-uk.co.uk
Daily living aids for adults and children. Wide range of products.

Sunrise Medical
01384 44 66 88
www.sunrisemedical.co.uk
Manufacturers of wheelchairs for adults and children. Child friendly designs available.

The Whistling Tortoise
42A Hamilton Place
EH3 5AX
0131 225 6365
www.whistlingtortoise.com
A disability equipment shop in Edinburgh.

Whizz Kidz
020 7233 6600
kidzservices@whizz-kidz.org.uk
www.whizz-kidz.org.uk
Provide customised wheelchairs, tricycles and other specialised mobility equipment, wheelchair training, information and advice to change the lives of disabled children across the UK. They also are working to raise awareness of the need of disabled children so that they get the support they deserve from the general public and from the Government. Their website has factsheets for parents and carers on a wide range of subjects, including choosing mobility equipment for children The waiting list can be very long.
Remember SNIP's 'funder-finder' if you wish to apply for funds to privately purchase a piece of mobility equipment for your child!

NAPPY SUPPLIERS

Listed below is a selection of mail order nappy suppliers. A more extensive list can be found on the Changeworks website at:
www.changeworks.org.uk

Companies including Greenfibres, Little Green Earthlets and The Natural Collection also sell nappies by mail order.

Tots Bots Ltd
Carntyne Industrial Estate
30 Camelon Street
Glasgow
G32 6AF
0141 778 7486
email@totsbots.com
www.totsbots.com
Shaped towelling nappies made in Scotland. Winner of numerous awards.

The Nappy Lady
15 The Stanley Centre
Kelvin Way
Crawley
RH10 9SE
0845 652 6532
info@thenappylady.co.uk
www.thenappylady.co.uk

Plush Pants
01865 408040
Nappies and related natural products.

TreeHugger Mums
91A High Street
Newport
TF10 7AY
01952 811 413
www.treehuggermums.co.uk

Twinkle Twinkle
Unit 5 Headley Park
9 Headley Road East
Woodley
Reading
RG5 4SQ
0118 969 5550
miranda@twinkleontheweb.co.uk
www.twinkleontheweb.co.uk
Comprehensive selection of washable nappies, potty training, bedwetting aids, natural toiletries, slings. Free advice, downloadable guide on using nappies.

SHOES ONLINE

If your child has very narrow or broad feet, or he/she has uneven sizes, you may need to have shoes made. This is not as expensive as it sounds, although it does cost slightly more than high street prices. It is also worth investigating specialist companies if you want a particular style but can't get it in the shops.

Charles MacWatt Handmade Boots and Shoes
7 Christmas Steps
Bristol
BS1 5BS
0117 921 4247
Made to measure and to order shoes, boots and sandals for children and adults.

Daisy Roots
01604 880 066
sales@daisy-roots.com
www.daisy-roots.com
Baby booties and toddler shoes for 0-4yrs.

Soled Out
Unit 14, Forge Lane
Moorlands Industrial Estate
Saltash
Cornwall
PL12 6LX
01752 841080
Made to measure shoes and boots for children and adults in bright coloured leather with crepe soles. Shoes made to fit each foot.

TOILETRIES & COSMETICS ONLINE

Arbonne Baby Care
juliekennedy@myarbonne.co.uk
www.arbonnesuccess.myarbonne.co.uk
Products for baby's skin.

Greenbaby
www.greenbaby.co.uk
Lovely organic skincare for wee ones.

Lavera
01557 870 567
info@lavera.co.uk
www.lavera.co.uk
Organic natural cosmetics, skin care and bodycare products for the whole family.

Milk & Honey Organics
www.milkhoney.co.uk
Luxurious natural and organic gifts for prenatal, postnatal and new baby gifts. Beautifully wrapped and delivered to your door.

Pharmacy2U
www.pharmacy2u.co.uk
Offers a complete range of high street pharmacy products and services online, including an 'ask our pharmacists' service.

TOYS & GIFTS ONLINE

There are plenty of websites available for children's toys. Below are some names of note. For a fuller list, go to a search engine such as Google.

Bright Minds
0870 44 22 124
www.brightminds.co.uk
Offer a range of educational toys, from 2+ yrs. For pre-school children, the range includes puzzles, games and interactive toys. Products for older children are divided into subject categories, such as maths, music, nature studies, chemistry etc.

The Flower Stork
www.theflowerstork.com
Beautiful gifts for new or expectant parents. Baby wear bouquets look pretty and contain essential items of baby wear.

Good Gifts Catalogue
020 7794 8000
www.goodgifts.org
Charitable gifts for all ages. From stocking fillers, to party bags and something for those with more to spend – gifts from the heart.

The Green Gift Company Ltd
07808 400 773
contact@greengiftcompany.com
www.greengiftcompany.com
Gifts for all the family. An Edinburgh based business that sources ethical products. Also offer Green Gift Parties for mums wanting to host a social event at home, or for playgroups looking to fundraise.

Hawkin's Bazaar
0870 444 6460
www.hawkin.com
Intriguing catalogue/online shop packed with amusing and unusual gifts, toys, novelties and gadgets. Very reasonably priced. Ideal for stocking fillers or difficult to buy for people.

Holz Toys
www.holz-toys.co.uk
Beautiful wooden toys from the website or by catalogue.

Insect Lore
www.insectlore-europe.co.uk
Great for presents.

Letterbox
0870 600 7878
www.letterbox.co.uk
Collection of games, gifts, wooden farms, arks, dolls' houses, dressing up clothes etc. Extensive range of personalised gifts, ranging from name boards, jack-in-the-boxes, to chairs and sleeping bags. Also bedroom accessories. Loads of stocking filler/ party bag ideas, many with age recommendations.

Mulberry Bush
www.mulberrybush.co.uk
Huge selection of traditional wooden toys and games.

Nic Nac Noo
0131 664 1724
www.nicnacnoo.com
Natural, wooden and organic toys. Nic Nac Noo will come to you, so arrange to get together with friends, others at an antenatal meet-up, or at a toddler group.

Ollie & Forbes
0131 208 0405
07974 591528
sales@ollieandforbes.com
www.ollieandforbes.com
Edinburgh based company offering a beautiful selection of toys. Perfect for giving as a present as they come packaged in a lovely gift bag.

Playsongs Publications
020 8778 0708
www.playsongs.co.uk
Music for the very young. CDs of all the best songs and nursery rhymes, sung and played by professionals. Action songs, lullabies, lively time and sleepy time songs.

Spirit of Nature
www.spiritofnature.co.uk
Reasonably priced wooden toys and organic baby clothes.

Super Tramp Trampolines
01884 841305
www.supertramp.co.uk
Outdoor garden trampolines and wooden garden play equipment.

Tridias Creative Toys
0870 2402104
www.tridias.co.uk
Inventive toy and game ideas for children. Catalogue available with over 400 toys and games, or view and order online.

MISCELLANEOUS

Able Labels
08443 712 423
www.able-labels.co.uk
Personalised labels, correspondence cards, nametapes, photo gifts, and much more.

Cash's Name Tapes
J&J Cash Ltd
Torrington Ave
Coventry
01203 466466
www.jjcash.co.uk
Woven name tapes available online. Also widely available from shops such as John Lewis, Clarks Shoes, Mothercare and Aitken and Niven department stores.

Easy2name
www.easy2name.com
Wide range of labels suitable for clothes and possessions, including dishwasher-proof and iron on. Also items which can be personalised with your child's name, including pencils, crayons and pens.

Identity Direct
08454 505 098
customerservice@identitydirect.co.uk
www.identitydirect.co.uk
Large range of personalised children's products. Gifts and adventure book series where children can feature in their own story.

Minilabel
www.minilabels.co.uk
All types of labels suitable for clothing, back packs, and dishwasher-proof labels for packed lunch equipment. Iron-on labels that actually stay on (the writer can confirm this!).

Personal Presents
01753 783371
info@personalpresents.co.uk
www.personalpresents.co.uk
Lots of personalised gift ideas for any special occasion, births, christenings, Christmas, birthdays and more.

Splash About
info@splashabout.com
www.splashabout.com
Children's safety swimwear. Products for keeping little ones warm and/or afloat in water. Also produce sun protection suits look after children's delicate skin in the sun.

Stardust Ceilings
07941 011263
stardustceilings@blueyonder.co.uk
www.startdustceilings.com
Magical glow-in-the-dark stardust hand painted ceilings for your home.

Stuck On You
08454 560 014
Sales.uk@stuckonyou.biz
www.stuckonyou.biz
Fun personalised gifts, name labels, wrist bands and lots more.

Thingimijigs
0844 884 5262
www.thingimijigs.co.uk
All kinds of thingimijigs.

Ed's Top Of The Shops.....

Books - The Children's Bookshop

Clothes – Edinburgh has lots to offer try Nippers or Kitschy Coo

Corstorphine Pram Centre – very friendly and helpful staff who'll help you find the product that's right for you

Edinburgh's local High Streets - Stockbridge, Morningside and Bruntsfield.....spoilt for choice

Gifts – Eero & Riley or Oh Baby! for great gifts

IKEA – lots to buy and a great café for kids

John Lewis – everything under one roof and still the best nappy changing facilities in the city

Maternity Wear – Pretty Pregnant and Vanilla Bloom for stylish outfits

Shoes – Maddie and Mark's and Wee Masons

Shopping Centres – The Gyle and Ocean Terminal have plenty of child friendly shops and the facilities to match

Don't forget NCT sales for great bargains too!

What would you recommend?
Tell Ed
email ed@efuf.co.uk

PARTIES

Parties whether at home, in a local church hall or at an all-inclusive venue do need some forward planning. If you need to book a venue most places recommend doing this at least 8 weeks in advance. Many church halls, public halls, schools, community centres and sports clubs will hire out their premises for an afternoon. Remember weekends tend to be busier.

Soft play centres also offer birthday packages, often with use of a party area: the actual soft play structures are usually open to everyone. However, some do offer times when you can book the soft play for your party's exclusive use for an extra cost. Younger children may be quite frightened if it is too crowded, especially in the more energetic venues.

We have listed some suggestions for party venues, and also offered some ideas regarding party entertainers, products and services that might come in handy, whether you decide to host the party at home or in a venue. Many of the venues listed in the 'Places To Go' section of this book offer party packages, look out for the present symbol.

PARTY VENUES

Biggar Puppet Theatre
Puppet Tree House
Broughton Road
Biggar
Lanarkshire
Ml12 6HA
01899 220631
admin@purvespuppets.com
www.purvespuppets.com
Special birthday party option is offered by this well-established company. Package including invitations, balloons, buffet, performance and finger puppets. Just bring the cake. Min. 10 people but that can include the adults.

Broxburn Swimming Pool
01506 775680
Soft play parties are hosted in the 'Pirates Cove' soft play area. Max 20 children. Party price includes exclusive use; just bring your own birthday tea.

The Children's Party Cruise
The Bridge Inn
Ratho
0131 333 1320
info@bridgeinn.com
www.bridgeinn.com
A children's party on board a cruising canal boat restaurant. A CD disco is provided just take your own CDs (a disco can be organised for extra cost). A video player is available at no extra cost and there is plenty of space to play. Bridge Inn will supply the food. Min 20 people, max 36.

Cramond Kirk Hall
0131 312 6911
07979 795331
Variety of room sizes available for parties and events.

Linlithgow Leisure Centre
McGinley Way
01506 775440
A soft play party followed by use of the dance studio area for your own catering. Max 20 children.

Livingston Leisure Centre (XCITE)
Livingston Leisure Pool
01506 777870
'Space Bugs' soft play party, for children up to 7yrs, includes two hours of fun on slides, chutes, ball pool and a birthday tea; just bring the cake, in a designated eating area. Invitations, party bags and thank you cards (voucher for free admission) are provided.

Mariner Leisure Centre
Glasgow Road
Camelon
Falkirk
01324 503750
Party lasts 1 hr and includes soft play and a birthday tea; just bring the cake.

The Melting Pot
5 Rose Street
EH2 2PR
0131 243 2623
enquiries@themeltingpotedinburgh.org.uk
www.themeltingpotedinburgh.org.uk
Provides a large, light and friendly space for parties. Located right in the city centre the venue is fully accessible with lift access.

North Berwick Sports Centre
01620 893454
Birthday parties available, contact centre for details.

Party Planet
39 Baileyfield Road
EH15 1NP
0131 669 1231
parties@partyplanetonline.co.uk
www.partyplanetonline.co.uk
Specialist party venue. Visit the website for details of the party services available.

Play Action Team
0131 311 7073 or 7077
Octobus is a colourful, fun-filled play activity bus, available for private hire for events such as children's birthday parties, fairs and gala days. Age and number restrictions apply and hire charges vary according to the event, location and day required.

Play Planet
Donibristle Industrial Estate
Dalgety Bay
01383 822288
Situated 5 mins from Forth Bridge
Party lasts 2hrs and includes 1hr in soft play (3 separate areas for 0-2, 2-5 and 5-12 yrs) and 1hr in themed party rooms. Live appearance by Zimmy the alien, birthday tea, complimentary coffee vouchers, personalised invitations and party bags are all provided.

St Ninian's Church Hall
St Ninian's Road
Corstorphine
0131 539 6204
Venue only. Large Hall with adjoining kitchen which can accommodate up to 30 children.

PARTIES AT HOME

Throwing your own party can be a lot of fun with a little planning. Remember to send out invitations at least 4 weeks ahead. 1-2 hrs is long enough for young ones' parties. Useful party planning books are available in libraries and the following points may provide you with some ideas. Asking guests to come in fancy dress can help get everyone in party mood. Use decorations to set the scene. Enlist adult help - ask other parents or grandparents to stay and help but make sure you let them know in advance that you want them to do this.

Games
Make a list (in the excitement you may just forget all those great ideas!) of lots of quick games as concentration spans are short; and organise music. Giving a sweet to each child when they are put out of a game can prevent anyone feeling upset! Also contriving to have each child win a game and awarding them a 'medal' keeps everyone happy.

Don't forget to let businesses know you saw them in the EFUF book!

Craft session
Stickers and crayons to decorate their own paper plate, crown or cheap wooden photo frame. Do avoid pens and glue so as not to spoil party clothes and to minimise mess! Remember some children will finish in two minutes while others may take 20 minutes so have another adult on stand by to take the quick finishers for some more games and try to keep the session short (only 10-15 mins) to stop children getting bored.

Birthday tea
Having a picnic on the floor can work well - keep food simple and in small portions as children are usually too excited to eat much. Have another adult on hand armed with a roll of kitchen paper and a pack of wet wipes to help with any accidents! Put out the savouries first (e.g. small sandwiches, sausages, crisps, cherry tomatoes, carrot sticks, cheese sticks, fruit chopped into small pieces etc) then bring out some small cakes, chocolate crispy cakes, marshmallow top hats, and then finally the birthday cake (don't forget to sing!).

Finale
There is a lot of pressure to provide party bags these days and if you decide to do this, try including just one inexpensive but quality toy suitable to the age group (e.g. small toy car, playmobile figure, hair accessories, or bouncy ball), a balloon and a small chocolate or sweet, instead of lots of small plastic toys that are never looked at again. Or, instead of handing out party bags try making a lucky dip or a pinata.
For the lucky dip fill a box with shredded newspaper and hide enough small gifts for everyone. If you have the time small children love helping to make a pinata. Cover a balloon with strips of papier-mache (newspaper soaked in a mixture of flour and water) and leave to dry for a couple of days then paint in bright colours. When fully dried burst the balloon, fill piñata with small named gifts or sweets (nothing too heavy!) and thread some string through so that you can either hang it up or hold it up for them all to take a turn at whacking it with a wooden spoon until it breaks and all the contents came tumbling out.

BOUNCY CASTLE HIRE

Bennetts Bouncy Castles
9 Meadowplace Road
EH12 7TZ
0131 334 4545
bennettshire@blueyonder.co.uk
www.bennettshire.co.uk
Bouncy castles delivered and set up. All sizes, suitable for indoor use or in your garden with a shower cover. Specialised designs for under 5s.

Kidbounce
9 Scarlett Park
Musselburgh
EH21 8BY
0131 653 6243
Operating throughout Edinburgh and the Lothians, hirers of bouncy castles and soft play equipment. This company has a number of products specifically designed for under 5s.

Sir-Bounce-A-Lot
07900 827 813
sir.bouncealot@yahoo.co.uk
www.sir-bounce-a-lot.co.uk
Inflatable ball ponds, bouncy castles, inflatable fun runs and a 50ft obstacle course available for under 5s.

DECORATIONS, FANCY DRESS & ACCESSORIES

Party Mania
30 West Nicolson Street
0131 667 6020
www.partypartyparty.co.uk
Tableware, party bag fillers, decorations, poppers, confetti, wigs, hats and helium balloon table decorations. Helium gas tanks can also be hired to fill your own balloons.

The Party Shack
140 North High Street
Musselburgh
0131 665 4287
www.thepartyshack.net
Specialises in items for themed parties. Stocks lots of party accessories, balloons and children's fancy dress.

ONLINE PARTY ACCESSORIES
There are hundreds of online companies out there to provide everything from invitations, tableware, hats, party bags, balloons to pinatas. Most have all the latest themes such as Disney Princesses, Scooby Doo, Thomas and Friends, Spiderman, etc. If you search for 'children's party supplies' you get thousands of results! We have listed a few tried and tested ones to get you started:

Party Pieces
www.partypieces.co.uk

Kids Party Shop
www.kids-partyshop.co.uk

Kidsparties4U
www.kidsparties4u.co.uk

Party Godmother
www.partygodmother.com

The Little Things
www.thelittlethings.info

CATERING & CAKES

Most parents provide their own food for home hosted parties and there are books in the library to inspire you, but do keep it simple as children are usually too excited to eat much. Most of the supermarkets can, with prior warning, provide trays of buffet food, such as sandwiches. Or why not try your local deli or sandwich shop?

Cakes are usually the centrepiece of any party tea and again libraries often have books with easy to follow recipes and ideas. A number of shops hire out cake tins and instructions. However, if you don't feel ambitious enough to tackle one, Edinburgh seems to be teeming with people with novelty cake making businesses. Local bakers, confectioners and many supermarkets can supply cakes with your photo of choice turned into edible icing. See Cakes & Cookery in the 'Shopping' section for some local recommendations.

ENTERTAINMENT

Many of the entertainers we contacted felt that their acts weren't suitable for under 5s and stressed that there was nothing worse than adults giving a running commentary to tots. It is most important when looking for an act to tell them the age span of the children and whether you have seen them before, as many entertainers have several routines. Some may even run the whole party if you want. Those listed below have acts/services suited to the under 5s age group.

Don't forget many of the people who run regular classes and weekly sessions are also happy to provide their services for parties. See the 'Activities and Classes' listings forThe Drama Studio, Jo Jingles, Monkey Music, Music For Wee Ones and others.

Beano The Clown
Unit 275
44-46 Morningside Road
EH10 4BE
07948 07 05 69
beanosab@hotmail.com
www.Beano.theclown.free.fr
Party consists of songs with the guitar, a magic show with a glove puppet, and balloon animals. This takes one hour and is usually enough for under 5s. Longer sessions are also available with extra games such as musical bumps and pass the parcel. He also does shows where he starts by putting his clown make up in front of the children. They look at themselves in the same mirror as him, and play with the squeaky red nose, so that they are not afraid of his clown face. He then plays the songs, juggles with juggling balls and spinning plates, does a trick with the puppet, and finishes with balloon animals. Beano has been a clown for over fifteen years. He speaks French, and can do shows in both languages when required. He is a member of Equity and Clown International and is Disclosed.

Carries-Matic Theme Parties
0131 336 3673
07952 945 749
carriesmatic@yahoo.co.uk
Party entertainment designed to suit your occasion, using stories, poems, song, dance, puppets, face-paint, balloons and games to give an interactive and educational experience. Parties suitable for all ages from tiny tots to teens and there are a wide variety of themes available including; Ballet, Wizards, Posh Princesses, Native American Indian and animals. Carrie is a professionally trained dancer, dance and drama teacher, children's theatre director, member of equity and mother, and is Disclosed.

Dinky Drama and Puppet Party
01236 736136
info@baba-boom.co.uk
Parties for 2-5yrs that are interactive as well as entertaining. Using a variety of upbeat, fun movement/dance action songs, percussion playing, puppet show, interactive role play and songs, props and parachutes, they offer a fun and energetic hour session. Longer sessions can be arranged at additional cost but one hour is recommended for this age group. There are no gimmicks or extras such as party bags, just a stream of activity to occupy and let the children enjoy themselves.

Flotsam and Jetsam Puppets and Stories
2 Summerhall Square
EH9 1QD
0131 662 9834
07813 70 58 40
flotsam@jetsam.wanadoo.co.uk
Lively puppets and stories designed to appeal to younger children (2+ yrs). Puppeteer and storyteller will come to your party wearing her magical blue 'story dress'. The dress has many pockets and in each one are puppets and props waiting to come out and tell their stories. Lots of joining-in fun and a special surprise for the birthday child. Call for a brochure and current prices. Shows based around the seasons are also available to playgroups and nurseries.

Gary James and Stone the Crow
46 Easter Drylaw Bank
EH4 2QN
0131 332 8321
0793 272 8695
g.james@blueyonder.co.uk
www.stonethecrow.co.uk
Magic fun shows for all events. Full time Professional Entertainer.

Gordon's Magic and Puppet Show
0131 652 2189
gordonhunt1@btinternet.com
www.gordonsmagicandpuppets.com
Entertainment for birthday parties and other events with puppets, magic, balloon animals and organised games. Packed with chances for party guests to participate in the action.

Jango the Clown
07932 087445
mail@clowncompany.co.uk
www.clowncompany.co.uk
Jango is multi-talented and puts on a real show to entertain kids of all ages. We've seen him cope with a party for a hundred under 5s and they all loved every minute.

Jimmy Craig
26 Muirfield Street
Kirkaldy
KY2 6SY
01592 261706
This experienced fun magician provides prize-winning fun-filled magical entertainment for children. He specialises in shows suitable for children of playgroup age and up.

Mr Boom
The Old Repeater Station
Libberton
South Lanarkshire
01555 84 11 68
info@mrboom.co.uk
www.mrboom.co.uk
The children's one-man band from the moon has been visiting Planet Earth for some 24 years now. He's written a wealth of science based songs well known to several generations of youngsters. He's a popular draw at fund raising concerts and visits schools and nurseries with his enchanting singing and dancing show for young children. Sing along all together now! Dance in a pixie ring! Be a planet going round the sun! If Mr Boom's there, you'll have lots of fun.

Tricky Ricky
10 Drum Brae Avenue
EH12 8TE
0131 339 8500
ricky@trickyricky.com
www.trickyricky.com
Edinburgh's multi award-winning children's entertainer & magician. Magic, songs and balloon modelling. A riot of fun and laughter, including Bingo the real puppet dog!

Where would you suggest?
Tell us -
ed@efuf.co.uk

Information & Support

Ed's Timeline...

With so much to think about in the early days of parenthood you might find yourself wondering about what happens when. Hopefully this handy timeline will help put a few things into context. The chapters of the book that follow provide details of places that provide futher information; more on nurseries, toddler groups and playgroups; handy information about childcare options; and heathcare contact details.

During Pregnancy	Find out from your midwife what antenatal classes you will be offered by the NHS and book into private antenatal classes, such as those run by the NCT, if you wish.
	If eligible (on benefits or you're pregnant and under 18) apply for Healthy Start vouchers which you swap for milk, fresh fruit, fresh vegetables and infant formula milk.
	Consider exercise classes for antenatal women, such as yoga and swimming.
	Try the free NCT bra-fitting service for help finding a comfortable and supportive bra.
After 25wks of pregnancy	After the 25th week of pregnancy ask for a claim form from your midwife for the Health in Pregnancy grant of £190.
After 29wks of pregnancy	After the 29th week of pregnancy (and before your child is 3mths old), apply for the Sure Start Maternity Grant if you are on a low income. This is a one-off payment of £500 to help towards the cost of a new baby.
	Consider purchasing a trial pack of real nappies from Edinburgh and Lothians Real Nappy Project (www.changeworks.co.uk).
	Find out about maternity and paternity pay from your employers. Look at private nurseries for when returning to work (enquire about childcare vouchers from your employer).
After 36 wks of pregnancy	You can buy a feeding bra after 36wks of pregnancy. Local NCT bra-fitters are there to help.
Birth	Non-routine immunisation against tuberculosis (TB) for babies more likely to come into contact with TB than the general population.
	Non-routine immunisation against Hepatitis B for babies where mothers are Hep B positive.
10 days	Usually discharged by the midwife around this time and your health visitor takes over.
By 21 days	Register the birth and name of your baby with local Registrar of Births.
	As soon as possible register your baby with a GP.
	Apply for Child Benefit.

2 months	1st routine immunisations to protect against diphtheria, tetanus, pertussis, polio, Haemophilus influenza type b and pneumococcal infection.	
	Make sure you have claimed for any Tax Credits you are due.	
3 months	2nd routine immunisations to protect against diphtheria, tetanus, pertussis, polio, Haemophilus influenzae type b and meningococcal C.	
4 months	3rd routine immunisations to protect against diphtheria, tetanus, pertussis, polio, Haemophilus influenzae type b, meningococcal C and pneumococcal infection.	
	Bookbug book bag supplied by health visitor.	
Around 6 months	Register your baby with a dentist.	
	Start weaning your baby onto solid foods.	
Around 12 months	Routine immunisation to protect against Haemophilus influenzae type b and meningococcal C.	
	Second set of bookbug books given out by health visitor.	
	Between 1-2yrs put your child's name on playgroup waiting lists if wishing them to attend later (most take children from 27-30mths).	
	If considering private education, start looking at the independent schools and putting your child's name on the waiting lists.	
Around 13 months	Routine immunisations to protect against measles, mumps and rubella (MMR) & pneumococcal infection.	
2 years	For council nurseries, put child's name on waiting lists as soon as 2yrs (eligible for free part-time place the term after their 3rd birthday).	
	Usually some time between 2 and 3yrs start potty training your child.	
3 years	Join The Children's Traffic Club, which helps parents/carers teach their children about road safety through a series of 6 books.	
	Bookbug Treasure Chest received by children in nurseries and from child and family centres.	
	Between 3 and 6yrs be alert to any apparent language delay, hearing or sight problems - contact your health visitor if any concerns.	
3yrs 4mths to 5 years	Routine immunisations to protect against diptheria, tetanus, pertussis, polio and MMR.	
3yrs 9mths +	Around November time, enrol your child for entry to your local school the folllowing August (look out for dates of enrolment days at the relevant school). Children who are 5yrs on or before the last day of February usually start Primary School in the previous August.	
	If applying to defer your child's school entry until the following year, an application for automatic deferral (your child's birthday is in January or February) should be submitted by end of February and for discretionary deferral (your child's birthday is between the first day of the Autumn term and the end of December) by the end of March.	

We hope you find this useful. The information was correct, to the best of our knowledge, at the time of going to print. However, details do change, so please let us know if you come across any information that needs updated for the next edition. Email info@efuf.co.uk. Visit our website for updates www.efuf.co.uk.

HELP & INFORMATION

This section is meant to be a starting point if you are looking for help or advice. It is not all-encompassing, but we have tried to list the names and addresses of organisations that can provide you with information, advice and support.

HEALTH

For details of emergency care, general practitioner services, hospital services, antenatal care, antenatal classes and support, postnatal support, dental care and complementary healthcare please see the 'Healthcare' section.

While this section is not able to cover all of the support and services available to families, it is hoped that the advice and information given may be useful. Do remember that a number of advice and information services are listed that families can contact for further information. SNIP (Special Needs Information Point), for example, is a very valuable resource for parents of children with special needs in the Edinburgh area looking for information or support.

Benefits and Social Security Information

There's a good deal of information online. A few useful resources are:

Benefit Enquiry Line
0800 88 22 00

A confidential telephone service for people with disabilities, their representatives and their carers.

Visit our website for updates:
www.efuf.co.uk

Benefits Now
www.benefitsnow.co.uk

The website has detailed information about claiming DLA, along with discussion lists where parents can exchange advice and information, as well as links to equipment suppliers and information about the Motability scheme. The site also contains the full text of the Disability Handbook, used by the Benefits Agency when assessing claims and which has useful information about the appeals process.

Parents at Work
www.workingfamilies.org.uk

Has a wide range of information including a Tax Credit online calculator and fact sheets about rights during maternity leave and flexible working. Aims to help children, working parents and their employers find a better balance between responsibilities at home and work.

Their Children with Disabilities Project produces a newsletter - "Waving not drowning", for parents of disabled children who work or want to work.

Department for Work and Pensions
www.direct.gov.uk

Provides details of all public services including the different types of benefits available and how to make a claim.

Child Tax Credit

For help or information regarding child tax credit see the relevant section of the public services website (and Child Benefit) which includes a tax credits online questionnaire to check eligibility. You can contact the helpline or write to the social security office. You will need your NI number (and your partner's if the claim is joint). The helpline can be extremely busy, but it's still quicker than writing.

Tax Credits Helpline
0845 300 3900
Textphone: 0845 300 3909
The helpline is open daily.
General queries are answered here:
www.hmrc.gov.uk/taxcredits

0845 3021444
National number for information regarding Child Benefit.

LOCAL SOCIAL SECURITY & JOBCENTRE PLUS OFFICES

Social Security Office
38 Castle Terrace
Edinburgh
EH3 9SJ
0131 229 9191
General information and advice about social security and child benefits.

More information concerning benefits can be found on the website of the Edinburgh City Council under Jobs and Careers:
www.edinburgh.gov.uk/internet/city_living/

Wester Hailes Jobcentre Plus
Westside Plaza
Edinburgh
EH14 2SP
0131 456 4300

High Riggs Jobcentre Plus
20 High Riggs
Edinburgh
EH3 9HU
0131 456 4000

Leith Jobcentre Plus
199 Commercial Street
Edinburgh
EH6 6QP
0131 555 8000

City Jobcentre Plus
11-13 South St Andrew Street
Edinburgh
EH2 2BT
0131 456 3300

The City of Edinburgh Council Advice Shop
85-87 South Bridge
Edinburgh
EH1 1HN
0131 225 1255
Consumer advice, debt advice and advice on welfare benefits.

SOCIAL WORK
For all first time contact with adult social care services contact Social Care Direct.

Social Care Direct
0131 200 2324
socialcaredirect@edinburgh.gov.uk

The opening hours for Social Care Direct are:
08.30 - 5.00 Monday to Thursday
08.30 - 3.40 Friday

Outside of these hours and on public holidays contact the Emergency Social Work Service.

Emergency Social Work Service
0800 731 6969

SOCIAL WORK CENTRES

Muirhouse Crescent Social Work Centre
34 Muirhouse Crescent
Edinburgh
EH4 4QL
0131 343 1991

West Pilton Gardens Social Work Centre
8 West Pilton Gardens
Edinburgh
EH4 4DP
0131 529 5400

Westfield House Social Work Centre
5 Kirk Loan
Edinburgh
EH12 7HD
0131 334 9933

Springwell House Social Work Centre
1 Gorgie Road
Edinburgh
EH11 2LA
0131 313 3366

Murrayburn Gate Social Work Centre
5 Murrayburn Gate
Edinburgh
EH14 2SS
0131 442 4131

Oxgangs Path Social Work Centre
4 Oxgangs Path
Edinburgh
EH13 9LX
0131 445 4451

Victoria Street Social Work Centre
11 Victoria Street
Edinburgh
EH21 2HE
0131 226 6731

Leith Social Work Centre
St John's House
71 Constitution Street
Edinburgh
EH6 7AF
0131 553 2121

Craigentinny Social Work Centre
Loaning Road
Edinburgh
EH7 6JE
0131 661 8291

Captains Road Social Work Centre
40 Captains Road
Edinburgh
EH17 8QF
0131 529 5300

Craigmillar Social Work Centre
171 Duddingston Park South
Edinburgh
EH15 3EG
0131 657 8500

Social Work services provide a range of services to support children with disabilities and illness. For more information about any of these services contact your nearest Social Work Centre (as above). Services and support offered may include:

Share the Care
Links families to carers who can offer regular care in their own home to give the families of children with disabilities a break.

Family Focus
Offers care at the child's own home. It might be help with bathing, toileting or feeding or accompanying the family on outings. Sometimes Family Focus staff 'sit' to allow parents to go out alone or with other children.

Residential Respite Care

Offered at Seaview, a centre where children with profound disabilities can go and receive the specialist care they need. Places are in high demand and are generally offered only to children who are unlikely to be matched to a Share the Care family.

Community Occupational Therapists (OTs)

Help people with disabilities make the most of their abilities. They teach people new ways of doing things, provide equipment and practical help where necessary, and give support and advice. They help people overcome the limiting factors of disability and help them to be as independent as possible.

Direct Payments

Direct payments allow people, including parents of disabled children, to purchase services to meet their community care needs instead of the local authority arranging services for them. If your local authority decides that you need community care or children's services, they must offer you direct payments as an alternative to arranging the services for you. Parents of a disabled child who has been assessed as needing children's services are now eligible for direct payments to enable them to purchase these services, however in reality few parents in some local authorities (including City of Edinburgh) are currently able to make use of direct payments, for a variety of reasons. If your child has not had a formal assessment of need carried out by a social worker, then contact your local social work centre and request that this happens. Once this assessment is completed, you may then be offered services for your child. If you are offered services you should also be given the option to receive direct payments to purchase these services yourself, if you are able to and choose to do so. You can contact Direct Payments Scotland for advice on receiving direct payments.

Direct Payments Scotland

27 Beaverhall Road
EH7 4JE
0131 558 5200 or 3450
info@dpscotland.org.uk
www.dpscotland.org.uk

Direct Payments Scotland can give advice by telephone and also publish a variety of useful factsheets on direct payments related issues, including 'A guide to receiving direct payments in Scotland'. Contact them if you're having difficulties trying to access direct payments or if you wish to know more about purchasing services with direct payments.

ADVICE CENTRES

Citizens Advice Bureaux Scotland

www.cas.org.uk

Citizens Advice Bureaux Edinburgh

www.citizensadviceedinburgh.co.uk

A free, confidential service providing general advice and information on topics such as housing, family, employment, benefits and consumer issues. Offers money advice and debt negotiation, representation at employment and social security tribunals, and some court representation. Most offices have legal clinics on a weekly basis.

Local offices throughout Edinburgh can be found at:

8a-8b Bath Street
Portobello
Edinburgh
EH15 1EY
0131 669 7138 (advice)
0131 669 9503 (appts)
portobello@citizensadviceedinburgh.co.uk

Fountainbridge Library
137 Dundee Street
Edinburgh
EH11 1BG
0131 474 8080 (advice)
0131 474 8081 (appts)
gorgiedalry@citizensadviceedinburgh.
co.uk

58 Dundas Street
Edinburgh
EH3 6QZ
0131 557 1500 (advice)
0131 558 3681 (appts)
central@citizensadviceedinburgh.co.uk

166 Great Junction Street
Edinburgh
EH6 5LJ
0131 554 8144
leith@citizensadviceedinburgh.co.uk

661 Ferry Road
Edinburgh
EH4 2TX
0131 332 9434
pilton@citizensadviceedinburgh.co.uk

Gingerbread Edinburgh and Lothian Project Ltd
117-119 Fountainbridge
Edinburgh
EH3 9QG
0131 478 1391
gingerbread@wwmail.co.uk
Information and advice centre for lone parent families. Also provides legal and informal counselling by appointment, childcare services and after school care clubs. Two-partner families welcome to use childcare facilities. Holiday information packs and leaflets on all of the above available on request.

Granton Information Centre
134-138 West Granton Road
Edinburgh
0131 552 0458
info@gic.org.uk
www.gic.org.uk
Information and advice on benefits, debts, housing, employment etc. Also available for development of local self-help/support groups. Youth and disability rights.

The Rights Office
Southside Community Centre
117 Nicolson Street
Edinburgh
EH8 9YG
0131 667 6339
Advice sessions, independent advice and representation on welfare benefits, disability rights, employment rights, debt and housing.

HOUSING

 For specific advice on housing and related issues:

City of Edinburgh Housing Department
www.edinburgh.gov.uk
Part of the official council website is devoted to housing issues. Links to sections on adaptations, information for tenants and details of houses available for exchange.

Ownership Options in Scotland
0131 661 3400
www.oois.org.uk
A charity providing information, advice and other support (although not financial) to disabled people, carers and professionals to improve access to housing in the owner occupied sector. This service is also provided for parents of disabled children and may be useful if you are considering home ownership or seeking more information on whether home ownership is a possibility for your family.

Council Tax Reduction

To qualify for the council tax reduction (which would move your council tax bill down by one band), households must include a child or adult who is substantially or permanently disabled. They must also either: use a wheelchair indoors; need a second bathroom, toilet or kitchen; or be the main user of one room, as a living space, for treatment or to store equipment.

The reduction is granted regardless of income or savings, and claims can be backdated indefinitely if applicants can prove that they met the criteria in the past. Contact your local council tax office for further information, you can do this by phoning your local council switchboard (for City of Edinburgh Council call 0131 200 2000).

MEDIA LISTINGS

The Scotsman Group

108 Holyrood Road
Edinburgh
0131 620 8620 (reception)
0131 620 8888 (advertising)
www.scotsman.com

The Scotsman

Carries birth announcements. Has daily section with details of exhibitions, theatres, art galleries, etc. Weekend section on Sat with 'What's on' information.

Evening News

Daily afternoon and evening paper full of local news.'Daily Plan-It' has details of events.

Scotland on Sunday

Scottish Sunday paper with events page.

Edinburgh Herald and Post

0131 620 8080
edinhp@scotsman.com
Published every Thu and delivered free to most homes in the city. Cinema listings and details of local arts and community events, sales, fetes etc. Large 'For Sale' columns. A different edition is printed for West Lothian (Tel 01506 503400 for enquiries or editorial).

Families Edinburgh

0131 622 0405
www.familiesmagazine.co.uk
Free bi-monthly magazine for families with young children. Distributed at playgroups, nurseries, leisure centres, etc. Local listings, advertisements, features.

The List

14 High Street
Edinburgh
EH1 1TE
0131 550 3070
editor@list.co.uk
www.list.co.uk
Published fortnightly and includes a small section 'Kid's List' which provides information about events in and around Edinburgh and Glasgow. It's worthwhile checking with the specific venues regarding times etc, as information can change after the publication has gone to press. Available at newsagents.

GUIDES TO EDINBURGH

City of Edinburgh Council

www.edinburgh.gov.uk
Council-run information website, which provides information about your local community and council departments.

A-Z guide

Produced by City of Edinburgh Council, listing contacts, community updates, council lists, and general information regarding the city.

Edinburgh For Under Fives

www.efuf.co.uk
An independent guide to Edinburgh specifically for families with young chldren, produced every two years by local parents. The best, of course!

Netmums

www.netmums.com/edinburgh
Includes information on events, activities and meeting local mothers.

Skootkidz

0131 317 1270
07827 930 830
linda@skootkidz.com
Local events guide available through an e-newsletter. Weekly updates on events, clubs, classes, workshops, special offers, family friendly eating out and shopping.To receive Skootkidz send your email address to linda@skootkidz.com.

SUPPORT & ASSISTANCE

This section contains alphabetical listings of organisations and voluntary groups who offer support and assistance on a wide range of issues.

Your local Community Education Centre and some of the Community High Schools also arrange Parents' Groups with crèche facilities; for more information see Community Education Centres in the 'Activities & Classes' section.

The Action Group

Norton Park
57 Albion Road
EH7 5QY
0131 475 2315
advice@actgroup.demon.co.uk
www.actiongroup.org.uk
The Action Group is a voluntary organisation that has developed a range of services for people with support needs and learning disabilities - and their carers throughout Edinburgh and the Lothians. They offer a family info and support service, playschemes, welfare rights advice, holidays, leisure schemes, sitter service, information and newsletters.

Advice guide

www.adviceguide.org.uk
This is the online advice service of the National Association of Citizens Advice Bureaux, offering online advice on a variety of topics.

AFASIC

0845 355 5577
www.afasic.org.uk
www.afasicscotland.org.uk
www.talkingpoint.org.uk
Telephone helpline Mon-Fri 10.30-14.30. Charity supporting children and young adults with speech, language or communication impairments and their parents/carers.

AFASIC Edinburgh
0131 557 9755
afasic.edinburgh@afasicscotland.org.uk
Local support group.

Allergy UK
3 White Oak Square
London Road
Swanley
Kent
BR8 7AG
01322 619864 (helpline)
www.allergyfoundation.com
UK charity providing information on all aspects of allergy.

Ask Nanny
Contact: Trudy
0131476 0004
ask@ask-nanny.com
www.asknanny.com
Ask Nanny offers parent coaching to advise parents on all stages of baby and childhood including sleep, feeding and behaviour.

Asthma UK Scotland
(formerly Asthma Campaign Scotland)
4 Queen Street
Edinburgh
EH2 1JE
0131 226 2544
08457 01 02 03 (helpline)
enquiries@asthma.org.uk
Helpline available Mon-Fri 9.00-17.00. An independent UK charity, based in London, Edinburgh, Cardiff and Belfast, which works to conquer asthma.

Barton Hill Advice Service
www.bhas.org.uk
This voluntary sector agency offers free online guides to claiming disability living allowance, attendance allowance and incapacity benefit.

BEMAS
Black and Ethnic Minorities Advice Service
The Action Group
Norton Park
57 Albion Road
EH7 5QY
0131 475 2315
The BEMAS team in the Action Group provide practical advice and assistance regarding social work services, education, health and housing to Black or Ethnic Minority families who care for children and adults with additional support needs. The service is free and confidential. Interpreters can be arranged upon request.

Capability Scotland Advice Service (ASCS)
11 Ellersly Road
Edinburgh
EH12 6HY
0131 313 5510
Text phone: 0131 346 2529
ascs@capability-scotland.org.uk
www.capability-scotland.org.uk
Provides information and advice on any disability matter.

The Compassionate Friends
53 North Street
Bristol
BS3 1EN
0845 123 2304 (helpline)
0117 9665202 or 0845 1203785 (office)
www.tcf.org.uk
A self-help group for parents and their families who have suffered the loss of a child of any age through any cause.

Child Brain Injury Trust
0131 229 1852
www.cbituk.org
CBIT works with children who have an acquired brain injury and their families. They have a number of new parents groups which meet to talk about brain injury, to share ideas and to have a night out. There are groups in Edinburgh, West Lothian and Glasgow.

Children in Scotland
www.childreninscotland.org.uk
National agency for voluntary, statutory and professional organisations and individuals working with children and their families in Scotland. It exists to identify and promote the interests of children and their families and to ensure that relevant policies, services and other provisions are of the highest possible quality.

Contact a Family Scotland
Craigmillar Social Enterprise & Arts Centre
11/9 Harewood Road
Edinburgh
EH16 4NT
0131 659 2930
0808 808 3555
www.cafamily.org.uk
Introduces and links families whose children have special needs through local mutual support and self-help groups.
Contact a Family is the only UK charity providing support and advice to parents whatever the medical condition of their child. Their web-site has information on a huge number of specific conditions and rare syndromes, along with details of support groups. They have a very useful helpline (see above) for information relating to parenting a child with additional needs; they aim to be a one-stop advice service for parents. Advice and information can be given on a wide range of topics, including: medical conditions affecting children (including very rare disorders), funding for holidays, benefits, putting you in touch with other parents with children with the same condition and details of local support groups for families of children with any disability.

Couple Counselling Lothian
9a Dundas Street
Edinburgh
0131 556 1527
admin@cclothian.org.uk
www.cclothian.org.uk
A range of counselling and other services for couples and individuals who are experiencing relationship difficulties.

Cruse Bereavement Care Scotland
3 Rutland Square
Edinburgh
EH1 2AS
0131 229 6275
www.crusescotland.org.uk
Bereavement counselling, advisory services and friendship groups for adults. Also offers bereavement counselling to children.

DAPeND Helpline
0845 1203746
Helpline available Mon-Fri 19.00-22.00. Offers support to those suffering from postnatal or antenatal depression. Run under the auspices of Depression Alliance.

Disability Rights Commission
08457 622 633
The Disability Rights Commission (DRC) is an independent organisation with the goal of 'a society where all disabled people can participate fully as equal citizens'. The DRC Helpline is there to give advice and information about the Disability Discrimination Act (DDA) 1995. If you feel your child has been treated unfairly because of their disability and want to talk to the DRC, then contact the helpline.

DisabledGo Edinburgh
www.disabledgo.info

A free internet guide offering people with different access concerns information about access to shops, pubs, restaurants, cinemas - all goods and services - throughout Edinburgh. The purpose of the guide is to empower people to get out and do what they want to do by making it much easier to check which places are accessible. Hundreds of shops, pubs, restaurants and other venues are taking part. It's hoped that this new guide will help open up Edinburgh to its thousands of disabled residents, and also make the area more accessible to Britain's 8.7 million disabled people.

Ed's Twin Tips.....

There are so many child-friendly businesses and venues in Edinburgh that most people are spoilt for choice. However, if you are a parent/carer of twins (or multiples) there will be particular favourites that make life that bit easier. Here's a few suggestions:

Activities - don't be afraid to phone in advance to ask about taking twins to classes and coached activities. Class leaders often welcome having an extra baby to involve in demonstrations and you get the opportunity to take turns spending quality time with each twin.

Eating Out - check venues have more than one highchair and plenty to entertain. Browns are fast for service and have plenty of high chairs.

Footwear - Shoos in Teviot Row offer an excellent fitting service and a twins discount on shoes. Clarks also offer a discount to members of the Edinburgh Twins club.

Greenspaces - for less stress try to avoid rivers and roads. Cammo near Barnton and Inveresk Lodge garden in Musselburgh are relatively enclosed. Saughton Park Winter Gardens are also worth a visit, the glass houses provide welcome warmth on a cold day.

Help - don't underestimate your health visitors, if you are struggling they will do their best to find someone to help you. Alternatively try Home-Start who will give help to parents of multiples to let you get out and have a breather (www.home-start.org.uk).

Nurseries - start looking early as it can be harder to get two spaces on the same days. Some nurseries (including Cranley's) offer a second child discount.

Playgrounds - opt for smaller facilities like Longstone Park or Harrison Park where there aren't huge climbing frames to worry about. Juniper Green has a more toddler friendly climbing frame.

Sales - it can be expensive buying everything in duplicate so visit NCT sales, the Polwarth Parish Church sale and OMNI car boot sales to save a few pennies.

Share - TAMBA (www.tamba.org.uk) and The Twins Club (www.edinburghtwins.co.uk) provide a range of ideas, help, support, social events and offer twin and multiple groups for different ages and areas.

Soft Play - Scrambles at Ratho is well supervised and it's possible for even parents with twins to get a wee break.

Down's Syndrome Scotland

158-160 Balgreen Road
Edinburgh
EH11 3AU
0131 313 4225
info@dsscotland.org.uk
www.dsscotland.org.uk
Provides support and information to parents of children with Down's Syndrome.

Edinburgh Adders

edinburghadders@aol.com
A group of parents have set up an ADHD/ADD support group in Edinburgh. If you are interested or would like to know more, please email them.

Edinburgh Twins Club

www.edinburghtwins.co.uk
Support group for families with twins, triplets etc, providing help, advice and friendship.
See also TAMBA.

Edinburgh Women's Aid

4 Cheyne Street
Edinburgh
0131 315 8110
Text: 0778 147 2043
info@edinwomensaid.co.uk
www.ewa.smartchange.org
Edinburgh Women's Aid is an all women, confidential organisation which provides information, support and, where appropriate, refuge accommodation for women and any accompanying children who have experience of or are at risk of domestic abuse.

Edinburgh Women's Rape and Sexual Abuse Centre

PO Box 120
Brunswick Road
Edinburgh
EH7 5WX
0131 556 9437
info@ewrasac.org.uk
Information, practical and emotional support for women who have been raped or sexually assaulted at any time in their lives. Run by women for women.

Enlighten Action for Epilepsy

28 Drumsheugh Gardens
Edinburgh
EH3 7RN
0131 226 5458
info@enlighten.org.uk
www.enlighten.org.uk
Offers information, advice, support and counselling to parents of children with epilepsy and parents with epilepsy who have young children.

Enquire

0845 123 2303
www.enquire.org.uk
Enquire is the Scottish advice and information service for additional support for learning. The service is available to parents and carers of children and young people with additional support needs, to children and young people themselves, and to professionals working with them. Enquire offers special educational needs advice and information, including advice and information to parents and carers of children attending nursery.
The telephone helpline is attended by trained advisors. Outwith these times there is an answering service.
Written responses will also be made to their online email forms and enquiries via the website. Enquire also offers training and talks, produces a range of free publications and has a legal subscription service.

Epilepsy Action Scotland

48 Govan Road
Glasgow
0141 427 4911
0808 800 2 200 (helpline)
www.epilepsyscotland.org.uk
Provide information on the causes and treatment of epilepsy and campaigns for more epilepsy services in Scotland.

ERIC - Enuresis Resource and Information Centre
34 Old School House
Britannia Road
Kingswood
Bristol
BS15 8DB
0117 960 3060 (helpline)
info@eric.org.uk
www.eric.org.uk
Helpline available Mon-Fri 10.00-16.00. ERIC provides advice and information to children, young people, parents and professionals on bedwetting, day-time wetting and soiling.

FAIR
Family Advice and Information Resource
25-27 West Nicolson Street
EH8 9DB
0131 662 1962
fair@fairadvice.org.uk
www.fairadvice.org.uk
Information and advice service for people with learning disabilities, parents, carers and people who work with them in Edinburgh. Call them or pop into their office.

Family Care - Birthlink Adoption Counselling Service
21 Castle Street
Edinburgh
EH2 3DN
0131 225 6441
mail@birthlink.org.uk
www.birthlink.org.uk
The adoption contact register for Scotland. Counselling, support and advice for adopted people, birth parents and adoptive parents.

The Family Fund
PO Box 50
York
YO1 9ZX
0845 1304542
www.familyfund.org.uk
Helps families of disabled or seriously ill children under 16. They give grants related to the care of the child including holidays, leisure, laundry equipment, driving lessons and lots more. They also provide a range of information on benefits, holidays, transport and lots more. If your income is £21,500 or less they may be able to help. Apply by phone, online or in writing. You'll need to give your child's name, date of birth, their disability and details of the help you need.

Family Mediation Lothian
37 George Street
Edinburgh
EH2 2HN
0131 226 4507
Lothian@familymediation.freeserve.co.uk
Helps separating and divorced parents to make arrangements for the future care of their children.

Family Support Group
Queensferry, Dalmeny & Kirkliston area
0131 319 3200
A group of parents of children with additional learning needs have started this support group for parents and relatives of children with additional learning needs, no matter what age. The aim of the group is for parents to get together, chat and exchange information.

Anything out of date?
Let us know -
info@efuf.co.uk

259

firsthand
39 Broughton Place
Edinburgh
EH1 3PR
0131 557 3121
admin@1sthand.org.uk
www.1sthand.org.uk
A voluntary organisation providing services to lone parents, carers, children and young disabled adults. Their services include a sitter service for parents of disabled children or young people. They offer a regular sit so that parents who have no other reliable sitter can count on a break. They work within the city of Edinburgh and are staffed by paid staff as well as volunteers (paid staff usually sit for children with complex needs).

First Step Community Project
37 Galt Avenue
Musselburgh
EH21 8HU
0131 665 0848
www.ellp.net/firststep/content/view/14/1/
Project for families with young children offering many services for parents as well as the children.

Grapevine
Norton Park
57 Albion Road
EH7 5QY
grapevine@lothiancil.demon.co.uk
www.lothiancil.org.uk
Provides free, confidential information to disabled people, their supporters and any organisation or individual looking for disability-related information in Edinburgh and Lothian. You can contact Grapevine about a wide variety of issues, including: disability benefits, transport, aids and equipment, access issues, community care and direct payments, housing and adaptations, holidays and leisure, education and employment, and the Disability Discrimination Act.

Homelink
Unit 5, Abbeymount Techbase
2 Easter Road
Edinburgh
EH7 5AN
0131 661 0890
www.homelinkbefriending.org
Provides emotional and practical support to young families, using trained befrienders.

Home-Start
0800 068 6368
www.home-start.org.uk

Leith and North East Edinburgh
2b Pirrie Street
Edinburgh
EH6 5HY
0131 553 7819
homestartleith@btconnect.com
www.homestartleith.co.uk
and
Edinburgh South Central
35 Guthrie Street
Edinburgh
EH1 1JG
0131 226 1331
homestart.edinsc@btconnect.com

Volunteers offer regular support and practical help in the home to young families who have at least one child under 5. Trained volunteers visit families once a week for 2-3 hours offering emotional support and practical help.

Humanist Society of Scotland
4 Scotland Street Lane West
Edinburgh
EH3
0131 556 0128
www.humanism-scotland.org.uk
Information about non-religious ceremonies, including baby naming ceremonies.

Like to be listed?
Get in touch -
business@efuf.co.uk

Hyperactive Children's Support Group
71 Whyke Lane
Chichester
West Sussex
P019 7PD
01243 539966
hyperactive@hacsg.org.uk
www.hacsg.org.uk
The HACSG considers non-drug therapies (dietary ones in particular), important for under 6s.

IndependentSpecialEducation Advice (ISEA) Scotland
164 High Street
Dalkeith
EH22 1AY
0131 454 0096 (general)
0131 454 0082 (helpline)
0131 454 0144 (advocacy/representation)
plofficer@isea.org.uk
www.isea.org.uk
Provides advice, information, advocacy and representation to parents throughout Scotland who have a child or young person with additional support needs.

LIBRA
4 Norton Park
Edinburgh
EH7 5RS
0131 661 0111
www.librascotland.org.uk
LIBRA specialise in counselling and groupwork for women worried about their own drinking or who are affected by someone else's drinking.

Link Support Group
PO Box 1883
West Calder
EH55 8WB
01506 873650
linksupport.wl@btinternet.com
www.linksupport.wl.btinternet.co.uk
Support group situated in West Lothian who are dedicated to providing information to parents of children with special educational needs.

Lothian Autistic Society
Unit 22, Castlebrae Business Centre
40 Peffer Place
Edinburgh
EH16 4BB
0131 661 3834
www.lothianautistic.org
Provides monthly support meetings for all parents of children on ASD.

Lothian Racial Equality Council
14 Forth Street
Edinburgh
0131 556 0441
admin@lrec.org.uk
www.elrec.org.uk
Aims to work towards the elimination of racial discrimination.

MAMA - Meet a Mum Association
54 Lillington Road
Radstock
BA3 3NR
0845 1203746
meet_a_mum.assoc@btinternet.com
www.mama.co.uk
Helpline available Mon-Fri 19.00-22.00. Friendship and support to mothers and mothers-to-be through local groups or individual contacts.

Mindroom
PO Box 13684
Musselburgh
EH21 1YL
0131 317 1016
moreinfo@mindroom.org
www.mindroom.org
Mindroom is a charity dedicated to raising awareness of learning difficulties as well as providing direct help and support for children and adults with learning difficulties and their families.

The Miscarriage Association
c/o Clayton Hospital
Northgate
Wakefield
West Yorkshire
01924 200799
www.miscarriageassociation.org.uk

Mosaic Down's Syndrome UK
www.mosaicdownsyndrome.org
This website offers support and information for parents of children and adults with Mosaic Down's Syndrome.

Muscular Dystrophy Campaign
61 Southwark Street
London
SE1 0HL
0800 652 6352 (information and support)
www.muscular-dystrophy.org

National Childbirth Trust
0844 243 6994
www.nct.org.uk
www.nctedinburgh.moonfruit.com
Provides classes, groups and counselling services, offering parents information and support during pregnancy and the early years of parenthood. Local bumps and babies groups, postnatal support groups, social events and Nearly New Sales.

NCT Breastfeeding Line
0300 330 0771
Helpline available 8.00-22.00.

National Deaf Children's Society Scotland
Second Floor
Empire House
131 West Nile Street
Glasgow
G1 2RX
0141 354 7850
ndcs.scotland@ndcs.org.uk
www.ndcs.org.uk
An independent UK charity supporting children and young adults with deafness, and their parents/carers.

National Domestic Violence Helpline
0808 808 9999 (24 hours)
www.national domesticviolencehelpline.org.uk

National Eczema Society
Hill House
Highgate Hill
London
N19 5NA
0870 241 3604
helpline@eczema.org
www.eczema.org
Telephone information line available Mon-Fri 8.00-20.00. An independent UK charity dealing with the management and treatment of eczema.

North West Carers Centre
0131 315 3130
Offers a free, flexible sitter service for people living in or caring for someone in North West Edinburgh. Trained paid support workers give people a short break from their caring responsibilities by providing support either to the carer or to the person being cared for.

Anything out of date?
Let us know -
info@efuf.co.uk

One Parent Families

www.oneparentfamilies.org.uk

One Parent Families has published a free guide "The Lone Parent Guide to Caring for a Child with Additional Needs" which includes sections about accessing support and financial help. They have also worked with Contact a Family to develop a telephone advice service.

One Parent Families Scotland

13 Gayfield Square
Edinburgh
EH1 3NX
0131 556 3899
info@opfs org.uk
www.opfs.org.uk
Information and help for lone parents.
National Lone Parent Helpline also available:
0808 801 0323

The Parent Centre

The Edinburgh Parent Centre
28 Kirk Brae
Edinburgh
EH16 6HH
0131 664 5388
info@theparentcentre.co.uk
Offers courses to support parents in the tasks of parenting. Fees apply.

Parenting Across Scotland

1 Boroughloch Square
Edinburgh
EH8 9NJ
0131 319 8071
pas@children1st.org.uk
www.parentingacrossscotland.org
A partnership of seven charities across Scotland working together to focus on issues affecting families. Visit the website to find out more about the information and support available to families.

Parentline Scotland

0808 800 2222
parentsupport@parentlineplus.org.uk
www.parentlinescotland.org.uk
Information, advice, or someone to listen to you on the telephone. Telephone support and advice for parents provided by trained volunteers. Lines open Monday, Wednesday, Friday 09:00 – 17:00, Tuesday and Thursday 09:00 – 21:00.

Parent Network Scotland

0141 339 0092
mail@parentnetworkscotland.org.uk
www.parentnetworkscotland.org.uk
Provide information, courses and workshops for parents to learn and develop parenting skills.

The PF Counselling Service

Eric Liddle Centre
15 Morningside Road
Edinburgh
EH10 4DP
0131 447 0876
info@pfcounselling.org.uk
Counselling is available for individuals and couples (over 18 yrs) on a wide range of problems and difficulties.

PINS

Pelvic Instability Network Scotland
01586 830323
info@pelvicinstability.org.uk
www.pelvicinstability.org.uk
A Scottish charity supporting women with Symphysis Pubis Dysfunction, also known as Pelvic Girdle Pain. Their aim is to provide support and information to women with this condition and to raise awareness of the condition amongst health professionals and the general public.

Positive Help

13a Great King Street
Edinbugh
0131 558 1122
www.positivehelpedinburgh.co.uk/
Voluntary organisation for people living with HIV.

Prison Advice and Care Trust Family Support Service
254 Caledonian Road
London
N1 0NG
0800 0853021
www.prisonadvice.org.uk
Advice, information and support for the families of those in prison.

The Rock Trust
55 Albany Street
Edinburgh
EH1 3QY
0131 557 4049
e.admin@rocktrust.org
www.rocktrust.org
This charity helps homeless and socially excluded young people in many ways, including providing supported accommodation for young mothers and babies.

Roundabout Centre
(YWCA Scotland)
4b Gayfield Place
Edinburgh
0131 558 8000
www.ywcascotland.org

The Roundabout Group
01875 615415
Parents whose lives are affected because family members have dyslexia, Asperger's syndrome, DAMP, dyspraxia, autistic spectrum disorders and ADD can attend a support group in Tranent. The group was set up to support parents having to deal with issues associated with these conditions.

RNIB Scotland
Dunedin House
25 Ravelston Terrace
EH4 3TP
0131 311 8500
rnibscotland@rnib.org.uk
www.rnib.org.uk
RNIB offers practical support and advice to anyone with a sight problem.

Saheliya
10 Union Street
Edinburgh
EH1 3LU
0131 556 9302
www.saheliya.pwp.blueyonder.co.uk
Supports and promotes the positive mental health and well-being of black and minority ethnic women and girls in the Edinburgh area.

SANDS
0207 436 7940
0207 436 5881 (helpline)
www.uk-sands.org
Offers support for those affected by stillbirth or the death of a baby in the early weeks of life.

SANDS Lothians
Craiglockhart Centre Tournament Building
177 Colinton Road
Edinburgh
EH14 1BZ
0131 622 6263 or 622 6264 or
07929 16 78 12 (helplines)
sandslothians@btconnect.com
www.sands-lothians.org.uk
Offers a range of befriending and counselling services and can also offer helpful advice with a baby's funeral.

Scottish Cot Death Trust
Royal Hospital for Sick Children
Yorkhill
Glasgow
G3 8SJ
0141 357 3946
www.sidscotland.org.uk
Gives personal support to bereaved families by letter, telephone and leaflets and may put parents in touch with other bereaved parents.

Scottish National Federation for the Welfare of the Blind

8 Netherlea
Scone
Perthshire
PH2 6QA
01738 626 969
www.snfwb.org.uk
Co-ordinates organisations working for blind people in Scotland.

Scottish Society for Autism

Hilton House
Alloa Business Centre
The Whins
Alloa
FK10 3SA
01259 720 044
autism@autism-in-scotland.org.uk
www.autism-in-scotland.org.uk
Seeks to ensure the provision of the best possible education, care, support and opportunities for people of all ages with autism in Scotland.

Scottish Spina Bifida Association

190 Queensferry Road
0131 332 0743 (office)
08459 111112 (support service)
www.ssba.org.uk
Phone the family support service for local contacts.

Sexual Health Information Line

0800 567 123

Shakti Women's Aid

Norton Park
57 Albion Road
Edinburgh
EH7 5QY
0131 475 2399
info@shaktiedinburgh.co.uk
www.shaktiedinburgh.co.uk
Offers information, practical and emotional support and safe, temporary accommodation to all black and ethnic minority women and their children who are being abused either physically or mentally by their partners, husbands or families.

Siblings of Children with Autism

Scotland Yard Adventure Centre
70 Eyre Place
0131 557 8199
A parent and toddler group for children 3yrs and under who have a brother or sister with autism.

Simpson House Drugs Counselling and Related Services

52 Queen Street
Edinburgh
EH2 3NS
0131 225 1054/6028
Opening times: Mon-Fri 9.00-17.00 Free and confidential counselling service to drug users, friends and families.

The Sleep Lady

Contact: Linda Russell
07827 930 830
www.thesleeplady.co.uk
One to one support in your own home either by telephone or home visits.

Visit our website for updates:
www.efuf.co.uk

INFORMATION & SUPPORT

Sleep Scotland
0131 651 1392
0845 0031212 (support line)
sleepscotland@btinternet.com
www.sleepscotland.org
Support line available Mon-Fri 9.30-23.30. Provides support to families of children with special needs and severe sleep problems.

Smokeline
0800 848484

SNIP: Special Needs Information Point
Royal Hospital for Sick Children
14 Rillbank Terrace
Edinburgh
EH9 1LN
0131 536 0583
Text phone: 0131 536 0360
snip@btinternet.com
www.snipinfo.org
Provides information, advice, contact addresses, advocacy and emotional support to parents/carers of children with additional support needs about the services available to them.
SNIP run therapeutic support groups in Edinburgh for parents/carers of children with special needs.

SNIP is an important contact for parents and carers of children with special needs. Based up at Rillbank Terrace, next to the Royal Hospital for Sick Children, Edinburgh – SNIP offer a variety of very valuable services. They provide advice and information on services available to children with special needs and their carers and welcome calls from parents, carers, professionals and anyone else with an interest in special needs. They don't charge for information and will call you back if you contact them by phone. As well as a helpline service they also run support groups, produce a monthly newsletter, have a very informative website and can carry out a 'funder finder' for families of children with additional support needs to apply for grants to purchase things like equipment and holidays.
Keep SNIP's contact details at hand – you're likely to need them!

Stepfamily Scotland
Gillis Centre
113 Whitehouse Loan
Edinburgh
EH10 1BB
0845 122 8655 (helpline)
0131 623 8951 (office)
info@stepfamilyscotland.org.uk
www.stepfamilyscotland.org.uk
Offers support and information to all members of stepfamilies and those working with them.

Stepping Stones (North Edinburgh)
10 Wardieburn Road
Edinburgh
EH5 1LY
0131 551 1632
A chance for young parents who live in the Greater Pilton area to meet together and participate in various activities.

TAMBA Twinline
0800 138 0509
A confidential listening support and information service run by trained volunteers all of whom are parents of twins or triplets.

VOCAL
Voice of Carers Across Lothian
0131 622 6666
www.vocal.org.uk
A carer-led organisation which campaigns for carers and their needs, giving them a real voice. It provides information and advice to carers & professionals and an advocacy and counselling service is available to carers free of charge. VOCAL also run courses for parents on lifting and handling – these can be very useful for parents and are provided free of charge.

Wellspring
13 Smith's Place
Edinburgh
EH6 8NT
0131 553 6660
mail@wellspring-scotland.co.uk
www.wellspring-scotland.co.uk
Offers psychotherapy and counselling to individuals, couples and groups, including families and young people.

West Lothian parent groups for children with communication difficulties or autism
01506 777598
louise.jarman@wlt.scot.nhs.uk
At this group parents of children with communication difficulties or autism have the opportunity to discuss various topics, including using a variety of visual strategies to improve communication. There is also a library with appropriate books on autism available and a creche.

Women's Groups
City of Edinburgh Council Equality Unit
12 St Giles Street
Edinburgh
0131 469 3603.
For more comprehensive information on Women's Groups.

Like to be listed?
Get in touch -
business@efuf.co.uk

Pre-school Play & Education

Pre-school Play and Education

There are many opportunities for under 5s to meet with others of the same age. Informal groups can provide a welcome break from the home, offering a large range of toys and space to play with them. This is a great way to meet others in a similar situation to yourself. There are also more structured pre-school options and nursery provision for those who are interested.

This section of the book provides some more information on the options available and details of the following:

• Sources of Information
• Toddler Groups
• Playgroups
• Choosing a Nursery
• Nurseries

OPTIONS AND TIMELINE FROM 0 – 5 YEARS

After becoming an expert on birthing options, travel systems, cots, and weaning, you will now find that you have to master the field of education and childcare available for your little one(s)! It can be overwhelming for the busy parent/carer, so we have tried to provide you with some useful information to help get you started.

Before Birth:
Consider submitting an application for private nursery if you know you will require childcare upon returning to work. Nurseries can have long waiting lists!

Age 0 – 1:

Parent and Baby Groups
These are informal groups that cater for parents and babies, and are generally held in health centres or in someone's home. Your health visitor, clinic or the National Childbirth Trust wcan put you in touch with other parents in your area. These groups are a good way to meet other adults in a similar situation to your own, and help provide support and friendship for you and your baby.

Private Nursery
Many of these offer childcare from thee months, and are usually open between 8.00 and 18.00, Monday to Friday, all year, and therefore useful for parents/carers who work outside the home. Spaces for under 2s can be hard to find, so try and register with the nursery as soon as possible – even before the baby is born as noted above! Fees are applicable, and will be higher for under 2s, as the staff/child ratio is higher. All private nurseries should be registered with the Care Commission, and are inspected once a year. Nurseries that provide education to pre-schoolers will also have an HMIE (Her Majesty's Inspectorate of Education) report available. Please refer to the 'Nursery Choice' section for information to consider when choosing a private nursery.

Age 1 – 2 ½:

Parent and Toddler Groups

These groups are generally set up by local parents and are held in church halls, community centres, or schools, and cater for babies and toddlers. The carer (parent, guardian, nanny or childminder) stays with the child throughout the session. Some groups separate the babies and the toddlers by age and have specific days for specific age ranges. Facilities and standards vary, but most have a selection of toys and puzzles, books, crayons and some larger pieces of equipment, such as climbing frames, chutes, play cookers, ball pits, wendy houses etc. It is best to check personally for the atmosphere and safety standards, particularly outdoor equipment, if you are attending these groups. Prices range from nothing to approximately £5-£7 or more per term depending on the venue. There is often a small charge for tea, coffee, juice, biscuits and so on. It's not unusual for groups to have a rota for making tea etc, and carers help set up and tidy away the toys.

Private Nursery

See above for more information.

Age 2:

If you are planning on sending your child to a Council Nursery, you should submit an application form around the time your child turns two years old. On the application form, you will be asked to list, in priority order, up to three nursery choices (there are no catchment areas for nurseries meaning you can send your child to any nursery in the city if a place is available). A nursery place will be offered as soon as possible after s/he becomes eligible.

Age 2 ½ - 5:

Important! At age three – four all children are eligible for a free, part-time place in nursery (term beginning after third birthday). This is funded by the Scottish Government, and is for up to a total of 475 hours per year, which usually means up to 5 x 2 ½ hour sessions per week. If claiming a funded part-time place through a Partner Provider Centre, complete a Pupil Information Form from the Centre in the term before your child becomes eligible for funding (usually term before turning three).

Playgroups

These are voluntary, non-profit-making groups, which provide more structured play/ education. They may be open mornings or afternoons, or both. Charges are usually low and parents may be expected to help on a rota basis. Many playgroups operate in partnership with the City of Edinburgh Council (through a "Partner Provider"), meaning that you will be able to receive a refund of all or part of your fees once your child is eligible (usually the term after their third birthday), or the place may be provided free. All groups that are Partner Providers are registered and inspected by the Scottish Care Commission and HMIE. Some playgroups may require your child to be toilet-trained.

City of Edinburgh Council Nursery (three years and older)
These are nursery schools and nursery classes based in primary schools across the city that are run by the City of Edinburgh Council. All provide free part-time places usually from the term after your child's third birthday. This means that children can attend five morning or afternoon sessions a week. If you need longer hours, wraparound care or full day-care, you may be able to purchase these at the nursery your child attends.

Private Nursery
If the nursery is a Partner Provider, you will be able to receive a refund of all or part of your fees once your child is eligible – usually the term after their third birthday.

Independent School Nursery
These are independent schools that have a nursery department. Most offer the choice of a morning, afternoon, or whole day placement. Fees are payable. If the nursery is a Partner Provider, you will be able to receive a refund of all or part of your fees once your child is eligible – usually the term after their third birthday.

Age 4:
Register for Primary School – usually in mid-November of the term before your child begins school. Look for local advertisements advising of exact registration dates and birthdate eligibility

Age 4 ½ - 5:
The entry date for children starting Primary School (P1) in Scotland is August. In general, children starting P1 in August must have either celebrated their fifth birthday in the preceding six months (from 1 March onwards) or are due to celebrate their fifth birthday in the following six months (birth dates up to 28 February). You should contact the Council if you have just arrived from England or Wales, where the admission ages differ.

Pre-school Play and Education – Sources of Information
Below we have listed some contacts that may be useful when researching childcare, pre-school and play options for your child.

GENERAL INFORMATION

Edinburgh Childcare Information Service
Waverley Court Level 1.2
4 East Market Street
Edinburgh EH8 8BG
0800 032 0323 (Mon-Fri 08.30-16.00)
childcareinformation@edinburgh.gov.uk
www.scottishchildcare.gov.uk
For full details of the service please see "Childcare section"
This is a great resource for finding current toddler, playgroup, and nursery information – you can do an online search using your postcode to locate childcare in your area.

PLAYGROUP INFORMATION

Scottish Pre-school Play Association (SPPA)
21 Granville Street
Glasgow G3 7EE
0141 221 4148
www.sppa.org.uk
At time of publication, there is no Lothian/East of Scotland office. For Edinburgh and West Lothian help and advice, you can contact above number Mon-Fri 10:00-14:30.

NURSERY AND SCHOOL INFORMATION

Edinburgh Nursery and School Guide
www.nurseryandschoolguide.co.uk
This magazine is for sale (£2.50) in many shops in Edinburgh, including Tesco, Sainsbury's, Waitrose, and Waterstones. It has a comprehensive list of Private Nurseries as well as editorial features to help you find the right nursery for you and your child.

The Scottish Commission for the Regulation of Care (The Care Commission)
Stuart House
Eskmills Business Park
Musselburgh EH21 7PB
0131 653 4100 or 0845 600 8335
www.carecommission.com
In Scotland, all private nurseries should be registered with the Care Commission, which can provide a list of registered groups (including nurseries), childminders and other daycare provision for children. For anyone relocating from England or Wales, Ofsted has no jurisdiction in Scotland. Nursery premises etc. are inspected once a year and reports are compiled after the inspection. These reports are compiled with the nursery in mind rather than the potential parent, so they may seem dry, but you can access them via the Care Commission website. The Care Commission updates the registration list regularly and if you cannot find a suitable nursery in your preferred area, it is worth phoning them.

National Day Nurseries Association Scotland
Level 2, 100 Wellington Street
Glasgow G2 6DH
0141 248 8694
Scotland@ndna.org.uk
www.ndna.org.uk
A national charity organisation that aims to enhance the development and education of children in their early years. The website provides information to parents about finding and choosing a nursery as well as information about the inspection of nurseries.

Her Majesty's Inspectorate of Education (HMIE)
Denholm House
Almondvale Business Park
Almondvale Way
Livingston
EH54 6GA
01506 600 200
www.hmie.gov.uk
Inspects and reports on the quality of pre-school education. Inspections are done at least every seven years and more often if necessary. Sometimes these inspections are done in conjunction with the Care Commission.

The City of Edinburgh Council Early Years and Childcare Team
Waverley Court
Level 1/4
4 East Market Street
Edinburgh EH8 8BG
0131 529 2412
www.edinburgh.gov.uk/internet/learning/CEC_pre_school_and_childcare
Provides information on pre-school and childcare options offered by the Council. You can download guides giving information about pre-school and primary school education, as well as a nursery application form from the website. Links to information about early years and nursery schools can be accessed via this website.

East Lothian Council Department of Education & Children's Services
John Muir House
Haddington EH41 3HA
01620 827 827
childcareinfo@eastlothian.gov.uk
www.eastlothian.gov.uk
Provides information about nursery education, and about moving from nursery to primary school. On the website, follow the links from "Education and Learning", and then to "Nurseries and Playgroups" to access relevant information and more specific contacts.

Midlothian Council Education Division
Midlothian House
Buccleuch St
Dalkeith EH22 1DN
0131 270 7500
enquiries@midlothian.gov.uk
www.midlothian.gov.uk
Provides information about nursery education offered by Midlothian council, as well as registered childcare options (childminders, private nurseries, playgroups, etc). Follow the links from "Learning and Libraries" to "Childcare and Early Years Partnership" as well as "Nursery Schools" to access relevant information from the website.

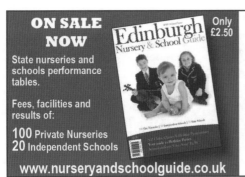
Scottish Council of Independent Schools

21 Melville St
Edinburgh EH3 7PE
0131 220 2106
info@scis.org.uk
www.scis.org.uk
Represents over 70 member independent, fee-paying schools in Scotland. Provides information about schools with nurseries, choosing a school, special needs education, financial considerations, etc. You can also find out information about fees, exam results, pupil numbers, etc.

GAELIC EDUCATION

Gaelic Education

Waverley Court
Business Centre 1/4
4 East Market Street
Edinburgh
EH8 8BG
0131 529 2415
www.edinburgh.gov.uk/learning/Programmes_and_initiatives/CEC_gaelic_education
There are two Gaelic toddler groups that operate in the city (Tollcross and Corstorphine – see toddler group listings), and an established nursery class at Tollcross Primary School (see below).

Gaelic Nursery and Primary School Education

Kenneth Neal (Head Teacher) 0131 229 7828 or Norma Martin 0131 529 2415
There is a Gaelic medium unit at Tollcross Primary School which caters for nursery and primary pupils from all over the city. There is no requirement for the parents to have any knowledge of Gaelic.

Toddler Groups

Name	Address	Phone Number (0131 +)	Contact Details	
EDINBURGH CENTRAL				
High School Yards Nursery	High School Yards off Infirmary Street EH1 1LZ	556 6536	Nicky Johnston or Alison Conroy	
King's Tots	The Kings Centre 11 Gayfield Street Edinburgh EH1 3NR			
St. Columba's Free Church	Johnson Terrace - entrance by hall door at Victoria Terrace	228 3782	Catriona Lamont	
Croileagan (Gaelic Parent and Toddler Playgroup)	Tollcross Community Centre Tollcross Primary School 117 Fountainbridge	529 2415	Norma Martin norma.martin@ edinburgh.gov.uk	
St Paul's and St George's Babies and Toddlers	St Paul's and St George's Church York Place	556 1335	Gemma Stoddart	
St. Mary's Episcopal Cathedral Toddler Group	Walpole Hall Chester St	476 0631	Alison Howard	

Day(s)	Time	Drop in?	Cost	Rota	Age Group	Other Information
W	9.15 - 11.30				0-3	Contribution to be made for refreshments. Sure Start Parent and Toddler Club.
Tu	10.00-12.00	Yes	£5 per family per term	Optional	0-3	www.kingschurch edinburgh.org
						No group at present but hopes to restart. Phone for details.
W,F	9.15-11.30	Yes		No	0-5	The group is open to any to join. Gaelic speaking play leader in place for language input. See also Corstorphine group.
Th	10.00-11.30	Yes	£1.50	No		Limited places. Phone to book a place. Snacks provided for children and coffee and biscuits for parents Mix of structured and free play plus song time.
F	10.00-11.30 all year	Yes	50p per family	Yes, casual.	0-3	Coffee/tea for carers. Biscuits and water for children.

Name	Address	Phone Number (0131 +)	Contact Details	
Palmerston Place Baby and Toddler Group	Annan House 10 Palmerston Place	447 9598	Rachel Wilson 663 8845	

EDINBURGH NORTH

Comely Bank Toddlers	St. Stephen's Comely Bank Church 10 Comely Bank Road			
Edinburgh Twins Club Bumps & Babies/ Toddler Group	St. Stephen's Comely Bank Church 10 Comely Bank Road		www.edinburghtwins. co.uk	
Dean Church Parent and Toddler Group	Dean Church 65-67 Dean Path EH4 3AT	225 5998	Jill Murray jill.murray@gmail.com	
Dean Tots	Dean Church 65-67 Dean Path EH4 3AT		Sharon 07751 429731 Antonia 07545 264523	
International Playgroup	St. Stephen's Centre St. Stephen's Street near Howe Street			
Davidson's Mains Parish Church Toddler Group	Quality Street	476 3519	Moira Harvey or lesleysevern@ blueyonder.co.uk	

Day(s)	Time	Drop in?	Cost	Rota	Age Group	Other Information
M	10.00-11.30 term time only	Yes	£1 per week			Coffee, juice etc provided.
Th	9.30 - 11.30 term time only					
M	10-11.30		£2 per family per session			Only for parents or carers with twins or more.
M	9.30-11.30	Yes	£2/week for 1 child. £3/wk for 2 or more children	Yes, organised on the day.	3mths-4yrs	Snacks and drinks for children and adults.
W,Th	9.30-11.45	No	Up to 1 year £20/term 1yr+ £40/term	No, but help tidy at end.	0-4	Playleader sets up toys, snacks and leads singing.
M,F	10.00-11.30	Yes	£2.50 per family	Yes, casual.	0-4	Large play area with quieter areas for babies. Lots of toys, activities, and books.
Th	9.30-11.30	No	£15 per term	Yes	0-4	Lots of toys and activities. Snack is provided for children and coffee and biscuits for grown-ups on a rota system. Please bring a cup/beaker for your child.

PRE-SCHOOL - TODDLER GROUPS

Name	Address	Phone Number (0131 +)	Contact Details	
Parent & Toddler Group	Cramond Kirk Hall Cramond Glebe Road	336 2036	Venue	
Blackhall Mother and Toddler Group	St Columba's Church Columba Road Edinburgh EH4 3QU	07718 500939	Su Lawrence	
Holycross Mother & Toddler Group	Holycross Church Hall	312 7670	Laurie Hawksey	
Trinity Toddler Group	Holy Cross Primary School School buildings Craighall Road	625 0165 or 07712 576469	Dawn Owen	
Inverleith Church Toddler Group	Inverleith Church Ferry Road	552 7615	Ann Tracy	
The Acorn Club	Inverleith Church Ferry Road	476 2067	Kath Drainer	
Forthview Primary School	West Pilton Place EH4 4DF	332 2468	Tracy Berry	
Muirhouse Toddlers	Craigroyston Community Centre 1a Pennywell Road			
EDINBURGH EAST				
Holyrood Abbey Church of Scotland Baby and Toddler Group	Marionville Road on corner with London Road	661 4230	Ann McTaggart	
Piershill Under-3 Project	New Restalrig Church Willowbrae Road	661 3109	Jacqui Cairney	

Day(s)	Time	Drop in?	Cost	Rota	Age Group	Other Information
Tu	10.00-12.00	Yes	Yes	No	0-4	
Tu	9.30-11.30	No	£15 per term	Yes	0-3	Tea, coffee. Snack for children.
M	9.30-11.30	Yes	£1		0-4	Coffee/tea for carers.
M-F	10.00-12.00	No	£1/ session plus £5/ quarter	Yes	0-4	Coffee and tea. Snack for children.
W	10.00-12.00	Yes	Free	Yes	0-3	Tea, coffee. Snack for children. Small charge.
Th	9.30-11.15	Yes	£1	Yes	0-5	Tea, coffee, snack. Craft based.
Th	9.00 - 11.00 term time only	Yes	Free	No	0-4	Run by a homelink teacher. Coffee and tea. Snack for children.
M-Th	9.00-11.00					
M	10.00-11.30	Yes	60p per family	No	0-3	Fruit and biscuits for children. Coffee/tea and biscuits for adults.
					0-3	Phone for details.

PRE-SCHOOL - TODDLER GROUPS

Name	Address	Phone Number (0131 +)	Contact Details	
St Philip's Church	Brunstane Road North			
Caring for Kids	Magdalen Community Centre 106b Magdalen Drive	669 8760		
Fort Drop-In	Fort Primary School North Fort Street	467 7131		
Fort Parent & Toddler Group	Fort Community Wing North Fort Street			
Little Leithers	Destiny Church 12 Casselbank Street Leith EH6 5HA	555 2707	Venue	
Mother and Toddler Group	North Leith Parish Church Madeira St Leith EH6 4AW	553 7378	Venue	
Pilmeny Group	Pilmeny Youth Centre 44 Buchanan Street EH6 8RF	554 0953	Venue	
Ripple Project Parent & Toddler Group	St Margaret's Church Hall Restalrig Road South	554 7400		
Greengables Toddler Group	8a Niddrie House Gardens	669 9083	Linda Jamieson	
Mother and Toddler Group	St Andrews Church Hall, 410 Easter Road EH6 8NT	553 8859	Venue	

Day(s)	Time	Drop in?	Cost	Rota	Age Group	Other Information
F	9.45-11.15	Yes	None			
Th	10-12					
W	12.30-3.30 term time only					
W	9.30-11.30					
M Tu Th	10.30-12.00 & 13.00-14.30 10.30-12.00 10.30-12.00	Yes	Donation	No	0-3 0-3 0-3 0-1	www. destinyedinburgh. com
M,Th	9.30-11.30	Yes	£10 per yr	No	0-4	
Tu,Th	9.30-11.00	No	£1 per child	No	0-2	dlmh@live.co.uk
T	9.30-11.15					
Th term time only	10.30-12.00	Yes	Donation	No	0-3	
Tu,Th	9.30-11.30	Yes	£1	No	0-3	

Name	Address	Phone Number (0131 +)	Contact Details	
Northfield and Willowbrae Toddler Group	Northfield and Willowbrae Community Centre 10 Northfield Road Northfield EH8 7PP	661 5723	Venue	
Toddler Group	St Christopher's Church Craigentinny Road EH7			
Parent and Toddler Group	Ocean Kitchen Area Ocean Terminal	557 6585	Health Visitors Bellevue Med Centre	
South Leith Parent Toddler Group	South Leith Church Halls Henderson Street EH6	82853 3024 or 07985 219527	Eve Nicola	
Braidwood Tots	Braidwood Centre 69 Dumbiedykes Road EH8 9UT			
Gilmerton Project Playgroup	Gilmerton Community Centre 4 Drum Street EH17 8QG	664 2335	Fiona elma@bueyonder.co.uk	
Valley Park Community Centre	37 Southhouse Road EH17 8EU	664 2210		
Liberton Kirk Baby and Toddler Group	5A Kirk Gate EH16 6RY	664 8264		

Day(s)	Time	Drop in?	Cost	Rota	Age Group	Other Information
M,W,F	9.45-11.30	Yes	Yes	No	0-3	
Th	9.30-11.30	Yes	£1.50	No	0-3	
Tu	2.30-4.30	Yes	No	No	0-3	
Tu	9.30-11.30	Yes	£1	No	0-4	eve.anna@ blueyonder.co.uk
Th	12.30-14.30				0-5	A small donation provides adults with tea/coffe and biscuit and a healthy snack and drink for your child. Free play with snack break, songtime at the end of the session.
Mon – Fri term times	9:00 – 11:30	No	£17 per week	Yes	2 1/5 – 5	www.gilmerton. btik.com
Tu	10.00-12.00		Free		0-3	This has replaced the Burdie House Community centre.
Tues	13.30-15.00		£2		0 – 5yrs	

Name	Address	Phone Number (0131 +)	Contact Details	
Inch Community Centre Play Plus Toy Library	225 Gilmerton Road EH16 5UF	664 4710		
Niddrie Baby and Toddler Group	Niddrie Community Church 12 Hay Drive EH16 4RY	669 9400	Lizzie Aylett	
Prestonfield Toddlers	Cameron House Community Education Centre 34 Prestonfield Avenue EH16 5EA	667 3762	Susan Ferguson at venue	

EDINBURGH SOUTH

Name	Address	Phone Number (0131 +)	Contact Details	
Blackford Toddler Group	Reid Memorial Church West Saville Terrace Blackford Edinburgh EH9 3HY	662 1203		
St Catherine Argyle Church Baby and Toddler Group	St Catherine Argyle Church 61 Grange Road	667 7220		
Duncan Street Parent Toddler Group	Baptist Church Hall 13 Duncan Street EH9 1SR	667 8097	duncanstreetplaygroup@googlemail.com	
Marchmont Playgroup	Inchcolm Hall 1A Kilgraston Road EH9 1TZ	447 2529	Vanessa Crowe	
Barclay Viewforth Church Toddlers	Barclay Viewforth Church Hall 1 Wright's Houses Bruntsfield EH10 4HR	229 6810	Katherine Ellis	
The Old Schoolhouse	140 Morningside Road EH10 4PX	447 2137		

Day(s)	Time	Drop in?	Cost	Rota	Age Group	Other Information
Tues	9.00-12.00	Yes	Free		0- 3+	
M	10.00-11.30	Yes	Yes	No	0-4	
W, F	10.30 - 12.30	No	50p per session			Centre membership required.
W	10.00-11.30		Snack and drinks for sale at nominal cost			
Tu	10.00-12.00	No	50p		0-3	www.stcatherines-argyle.org.uk
M-F	9.00-11.45		Contact provider		2 1/5 – 5	www.duncanstreet.co.uk
Tu, W, Th	9.30-12.30	No	50p		2 1/4 - 4	www.marchmontstgiles.org.uk
Tu	10.00-12.00	Yes		No	0-3	Coffee and tea. Snack for children.
Th	9.30-11.30		£1.50 per week		0 – 4	

Name	Address	Phone Number (0131 +)	Contact Details	
Next Step Parent & Toddler Group	Rudolph Steiner School 60 Spylaw Rd EH10 5BR	337 3410	Venue	
Morningside Parish Church Baby and Toddler Group	Cluny Centre Cluny Drive EH10 6DN	447 6745	http://www. morningside parishchurch.org.uk/	
Morningside Minis	Morningside Baptist Church Lower Hall Morningside Road EH10 4DB	447 9787	Liz Scott www.mbc.org.uk/ church-life/children- and-families/ morningside-minis	
Fairmilehead Toddler Group	Fairmilehead Parish Church 1a Frogston Road EH10 7AA	445 2374	fairmileheadtoddlers @googlemail.com	
PEEP Baby and Toddler Group	Paradykes Community Centre Mayburn Walk Loanhead EH20 9HG	448 0103	Joanna McLean	
Loanhead Parents 'n' Tots	Loanhead Community Learning Centre 5 Mayburn Walk EH20 9HG	440 3169	www.lclc.org.uk/ activities.htm	
EDINBURGH WEST				
Messy Monsters	Dreghorn Barracks Community Centre			
Mums Babes and Tots	Dreghorn Barracks Community Centre	310 2730	Kelly Nichols	
Balerno Toddlers	Balerno Parish Church Hall (Opposite Scotmid) Dean Park Brae Balerno	07795 528341	Charlotte Fleming	

Day(s)	Time	Drop in?	Cost	Rota	Age Group	Other Information
M-F	10.15-12.30					Contact venue for details.
M	10:00 – 11:30	Yes			0 – 3	
M, Tu	9:30 – 11:30	Tues only	£1		0 – 3	Free play, snack (and coffee for carers), story time, craft/construction, and singing.
M,Tu, Th,F	10.00-11.30	No			0-5	www.fhpc.org.uk
M, W					6-12 mth 1-2	
M,W,F	9.30-11.30		£1		2 1/2 - 5	
W	13.00-15.00		£1			
M	10.00-12.00	Yes	£1	No	0-4	Coffee and tea. Snack for children.
Th	9.45-11.30	Yes	£1 per session and £4 per term	Yes	0-3	Coffee and tea. Snack for children.

Name	Address	Phone Number (0131 +)	Contact Details	
St Mungo's Minis .	St Mungo's Church St Mungo's Ministry Centre 46B Bavelaw Road Balerno EH14 7AE	449 9903	Kate Yates	
Colinton Toddler Group	St Cuthbert's Church Hall Westgarth Avenue	07730 102327	Ally	
Stableroom Toddler Group	Colinton Parish Church Hall Spylaw Bank Road	477 9494	Fiona Blair	
Happy Faces Toddler Group	Stableroom Playgroup Colinton Parish Church Dell Road Colinton	07773 928337	Sarah Rynas	
Craiglockhart Toddler Group	Craiglockhart Church Hall Craiglockhart Drive North EH14 1HS	455 8229	Emily Langrish emilylangrish@ hotmail.co.uk	
Carrick Knowe Church	118-132 Saughton Road North EH12 7DR	334 1505	Venue	
Oxgangs Brae Toddlers	Oxgangs Neighbourhood Centre 71 Firrhill Drive EH13 9EU (off Oxgangs Cres)	441 7558	Elizabeth Brash	
St Peter's 0-5s	St Peter's Church Lutton Place	667 6224		

Day(s)	Time	Drop in?	Cost	Rota	Age Group	Other Information
Tu,W	10-11.30	Yes	50p	No	0-4	Coffee and tea. Snack for children.
M	9.15-11.15	Yes	£2.50 per session or £1.50 per session if paid for by the term in advance	No	0-3 1/2	Coffee and tea. Snack for children.
Th	9.15-11.15	Yes	£20 per term in advance	No	0-3	Coffee and tea. Snack for children.
Tu	9.30-11.30	Yes	£1	Yes	0-4	Coffee and tea.
M	10:00-11:45		£2 per session (snack included)		Baby-4	
Th,F	10.00-11.30	Yes	Donation	No	0-4	Runs during school holiday.
Tu	10.00 - 12.00				0-4	
M,Th	9.30 - 11.00		80p			Well established group. Small charge for refreshments.

Name	Address	Phone Number (0131 +)	Contact Details	
Oxgangs Sure Start Project	Colinton Mains Community Centre 1 Firrhill Loan Edinburgh EH13 9LS	441 7318	Sue Christie	
Edinburgh Twins Club Bumps & Babies/ Toddler Group	Oxgangs Neighbourhood Centre 71 Firrhill Drive EH13 9EU (off Oxgangs Cres)	441 7558		
Polwarth Parent, Baby and Toddler Group	Polwarth Parish Church 36-38 Polwarth Terrace Edinburgh EH11 1LU	346 2711		
Murrayfield Parish Church	Ormidale Terrace	467 3548	Gail Bruce	
Murrayfield Parish Church	Ormidale Terrace	337 2935	Beverley Kerr	
Croileagan Gaelic Medium Parent and Toddler Group	Corstorphine Youth and Community Centre Kirk Loan	529 2415	Norma Martin norma.martin@ edinburgh.gov.uk	
Parkgrove Parent & Toddler Group	The Munro Centre Parkgrove St	539 7179	Venue	§
Jack and Jill Mother and Toddler Club	St Anne's Church Hall Kaimes Road	334 2039	Frances Tennant	
St Ninian's Church Hall	St Ninian's Road	334 7301	Venue	

Day(s)	Time	Drop in?	Cost	Rota	Age Group	Other Information
					0-4	Phone for up to date information.
Th	10.00 -11.30		£2			Only for families or carers with twins or more.
Tu Th	10.00 - 12.00 14:30 - 16.30					
W	10-00- 12.00	No	£6 per term/£1 per week	No	0-4	Coffee and tea. Snack for children.
F	10-30- 12.00	Yes	£1 per session	No	0-3	Coffee and tea.
M	10.00- 12.30	Yes		No	0-5	The group is open to any to join. Gaelic speaking play leader in place for language input. See also Tollcross group.
Th	9.15- 11.30	Yes	Yes	No	0-4	
W	9.30- 11.30	No	Yes	No	0-4	
Tu, F	10.00- 11.30	No	£5 per term	Yes	0-3	

Name	Address	Phone Number (0131 +)	Contact Details	
St Thomas Church Toddler Group	Gyle Hall 79 Glasgow Road EH12 8LJ	316 4292	Venue	
Gorgie Memorial Hall	Gorgie Road	337 9098	Venue	
Gorgie Salvation Army Toddler Group	431 Gorgie Road EH11 2RT	346 2753	Mrs Barber Children's Development Officer	
Gorgie Tots	Destiny Church 52 Gorgie Road EH11 2NB	555 2707	Destiny Church Leith	
St Bride's Centre Toddler Group	10 Orwell Terrace EH11 2DZ	346 1405	Venue	
East Craigs Mother & Toddler Group	East Craigs Church Centre 2 Bughtlin Market	339 8336	Venue	
Slateford Green Parent and Toddler Group	Slateford Green Community Centre	443 1207	Venue	
Broomhouse Mother and Toddler Group	St David's Church Broomhouse Road	443 1207	Call Slateford Green Community Centre for details	
Craigmount Community Wing	Craigs Road EH12 8DH	339 6823	Venue	
Carrickvale Parent and Toddler Group	Carrickvale Community Education Centre 2 Saughton Mains Street EH11 3HH	443 6971	Venue	
Ratho Community Centre	1 School Wynd Ratho EH28 8TT	333 1055	Venue	

Day(s)	Time	Drop in?	Cost	Rota	Age Group	Other Information
Tu	10.00-11.30	Yes	No	Yes	0-3	
Tu,W, Th,F	9.30-15.00 9.30-12	Yes	£1	No	0-4	
Tu	9.30-11.30	Yes	£1	Yes	0-4	
Th	10.30-12.00	Yes	Donation	No	0-3	
Fri	9.30-11.30	Yes	No	No	0-4	
Tu,Th	10.00-11.30	Yes	Yes	No	0-3	
W	9.30 - 11.30	Yes	Donation	No	0-4	
					0-3	
W,Th, F	9.30-12.00	Yes	£1.	No	0-4	
M,Tu, Th,F	9.30 - 11.30	Yes	Donation	No	0-4	
Tu,Th	10.00 - 12.00	Yes	50p members £1 others	No	0-4	

Name	Address	Phone Number (0131 +)	Contact Details	
Westfield Court Nursery School Parent and Child Club	Westfield Court Nursery School Alexander Drive EH11 2RJ	337 4914	Venue	
St Nicholas Toddler Group	St Nicholas Church 12 Calder Gardens EH11 4JD			
Kirkliston Project Parent and Toddler Group	Kirkliston Community Centre 16-18 Queensferry Road EH29 9AQ	331 3574	Community Centre Office	
South Queensferry Under Fives Mother and Toddler Group	South Queensferry Community Centre Kirkliston Road South Queensferry	331 3574	Community Centre Office	
South Queensferry Under Fives Childminders' Group	South Queensferry Community Centre Kirkliston Road South Queensferry	331 2113	Community Centre Office	

Any information missing or incorrect?
Tell Ed.

Contact Ed via our website
www.efuf.co.uk

or send an email
info@efuf.co.uk

Day(s)	Time	Drop in?	Cost	Rota	Age Group	Other Information
W		Yes	No	Yes	0-5	Telephone for details of times.
Tu, W, F	9.30-11.30	Yes	Small charge	Yes	0-3	
M,W	9.00-11.30	Yes	Donation	No	0-4	
		Yes	Donation	Yes	0-4	
M, W	9.00-11.30	Yes	Donation	No	0-4	
Th	9.30-11.30	Yes	Yes	No	0-4	

Playgroups

We have compiled as comprehensive a list of playgroups as possible. A listing below is not a recommendation by Edinburgh for Under Fives – we encourage you to make contact and see if the group fits your child's needs. All the details were correct at time of checking. However, details do change, so please let us know if you come across any information that needs updated for the next edition. And if you come across any playgroups that aren't listed below, please let us know - we haven't left any out intentionally!

Name	Address	Phone Number (0131 +)	Email/ website	
Playgroups - Central				
Nari Kallyan Shangho Project	Darroch Annexe 7 Gillespie Street EH3 9NH	221 1915	nks@nkshealth.co.uk www.nkshealth.co.uk	
Edzell Nursery Ltd	St. James Scottish Episcopal Church 57b Inverleith Row EH3 5PX	551 2179	sarah.sutherland@ blueyonder.co.uk	
Playgroups - North				
Cramond Playgroup	Cramond Kirk Hall Cramond Glebe Road EH4 6NS	07913 819 085	cramond.playgroup@ hotmail.co.uk	
Blackhall Playgroup	St Columba's Parish Church Columba Road Blackhall EH4 3QU	332 4431	www.blackhallstcolumba. org.uk	
Reindeer Playgroup	Holy Cross Church Hall Quality Street EH4 5BP	07906 518 747		
Parkgrove Playgroup	Munro Centre Parkgrove Place Clermiston EH4 7NR	539 7179		

Visit our website for updates:
www.efuf.co.uk

Contact Name	Day(s)	Time	Cost	Age Group	Other Information?
	M-F	9-11:45 12:15-15:00	£3/session or £6/day	2-5	
Sarah Sutherland	M-F Part time; Term times	9-11:50	£158/term; £93/term part time	2 1/2-5 1/2	
Louise Stevens	M-F	9:05-11:55	£8/session £3/month snack	2-5	Application forms available from playgroup from 18 months.
	M,W,Th Tu	9:30-12.00 12.00-14:30		2 1/2-5	
Ruth McKenzie	Tu-Fr	9:15-11:45	£6/morning + 15p for snack	2 1/2-5	
Mrs O'Flaherty	M,W,Fr	9:15-11:30	£3.50/day	2 1/2-5	

Name	Address	Phone Number (0131 +)	Email/ website	
Prentice Centre Playgroup	The Prentice Centre 1 Granton Mains Avenue EH4 4GA	552 0485	prenticecentre@hotmail.com	
Blackhall Nursery	Ravelston Park Pavilion Craigcrook Road EH4 3RU	332 8296	www.blackhallnursery.com blackhallnursery@fsnet.co.uk	
Edinburgh Pre Nursery Services Funtime Playgroup	Royston/Wardieburn Community Centre Pilton Drive North EH5 1NF	552 5700	elma@blueyonder.co.uk	
Wardie Nursery	Wardie Residents Club 125 Granton Road EH5 3NJ	07969 099 340		
Trinity Nursery	Wardie Church Primrose Bank Road EH5 3JE	551 3847		
Leith St Andrew's Playgroup	Leith St. Andrews Church 410 Easter Road EH6 8HT	07792 493 359		
Craigentinny/Lochend Playgroup	Craigentinny Community Centre 15 Loaning Road EH7 6JE	661 8188	Wendy.spencer@sppa.org.uk	
St Mary's Playgroup	St. Mary's RC Primary School 63 East London Street EH7 4BW	556 1634	stmarysplaygroup@aol.com	
Tom Thumb Nursery	Vennel Church Hall Smithsland South Queensferry EH30 9HU	331 4273 07713 154 144		

Contact Name	Day(s)	Time	Cost	Age Group	Other Information?
Mary Rae	M-Th All year	9:30-11:30; 12:30-2:30	£1/session	2-5	
	M-F	8:55-11:30 12:15-14:45	Funded places	3-5	
	M-F term times	9:15-11:45	£8/wk	2 1/2-5	
Joyce Gladstone	M-F	9:00-11:35	Funded places + minimal top up fee	3-5	Parent run.
Pam Johnston	M-F	9:00-12:00	£12/morning	2 1/2-5	Partner provider.
Christine Anderson	M-F	9:15-11:45	£5/morning snack included	2-5	Minimum 2 days/week.
	M-F	9:15-11:30		2 1/2-5	
Mrs Gail Dempster	M-F	9:00-12:00	£5/morning	2 1/2-5	Yoga Tuesday £1 extra.
Debbie Urquhart	M-F M-Th	9:00-11:30 12:15-14:45	£4.40/session	2-5	

PRE-SCHOOL - PLAYGROUPS

Name	Address	Phone Number (0131 +)	Email/ website	
Playgroups - East				
Northfield/Willowbrae Nursery Playgroup	Northfield & Willowbrae Community Centre 10 Northfield Road EH8 7PP	661 5723	jill.om@btinternet.com	
Portobello Toddlers Hut Playgroup	The Toddlers Hut 28 Beach Lane Portobello EH15 1HU	669 6849		
St James' Playgroup	St James' Church Hall Rosefield Place EH15 1AD	07722 107 065		
EPNS - Gilmerton Project Playgroup	Gilmerton Community Centre 4 Drum Street EH17 8QG	664 2235	elma@blueyonder.co.uk	
Playgroups - South				
Marchmont Playgroup	Marchmont St. Giles' Parish Church 1a Kilgraston Road EH9 2DW	447 4359 ext.24	marchmontplaygroup@hotmail.co.uk www.marchmontstgiles.org.uk	
Duncan Street Pre-School Playgroup	Baptist Church Hall 13 Duncan Street EH9 1SR	667 8097 (pm only)	duncanstreetplaygroup@googlemail.com	
Mayfield/Salisbury Playgroup	Mayfield Salisbury Parish Church Hall 18 West Mayfield EH9 1TQ	07753 163 168		

Contact Name	Day(s)	Time	Cost	Age Group	Other Information?
Jill O'Malley	M-F term times	9:15-11:45	Funded places for over 3s; Under 3s £25/week plus £2/week snack	2 1/2-5	
	M-F Tu-Th	9:00-11:30 13:00-15:30	£5/session	2 1/2-5	Can go on waiting list from 2 yrs.
Jane Peden	M,Tu,Th,F term times	9:00-12:10	£5/morning or £20/week	2 1/2-5	Cost may increase in 2010.
	M-F term times	9:00-11:30	£17/week	2 1/2-5	
	T, W, Th	9:30-12:00 term times	£18/week	2yr3m-4	Community based playgroup Can put name on waiting list from birth.
Lorraine Adam	M-F part time; term times	9:00-11:45	Contact venue	2 1/2-5	
Freda Mitchell	M-F	9:10-11:40	£6/session Discount for 4+ sessions	2-5	

Name	Address	Phone Number (0131 +)	Email/ website	
Holy Corner Community Playgroup	Christ Church Hall 6a Morningside Road EH10 4DD	228 2768	playgroup@holycorner.plus.com	
Greenbank Preschool	Greenbank Church Braidburn Terrace EH10 6ES	447 8068	www.greenbankpreschool.org	
Nile Grove Community Playgroup	Morningside Parish Church 1 Nile Grove EH10 4RE	447 9430 07871 538 210		
St Fillan's Playgroup	St. Fillans Church 8 Buckstone Drive EH10 6PD	07790 067 927	stfillansplaygroup@hotmail.com	
Bruntsfield Community Nursery	Bruntsfield Primary School 12 Montpelier EH10 4NA	228 1526		

Playgroups - West

Name	Address	Phone Number (0131 +)	Email/ website	
EPNS - The Patch Baby Room/Creche	The Patch Creche 5 Calder Park EH11 4NF	476 2279 07804 323 064	elma@blueyonder.co.uk	
Edinburgh Pre Nursery Services The Patch Playgroup	Sighthill Primary School 5 Calder Park EH11 4NF	476 2279 07804 323 064	elma@blueyonder.co.uk	
Balgreen Playgroup	Balgreen Bowling Club 167 Pansy Walk Balgreen Road EH11 3AT	313 5097 07972 352 591		
Broomhall Playgroup	81 Broomhall Avenue EH12 7NW	07749 765 104		

Contact Name	Day(s)	Time	Cost	Age Group	Other Information?
Alison Kirkwood	M-F term times	9:10-11:45	£6/session	2 1/2-5	Partner provider.
	M-F	9:00-11:35 12:35-15:10	Funded places – contact venue	3-5	
Elaina Johnsosn	M-F term times	9:15-11:45	£7/session	2yr3m -5	
Mary Wong	M-Th	9:15-11:45	£7.50/ session	2-5	Can put name on waiting list at one year.
Fiona Anderson	M-Th F	9:00-11:45 9:00-11:30	Funded places – contact venue	3-5	
	M-F M-Th	9:00-11:45 12:30-14:45	£3/session	4mths -2	
	M-Th F term times	9:30-12:00 12:30-15:00 9:30-11:45	£10/week	2-5	
Debbie Akroyd Taylor	M-F	9:15-11:45	£20/week	2-5	Do not have to be toilet trained.

Name	Address	Phone Number (0131 +)	Email/ website	
Harrison Playgroup	Phoenix Youth Club 1 Harrison Place EH11 1SQ	07769 686 129	info@harrisonplaygroup. co.uk www.harrisonplaygroup. co.uk	
Corstorphine Village Playgroup	2 A (Old Parish Church High Street Halls) Corstorphine High Street EH12 7ST	07707 695 426	www. corstorphinevillageplaygroup. co.uk	
Gylemuir Community Playgroup	Children's Centre 10 Wester Broom Place EH12 7RT	07704 140 071	Mcmillan9371@hotmail.com	
Craigsbank Church Playgroup (A)	Craigs Bank Church Craigs Bank EH12 8HD	334 6365		
Craigsbank Church Playgroup (B)	East Craigs Church Centre Bughtlin Market EH12 8XP	334 6365		
Fox Covert Nursery	Fox Covert Primary School Clerwood Terrace EH12 8PG	467 7294	fcnursery@hotmail.co.uk www.foxcovertnursery.ik.org	
Forrestine's Playgroup	St. Augustines High School 208 Broomhouse Road EH12 9AD	07914 076 782		
Dreghorn Pre-School Playgroup	25/27 Dreghorn Gardens EH13 9NW	441 5974		

Contact Name	Day(s)	Time	Cost	Age Group	Other Information?
Tor Bretherton	M-F	9:15-11:30	£5/session part time; £4.50/ session full-time	2-5	Do not have to be toilet trained.
Mrs Jean Howe	M-F term times	9:15-11:45	£5.75/ session payable per term	2 1/2-5	Can put on waiting list from one year.
Susan McMillan	M-F term times	9:00-11:45 11:45-12:30 (lunch club)	£5/morning £5/day (lunch club)	2-5	Do not need to be toilet trained.
Liz Walls	Tu,W,Th, F	9:15-11:45	£5/session	2yr3m -4	
Karen Ross	Tu,W,Th, F	9:15-11:45	£5/session	2yr3m -4	
	M-F term times	9:00-11:30	Funded places	3-5	For children planning to attend Fox Covert School.
Sandra Davidson	M-F	9:15-11:45	£4/session	2-5	Moving to a new venue in 2010 – contact mobile number for current information.
Helen Mullen	M-F	9:15-11:45	£10/session – 9 months-2yrs £8.50/ session – 2yr and older	6mths -5	

Name	Address	Phone Number (0131 +)	Email/ website	
Colinton Mains Playgroup	Colinton Mains Community Centre 1 Firhill Loan EH13 9EJ	441 6597		
Stableroom Playgroup	Colinton Parish Church Dell Road EH13 0JR	477 9494	stableroom@hotmail.co.uk	
Riccarton Playgroup	59a Curriehill Road EH14 5PU	07814 568 635 (am only)		
The Village Playgroup	7-11 Main Street Balerno EH14 7EQ	451 5756		
Juniper Green Nursery Playgroup	Juniper Green Village Hall 1 Juniper Park Road Juniper Green EH14 5DX	453 4427 07948 554 889	junipergreenplaygroup@ hotmail.com www.junipergreenplaygroup. vpweb.co.uk	
Currie Playgroup	Baptist Church Hall 16 Kirkgate EH14 6AN	449 2016		
Compass Playgroup	Deanpark Primary Preschool Centre 1 Main Street Balerno EH14 7EQ	449 4529		
Cranley Nursery	Paties Road Pavilion Katesmill Road EH14 1JF	441 3804	lorna@cranleynursery.co.uk	

Contact Name	Day(s)	Time	Cost	Age Group	Other Information?
Kerena Mitchell	M,W,F	9:15-11:45	£6/session	2 1/2-5	Partner provider.
Janice Rew	M-F	9:00-12:30	£5.50/ session £2.50 lunch club/ £4 wrap around service	2-5	New facility beside school.
Alice Anderson	M-Th Fr	8:00-12:00 13:00-16:00 8:00-13:00	£10/session	2-5	
Julie Valentine	M-F	9:15-12:00	£6/session	2-4	
Amanda Gillespie	M-F	9:00-11:45	Contact venue	2-5	Lunch club and wrap around service with Currie School Nursery at additional charge.
Lindsay Costello	M-Th	9:00-11:45 11:45-12:30 (lunch club)	£4.75/ session	2-5	Lunch club and nursery transfer at additional charge. Duty rota.
Lorna Smith					

Name	Address	Phone Number (0131 +)	Email/ website	
Littleflyers Playgroup	Thomas Chalmers Church Centre The Square Kirkliston EH29	333 4088 01506 854 066		
Kirkliston Playgroup	The Pavilion Allison Park Carmel Road Kirkliston EH29 9DD	07952 284 532		

Accessible Pre-school

Parents with disabled children can experience difficulties trying to find appropriate and affordable childcare for their child. If you are experiencing problems finding childcare for your child remember that you are not alone and it is not impossible!

The current situation is that many childminders may not feel they are in a position to accommodate a child with additional needs as they may have to limit their numbers if they do so, or they may feel they do not have the appropriate training. It is also unusual for additional support to be available for children with special needs in private nursery settings. There are, of course, childminders and nurseries who are willing and able to accommodate children with additional needs – so how do you go about finding them?

Edinburgh Childcare Information Service
0800 032 0323
www.childcarelink.gov.uk
Provide information on childminders, nurseries and play-schemes that accommodate children with special needs. However, details are limited and no information is given on the kind of special needs the childcare provider can accommodate or on the special needs training and experience of the staff. While some of the providers indicate that they can accommodate special needs, they may also indicate that their premises are not wheelchair accessible.

The Edinburgh Childcare Partnership
0131 270 6061 or 6064
www.edinburghchildcare.co.uk
Have an Inclusion Officer who deals with funding applications from providers seeking to provide care for children with additional support needs. Funds may be available to enable mainstream childcare providers to cover the extra costs of looking after a disabled child. Don't assume that the childcare provider you're interested in is aware of these funds!

If your child attends a local authority nursery school, it may be that they are provided with additional support to enable their inclusion. The support may be for a few hours a week or for all of the time they attend, depending on their needs. You should put your child's name down for your chosen nursery school as soon as you can.

Other options include Child and Family Centres which offer support to vulnerable and disadvantaged families with children under five. Support may be offered within the centre or the family home. Centres also offer a range of services, for example mother and toddler groups and community groups. Children with disabilities can attend the Centres, supported by community occupational therapists and physiotherapists, and have access to a range of medical and social work services. Ask your social worker (if you have one, or the duty children and families social worker) for further information.

Contact Name	Day(s)	Time	Cost	Age Group	Other Information?
Michelle Stevens	W,Th,F	9:15-11:45	£7.75/ session or £19.38 for 3 sessions	2-5	
Janet Dall	Tu,Th,F	9:30-11:30	£4.50	2-3	

The Barrie Nursery
Canaan Lane
0131 446 3120
Partnership nursery based at the Canaan Lane Campus of the Royal Blind School. This is a purpose built educational and residential facility for children and young adults with multiple disabilities in addition to their visual impairments.
Offers: small group and individual teaching; high staff ratio; elaborated and adapted 3-5 curriculum; therapists as an integral part of teaching team; access to specialist teaching for all pupils in mobility, music therapy and physical education; adapted and accessible outdoor play area. Also offers early education to children aged two years eleven months to four years. The Early Years Play Group meets weekly and includes a toy library, access to hydrotherapy pool and the services of a parent counsellor.

The Westerlea Early Education Centre
Ellersly Road
Murryfield
0131 337 9467
www.capability-scotland.org.uk
An early learning support service for children with additional needs. It is open to anyone who feels their child will benefit from any of the services on offer. Services include group and individual work on play, movement, communication and sensory development, massage, hydrotherapy and music therapy (for music therapy see below).

Westerlea offers centre based work and outreach, as well as a playscheme. They cater for children from birth to three years. For more information, see contact details above.

Bright Sparks
01875 823699
Weekly Midlothian special needs playgroup at Brown Buildings in Gorebridge. Everyone is welcome. Activities include a soft play area and music therapy. Transport can be provided.

Spectrum
St Giles Centre
Broomhouse Crescent
EH11 3UB
0131 443 0304
Offers teaching programmes for pre-school children with autism and helps families to use them with their child. Support can be either at home, a children's centre or nursery depending on the child's and the family's needs.

Edinburgh Visiting Teaching and Support Service
154 McDonald Road
EH7 4NN
0131 469 2850
This specialised early intervention and support service may be able to offer a home visiting teacher for your child, to work on a one-to-one basis with them to support them in pre-school learning.

Nursery Choice

Things to Consider

When choosing a nursery, it is sometimes hard to know where to start! If possible, get recommendations from other parents. Your child is likely to be spending a good deal of time at nursery, and it may be the first time you have left her/him with another carer, so it is important that you feel confident in the care s/he is receiving. Visit several alternatives, ideally with your child, so that you can get an idea how s/he feels about them too. Make a list of questions you would like to ask. Then, in order to get a realistic picture of a nursery, drop in unannounced on more than one occasion at different times of the day. Ultimately, the choice is a personal one, and depends on your individual family needs. However, we have provided some points you may find it helpful to consider when making your decision.

Starting Out – What kind of nursery place?

- Do you require a private nursery or a nursery class in an independent school? If so, it is best to enquire as soon as possible, as waiting lists can be long.
- Do you require a nursery place in a Council nursery when your child turns three? If so, make sure you submit a nursery application form around the time your child turns two. (Remember, there are no catchment area restrictions for Council-run nurseries, so you can send your child to any nursery in the city if a place is available).
- Does your workplace offer nursery care? If so, is there a waiting list?
- Does your college or university offer nursery care? If so, is the care year-round or term-time only?
- Does your child require additional support? If so, you should discuss your needs with the head teacher or staff centre manager to make sure these needs can be met.

Activities

- How is the day structured? Ask to see the daily planner. This should give you an idea of the activities and experiences offered to the children.
- Are the children happily occupied during your visit?
- Do you feel the atmosphere is chaotic or calm and what do you think will best suit your child?
- What activities are available during free play periods?
- Do children have access to a TV, or is a radio on during your visit – and how do you feel about this?
- Are outside trips/visits/activities/classes provided? Is there an additional charge for these? How are they supervised?
- How much outside time is provided during the day, and when/where does this take place?
- Are there specific activities you would like your child to take part in and are these available?

Facilities

- Does the nursery seem friendly, inviting, and light?
- Is it brightly decorated with children's artwork?
- Is there room for a variety of activities?
- Where are naps taken, and what sleeping facilities are provided?
- Is there a garden or safe outdoor play area? How often do the children go outside?
- Do you feel confident about the security measures in place?
- Are there different activity areas for children of different ages? Does this arrangement benefit your child?

Feedback and Communication

- What sort of report do parents receive at the end of the day (nappies, sleeps, meals, activities) and is this verbal or written?
- Is your child assigned a key worker with whom you can discuss daily matters and general progress?
- What opportunities do parents have to discuss their child's needs and other matters with the nursery staff and management?

Staff and Education

- Who is in charge of the nursery, and are they available during your visit?
- What qualifications are held by staff?
- Are staff/child ratios being complied with?
- What is the staff turnover like?
- How do staff members manage challenging behaviour?
- Does the nursery follow the "Curriculum for Excellence" ?
- What does the HMIE report say about the nursery?
- What does the Care Commission report say about the nursery?

Financial Considerations

- Does the weekly charge include meals, milk, nappies, wipes, etc.?
- Are any free settling-in sessions provided?
- Are there any discounts available for students, families on low incomes, companies and siblings? Remember, if you spend money on childcare while you work and you qualify for the Working Tax Credit, you might be entitled to financial help with childcare costs (see 'Information & Support' section).
- Does the nursery accept childcare vouchers?
- If it is a private nursery and your child will still be attending at age three – is the nursery a Partner Provider?
- How are nursery fees collected?
- If your child attends on a part-time basis, are you able to purchase "extra sessions" if necessary?

Practicalities

- Is there a waiting list and, if so, how long is it?
- Does the nursery welcome expressed milk?
- Are meals and/or snacks provided? If so, ask to see a week's menu to make sure you are happy with the range of food on offer.
- What are the food preparation facilities like?
- What provision is made for vegetarian children or those with allergies etc?
- Are real nappies accepted?
- For part-time places, is there a minimum number of sessions your child has to attend?
- What sort of settling-in process does the nursery adopt, and is this sufficient for your child?
- Does the fee for part-time sessions include snacks and meals?

Timetable

- Do opening times fit in with your schedule? Remember, at private nurseries you are paying for the service, and shouldn't have to drop-off at precise opening times if it doesn't suit your schedule.
- Are pickup times flexible?
- Is there an after school club for older children?
- Is there parking available at busy times?

This is not an exhaustive list of questions, but we hope we have given you a good starting point. As a final consideration, don't ignore your instinct when choosing a nursery – chances are that if you get a "good feeling" from your visit at a nursery, your child will too. Good luck!

Council-run Nurseries and Centres

Instead of listing all of these here, we direct you to the excellent booklet produced by the City of Edinburgh Council, "Pre-school Education in Edinburgh." This lists addresses and contact phone numbers for nurseries, nursery classes in primary schools, nursery classes in special schools, child and family centres, and early years centres. There is also a list of Partner Provider centres.

The booklet is available in some nurseries, by calling 0131 529 2412, or by downloading it from the City of Edinburgh Council website:
www.edinburgh.gov.uk/internet/learning/CEC_pre_school_and_childcare

Private Day Nurseries

We have compiled as comprehensive a list of nurseries as possible from a variety of sources. A listing below is not a recommendation by Edinburgh for Under Fives – we encourage you to make contact and see if the nursery fits the needs of you and your child (please refer to the previous section, "Nursery Choice"). All the details were correct at time of checking. However, details do change, so please let us know if you come across any information that needs updated for the next edition. And if you come across any nurseries that aren't listed below, please let us know - we haven't left any out intentionally!

When you join us at The Edinburgh Nursery you can be assured by our 22 years experience of providing a child lead learning environment supported by professional and highly skilled childcare practitioners. All our staff are qualified or in training, and registered with the Scottish Social Services Council. Our Nursery Manager has been with the company 17 years.

Our creches based at 13 East London Street and 79a Broughton Street provide a home from home environment where our focus is on encouraging your child to become confident and form strong bonds with their carers. We aim to take the children outdoors all through the year to use our Gardens and enjoy story telling and snacks outside. We provide a hot nutritionally balanced meal at lunchtime, breakfast and a Nursery Tea. We support breast feeding mothers and the real nappy initiative.

Contact us: www.edinburghnursery.com
Telephone 0131 557 5675

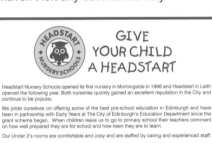

GIVE YOUR CHILD A HEADSTART

Headstart Nursery Schools opened its first nursery in Morningside in 1996 and Headstart in Leith opened the following year. Both nurseries quickly gained an excellent reputation in the City and continue to be popular.

We pride ourselves on offering some of the best pre-school education in Edinburgh and have been in partnership with Early Years at The City of Edinburgh's Education Department since the grant scheme began. When children leave us to go to primary school their teachers comment on how well prepared they are for school and how keen they are to learn.

Our Under 2's rooms are comfortable and cosy and are staffed by caring and experienced staff.

The majority of our staff are fully qualified and the small number of Nursery Assistants we have are in training to gain their full qualification. We staff well above the minimum guidelines and continue to offer a 1 to 5 staff to child ratio (but many of our competitors have increased their ratio to 1 to 8.

Many of our staff have been with Headstart for a long time and a number of parents are returning to us with their third child.

To find out why parents are so pleased with the care and education we provide please contact the nurseries to arrange a visit or visit our website.

Leith	Morningside
0131 555 0700	0131 447 4778
leith@headstartnursery.co.uk	morningside@headstartnursery.co.uk
16 Queen Charlotte Street	64-68 Morningside Drive

www.headstartnursery.co.uk

"We find the quality of care at Headstart excellent. Our daughter really enjoys her time there. The staff are friendly and always welcoming on arrival. There are plenty of interesting activities from a young age and we feel that our daughter has developed wonderfully both socially and creatively."

Mrs F

"As doting parents of our only child, my husband and I were endlessly reassured by the staff when our daughter first began to attend Headstart. They never objected to our phoning to check on her: and they helped her to settle in so quickly that we were soon entirely comfortable with leaving her in their care. We have never worried about her, because she has been very keen to get to Nursery, and has always been happy and content when we have gone to pick her up. Once or twice she has been unwell, and they have contacted us when she was really needed to be taken home: knowing we could trust their judgement on that has been deeply reassuring. They know our little girl very well and really care for her. We are grateful to them for handling this first phase of her care and development so well. We would recommend Headstart with utter confidence to any parent: and wish the Nursery the very best for the future."

Mr & Mrs L

Name	Address	Phone Number (0131 +)	Contact Name	
Nurseries - Central				
Bright Horizons Family Solutions - Rutland Nursery	4a Rutland Square EH1 2AS	229 8888	Tracy Cameron	
Royal Mile Nursery (Bothwell)	Stamp Office Close 215 High Street EH1 1PX	226 6574	Sharon Elliot	
Cowgate Under 5's Centre	7 Old Assembly Close 172 High Street EH1 1QX	225 7251	Lynn McNair	
Edinburgh Nursery Creche 2	71a Broughton Street Edinburgh EH1 3RJ	556 3373	Claire Brown	
Busy Bees Nursery	20 Valleyfield Street EH3 9LR	229 7889	Jessica Van Lieshout	
Rainbow Kindergarten	72 Gilmore Place EH3 9NX	228 1668	Lorraine McConnell	
New Town Nursery Too	4 Forres Street EH3 6BJ	226 5692 07718 912 221	Gary Peattie	
Baby Rainbow Nursery	68 Gilmore Place EH3 9NX	229 8742	Jackie Bell	
Wonder Years Nursery	29 Inverleith Row EH3 5QH	552 5000	Sheila Powis	
Nari Kallyan Shangho Playgroup	Darroch Anexe 7 Gillespie St EH3 9NH	221 1915 07738 202 614		

Anything out of date?
Let us know -
info@efuf.co.uk

E-Mail/Website	Days	Times	Ages
rutland@brighthorizons.com www.brighthorizons.co.uk	M-F	8:00-18:00	3mths-5
www.edinburghdaynurseries.com	M-F	8:00-18:00	3mths-6
www.cowgateunder5s.co.uk	M-F	8:00-17:45	3mths-5
edinnursery@aol.com www.edinburghnursery.com	M-F	8:00-18:00	0-2
info@busybeesnursery.co.uk www.busybeesnursery.co.uk	M-F	8:15-17:45	1 1/2-5
rainbow.kindergarten@tiscali.co.uk www.rainbowkindergarten.com	M-F	8:00-18:00	2-8
ygary@newtownnurseries.com www.newtownnurseries.com	M-F	8:00-17:45	3mths-5
rainbow.kindergarten@tiscali.co.uk www.rainbowkindergarten.com	M-F	8:00-18:00	3mths-2 1/2
wonderyears1@btconnect.com	M-F	8:00-18:00	3mths-5
nks@nkshealth.co.uk www.nkshealth.co.uk	M-F	9:00-15:00	3mths-5

Visit our website for updates:
www.efuf.co.uk

Name	Address	Phone Number (0131 +)	Contact Name	
Doune Terrace Nursery	9c Doune Terrace EH3 6DY	225 3805 07789 937 055	Maureen Crandles	
Careshare at Port Hamilton	69 Morrison Street EH3 8BU	228 1221	Kirsty Grant	
Walker Street Nursery School	17 Walker Street EH3 7NE	220 2699	Laura Crandles	

Nurseries - North

Name	Address	Phone Number	Contact Name	
Orchard Nursery	Royal Victoria Hospital 13 Craigleith Road EH4 2DN	343 6617	Melanie Aspen	
North Edinburgh Childcare Pre-School Provision	North Edinburgh Childcare 18b Ferry Road Avenue EH4 4BL	332 8001	Beverly Malcolm	
Bright Horizons Family Solutions at Cramond Nursery	26 Whitehouse Road EH4 6PH	336 3222	Karen Duguid	
Barnton Nursery	534 Queensferry Road EH4 6EE	339 6340	Audrey Bauldwin	
Arbor Green Nursery	22 Arboretum Avenue EH4 1HP	343 2345	Natalie Clark	
New Town Nursery	12 Dean Terrace EH4 1ND	332 5920 07718 912 221	Yvonne Mclellan	
Chapter One Childcare	5 Douglas Gardens EH4 3DA	220 0707	Diane Pearson	
Leaps and Bounds Nursery Ltd	56a Drum Brae North EH4 8AZ	339 1490	Jacqui Glasgow	

E-Mail/Website	Days	Times	Ages
contact@douneterracenursery.org.uk	M-F	8:00-18:00	0-5
porthamilton@caresharenurseries.com www.caresharenurseries.com	M-F	7:30-18:00	6 wks-5
contact@walkerstreetnursery.org.uk	M-F	8:00-18:00	3-5
edinburgh@orchard-nursery.co.uk www.scottishnurseries.com	M-F	7:00-18:00	3mths-5
www.northedinburghchildcare.co.uk	M-F	8:00-18:00	4mths-12 (after school club)
cramond@brighthorizons.com www.brighthorizons.com	M-F	7:30-18:00	3mths-5
www.edinburghdaynurseries.com	M-F	7:30-18:30	0-5
www.aborgreennursery.com	M-F	7:45-17:45	3mths-5
yvonnemclellan@btconnnect.com	M-F	8:00-17:45	0-5
diane@chapteronechildcare.com www.chapteronechildcare.com	M-F	8:00-18:00	3mths-5
jacquiglasgow@msn.com www.leaps-n-bounds.co.uk	M-F	8:00-18:00	0-5

Name	Address	Phone Number (0131 +)	Contact Name	
Peek-a-Boo Nursery	12 Parkgrove Loan EH4 7QX	339 9161 07775 623 885	Sally-Anne Peek	
Crewe Road Nursery Ltd	122 Crewe Road South EH4 2NY	332 8392 07748 464 035	Lorraine Suggit	
Mr Squirrel's Nursery	27 Cargil Terrace EH5 3NF	552 0499	Bernadette Campbell	
Trinity Tots Nursery	9 Granton Road EH5 3QJ	551 3020	Linda Kane	
Waterfront Nurseries	Edinburgh Telford College 350 West Granton Road EH5 1QE	559 4080	Julie Petit	
Leith Academy Community Nursery	Leith Academy 20 Academy Park EH6 8JQ	554 0606		
Summerside Kindergarten	1 Summerside Street EH6 4NT	554 6560	Carol-Anne McLeod	
Headstart Nursery School - Leith	Headstart Nursery 16 Queen Charlotte Street EH6 6AT	555 0700	Caroline Gilhooley	
Forbes Children's Nursery Claremont Park	12 Claremont Park EH6 7PJ	553 5068 07957 293 494	Theres Durieze	

Anything out of date?
Let us know -
info@efuf.co.uk

E-Mail/Website	Days	Times	Ages
peekabooinfo@virgin.net www.peekaboonursery.net	M-F	8:00-18:00	3mths-5
www.scottishnurseries.com	M-F	8:00-17:45	0-5
BJ.Campbell@btconnect.com www.mr-squirrel.co.uk	M-F	8:15-17:30	3-5.5
TrinitytotsLJK@aol.com	M-F	8:00-17:45	2mths-5yr11m
	M-F	8:00-18:00	3mths-5
cathy.carstairs@leith.edin.sch.uk www.leith.edin.sch.uk	M-F	8:00-17:00	1mth-5
summersidekindergarten@blueyonder.co.uk	M-F	8:00-18:00	3mths-5
leith@headstartnursery.co.uk www.headstartnursery.co.uk	M-F	8:00-18:00	3mths-5
forbescncp@btconnect.com www.forbesnursery.com	M-F	8:00-18:00	3mths-5

Visit our website for updates:
www.efuf.co.uk

Name	Address	Phone Number (0131 +)	Contact Name	
Careshare - Newhaven Nursery	Next Generation Health Club Newhaven Place EH6 4LX	467 4647	Nicola Buchan	
The Rowan Tree Nursery	94 Pilrig Street EH6 5AY	554 3377		
Bright Horizons Family Solutions at Annandale	37 Annandale Street Lane EH7 4LS	557 5567	Cathrine Buchannan	
Heriot Hill Nursery	32/34 Heriothill Terrace EH7 4DY	557 9907	Charlie Wardill	
Edinburgh Nursery	129 Broughton Road EH7 4JH	557 5675	Laura Grieve	
Edinburgh Nursery	3 Beaverhall Road EH7 4JQ	556 9252	Karen Fairlamb	
Edinburgh Nursery Creche 1	13 East London Street EH7 4BN	557 9014	Claire Brown	
Nippers Nursery Ltd	Scotstoun Avenue South Queensferry EH30 9TG	319 1778 07973 102 312		
Nurseries - East				
Elsie Inglis Nursery (Bright Horizins Family Solutions)	1 Waverley Park Spring Gardens EH8 8EW	661 8551	Caroline Thronborrow	
University of Edinburgh	Psychology Department 7 George Square EH8 9JZ	650 3448	Audrey Cameron	
Little V.I.P's	2 Windsor Place EH15 2AA	669 5040	Diane Brown	

E-Mail/Website	Days	Times	Ages
Newhaven@caresharenurseries.com www.caresharenurseries.com	M-F	7:30-18:00	0-5
	M-F	8:00-18:00	3mths-5
annandale@brighthorizons.com www.brighthorizons.co.uk	M-F	8:00-18:00	3mths-5
liz@heriothillnursery.com www.heriothillnursery.com	M-F	8:00-18:00	0-5
edinnursery@aol.com www.edinburghnursery.com	M-F	8:00-18:00	3-5
edinnursery@aol.com www.edinburghnursery.com	M-F	8:00-18:00	1 1/2-3
edinnursery@aol.com www.edinburghnursery.com	M-F	8:00-18:00	0-2
nippers.nursery@btinternet.com www.nippersnursery.com	M-F	7:30-17:30	3mths-5
elsies@brighthorizons.com www.brighthorizons.co.uk	M-F	8:00-18:00	3mths-5
a.cameron@ed.ac.uk www.unitots.psy.ed.ac.uk	M-F	8:30-17:00 term times	2 1/2-5
littlevips@btconnect.com www.little-vips.com	M-F	8:00-18:00	3mths-5yr11m

Name	Address	Phone Number (0131 +)	Contact Name	
Brighton Nursery	9C Bellfield Lane EH15 2BL	308 8589 07903 890 131	Jenny Allison	
Rocking Horse Nursery	60a Duddingston Road EH15 1SG	669 0819	Linda Smith	
Highland Fling Nursery	11 Brighton Crescent East EH15 1LR	468 3456 07870 666 424	Patricia Chisholm	
Cherrytrees Nursery	1c Duddingston Park EH15 1JN	669 0405	Frances Kay	
Seabeach Day Nursery	27 Straiton Place EH15 2BA	657 3249	Lucille Watt	
Blossom Day Nursery	15 B/C Bath Street EH15 1EZ	657 2233	Joan Simeleyson	
Little Monkeys Nursery	28 Kilmaurs Road EH16 5DP	667 5544	Valerie Broomfield	
The Owl and the Pussycat Children's Nursery	1 Claverhouse Drive EH16 6BR	664 1345	Kelly Parket	
Mother Goose Nursery 3	50 Howden Hall Road EH16 6PJ	620 4380	Laura Mcaulay	
Chapter One Childcare	50 Kirk Brae EH16 6HT	664 3031	Lauren Gloydek	
Acorns Nursery - Careshare	Edinburgh Royal Infirmary 51 Little France Crescent EH16 4SA	664 7621	Joanne Lamb	

Anything out of date?
Let us know -
info@efuf.co.uk

E-Mail/Website	Days	Times	Ages
brightonnursery@btconnect.com	M-F	8:00-18:00	6mths-5
rockinghorse60a@btconnect.com www.rockinghorse-nursery.co.uk	M-F	7:45-18:00	3mths-8
pat@highlandflingfreedom.com www.scottishnurseries.com	M-F	8:00-18:00	2-11
cherrytrees.littleacrorns@virgin.net	M-F	8:00-17:30	3mths-5
seabeachnursery@btconnect.com	M-F	8:00-16:00	3mths-5
admin@blossomdaynursery.co.uk www.blossomdaynursery.co.uk	M-F	8:00-18:00	2-8
kilmaurs@littlemonkeysnursery.com www.littlemonkeysnursery.com	M-F	7:00-19:00	3mths-5
owlandpussycatuk@aol.com www.owlandpussycat.net	M-F	8:00-18:00	6mths-5
mothergoose3@live.co.uk	M-F	8:00-18:00	3mths-5
info@chapteronechildcare.com www.chapteronechildcare.com	M-F	8:00-18:00	0-5
acorns@caresharenurseries.com www.caresharenurseries.com	M-F	7:30-18:00	6 wks-5

Visit our website for updates:
www.efuf.co.uk

Name	Address	Phone Number (0131 +)	Contact Name	
Playdays Kindergarten	17 East Suffolk Road EH16 5PH	662 0010 07919 442 786	Ali Mohamed	
The Edinburgh Montessori Nursery	98 Lasswade Road EH16 6SU	664 3434 07791 417 201	Rachael Holt	
Priestfield House Nursery	Prestonfield 89 Priestfield Road EH16 5JD	620 2379		
The University of Edinburgh Day Nursery	79-81 Dalkeith Road EH16 5AL	667 9584	Rhona R Connell	
Kidzcare@Haystax	Hay Avenue EH16 4AQ	657 0590	Sue Kirditson	
Mother Goose Nursery	6 Ferniehill Road EH17 7AB	664 3276		
Chapter One Childcare	1b Drum Street EH17 8QQ	664 5376	Elizabeth Coyle	

Nurseries - South

Name	Address	Phone Number (0131 +)	Contact Name	
Kidzcare@Norwood House	Norwood House 9 Kilgraston Road EH9 2DX	668 2797	Magda Widera	
Grange Private Nursery	180 Grange Loan EH9 2EE	667 9547	Stacey Gilchrist	
Meadows Nursery	5 Millerfield Place EH9 1LW	667 5316 07913 061 023	Karen Johnston	
Stepping Stones Nursery	21a Millerfield Place EH9 1LW	668 4249		
Strawberry Hill	13 Minto Street EH9 1RG	668 3300 07888 696 264	Farina Tavasolian	

E-Mail/Website	Days	Times	Ages
iplaydays@aol.com www.playdayskindergarten.co.uk	M-F	8:00-18:00 (Fridays until 17:30)	3mths-5
info@edinburghmontessorinursery.co.uk	M-F	8:00-18:00	3mths-5
www.priestfield.scottishnurseries.co.uk	M-F	8:00-18:00	3mths-5yr11m
day.nursery@ed.ac.uk www.nursery.ed.ac.uk	M-F	8:30-17:30	6 wks-5
haystaxnursery@btconnect.com www.kidzcare.org	M-F	8:00-18:00	3mths-3
www.scottishnurseries.com	M-F	8:00-18:00	0-14
info@chapteronechildcare.com www.chapteronechildcare.com	M-F	8:00-18:00	0-5
www.kidzcare.org www.astleygrangenurseries.co.uk	M-F	8:00-18:00	3mths-5
info@colinton.org.uk www.colinton.org.uk	M-F	8:00-18:00	3mths-5
info@meadows-nursery.co.uk www.meadows-nursery.co.uk	M-F	8:00-18:00	3mths-6
jnt_burns@yahoo.co.uk www.steppingstones-nursery.com	M-F	7:00-18:00	0-5
strawberryhillnursery@yahoo.co.uk www.strawberryhillnursery.co.uk	M-F	7:45-18:00	3mths-5

PRE-SCHOOL - NURSERIES

Name	Address	Phone Number (0131 +)	Contact Name	
Royal Hospital for Sick Children Day Nursery	11 Millerfield Place EH9 1LW	536 0683	Rosie Allanson	
Kidzcare Tweenie Nursery	133 Grange Loan EH9 2HB	668 2797	Hannah Kay	
Headstart Nursery School Morningside	64-68 Morningside Drive EH10 5NU	447 4778	Susan Cleghorn	
Morningside Montessori Nursery	3 Greenhill Park EH10 4DW	446 0777 07834 163 446	Emma Wardell	
Florence House	46 Bruntsfield Place EH10 4HQ	229 1970	Mrs Nancie Kelly	
Fairmile Kindergarten	2a Oxgangs Road EH10 7AU	445 1566	Christina Ritchie	
Cranley Buckstone Nursery	226 Braid Road EH10 6NZ	445 2227	Vikki Connolly	
The City Nursery	47 Greenbank Drive EH10 5SA	446 0088	Tony Houghton or Sam Collie	
Childsplay Nursery	8 Falcon Road EH10 4AH	447 0077	Kimberley Morris	
Bright Horizons Family Solutions at Bruntsfield Nursery	7 Blantyre Terrace EH10 5AD	447 9797	Sheana Taylor	
Bright Horizons Family Solutions at Morton Mains Farmhouse Nursery	37 Winton Loan EH10 7AW	445 4450	Sarah Woods	

Anything out of date?
Let us know -
info@efuf.co.uk

E-Mail/Website	Days	Times	Ages
rosie.allanson@luht.scot.nhs.uk	M-F	7:30-18:00	3mths-5
info@kidzcare.org www.kidzcare.org	M-F	8:00-18:00	3mths-5
morningside@headstartnursery.co.uk www.headstartnursery.co.uk	M-F	8:00-18:00	9mths-5
enquiries@morningsidemontessori.co.uk www.morningsidemontessori.co.uk	M-F	9:00-12:00 & 13:00-16:00 term times only	2-5
florencehouse46@hotmail.com	M-F	8:00-18:00	3mths-5
ritchie.res@virgin.net www.fairmilekindergarten.com	M-F	8:00-18:00	3mths-5
vikki@cranleynursery.co.uk www.cranleynursery.co.uk	M-F	8:00-18:00	3mths-5
citynursery@yahoo.co.uk www.city-nursery.co.uk	M-F	7:30-18:00	2-5
childsplaynursery@btconnect.com www.childsplaynurseries.com	M-F	8:00-18:00	0-5
bruntsfield@brighthorizons.com www.brighthorizons.com	M-F	8:00-18:00	3mths- 5yr11m
morton@brighthorizons.com www.brighthorizons.co.uk	M-F	7:30-18:00	3mths-5

Visit our website for updates:
www.efuf.co.uk

PRE-SCHOOL - NURSERIES

Name	Address	Phone Number (0131 +)	Contact Name	
Little City Nursery	2a Rattray Drive EH10 5TH	446 0101	Kelly Culbard	
Hermitage Day Nursery (Edinburgh) Ltd	2 Hermitage Terrace EH10 4RP	447 5202	Mary Cumming	
Forbes Children's Nursery	5 Forbes Road EH10 4EF	229 5511 07957 293 494	Theres Durieze	
The Corner House Day Nursery	2 South Gillsland Road EH10 5DE	447 4050	Jacqueline Drinkwater	
The Corner House Day Nursery 2	2 Spylaw Road EH10 5BN	229 1500	Jacqueline Drinkwater	
Haci Ali Avsar	75 Viewforth EH10 4LL	229 8627		
Little Hawthorn Organic Nursery	16 Hawthorn Gardens Loanhead EH20 9EG	440 3057	Natalie Hollerin	

Nurseries - West

Name	Address	Phone Number (0131 +)	Contact Name	
Smilechildcare - Calder Centre	Smilechildcare 17 Calder Grove EH11 4LZ	476 7800	Donna Rodger	
Childcare Scotland Ltd Melville House Nursery	41 Polwarth Terrace EH11 1NL	313 0111	Kay Thompson	
Kath's Kindergartens Too	14 Angle Park Terrace EH11 2JX	337 4157	Andy or Kath Eadie	
Bright Sparks Nursery	58 Saughton Crescent EH12 5SP	313 1280	Anne Oberlander	
The Murrayfield Nursery	52 Saughton Crescent EH12 5SP	346 4459	Maxine Simpson-Smith	

E-Mail/Website	Days	Times	Ages
citynursery@yahoo.co.uk	M-F	7:30-18:00	0-2
marycumming@hotmail.com www.hermitagenursery.co.uk	M-F	7:30-18:00	0-5
forbescnbr@btconnect.com www.forbesnursery.com	M-F	8:00-18:00	3mths-5
	M-F	8:00-18:00	3mths-5
info@cornerhousenursery.co.uk www.cornerhousenursery.co.uk	M-F	8:00-18:00	3mths-5
	M-F	8:00-18:00	3mths-5
littlehawthorn@btinternet.com	M-F	8:00-18:00	0-5
www.smilechildcare.org	M-F	8:00-18:00	2-5
melvillehouse@aol.com www.childcarescotland.co.uk	M-F	8:00-18:00	6mths-5
ae011g4080@blueyonder.co.uk	M-F	8:00-17:30	2-5
info@brightsparks-nursery.com www.brightsparks-nursery.com	M-F	8:00-18:00	0-5
maxinesmith1@btconnect.com	M-F	8:00-18:00	6 wks-5

Name	Address	Phone Number (0131 +)	Contact Name	
Early Days Nursery School	36 Palmerston Place EH12 5BJ	226 4491 07789 937 055	Maureen Crandles	
Wester Coates Nursery School	13 Wester Coates Terrace EH12 5LR	346 7398	Alison Hawkins	
The Montessori Nursery School	Church of the Good Shepherd Hall Murrayfield Avenue EH12 6AU	346 8921	Mrs Park	
Edinburgh Day Nursery and Creche	The David Lloyd Club 89b Glasgow Road EH12 8LH	334 8055	Clare Barr	
Croileagan Nursery	6A Featherhall Avenue EH12 7TQ	334 2960	Catherine Groat	
Edinburgh Park Careshare	1 Lochside Place EH12 9DF	339 1245 07740 838 890	Judith Moncure	
Jigsaw Childcare	40 Turnhouse Road EH12 8LX	339 5557	Joanne Morrice	
The Tower House Montessori Nursery	438 Lanark Road EH13 0NJ	441 2200	Lisa Stuart	
Colinton Private Nursery	22 Dreghorn Loan EH13 0DE	477 7330	Marion Towers	
Colinton Village Nursery	6 Bridge Road EH13 0LF	477 4518	Karen Smtyh	
Lanark Road Nursery	305 Lanark Road EH14 2LL	441 5678	Sheila Anderson	
Cranley Nursery (Colinton)	Paties Road Football Pavilion 66 Katesmill Road EH14 1JF	441 3804	Lorna Smith	

E-Mail/Website	Days	Times	Ages
earlydaysnursery@btconnect.com	M-F	8:00-18:00	6mths-3
	M-F term times	8:50-12:00	
jpark@montessori-edinburgh.org.uk	M-F	9:00-12:30	2 1/2-5
edinburgh@asquithnurseries.co.uk www.asquithnurseries.co.uk	M-F	8:00-18:00	3mths-5
chris@croileagan.com www.croileagan.com	M-F	8:00-17:45	0-5
edinburghpark@caresharenurseries.com www.caresharenurseries.com	M-F	7:30-18:00	0-5
joanne@jigsaw-childcare.com www.jigsaw-childcare.com	M-F	7:30-18:00	3mths-5
towerinfo@btinternet.con www.thetowerhousenursery.co.uk	M-F	7:30-12:30 12:30-17:30 13:00-18:00	0-5
info@colinton.org.uk	M-F	8:00-18:00	3mths-5
info@colinton.org.uk	M-F	8:00-18:00	3mths-5
douglasanderson@blueyonder.co.uk	M-F	8:00-18:00	6 wks-5
lorna@cranleynursery.co.uk www.cranleynursery.co.uk	M-F	8:00-18:00	2-5

Name	Address	Phone Number (0131 +)	Contact Name	
Cranley Nursery Craiglockhart	38 Craiglockhart Avenue EH14 1LT	444 0880	Carron Halleran	
Juniper Green Tots	18 Foulis Crescent EH14 5BN	453 4229 07707 901 561		
Juniper Green Private Nursery	Juniper Green Private Nursery 6-8 Woodhall Drive EH14 5BX	458 3003		
Pinocchio's Childrens Nurseries Ltd	First Gait Heriot Watt University EH14 4AS	451 5236	Claire Moffatt	
Smilechildcare - Hailesland	83/84 Dumbryden Gardens EH14 2NZ	476 7806	Diane Wright	
Little Monkeys Limited	1 Craiglockhart Terrace EH14 1AJ	443 8701	Grace Kerr	
Scallywags Nursery	62 Longstone Road EH14 2BA	443 2002	Rachel Craig	
Currie Children's Nursery	79 Riccarton Mains Road EH14 5NB	07711 302 304	Jane Gilburt	
Jigsaw Nursery	5 Main St Balerno EH14 7EQ	449 4516	Diane Alexander	
Jigsaw Babies	32 Main St Balerno EH14 7EQ	624 4517	Diane Alexander	

Anything out of date?
Let us know -
info@efuf.co.uk

E-Mail/Website	Days	Times	Ages
carron@cranleynursery.co.uk www.cranleynursery.co.uk	M-F	8:00-18:00	6 wks-5
pamelagt@aol.com	M-F	8:00-18:00	6mths-3
www.scottishnurseries.com	M-F	8:00-18:00	2-5
heriot-watt@pinocchiosnursery.co.uk www.pinocchiosnursery.co.uk	M-F	7:30-18:00	3mths-5
mailbox@smilechildcare.org www.smilechildcare.org	M-F	8:00-18:00	0-2
craiglockhart@littlemonkeysnursery.com www.littlemonkeysnursery.com	M-F	7:00-19:00	3mths-5
scallywags2008@hotmail.co.uk www.scallywagsnursery.com	M-F	8:00-18:00	6 wks-5
currienursery@btinternet.com www.currienursery.co.uk	M-F	7:30-18:00	0-5
mairead@jigsaw-nurseries.co.uk	M-F	8:00-18:00	2-5
	M-F	8:00-18:00	0-2

Visit our website for updates:
www.efuf.co.uk

Name	Address	Phone Number (0131 +)	Contact Name	
Little Flyers Nursery	4A Ingliston Road EH28 8AU	335 3679		
Claylands Nursery	Claylands Farm Near Newbridge EH28 8LZ	333 4701 07711 302 304		

E-Mail/Website	Days	Times	Ages
littleflyersnursery@hotmail.co.uk	M-F	8:00-18:00	3mths-5
claylandsnursery@btinternet.com www.claylandsnursery.co.uk	M-F	7:30-18:00	0-5

Independent School Nurseries

The independent schools in Edinburgh with nursery departments are listed below.

Name	Address	Phone Number (0131 +)	E-Mail/Website	
The Edinburgh Academy Nursery	Arboretum Road EH3 5PL	552 3690	enquiriesjs@ edinburghacademy.org.uk www.edinburghacademy.org. uk/nursery	
George Heriot's School Nursery	Lauriston Place EH3 9EQ	229 7263	enquiries@george-heriots.com www.george-heriots.com	
The Mary Erskine and Stewart's Melville Junior School	Queensferry Road EH4 3EZ	311 1111	admissions@esmgc.com www.esms.edin.sch.uk	
Cargilfield School Nursery	Barton Avenue EH4 6HU	336 2207	admin@cargilfield.com www.cargilfield.com	
Loretto Junior School	North Esk Lodge, North High Street, Musselburgh EH21 6JA	653 4570	juniorschool@loretto.com www.loretto.com	
Rudolph Steiner School Kindergarten	60 Spylaw Road EH10 5BR	337 3410	www.steinerweb.org.uk	
George Watson's College Nursery	Colinton Road EH10 5EG	446 6040	info@gwc.org.uk gwc.org.uk	
St George's School for Girls	Garscube Terrace EH12 6BG	311 8000	office@st-georges.edin.sch.uk www.st-georges.edin.sch.uk	
Clifton Hall School Nursery	Newbridge EH28 8LQ	333 1359	office@cliftonhall.org.uk www.cliftonhall.org.uk	
The Compass School Nursery	West Road Haddington EH41 3RD	(01620) 822 642	office@thecompassschool. co.uk www.thecompassschool.co.uk	

All details were correct at time of checking, however, details do change, so please let us know if you come across any information that needs updated for the next edition.

Contact us via the www.efuf.co.uk website or email info@efuf.co.uk.

Contact Name	Days	Times	Ages
Admissions Secretary	M-F term time and holiday clubs	8.30-15.00 (wrap around care available from 8.00-18.00 for 3+)	2-5
Clare Roberston	M-F term Time	8.15-14.00	4-5
Barbara Wood	M-F term time and holiday clubs	8.30-12.30 (wrap around care available from 7.50- 18.00 term time and 8.15- 18.00 during holidays)	3-5
John Elder	M-F term time	8.30-15.00 (wrap around care available from 8.00-18.00)	3-5
Mairi Gillies	M-F term time	9.00-15.00	3-5
Admissions secretary	M-F term time	8.45-12.40	3 1/2-6
Admissions Secretary	M-F	8.45-15.00 (wrap around care available from 8.00-17.45)	3-5
Admissions Secretary	M-F term time	7.45-18.00	2-5
Rod Grant	M-F term time	8.20-15.15 (additional care available till 17.30)	3-5
Mark Becher	M-F term time	8.40-15.00 (additional care available till 18.00)	4-5

Childcare

Childcare

The search for, and selection of, the right type of childcare for you and your family can be not only stressful and time consuming but also a period when you may have to make some compromises and decisions you might not have considered previously. If involving extended/immediate family is not a viable option, choices include taking your child to a childminder, employing someone to come to you, or enrolling your child in a nursery.

Irrespective of the type of childcare you are considering, try to give yourself as much time as possible to check out the options; the more time you have, the less likely you are to feel that you've been unnecessarily pressured into making a decision.
Talk to as many people as you can about their experiences of childcare: their good accounts will reassure you and their 'horror stories' will help you to be aware of what to look out for. Keep an open mind, and above all, have faith in your instinct for what makes sense for both yourself/selves and your child. There are various good solutions and at least one of them will make the most sense for your situation.

If you feel happy and relaxed about your childcare arrangements, then you can use your time away from your child much more effectively. While your child may seem so vulnerable, remember that other adults outside the family can be a very positive part of their life.

For impartial and comprehensive advice on local childcare of all forms, contact:

Edinburgh Childcare Information Service
Waverley Court Level 1.2
4 East Market Street
EH8 8BG
0800 032 0323 (Freephone)
0131 529 2110
childcareinformation@edinburgh.gov.uk
www.scottishchildcare.gov.uk

As part of the Government's National Childcare Strategy, the City of Edinburgh Council runs the Childcare Information Service. The service aims to provide free and impartial information about registered childcare. Parents and carers can contact the Service to find out about the most suitable childcare for their family's needs.

Information is available on all different types of registered childcare – whether provided by the independent, voluntary or statutory sectors, including: childminders; independent nurseries; local nurseries; out of school care; playgroups; crèches and holiday play-schemes. Lists and profiles of childcare provision can also be tailored to meet each family's specific needs, such as services for a particular age group or geographical area. Information is regularly updated.

For information and support about returning to work, your local NCT branch may have a working mothers' group, or you could contact:

Working Families
1-3 Berry Street
London
EC1V 0AA
020 7253 7243
0800 013 0313 (low income families help)
advice@workingfamilies.org.uk
www.workingfamilies.org.uk

Working Families help children, their parents and employers with information about childcare and flexible working including advice on workplace violence, maternity rights and tax credits, as well as benefits, tax credits and childcare for parents of children with disabilities.

If your circumstances are particularly difficult, your local Child and Family Centre may be able to assist, or contact the Children and Families Resource Team:

Children and Families Social Care Direct

Children & Families Resource Team
Level 1 Waverley Court
4 East Market Street
EH8 8BG
0131 316 5070
0131 200 2327
socialcaredirect@edinburgh.gov.uk

The Children and Families Department can help with childcare in the form of Children's Centres, day carers and places at specially approved private nurseries. The service is free but is only available to families who are in need of help for social, financial or health reasons.

For independent local information, you may wish to consider the annual 'Edinburgh Nursery and School Guide' publication.

Mother's Helps

If you do not need someone to take full responsibility for your child/ren on a regular basis, but feel that you need some help in the home with general housework, as well as childcare, a mother's help may fit the bill. Mother's helps do not need any qualifications or experience and you can specify what you want them to do to help you, but remember the emphasis is on the word 'help'.

Au Pairs

Changes in the UK Home Office closed the official immigration category of 'au pair' in November 2008 which means that non-UK nationals who are part of the Youth Mobility Scheme can apply for an au pair placement under the Scheme. To be eligible, you must be aged between 18 and 31 and be a national of one of the following countries: Australia, Canada, Japan and New Zealand. An au pair can stay in the UK for up to two years. They do not need to remain with the same family, but they must ensure that all families they stay with fulfil legal requirements. Citizens from the European Union do not need work permits or to apply under such a scheme to get an au pair placement.

You can review the latest rules on the Home Office/ UK Border Agency website:
www.ukba.homeoffice.gov.uk/ workingintheuk

Border and Immigration Agency
Lunar House
40 Wellesley Road
Croydon
CR9 2BY
0870 606 7766
UKBApublicenquiries@ukba.gsi.gov.uk

Traditionally, au pairs live with an English-speaking host family, and should have the opportunity to study, and in return for board and lodging with a room of their own and a reasonable allowance (about £80- £100wk), they should help in the house for up to 5 hours a day, 5 days a week. So, there should be at least 2 full free days per week (this includes evenings), and the help can include light housework and childcare. There should be 1 week's paid leave for every 6 months worked, if you decide to go on holiday and not to take the au pair with you, they must be paid in your absence, and they are entitled to public holidays as free days without loss of pay.

Anything out of date?
Let us know -
info@efuf.co.uk

You will probably find when you are looking for childcare that many well-meaning acquaintances suggest having an au pair. However you should think very carefully about whether this form of help would suit you. Au pairs are not qualified in childcare and their main reason for being with you is to learn about the language and the country, not to care for your children.

Whilst many au pairs have extremely successful placements, you must remember that you have a responsibility as a host family: many au pairs are desperately unhappy as they are asked to work very long hours, and are treated as a servant rather than as one of the family. Their English may be limited on arrival; they can be very young and inexperienced, not only in domestic matters, but in life in general. You may find yourself having to explain to them the most basic elements of childcare, as well as possibly having to deal with unanticipated issues, such as anti-social behaviour, romantic dramas, homesickness, etc. And remember, an au pair is not a nanny and should be left in sole charge of the children only at the family's discretion.

Many parents find that, although they have help with housework, childcare and babysitting, they have also acquired the equivalent of an extra (teenage) child with all the responsibilities that entails!

Au pairs are not a cheap solution for regular childcare if you have very young children, but they can be perfect as a help around the house or for part-time care for older children. Au pairs can be found through agencies or contacts with the language departments of local schools, colleges and universities. Going through an agency does not guarantee a better au pair, but the advantage is that the good agencies will ensure that they keep you informed of any and all legal requirements in terms of immigration and employment, which may be one hassle you could do without.

The Edinburgh Au Pair Agency
The Walled Garden
Rosewell
EH24 9EQ
0131 440 0800
aupairs@rosewell.co.uk
Long-established, locally-based agency.
Three types of placements are available depending on the amount of hours you would like your au pair to work. There is a small registration fee and a one-off placement fee.

Au Pair Ecosse
6 Park Place
King's Park
Stirling
FK7 9JR
01786 47 45 73
ruth@aupairecosse.com
www.aupairecosse.com

Based in Stirling, this company can provide au pairs to anywhere in Scotland. Au pairs come from throughout the EU as well as Canada and other countries. Placements can be arranged from 3mths to 1yr. One-off placement fees apply. The company can also arrange short term holiday placements, as well as facilitating gap year and year-abroad placements for language students in Scottish schools and universities. They also help UK applicants find placements in other countries.

Babysitters

Some nanny agencies can help you find babysitters, although this is a more expensive option than the traditional options of friends, family or word of mouth. You can, if you wish, employ a neighbouring teenager to babysit but bear in mind that he or she must be over sixteen. Current rates range between £6 - £7.50/hr, more after midnight and if you are out late you should ensure that they get home safely, either by taking them yourself or giving them the taxi fare.

Don't forget to let businesses know you saw them in the EFUF book!

There are online options, but a few words of caution: 'national' often means England and Wales, so check the geographical area the company or organisation covers. Some state that they have screened the babysitters, others do not, so the onus is on the parent/carer to decide whether they are happy with the arrangement. By this point you might be just as lucky posting an ad and interviewing a few candidates yourself so you can have a few people on file. Fees for agencies are better kept for nannies, au pairs and maternity nurses.

Babysitting Circles

These are groups of parents who get together to provide a babysitting circle. To find out about circles in your area ask neighbours, parent and toddler groups, local parents, your Health Visitor, or your local NCT group. All these circles are organised on a purely informal basis and it is up to you to decide if you are happy with the way the circle is run. Many arrange for the parents and the children to meet together at regular intervals so that you can get to know each other better and if the circle is large enough similar families are matched together so that a new mother with one baby, for example, can avoid the happy bedtime chaos of a larger family with toddlers and older children!

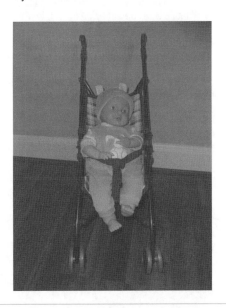

Babysitting Agencies

(see also Nanny Agencies further on in this section)

firsthand
39 Broughton Place
EH1 3RR
0131 557 3121
admin@firsthand.org.uk
www.1sthand.org.uk

firsthand is a voluntary organisation providing services to lone parents, carers, children, and young disabled adults, who live in the city of Edinburgh. Formerly known as Edinburgh Sitters, one of firsthand's services is a Sitter Service for lone parents and carers of disabled children, who do not have regular or reliable means of getting a break. Families are matched with a volunteer or paid sitter who looks after the child(ren) in the family home, for up to 4hrs at a time, on a regular basis. The aim is to give a regular break to lone parents and carers who may not otherwise have one. firsthand offers support to families with children under 3 through Sure Start funding. Eligible parents or carers should contact firsthand to ask for an application form.

Childminders

Childminders care for children in their own homes. They can offer a child a homely, family environment; most will have had first-hand experience with their own children, and may well be involved with the local toddler/play groups and schools, which may be an advantage for your child later on.

Childminders are self-employed and are legally required to register with the Scottish Commission for the Regulation of Care. Registration involves health, police, fire and home safety checks and is reviewed regularly. Registration is not, however, an evaluation of their skills as a childminder – these are for you to assess.

Childminders are approved to care for a maximum of six children up to and including the age of 12yrs, of whom no more than three are under 5yrs and only one is under 1yr; these figures include their own children. You must use a registered childminder: if in doubt ask to see a registration certificate, and check that it is up to date.

CHILDCARE

Finding a Childminder

A list of all registered childminders is available from the:

Childcare Information Service

08000 32 03 23
childcareinformation@edinburgh.gov.uk

There are online lists using the search options at www.scottishchildcare.gov.uk.
Your health visitor may have a list (check it is up to date) and other parents who use a childminder may know of any local vacancies.

How Much Will it Cost?

There is no national rate for childminders, and rates vary according to area, but across Edinburgh the average rate is around £4/hr per child. The SCMA (Scottish Childminding Association) produce a guide highlighting pay and conditions within various areas. Rates for part-time places may carry a premium, and some minders offer a reduced rate for siblings. Childminders are responsible for their own tax and National Insurance payments and also for Public Liability and Accident Insurance cover. You should check that they are either covered by their domestic insurance or that they have a special childminder's insurance policy.
Payment for holidays and sick pay vary: often a childminder will not charge if unavailable due to holidays or illness, but if you do not attend you should pay the normal rate or at least a percentage of it.

Choosing a Childminder

You will need to decide where you want your childminder to be based: someone close to home may mean that your child can make friends locally which will carry on to school, and enforced change in the long term is less likely to be necessary if your childminder is willing to continue caring for your child once he or she has started school. It is also more convenient to have someone nearby who can take your child, if, say, you are ill. Alternatively, you may prefer a childminder who lives closer to your place of work.

Once you have selected the names in your chosen area from the list, you will need to phone around to find out who has vacancies. Be prepared to find few vacancies – in many areas in Edinburgh demand outstrips supply. Most childminders are very helpful in telling you of any vacancies they are aware of, so do ask.

Always visit anyone who sounds suitable in their home and prepare yourself with a list of information for the childminder about you and your child and also questions you want to ask about the childminder. You need to establish the practicalities of hours, rates, holidays, sick pay, overtime (if required) and notice and whether you need to provide food and nappies.

You might also want to think about the following during your visit:
- Will your child have plenty of play opportunities – indoors and outdoors?
- Will there be outings to the park, playgroup, library etc?
- Will your child be able to rest during the day? If so where?
- What are the arrangements for meals and snacks?
- Are there other children for your child to play with and are they happy, settled and busy?
- What time will be set aside for you to discuss your child with the childminder?
- Will your wishes for the care of your child be accepted and respected?

When you do decide ensure you have a written contract summarising your agreement with the childminder.

 Visit our website for updates:
www.efuf.co.uk

Scottish Childminding Association

7 Melville Terrace
Stirling
FK8 2ND
01786 44 53 77
information@childminding.org
www.childminding.org

The only Scottish dedicated support organisation for registered childminders. It promotes good quality childcare within a home environment. It provides support, advice and information to all who are interested in childminding. It produces several useful publications for parents and childminders, some of which are free of charge, some of which are not. The SCMA also has comprehensive guides and advice sheets available online.

Nannies

You may prefer to employ someone to look after your children in your own home. Nannies may 'live in' or 'live out'. The choice between these options will depend on the nature of your childcare needs, your available accommodation, how you feel about having someone in your home and also on your financial resources.

Nannies are not required to be registered in the same way that childminders are, so you must follow through on references thoroughly. Remember that whether you choose to search via an agency or through local advertising/word of mouth – you will still need to spend time interviewing and checking references. Do not rely on references provided by the agency only – make the calls yourself.

It is worth thinking beforehand about the sort of person you are looking for and to specify your requirements with regard to training, qualifications, experience, age, etc.

Conditions of Service

Be clear in your own mind about your conditions of service in terms of hours, holidays, pay, duties, sick pay and so on. Must your nanny: be able to drive; be a non-smoker; understand a vegetarian diet; understand allergies; observe certain religious practices – and so on?
In the case of live-in help you should also think about any restrictions you wish to place upon the use of your home, such as having friends to stay, using the phone, etc.

Apart from looking after the children, duties can include babysitting, cooking, being responsible for the cleanliness of the nursery and laundry for the children. Nannies with qualifications and experience may not take kindly to being asked to clean a bathroom unless it is the one attached to the nursery! The priority for a nanny is the children and if there is downtime during naps – then the nanny is deserving of a break and can also focus on upcoming activities. A nanny's job should not be mistaken for that of a domestic cleaner, but depending on the individual, the nanny may do some light cleaning to help out.

Rates vary widely depending on qualifications, age and experience: full-time live-out care can range from £280-350/wk net*, or around £7-£9+/hr part-time. Live-in pay can be less (£200-300/week), but don't forget to take account of the 'hidden' domestic costs. When deciding what to pay take into account training, experience, number of children and level of responsibility required.

*Remember too the additional cost to you of National Insurance contributions and income tax payments, which can equal up to one third of the person's take-home pay.

Although a controversial issue, keep in mind that your nanny may wish to become pregnant herself. Nannies are NOT regarded as self-employed by the HMRC (unlike childminders and maternity nurses), you need to be clear on what your obligations as an employer are to a pregnant woman. (see Nanny Tax).

Employing a nanny

When you do appoint someone, it is up to you to contact your local Inland Revenue office to let them know you are an employer, and they will send you the necessary paperwork for you to fill in. Alternatively you can sign up for a membership with a payroll service that sorts out all of the paperwork on your behalf ensuring that the nanny receives the correct PAYE pay slips and that you pay the correct quarterly payments to the Inland Revenue.

This route is highly recommended (unless you or your partner are accountants) because it saves time, it is efficient and you have access to legal and tax advice as part of your membership fee should you have any questions regarding your obligations as an employer of a nanny, including what to do about sick pay, holidays, contracts and pregnancy. An example of such an organisation is:

Nanny Tax
PO Box 988
Brighton
BN1 3NT
0845 226 2203
mailbox@nannytax.co.uk
www.nannytax.co.uk

The following suggestions may help you find the right person:
Local contacts or friends may be able to recommend someone suitable – nannies usually know other nannies, or parents with children at private nurseries may hear that a member of staff is looking for a move. Take advantage of anyone's experience of employing a nanny – ask them about what they like about their nannies, and if there is anything they would have done differently.

You can place advertisements on Gumtree, in the Scotsman and/or the Evening News on Fridays (contact the papers at least two days in advance). Be prepared for a good number of responses, but if response is by phone in the first instance have a short list of questions handy to filter out unsuitable candidates quickly and only interview those who meet your criteria of experience and qualifications. You could also place notices in health centres where they have a general notice board.

If you seek someone with childcare qualifications, but don't mind if they do not have experience, contact the local colleges which offer Early Education and Childcare training courses:

Jewel & Esk Valley
0131 344 7100

Stevenson
0131 535 4700
The final term (Apr/May) is the best time to do this.

You may also wish to use an employment agency and there are a few in the Edinburgh area which specialise in finding nannies. They will usually charge a registration fee and then once they have your details they try to match you with someone suitable. If you are looking for a part-time nanny, some will try to set up a nanny-share scheme with other clients.

If you do appoint someone, you then pay an appointment fee to the agency. If you use an agency, find out before signing up what they offer in terms of service to you: some provide useful fact packs on registration which will help you with interviewing, contracts, conditions of employment, tax and National Insurance etc. They should also give some sort of guarantee to find temporary cover if you need it. Go for an agency that you feel will give you a dependable service, but remember it can only be as good as the nannies on its books, and sometimes cannot come up with anyone suitable.

Interviews

Ask all candidates to send you their CV in advance or, if that's not possible to bring it with them to the interview – this will give you a good starting point. Prepare your list of questions in advance and don't feel embarrassed to ask searching questions – you need to find out as much as you can in a very short time! Don't forget to give the candidates a chance to ask you questions and to tell you about themselves – they need to assess whether you will be the right family for them too and you can find out a lot about someone by listening carefully to what they have to say.

Be sure to obtain references from previous employers or from college tutors and follow them up (even if it means phoning Australia!) – again have a short list of questions ready to ask referees but also give them an opportunity to volunteer their own information.

Contract

It is important to have mutual expectations clear at the outset. A written contract stating the terms and conditions of service and the duties and responsibilities of the job is extremely helpful in preventing problems later on, or at least making them easier to sort out, for both parties and the law requires employers to provide certain written particulars.

Nanny Agencies

The following agencies are not the only ones available in the area, but they did provide full information regarding contact details and the services they provide. All such agencies are supposed to ensure that all people on their books have their Disclosure Scotland document.

Butterfly Personnel
7 Earlston Place
EH7 5SU
0131 659 5065
enquiries@butterflypersonnel.co.uk
www.butterflypersonnel.co.uk
This agency specialises in providing permanent nannies and maternity nurses, these ladies provide support to mothers and their newborn babies. Butterfly Personnel can also register private nannies for the use of childcare vouchers. Other services include experienced babysitters and supply nursery staff.

A & H Childcare Consultancy Ltd.
Suite 144
Baltic Chambers
50 Wellington Street
Glasgow
G2 6HJ
0141 248 6444
info@aandhchildcare.couk
www.aandhchildcare.co.uk

Although based in Glasgow, this agency can place people across the central belt and have no problem coming to visit your home for a consultation.

CHILDCARE

Norland Agency

York Place
London Road
Bath
BA1 6AE
01225 787 090
agency@norland.co.uk

The Norland College has a strong tradition of well trained nannies since 1892. Norland has recently started placing nannies in Scotland and they are well placed to provide temporary nanny care if you need to travel down south or plan to vacation within the EU.

OTHER SOURCES OF HELP WITH CHILDCARE

Edinburgh Crèche Co-op

297 Easter Road
EH6 8LH
0131 553 2116 (Mon-Fri 9.00-16.00)

Specialises in delivering flexible, professional childcare services including setting up and running crèche facilities, training, consultancy and staff cover. You need to provide a suitable room and the crèche workers are vetted, trained and experienced in organising stimulating and educational play activities, with an emphasis on child-centred care. It has full public liability insurance and complies with all relevant legislation and can be fully operational with only a few days notice.

> Make your business stand
> out from the rest
>
> Place an advert in the
> next edition of EFUF
>
> Visit the buiness section of our
> website for more information
>
> or email business@efuf.co.uk
>
>   www.efuf.co.uk

North Edinburgh Childcare

Crèche Services
18b Ferry Road Avenue
EH4 4BL
0131 332 8001
info@northedinburghchildcare.co.uk
www.northedinburghchildcare.co.uk

A childcare facility which gives quality, affordable crèche cover, to enable parents to access either leisure or business opportunities. The crèches provided are safe, stimulating and above all, fun. Available for bookings by any group or organisation which is planning an event – anytime, anywhere, on a one-off booking or cover for a regular event. North Edinburgh Childcare can accommodate up to 12 children between the ages of 0-12yrs (under 1s can be catered for if there are less than 6 other children). Rates vary, depending upon staffing ratios and the venue.

Smilechildcare

17 Calder Grove
Edinburgh
EH11 4LZ
0131 476 7800
mailbox@smilechildcare.org
www.smilechildcare.org

Smilechildcare's crèche service is designed to respond to the needs of a broad range of clients, such as: families – assisting with childcare at weddings, parties and other family occasions; businesses; and organisations – providing a crèche for AGMs, training events, conferences and other corporate events. Each crèche or childcare service is organised to best meet the needs of the individual family or company, including play and care for children with special needs.
Services can be provided in and around Edinburgh, either on a long or short-term basis or as a one off event. Smilechildcare will provide qualified childcare staff in the correct ratios; provide or come to a suitable location; complete a risk assessment of your chosen venue; provide play materials and a healthy snack.

Doula UK
0871 433 3103
info@doula.org.uk
www.doula.org.uk
Doula UK is the non-profit association for doulas. It provides information about the services they provide and can help you find a local doula.

Scottish Doula Network
info@scottishdoulanetwork.co.uk
www.scottishdoulanetwork.co.uk
This is a peer support network for doulas working in Scotland. It provides contact details but is not accountable for individual doulas.

A birth doula will work with a pregnant woman to help prepare her for the birth and offer to be one of the attendants during delivery.

A post-natal doula will work with a mother and her family for a mutually agreed period of time – usually about 6 weeks after the birth of a baby, although the extent of the support can vary according to the mother and her family's needs. This will usually be a set number of hours each day for a set number of days each week.

A post-natal doula provides physical and emotional support to a mother and her family. She will also help a mother to locate information and support from other sources. She can also free the mother from some domestic chores so that the mother has time to meet her own and her baby's needs.

Edinburgh Doulas
Contact: Kim Bradie
0131 554 6620
info@edinburghdoulas.co.uk
www.edinburghdoulas.co.uk
Provides birth and postnatal support. Postnatal support normally lasts between 10 days and 2 months depending on your needs. Minimum request is 4 hours of support a week.

Mother to Mother
Ante and Post-Natal Doula Support
Contact: Clare Bartos
0131 445 4445
clare@mothertomother.co.uk
www.mothertomother.co.uk
Provides postnatal doula services for families, as well as one-to-one breastfeeding support for those who do not want full doula support.

Nicola Goodall
Birth and Post Natal Doula
0131 478 0533
nicolagoodall@googlemail.com

Maternity Nurses
Maternity Nurses can be found via the same routes as finding a nanny. Maternity Nurses are expensive as they tend to live in for the first 4–8wks of a baby's life to help the mother adjust to her new situation. The maternity nurse is on hand to help the mother establish a routine (if required) as well as provide support with breast feeding, sleep and generally ensuring that the mother is pampered during the crucial first weeks after birth.

HELP IN THE HOME

Home Sweet Home
0131 476 3276
enquiries@home-sweet-home.co.uk
www.hshcleaning.co.uk
The Home Sweet Home Agency provides insured regular household services, such as cleaners and ironers, and can also find you tradesmen for specific home maintenance at a 10% discount. Registration fee for use of service - you pay the tradesmen/ women directly.

Healthcare

Healthcare

This section includes local NHS, voluntary and complementary health care services. It cannot claim to be comprehensive; however it should provide you with sources of more detailed information.

Emergency Numbers

If your child requires emergency treatment call
999 or 112

Or go direct to
Royal Hospital for Sick Children
9 Sciennes Road
Edinburgh
EH9 1HF
0131 536 0000

Or contact your GP
Or, if out of hours, call
NHS 24 Scotland
08454 242424

NEW TO THE AREA?

NHS Lothian
0131 537 8488
www.nhslothian.scot.nhs.uk
Visit the website or phone to find a GP, pharmacist or optician. Your local library will have a list of GP practices too. If you are new to the area, you should register with a local General Practitioner (GP) as soon as possible.

Dentists
0131 537 8444
Phone to find details of local dentists or contact NHS 24 on 08454 242424.

GP SERVICES

If you think your child has a medical problem, the normal first contact is your GP. As well as treating most common conditions and referring your child on to a specialist (should this be necessary), most GPs in Edinburgh provide special services for under 5s. These include a Child Health Surveillance Programme, often in conjunction with your health visitor, in which your child will be called for routine medical and developmental checks. In addition, your GP is likely to administer much of your child's basic immunisation programme.

If you want to change your GP practice, you can register with a new one directly, or you can telephone NHS Lothian on 0131 537 8488 for advice. If you have been removed from a GP's list, and cannot get another doctor to accept you, then telephone 0131 537 8473.

Out of Hours/Night Care

Lothian Unscheduled Care Service provides out-of-hours medical services for all of Lothian. You can access these by telephoning NHS 24 on 08454 242424. Your call will be answered by a call handler who will take some basic details. Then you will be forwarded to a nurse advisor who will assess the condition of your child and offer advice. You may be asked to attend an appointment at an out-of-hours centre, or to go to the hospital Accident and Emergency (A&E) department. If you need to take your child to A&E, NHS24 will call ahead and give them your details. NHS 24 works with the Scottish Ambulance Service, GP services, and A&E departments.

In emergencies dial 999 or 112

Immunisations

The National Health Service aims to immunise as many babies and children as possible to promote "herd immunity" and to prevent outbreaks of common, but serious, diseases. Most of the routine vaccines are administered through GP practices, sometimes in conjunction with health visitors. Assuming your child has been registered with a GP, you will be sent an automatic appointment notice when each vaccine is due. If you have any questions or concerns about immunisation your GP should be able to help you.

www.healthscotland.com/topics/health/ immunisation

Website for up-to-date information and descriptions of each vaccine, plus details of when they are offered. At the time of writing, the immunisation timetable for the under 5s is:

2 months – 2 injections: one protects against diphtheria, tetanus, acellular pertussis (whooping cough), polio and Hib (known as DTaP/IPV/Hib). The other protects against pneumococcal disease (PCV).

3 months – 2 injections: one for DTaP/IPV/Hib and one to protect against meningitis C (MenC)

4 months – 3 injections: DTaP/IPV/Hib, PCV and MenC.

12 months – 1 injection: Hib/MenC booster

13 months – 2 injections: one to protect against measles, mumps and rubella (MMR) and PCV booster

3 years 4 months to 5 years – 2 injections: DtaP/IPV booster and MMR booster

Minor Ailments Service

It is worth registering with your local pharmacist's "minor ailments service". This is a new NHS service for people who do not pay prescription charges, such as children. It means that if the pharmacist thinks it necessary, they can give you a medicine for no charge, without you having to make an appointment with your GP just to get a prescription. There are a wide range of minor illnesses and ailments which can be treated under the service.

Pharmacies (Chemists)
0131 537 8488
www.nhslothian.scot.nhs.uk
Phone or visit the website above to find the pharmacy nearest to where you are. To find a pharmacy that is open out of hours, telephone NHS 24 on 08454 242424.

Your local pharmacist can give advice on common health problems and can answer questions about medicines.

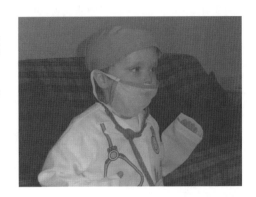

HOSPITAL SERVICES
(excluding maternity)

Royal Hospital for Sick Children
9 Sciennes Road
Edinburgh
EH9 1LF
0131 536 0000

This hospital, also known as 'Sick Kids', is focussed on the needs of children. It is located in Sciennes, south of the Meadows, but it is expected to relocate to the same site as the Edinburgh Royal Infirmary, Little France by 2013.

Clinics, waiting areas and the A&E department are all stocked with toys and books for all ages. All parents who wish to stay with their child can do so, and attempts will be made to find beds for as many as possible. These may be on the ward, or in separate areas. Priority is given to parents of very sick children, those who have travelled long distances and breast-feeding mothers. There are no specific visiting times for parents and guardians, and other visitors are welcome until 19:00 at the discretion of the ward charge nurse.

Specialist members of staff ensure that children are encouraged to play during their hospital stay, as well as helping children to understand the treatments and investigations they are undergoing. Volunteers work with the play specialists for example, guiding families around the hospital, taking the mobile library around the wards, befriending a child and reading bedtime stories to the children. Pre-operative Play Coordinators run pre-admission visits for children who are due to have surgery. These are recommended in order to alleviate stress and anxiety surrounding a hospital admission. Visits can also be organised for small groups of nursery/primary school children wishing to find out more about hospitals.

With prior arrangement the hospital nursery can accommodate a number of young children of parents visiting the hospital. The nursery is open Mon-Fri 08:00-18.00. For further information contact Play Services Coordinator, 0131 536 0000.

St John's Hospital at Howden
Howden Road West
Livingston
EH54 6PP
01506 523000

St John's is a modern teaching hospital for adults and children with an A&E department. It provides a full paediatric service including an acute receiving unit, special baby unit, paediatric ward and a range of outpatient services. Parents are welcome to stay and their needs are accommodated where possible on the ward. Siblings are welcome but appropriate adult supervision is appreciated. Visiting times for parents are open; for friends and relatives the hours are 11.00-19.00 and at the discretion of the Ward Sister. There is a playroom staffed by play leaders during the week and open at the weekend, nursing staff permitting. There are play facilities coordinated by play leaders when available.

Western General Hospital
Minor Injuries Clinic
Crewe Road
Edinburgh
EH4 2X
0131 537 1330 or 537 1331

This clinic is open 09:00 – 21:00 daily for anyone with a minor injury, for example, sprains, cuts, bites, minor burns, and small bone breaks (from shoulders to fingers and knees to toes). No appointment is necessary and telephone advice is also available. The specialist staff (nurse, physiotherapy, paramedic) can assess, diagnose and treat your child, and refer them for further treatment if required.

Anything out of date?
Let us know -
info@efuf.co.uk

DENTAL CARE

NHS dental care is free for mothers throughout pregnancy and until the baby's first birthday, as well as children under 18yrs. Regular attendance is needed to stay registered as an NHS patient. If you wish to change your dentist, you should check whether the new dentist will accept you as an NHS patient. Alternatively there are many dentists offering private treatment in Edinburgh.

It is a good idea to register your child with your family dentist as soon as they are born. If they accompany you on your own dental visits then they will become used to the surgery from an early age. The water supply in Lothian does not contain sufficient fluoride to benefit teeth. Your child's teeth should be cleaned as soon as they appear using a small headed brush and a fluoride toothpaste containing no less than 1000 parts per million fluoride. Only a smear of paste should be applied to the brush. For children at high risk of dental decay, dentists may prescribe fluoride tablets or drops.

Dental Emergencies

If your child is registered with a dentist then contact their dental surgery for emergency treatment.

If your child is not registered with a dentist, you can take them to the Children's Department at the

Edinburgh Dental Institute
Level 3, Lauriston Building
Lauriston Place
Edinburgh
Clinics run Monday-Friday 09:00 – 11:00 and 14:00 – 15:00. No appointment is necessary.

Lothian Dental Advice Line
0131 536 4800
If your child is not registered with a dentist, and needs out-of-hours treatment, you can get advice from the Lothian Dental Advice Line. This operates during evenings and at weekends. A dental nurse adviser will take your call and assess the urgency of the symptoms.

ANTENATAL CARE

www.readysteadybaby.org.uk

As soon as you find out you are pregnant you should call your GP surgery or health centre and ask for an appointment with a midwife. Usually you will be asked to choose where you would like to have your baby, at home or in hospital. A home birth can be arranged with the community midwives in your local area, depending on your medical history.

Maternity services are community based, with most women receiving care in their local area. NHS antenatal care is provided by the local midwifery team, your GP or, if necessary, a consultant obstetrician. This means that most women only attend hospital for the birth of their baby. The midwives provide information and support on all aspects of pregnancy, birth and postnatal care including breastfeeding. This includes providing information about health in pregnancy, screening tests, parenting skills, and your options for delivery.

You should be offered an opportunity to attend NHS antenatal classes provided by your community midwives along with other health professionals such as health visitors. Courses vary and, depending on your area, may include: women only classes; women and partner classes; teenage classes; aqua-natal classes; hypnotherapy and physiotherapy.

Unlike other parts of the UK, a 20-week anatomy scan is not offered by NHS Lothian as routine. However several companies offer this service privately, as well as the popular 3D and 4D scans.

You may wish to engage the services of an independent midwife or a doula. (Additional information available in the Childcare section.)

A doula (pronounced doo-la) provides emotional and practical support for the mother/parents before, during and/or after the birth of their child. She is also a mother's advocate in whatever situation she chooses to give birth, be it in hospital, at home, with or without medical intervention. A doula will assist the woman, and will work within her chosen environment as a birth assistant, adapting to the woman's changing needs during labour and birth. Doulas do not offer medical advice.

Independent Midwives UK
www.independentmidwives.org.uk
Independent Midwives have chosen to work outside the NHS in a self employed capacity. This website provides information and a search facility to find a local independent midwife. You can also find Scottish independent midwives at:

www.scotbirth.co.uk

Independent midwives provide antenatal and postnatal care, and support home births. They are fully qualified midwives, who like their NHS colleagues, are registered with the Nursing and Midwifery Council. If you plan a home birth and need to go to the hospital an independent midwife can remain with you as an advocate, supporter and friend, but may not have a contract with the hospital to provide midwifery services.

AIMS
Association for Improvements in the Maternity Services
0300 365 0663
helpline@aims.org.uk
www.aims.org.uk
AIMS provides information and support to parents about their choices in maternity care. A range of booklets on how to make the right decision for you, the second and third stages of labour, the pros and cons of induction, VBAC, breech birth, home birth, water birth, twins etc, plus a quarterly journal are available. Send SAE for free publications list. If you contact the AIMS helpline by email or telephone, you will be connected to volunteers who will respond as soon as possible.

National Childbirth Trust
0300 330 0772 (pregnancy and birth line)
0300 330 0770 (enquiries)
0844 243 6994 (antenatal classes)
www.nct.org.uk
www.nctedinburgh.moonfruit.com
The NCT provides support and evidence-based information about pregnancy, birth and the early days of parenthood. The philosophy of NCT antenatal classes is to empower women and their partners to make informed choices in managing pregnancy and labour. The classes are informal and friendly and many groups stay in touch after their babies are born. Classes run over 8 weeks and include relevant anatomy and physiology, preparation for labour including breathing and other relaxation exercises, and practicing postures for assisting the labour and birthing process. Breastfeeding and early parenting skills are also discussed. There are also intensive weekend courses available.

For more information and to book antenatal classes in Edinburgh email:

bookings1c@nct.org.uk

Pregnancy and Parents Centre
10 Lower Gilmore Place
Edinburgh
EH3 9NY
0131 229 3667
www.birthresourcecentre.org.uk
This centre (previously called the Birth Resource Centre) is a charitable organisation that aims to provide emotional and practical support and information. The centre provides a variety of classes and workshops for parents during pregnancy and after birth. All sessions provide parents with the information they need to enable them to make decisions about their pregnancies, birth and care of their babies, as well as an opportunity to meet others in similar circumstances. Birth pools, birth balls, library and a newsletter are available.

 Visit our website for updates:
www.efuf.co.uk

There are two hospitals offering maternity services in the Edinburgh area; Edinburgh Royal Infirmary and St John's Hospital at Howden.

Simpson Centre for Reproductive Health
Royal Infirmary of Edinburgh
Little France
51 Little France Crescent
0131 536 1000

St John's Hospital
Howden Road West
Livingston
EH54 6PP
01506 523000

NEONATAL CARE
Both Simpsons and St John's have neonatal units to provide specialist care for babies. Parents are encouraged to visit and to participate in their baby's care; siblings are also welcome. Parents may stay if accommodation is available, with priority given to those whose babies are acutely ill or whose babies have been transferred to the unit from another hospital. Breastfeeding is encouraged and necessary facilities are provided. Parents and siblings may visit anytime but supervision of children is required.

Simpsons Special Care Babies (SSCB)
Simpsons Special Care Babies
PO Box 12258
North West DO
Edinburgh
EH4 1YB
www.sscb.org
SSCB is a charity that supports the neonatal unit based in the Simpsons maternity unit of the Royal Infirmary of Edinburgh. It is dedicated to the care of premature or sick newborn babies, and the support of their parents. The charity is run by volunteers who either work in the unit, or have had a child (or children) go through it.

BabyView
www.babylink.info/edinburgh/
NeonatalUnit
If your baby is treated within the neonatal unit at the Royal Infirmary of Edinburgh you can use this website to access information about the care and treatment your baby will receive. It has two sections: the first is a public section that covers general information relevant to babies needing neonatal care and what happens within the Simpsons neonatal unit; the second section contains secure pages. The secure pages can only be accessed by parents of children. It enables parents to see medical reports and receive information written by nursing staff about their baby, and if they choose, to share access to this with other members of the family.

POSTNATAL & BREASTFEEDING SUPPORT

Postnatal care is provided at home by the local midwifery team. Community midwives visit you at home after the birth of your baby and will attend the delivery if you have a home birth. They will visit every day until the baby is 10 days old (or for longer if there are any problems). From this point, the health visitor will take over. Both midwives and health visitors will provide breastfeeding support.

Health visitors are all registered nurses who have undertaken further extensive training. The focus of much of their work is centred on families and children. This is achieved through home visits, clinic contact and parenting programmes, and involves helping parents develop an understanding of their child's health and development as well as offering wider support for the family. They have a sound knowledge of the local community and the resources available and can therefore direct families to relevant agencies, e.g. Children and Families Services, and local groups to obtain the help and support they might require. Health visitors also work closely with other members of Primary Health Care teams such as midwives, doctors, practice nurses, district nurses, community psychiatric nurses and school nurses.

Postnatal doulas provide support for between ten days and two months after birth. They can provide physical and emotional support to a mother and her family. This may include specific help with breastfeeding, as well as help with domestic chores. See Childcare section for further information.

NCT Postnatal Support
0300 330 0773 (postnatal support)
0844 243 6123 (Edinburgh North)
0844 243 6124 (Edinburgh South)
www.nct.org.uk
www.nctedinburgh.moonfruit.com
The NCT offers extensive postnatal support in the form of local groups of parents who meet on a regular basis. If you go to NCT antenatal classes your name will be given to your local group representative who should contact you around the time your baby is due, if not before. She will give you details of local meetings and may be able to advise you whom to contact if you have any specific problems. You are welcome to join a postnatal support group even if you have not been to NCT antenatal classes. Activities include coffee mornings or afternoons, evening talks, discussion groups, bumps and babies groups, fund-raising events, picnics, local newsletter, etc. Members receive a quarterly magazine.

Breastfeeding Support
www.realbabymilk.org
Midwives and health visitors provide support for breastfeeding and can put you in touch with local support groups. Several are listed in the Edinburgh area on the above website.

The Simpson Centre for Reproductive Health has Baby Friendly status awarded by UNICEF for its support of breastfeeding. There is a weekly drop-in clinic for those with breastfeeding problems. There are two play areas situated on the ground floor of the centre. A selection of toys and children's books are available. Parents are asked to keep children under supervision at all times.

Breastfeeding Network (BfN)
0300 100 0210
www.breastfeedingnetwork.org.uk
The Supporterline is a helpline staffed by volunteers who have breastfed their own babies and who have received training in breastfeeding.

La Leche League
0845 120 2918 (UK Helpline)
01620 822260 (East Lothian Leader)
www.laleche.org.uk
http://llledinburgh.wordpress.com/
LaLeche(pronounced"lalay-chay")isaninternational organisation that provides breastfeeding support, encouragement and information. The helpline provides telephone counselling from trained volunteers who have personal breastfeeding experience. There are local groups across the UK for pregnant and breastfeeding mothers to meet informally, accompanied by their children as well as female friends and relatives.
The Edinburgh group is based at the Pregnancy and Parents Centre and meets monthly, with separate sessions for those breastfeeding toddlers. There is no need to book.

NCT Breastfeeding Line
www.nct.org.uk
0300 330 0771 (breastfeeding support)
The NCT provides information, support and encouragement for breastfeeding through its network of breastfeeding counsellors who have all breastfed their own children and been through intensive training. They can also arrange the hire of electric breast pumps and valley cushions.

National Breastfeeding Helpline
0300 100 0212
Funded by the Department of Health, this helpline is provided by the Breastfeeding Network and the Association of Breastfeeding Mothers. It is staffed by volunteers who have breastfed and received intensive training in order to provide support.

Perinatal Depression

Perinatal depression occurs either before (antenatal) or after (postnatal) the birth of a baby. Do not hesitate to ask for help; it is not uncommon and it is a treatable illness. Your GP or health visitor will provide support and advice, including helping you to access other support services.

Bluebell at Parentline Scotland
0800 3457 457
Helpline for postnatal depression. Lines are open from 09:00 – 17:00 Monday, Wednesday and Friday and from 09:00 – 21:00 on Tuesdays and Thursdays.

Edinburgh Postnatal Depression Project
Wallace House
3 Boswall Road
Edinburgh
EH5 3RJ
0131 538 7288

8a Palmerston Place
Edinburgh
EH12 5AA
0131 220 3547

pnd@crossreach.org.uk
www.bluebellday.org.uk

This project aims to provide support to women, men and their families with a child under three years old. You can contact the project direct, or be referred via a health visitor, GP or other health professional. It offers a range of services to families suffering with postnatal depression including: couple and individual counselling, women's therapy groups and baby massage classes. All services supported with crèche facilities.

THERAPY CENTRES

Bobath Scotland
0141 435 3270
www.bobathscotland.org.uk

Bobath Centres specialise in the treatment of cerebral palsy and acquired neurological conditions in children & adults. There are centres throughout the UK, including The Scottish Bobath Centre in Glasgow. If you feel your child would benefit, speak to their consultant and physiotherapist, or call the centre directly.

Craighalbert Centre
01236 456100
www.craighalbert.org.uk

The Scottish Centre for Children with Motor Impairments, known as the Craighalbert Centre, is Scotland's national centre for young children with cerebral palsy. The centre is a nursery and a school, although children can also attend the centre on periodic placement or join one of the clubs that runs regularly – for example the Saturday group. This is conductive education therapy, based on methods devised at the Peto institute. For more information contact the centre on or have a look at their website.

Like to be listed?
Get in touch -
business@efuf.co.uk

COMPLEMENTARY HEALTHCARE

There are many complementary/alternative therapists offering a range of treatments in the Edinburgh area, but not all of these would be suitable for children or pregnant women. Individual practitioners offer most of these services privately and fees for consultation and treatment vary widely. It is strongly recommended that you check that any therapist is registered with their appropriate professional body. It would not be practical to include all therapists here; your local library may be able to direct you to a national organisation or professional body who can provide details of local therapists. An entry below is not necessarily a recommendation.

You can request an NHS referral to the Homeopathic hospital if you think this would be helpful for you or your child. While the hospital is in Glasgow, it operates outreach clinics in St John's at Howden.

YOGA AND MASSAGE THERAPIES

Birthlight
www.birthlight.com
Birthlight is a charity that focuses on the use of yoga and breathing methods to enhance the wellbeing of you and your baby. The website provides details of local baby massage and baby yoga instructors.

Daisy Days
Contact: Liz Foster
0131 478 1935
infantmassage@daisydays.org.uk
www.daisydays.org.uk
Baby massage courses for babies from 6wks until crawling. Antenatal classes are run for expectant mums who use a doll to practise technique.

Edinburgh Baby Massage
Contact: Anne Nash
07879 448181
anne@nashes.co.uk
www.edinburghbabymassage.co.uk
5 week baby massage courses for babies from 6wks until crawling. Courses are available in Anne's home in south Edinburgh or at your own home.

Knotstressed
Contact: Onie Tibbitt
07717 783230
onie@knotstressed.com
www.knotstressed.com
Workshops and therapeutic treatments for couples, parents and children, including baby massage, baby signing, doula support, birth preparation, hypnobirthing and massage during pregnancy.

Massage Therapies
Contact: Benedetta Gaetani d'Aragona
30A Hermitage Gardens
Edinburgh
EH10 6AY
0131 447 4421
massage@easynet.co.uk
www.massagetherapies.co.uk
Benedetta also practices from Neal's Yard Remedies.

KnotStressed
PARENT & BABY

- Baby Massage and Baby Signing
- HypnoBirthing® and Birth Preparation
- Pregnancy and Postnatal Massage
- Therapeutic Massage for Parents

www.knotstressed.com
07717 783 230
relax@knotstressed.com

OTHER SERVICES

Craniosacral Therapy
Contact: Ewan Kenny
The Sangha
14a Broughton Street Lane
Edinburgh
EH1 3LY
0131 557 9567
07962 224677
info@ewankenny.com
www.ewankenny.com
www.thesangha.co.uk
Ewan also practises from Mulberry House.

Discover Chiropractic
240 Queensferry Road
Edinburgh
EH4 2BP
0131 332 0063
Child-friendly family-run business, focused on family care. Consultations are available from birth. Toys, books and videos available. Nappy changing room with nappies provided. Breastfeeding welcome and premises accessible to pushchairs. Usually a member of staff can look after children during a parent's consultation.

The Edinburgh Natural Health Centre
GP Plus
1 Wemyss Place
Edinburgh
EH3 6DH
07950 012501
www.enhc.co.uk
Appointments at Wemyss Place on Mondays only. Acupuncture, homeopathy, acupressure massage, Chinese herbal medicine and nutrition are available with advice on and treatment for vaccinations. Consultation by appointment.

Elemental Birth
07891 059677
admin@elementalbirth.co.uk
www.elementalbirth.co.uk
Services include waterbirth pool hire, birth preparation workshops and YogaBirth classes.

Glovers Integrated Healthcare
10 William Street
Edinburgh
EH3 7NH
0131 225 3161
info@glovers-health.co.uk
www.glovers-health.co.uk
Homeopathic consultations and remedies for adults and children. Offers homeopathic support package for pregnancy and childbirth.

Health All Round
Springwell House, Ardmillan Terrace
Edinburgh
0131 537 7530
This is a local charity identifying and responding to a range of health needs and issues within the community of Gorgie, Dalry and surrounding areas. Offers counselling, complementary therapies, exercise groups and yoga. There is a weekly parent support group and a weekly multicultural women's group.

Healthcare Now
12 Stafford Street
Edinburgh
EH3 7AU
0131 220 1300
edinburgh@healthcarenow.co.uk
www.healthcarenow.co.uk
Private healthcare practice offering a range of services. Can be used as an addition to existing NHS provision and self-referrals are welcome. Services provided include a range of obstetric scans for every stage of pregnancy.

Herbal Medicine
Contact: Julie McGregor
0131 225 5542 or 315 2130
Herbal remedies for pregnancy, birth, postnatal support, babies and children. Weekly clinics at Napiers.

Homeopath
Contact: Linda Bendle
13 Polwarth Grove
Edinburgh
EH11 1LY
0131 622 0722
Professional homeopath, specialising in working with mothers and their children.

Contact: Robyn McDonald
0131 554 0389
Professional homeopath who is also training as a Doula to provide practical and emotional support before, during and after childbirth.

Lothian Homeopathy Clinic
Dalkeith Medical Centre
St Andrew Street
Dalkeith
EH22 2AP
0131 561 5513
Homeopathic treatment is available on the NHS at clinics held at both Dalkeith Medical Centre and the Leith Community Treatment Centre in Edinburgh. Patients referred by their GPs are able to consult homeopathically-qualified doctors. Treatment is free.

Medicalternative
Waterside House
19 Hawthornbank Lane
Edinburgh
EH4 3BH
0131 225 5656
reception@medicalalternative.com
A private health care centre, which encompasses both conventional and alternative care. You can walk in off the street and see a qualified GP (no referral or appointment needed). There are numerous alternative therapists, all highly qualified and specialists in their own field. Nappy changing facilities.

Mulberry House
39 Manor Place
Edinburgh
EH3 7EB
0131 225 2012
enquiries@mulberryhouse.co.uk
This is Edinburgh's largest complementary health centre offering many types of complementary therapies.

Napiers Dispensary
18 Bristo Place
Edinburgh
EH1 1EZ
0131 225 5542

35 Hamilton Place
Stockbridge
Edinburgh
EH3 5BA
0131 315 2130
www.napiers.net
Parent/child herbal clinic by appointment. Baby/child homeopathic clinic (monthly) by appointment. Consultations in herbal medicine, aromatherapy, osteopathy, homeopathy, acupuncture and counselling. The parent and child herbal clinics provide dedicated support for pregnant women, babies and children. Specialists in women's health problems also available. The shops stock a range of traditional herbal remedies, nutritional supplements, aromatherapy products and organic skin care as well as their own mother and baby range. Mail order available.

Neal's Yard Remedies
102 Hanover Street
Edinburgh
EH2 1DR
0131 226 3223
edinburgh@nealsyardremedies.com
Neal's Yard stocks organic skin care, aromatherapy, homeopathic, herbal and flower remedies. A wider variety of complementary therapies are offered through its treatment rooms. Mail order available.

The Osteopathic Practice
(for Adults, Babies and Children)
Contact: Tom Kelman
1 Wester Coates Avenue
Edinburgh
EH12 5LS
0131 346 0134
07866 299 250
tom@osteopathedinburgh.co.uk
Registered Osteopath with a postgraduate Diploma in Paediatrics, who specialises in paediatric and family care. He also helps mothers with gentle and effective relief from aches and pains before or after birth.

SOMA Osteopathy
21 Queen Charlotte Street
Edinburgh
EH6 6BA
0131 553 3388
www.somauk.com
Healthcare clinic specialising in the physical well-being of the whole person. Offer maternity support for mother and child - osteopathy, massage, reflexology, acupuncture, postnatal pelvic checks, and cranial osteopathy. Mother and baby discounts available.

The WholeWorks Complementary Therapy and Counselling Centre
Jackson's Close
209 Royal Mile
Edinburgh
EH1 1PZ
0131 225 8092
enquiries@thewholeworks.co.uk
www.thewholeworks.co.uk
Offers a range of complementary health therapies, counselling and psychotherapy services, including craniosacral therapy, massage, homeopathy, chiropractic, acupuncture and herbal medicine.

USEFUL ADDRESSES

This list is not intended to be exhaustive but it may help point you in the right direction if you are seeking local information. (See also the Information & Support section.) Your local GP, health visitor, NCT group, library and community centre are also useful sources for contacts.

Action for Sick Children (Scotland)
22 Laurie Street
Edinburgh
EH6 5AB
0131 553 6553
www.ascscotland.org.uk
A charity for all children in hospital and for adults caring for them. It provides information for parents with babies in special care units and parent packs to help children prepare for a hospital visit. A hospital play box is available for loan to local playgroups which helps parents to prepare children (3-6yrs) for a hospital visit; includes toys, books, real medical equipment and mini uniforms.

Chatterbox
Private Speech Therapy Services
Contact Jane Armstrong
0131 445 7385
07952 719609
janec.armstrong@virgin.net
www.chatterbox-speechtherapy.co.uk
Chatterbox offers a range of assessments which can be used to determine what is wrong with a child's speech and/or language skills. It is a mobile service, coming to your house where a thorough investigation is made of your child's communication skills. Jane also runs a clinic at Murrayfield Hospital (call 0131 316 2596 for appointments).

Child Accident Prevention Trust
0207 608 3828
safe@capt.org.uk
www.capt.org.uk
A national charity committed to reducing the number of children and young people killed, disabled and seriously injured as a result of accidents. Their website provides safety advice for babies, toddlers, and children aged 3-5 years.

Family Planning and Well Woman Services
Dean Terrace Clinic
18 Dean Terrace
Edinburgh
EH4 1NL.
0131 332 7941 or 343 6243
Offers all forms of contraception, pregnancy testing and gynaecology services. Open Monday-Friday and there is a drop-in clinic for under-25s on Saturday mornings.

NHS 24
08454 242424
www.nhs24.com
NHS 24 provides up-to-date health information and advice for people in Scotland. The telephone service operates 24/7 and can help you if your GP surgery is closed but you need help before it re-opens. The email enquiry service, accessed from the website, provides information about named health conditions, treatments and NHS services within 5 days.

NHS Lothian Library and Resource Centre
Deaconess House
148 The Pleasance
Edinburgh
0131 536 9451/2/3
library@nhslothian.scot.nhs.uk
No appointment is necessary and it is possible to leave a message outside these hours. The centre can provide leaflets and posters on a wide range of health issues free of charge. Resources for teaching and training purposes are also available for loan. The centre has several databases, which have information about specific conditions and related support and self-help groups. These are updated regularly and information can be printed out on request.

Lothian Community Health Projects' Forum
Contact: Lesley Blackmore or Laura Mitchell
LCHPF c/o Health Promotion
Third Floor, Lauriston Building
Lauriston Place
Edinburgh
EH3 9HA
0131 536 3540
lesley.blackmore@nhslothian.scot.nhs.uk
laura.mitchell@nhslothian.scot.nhs.uk
www.lchpf.co.uk
The forum provides information on various community health initiatives across Lothian.

St Andrew's First Aid
Edinburgh, Lothian and Borders
Strachan House
16 Torpichen Street
Edinburgh
EH3 8JB
0131 229 5419
www.firstaid.org.uk
St Andrews First Aid offers courses to the public including baby and child first aid.

Index

INDEX

INDEX

INDEX

M

INDEX

INDEX

INDEX

Y

Z

Extras & Thanks

Space for your thoughts and doodles...

We'd love to hear from you.
- Let us know what you think of the book.
- Tell us how we can improve it.
- Suggest places that should be included in the next edition.
- Offer to get involved as a researcher.

Visit our website at www.efuf.co.uk   **or**   **email** info@efuf.co.uk

Ed says, "Get your crayons and colouring pencils out and colour me in."

EXTRAS & THANKS

Thanks to our advertisers...

A huge thanks and a big shout out to all our supporters, and in particular those who have advertised in this edition.

EFUF was born in 1986 when a group of National Childbirth Trust (NCT) Members formed a committee and asked for a loan from Edinburgh NCT. Originally conceived as a pamphlet the publication quickly grew into a book. It was first published in 1987 and was such a success it had to be reprinted that year (and the loan was paid back in full). Sales of the book ensure we can produce future editions and any profits are used to support the NCT locally. Over the years the profits from the book have been there to help pay for things like supporting the former Edinburgh Office at the Stockbridge Health Centre and training NCT Antenatal Teachers and NCT Breastfeeding Counsellors.

Advertising revenue helps the EFUF committee to ensure we are able to print this helpful resource edition after edition, and continue our support of the NCT.

Thanks to:

Ceramic Experience	**Edinburgh Nursery**
Edinburgh Libraries	**Headstart Nursery**
Parents Like Us	**Heriot Hill Nursery**
Real Nappy Project	**Monkey Music**
Edinburgh Academy Nursery	**NCT**
Maddie and Mark's	**Water Babies**
Almond Valley	**Edinburgh Nursery & School Guide**
Butterfly Personnel Childcare	**KnotStressed**
Doodles	**Rugbytots**

Special thanks to Graeme McKirdy and George Eunson at Standard Life Plc who helped us to get this edition into print.

Thanks to our researchers...

Aileen Kelly
Alison Grahamslaw
Alison Macdonald-Ewen
Andrea Barlow
Anne Cameron
Antonia Delaney
Amy Reilly
Christine Carlow
Dani Dinwoodie
Diahann Whitefield
Elizabeth McCandlish
Emma Roberts
Heather Cameron
Helen Maguire
Jane Boardman
Jane Ziemons
Jen Farquharson
Joan Bundulis
Joanne Finnie
Jo Drew
Jude Thomas
Judy Rintoul
Kate Marriott
Kathy McGlew

Katie McGlew
Larissa Russell
Lindsay Isaacs
Lisa Pirrie
Ljupka Veloska Lynch
Lucy Barnett
Lynne Arnot
Marie-Amelie Viatte
Mary Ross
Melissa Corkhill
Morag Burnet
Nadine Roberts-Leivesley
Nicola Hearnden
Nina Abeysuriya
Philippa Coles
Rachel F Freeman
Rachel Kerr
Rhian Hastie
Rhona Bennett
Ruth Dawkins
Saara Reid
Sally Pryde
Sarah Joss
Sophie Kelsall
Sue Widdicombe

... and all their under fives!